lonely planet

SOUTHWEST USA'S
BEST TRIPS

32 AMAZING
ROAD TRIPS

Hugh McNaughtan, Amy C Balfour, Stephen Lioy,
Carolyn McCarthy, Christopher Pitts,
Ryan Ver Berkmoes, Benedict Walker

SYMBOLS IN THIS BOOK

✓ Top Tips   📖 History & Culture   📷 Essential Photo

🔗 Link Your Trips   👪 Family   🏃 Walking Tour

⊙ Tips from Locals   🍷 Food & Drink   ✖ Eating

↱ Trip Detour   🌳 Outdoors   🛏 Sleeping

☏ Telephone Number   @ Internet Access   🇬🇧 English-Language Menu

⊙ Opening Hours   📶 Wi-Fi Access   👪 Family-Friendly

P Parking   🥗 Vegetarian Selection

⊖ Nonsmoking   🐾 Pet-Friendly

❄ Air-Conditioning   🏊 Swimming Pool

MAP LEGEND

Routes
- Trip Route
- Trip Detour
- Linked Trip
- Walk Route
- Tollway
- Freeway
- Primary
- Secondary
- Tertiary
- Lane
- Unsealed Road
- Plaza/Mall
- Steps
- Tunnel
- Pedestrian Overpass
- Walk Track/Path

Boundaries
- International
- State/Province
- Cliff

Hydrography
- River/Creek
- Intermittent River
- Swamp/Mangrove
- Canal
- Water
- Dry/Salt/ Intermittent Lake
- Glacier

Route Markers
- 97 US National Hwy
- 5 US Interstate Hwy
- 44 State Hwy

Trips
- 1 Trip Numbers
- 9 Trip Stop
- 🚶 Walking tour
- ↱ Trip Detour

Population
- ✪ Capital (National)
- ◉ Capital (State/Province)
- ● City/Large Town
- ● Town/Village

Areas
- Beach
- Cemetery (Christian)
- Cemetery (Other)
- Park
- Forest
- Reservation
- Urban Area
- Sportsground

Transport
- ✈ Airport
- Ⓑ BART station
- Ⓣ Boston T station
- 🚡 Cable Car/ Funicular
- Ⓜ Metro/Muni station
- Ⓟ Parking
- Ⓢ Subway station
- 🚉 Train/Railway
- 🚊 Tram
- Ⓤ Underground station

Note: Not all symbols displayed above appear on the maps in this book

---

PLAN YOUR TRIP

ON THE ROAD

CONTENTS

Utah, Colorado & Nevada p269

Arizona p59

New Mexico p137

Texas p227

Contents cont.

ROAD TRIP ESSENTIALS

COVID-19

We have re-checked every business in this book before publication to ensure that it is still open after the COVID-19 outbreak. However, the economic and social impacts of COVID-19 will continue to be felt long after the outbreak has been contained, and many businesses, services and events referenced in this guide may experience ongoing restrictions. Some businesses may be temporarily closed, have changed their opening hours and services, or require bookings; some unfortunately could have closed permanently. We suggest you check with venues before visiting for the latest information.

Right: **Utah** Arches National Park

WELCOME TO
SOUTHWEST USA

Mother Nature had some fun in the Southwest. Red rock canyons crack across ancient plateaus. Hoodoos cluster like conspirators on remote slopes. Whisper-light sand dunes shimmer on distant horizons. Wildflowers, saguaros and ponderosa pines add the artistic flourish, luring you in for a closer look.

The 32 road trips in this book take you through the best this fabulous land has to offer, from trackless deserts to the majestic Grand Canyon. We'll guide you through the sandstone charms of Utah to the artistic sparkle of New Mexico, and from the wildflowers of Texas Hill Country to the ancient cliff towns of Colorado and Nevada's vast open spaces.

But it's not just about the scenery. Dinosaur tracks, spectacular caverns, Old West towns, kitschy attractions, BBQ joints and wine-tasting rooms add history, geology and all-round oomph. If you've only got time for one trip, make it one of our seven Classic Trips – essential playlists of the Greatest Hits of the Southwest.

Monument Valley Navajo Tribal Park
TRAVELLIGHT/SHUTTERSTOCK ©

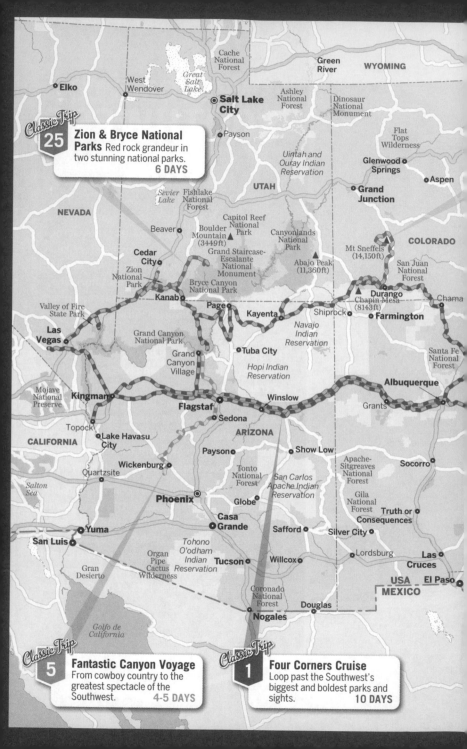

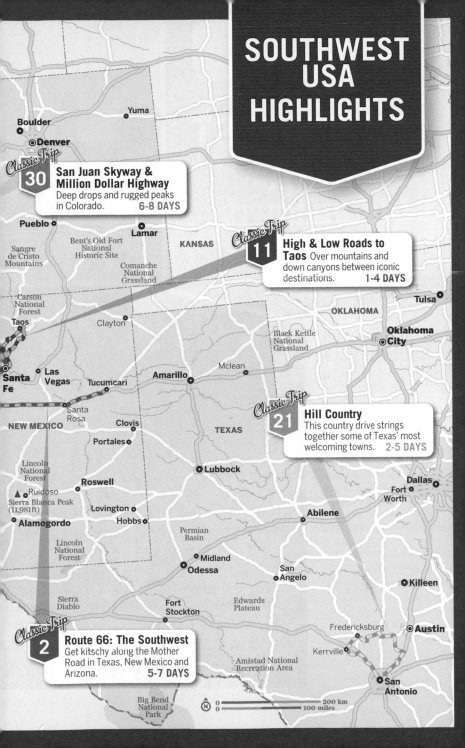

SOUTHWEST USA HIGHLIGHTS

Classic Trip
30 **San Juan Skyway & Million Dollar Highway**
Deep drops and rugged peaks in Colorado. **6-8 DAYS**

Classic Trip
11 **High & Low Roads to Taos** Over mountains and down canyons between iconic destinations. **1-4 DAYS**

Classic Trip
21 **Hill Country**
This country drive strings together some of Texas' most welcoming towns. **2-5 DAYS**

Classic Trip
2 **Route 66: The Southwest**
Get kitschy along the Mother Road in Texas, New Mexico and Arizona. **5-7 DAYS**

Yuma
Boulder
Denver
Pueblo
Sangre de Cristo Mountains
Bent's Old Fort National Historic Site
Lamar
KANSAS
Comanche National Grassland
Carson National Forest
Taos
Clayton
Black Kettle National Grassland
OKLAHOMA
Tulsa
Oklahoma City
Santa Fe
Las Vegas
Tucumcari
Santa Rosa
Amarillo
Mclean
NEW MEXICO
Clovis
Portales
TEXAS
Lincoln National Forest
Roswell
Ruidoso
Sierra Blanca Peak (11,981ft)
Lovington
Hobbs
Alamogordo
Lincoln National Forest
Lubbock
Dallas
Fort Worth
Abilene
Permian Basin
Midland
Odessa
San Angelo
Killeen
Sierra Diablo
Fort Stockton
Edwards Plateau
Fredericksburg
Austin
Kerrville
Amistad National Recreation Area
San Antonio
Big Bend National Park

0   200 km
0   100 miles

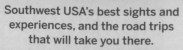
Southwest USA's best sights and experiences, and the road trips that will take you there.

SOUTHWEST USA
HIGHLIGHTS

Grand Canyon National Park

The sheer immensity of the canyon is what grabs you at first: it's a two-billion-year-old rip across the landscape that reveals the Earth's geologic secrets with astonishing clarity. But as you'll discover on **Trip 4: Grand Canyon North Rim & Lake Powell** and **Trip 5: Fantastic Canyon Voyage** it's the smaller details – sun-dappled ridges, crimson mesas, snowcapped junipers – that provide the final captivating flourishes.

Trips

Grand Canyon National Park Point Imperial, North Rim

Canyonlands National Park Mesa Arch

Sedona

The beauty of Sedona's red rock country startles everyone that comes this way. Yes, the jeep tours, crystal shops and chichi galleries are fun, but it's the brick-red buttes and canyons – strange yet familiar – that are unforgettable. On **Trip 8: Highway 89A: Red Rock Country**, soak up the beauty of the region by hiking to Airport Mesa, bicycling beneath Bell Rock or sliding through Oak Creek.

Trips 5 8

Zion National Park

The soaring red-and-white cliffs of Zion Canyon are one of Utah's most dramatic natural wonders. But **Trip 25: Zion & Bryce National Parks** also reveals more delicate beauties: weeping rocks, tiny grottoes, hanging gardens and meadows of mesa-top wildflowers. This lush vegetation, and the low elevation, distinguish Zion from more barren parks to the east.

Trips 1 25

Moab

Bike-thrashing slickrock. Class IV rapids. Hikes to sheer cliffs. It's just another day at the office for outdoor outfitters in this rugged playground. And as **Trip 27: Moab & Southeastern National Parks** proves, with activities this tough, you gotta have the appropriate support system: a sunrise java joint, a cool indie bookstore and a post-ride brewery that smells of beer and adventure.

Trips 27 29

Zion National Park The Virgin River and the Watchman

BEST SMALL TOWNS

Bisbee This once wild mining town is now a bohemian haven. **Trip** 3

Jerome Gallery hopping and wine tasting come with central Arizona views. **Trip** 5

Marfa An art scene with heart lures crowds to west Texas. **Trip** 22

Springdale Savor a locally sourced meal before canyoneering. **Trip** 25

Silver City Billy the Kid and summer monsoons keep things wild. **Trips** 17 18

Mesa Verde National Park

At Mesa Verde, the site of 600 ancient cliff dwellings, you explore the past by scrambling up ladders, scaling sheer rock faces and crawling through knee-worn tunnels. As you'll discover on **Trip 30: San Juan Skyway & Million Dollar Highway**, the park is also a place for contemplation. Ancestral Puebloans vacated it in AD 1300, perhaps displaced by climate change.

Trips 1

Taos Earthship

Taos

Ruggedly beautiful Taos has drawn a range of admirers over the years. Nineteenth-century mountain man Kit Carson had a home downtown and creative types like Georgia O'Keeffe and DH Lawrence also stayed awhile. And Carl Jung and Dennis Hopper? Maybe they came for the quirky individualism, which you can experience on **Trip 15: Enchanted Circle & Eastern Sangres** in the wonderfully eccentric Adobe Bar and off-the-grid Earthship community.

Trips **11** **15**

BEST SCENIC ROUTES

Highway 89/89A Old West meets the New West.
Trips **1** **4** **5** **8** **10** **25**

High Road to Taos Paint your own adventure on a picturesque mountain romp. **Trip** **11**

Million Dollar Highway Thar's gold in them thar views. **Trip** **30**

Highway 50 In the spring, snowcapped peaks are the backdrop. **Trip** **32**

Scenic Byway 12 Cruise forested plateaus and red rock canyons. **Trip** **26**

Carlsbad Caverns Stalagmites and stalacties

White Sands National Monument Unique sand dunes

Carlsbad Caverns National Park

The elevator drops the length of the Empire State Building then opens onto a subterranean village that holds a snack bar, water fountains, restrooms and the impressive 255ft-high Big Room, where geologic wonders are all around. Explore the inky depths on **Trip 16: Las Cruces to Carlsbad Caverns**.

Trip

White Sands National Monument

Frisbee on the dunes, umbrellas in the sand, kids riding wind-blown swells – the only thing missing is the water. But you won't mind, not with 275 sq miles of gypsum draping the landscape with a hypnotic whiteness. For full immersion on **Trip 16: Las Cruces to Carlsbad Caverns**, buy a disc and sled down the slopes.

Trip

American Indian Art

The most compelling works of today, from rugs to jewelry, put a fresh spin on ancient traditions. At Phoenix's Heard Museum on **Trip 10: Southwest Indian Nations Sojourn**, you'll even see Harry Potter–themed pottery. From Hopi kachina dolls to Navajo rugs to Zuni jewelry, art is a window into the heart of native Southwest peoples.

Trips

17

Green Chiles & Texas BBQ

In the Southwest, gift stores are filled with chile-themed gifts and homes are hung with dried-chile ristras. As you'll see on **Trip 12: El Camino Real & Turquoise Trail**, New Mexican restaurants rely on chiles as a key ingredient. In Texas, the emphasis is on barbecue, and on **Trip 21: Hill Country** the fun is in sampling the variations in preparation and sauce.

Trips

Canyon de Chelly

This remote, multipronged canyon feels far removed from time and space. Used as a stronghold by the Navajo, it has been the site of great violence. But families still farm the canyon, and it remains a beautiful sight, with walls soaring 1000ft from the canyon floor. The last stop on **Trip 10: Southwest Indian Nations Sojourn**, it's a compelling place to consider the Southwest's native people.

Trip 10

(left) **Canyon de Chelly** Spider Rock
(below) **New Mexico** Chile ristras

Hoover Dam

Before you begin the Hoover Dam tour on **Trip 1: Four Corners Cruise**, the guide points out the window, gesturing toward a tiny opening on the face of the 726ft-tall dam. It looks very far away. As you're smushed into the elevator, you pause, 'Do I really want to do–' and whoosh, you're dropping 50 stories into this concrete beast. Pretty cool.

Trips

BEST ROADSIDE ODDITIES

Cadillac Ranch Ten Cadillacs are jammed in the dirt. **Trip** 2

Wigwam Motel Sleep in concrete tipis on Route 66. **Trip** 2

Very Large Array Radio Telescope Is anybody out there? **Trip** 18

Show Low Card Game Statue memorializes a town legend. **Trip** 6

Southwest cuisine Tex-Mex tacos

Southwest Cuisine

From green-chile cheeseburgers to vegan BLTs and hefty Navajo tacos, eating in the Southwest is as diverse as its landscapes.

7 Southern Desert Wanderings Oh, Tucson, we love how you eat: Sonoran hotdogs, breakfast burritos and nuevo-Mexican masterpieces.

10 Southwest Indian Nations Sojourn Savor American Indian dishes at Kai, give frybread a try in Phoenix and enjoy lamb-and-hominy stew on the Hopi Reservation.

12 El Camino Real & Turquoise Trail Cheeseburger topped with Hatch's famous green chiles? A match made in New Mexico.

24 Heart of Texas Laredo serves great Mexican eats while big steaks are the bait in Amarillo.

History & Culture

Ancient civilizations left behind cliff dwellings, gunslingers left bullet holes and the heroes of the Alamo left legends to fill a hundred books.

3 A Taste of the Old West Boothill Graveyard and the OK Corral spotlight miningtown lore in Tombstone.

10 Southwest Indian Nations Sojourn Cliff dwellings and petroglyphs provide clues about prehistoric lifestyles while museums cover the Indian Wars and native cultural treasures.

11 High & Low Roads to Taos Santa Fe recently celebrated its 400th birthday, but Taos Pueblo is older by 200+ years.

21 Hill Country Remember the Alamo then learn about President Lyndon Johnson at his ranch and his boyhood home.

The Open Road

When people hear the term 'Open Road,' an image from the Southwest is what likely comes to mind: sandstone canyons, big skies, saguaro-dotted deserts and twisty mountain ridges.

2 Route 66: The Southwest Long, uninterrupted stretches of the Mother Road unfurl across Arizona, with nary a stoplight in sight.

5 Fantastic Canyon Voyage Curve over mountains, roll past red rocks then zip through pine trees.

22 Big Bend Scenic Loop With the Marfa Lights and a renegade Prada store, things get weird on this lasso loop.

32 Highway 50: The Loneliest Road In spring, this highway across the white-hot belly of Nevada is flanked to the east by snow-capped peaks.

Sedona A drink with a view

Bringing the Kids

Adventurous families or those in search of something quieter – both will have a blast in the Southwest.

3 **A Taste of the Old West** Ride a stagecoach, watch a shoot-out and explore an old copper mine.

16 **Las Cruces to Carlsbad Caverns**
Enjoy livestock-milking demos, sled rides down a sand dune, and a cavernous wonderland.

27 **Moab & Southeastern National Parks**
Welcome active families! Kids keep busy with junior ranger programs at two national parks and there's low-key rafting and hiking.

29 **Dinosaur Diamond Prehistoric Byway**
Dinosaur bones and footprints are bait for budding paleontologists in Utah and Colorado.

Wine & Beer

Whether it's a post-hike microbrew in Flagstaff or a glass of wine after shopping in Sedona, it just feels right to celebrate your adventures.

2 **Route 66: The Southwest** Savor history and beer at Kelly's Brewery and the Museum Club.

5 **Fantastic Canyon Voyage** Wine-tasting rooms hug Hwy 89 while the Flagstaff Ale Trail loops past microbreweries.

7 **Southern Desert Wanderings** A special microclimate encourages fine grapes around Sonoita and Elgin.

11 **High & Low Roads to Taos** The art and the wine are locally grown in Dixon.

Hiking

The Southwest is a hiker's paradise, with scenery to satisfy every type of explorer: mountain, riparian, desert and red rock.

5 **Fantastic Canyon Voyage** To fully appreciate the age and immensity of the Grand Canyon, hike into its depths.

22 **Big Bend Scenic Loop** There are more than 200 miles of trails at this enormous park, with many good sunrise and sunset vistas.

25 **Zion & Bryce National Parks** Slot canyons, hidden pools and lofty scrambles are Zion highlights, and a Tolkien-esque forest of hoodoos wows 'em at nearby Bryce.

31 **Colorado's High Country Byways**
Ramble through the Rockies or slide over sand dunes.

NEED ᵀᴼ KNOW

CURRENCY
US dollar ($)

LANGUAGE
English, Spanish

VISAS
Generally not required for stays of up to 90 days for countries in the Visa Waiver Program. ESTA (Travel Authorization) required; apply online in advance.

FUEL
Gas stations are ubiquitous in urban areas and along interstates. They can be few and far between in isolated areas. Expect to pay $2 to $3 per gallon.

RENTAL CARS
Avis (www.avis.com)
Enterprise (www.enterprise.com)
Hertz (www.hertz.com)

IMPORTANT NUMBERS
AAA (☎800-222-4357)
Emergency (☎911)
Road Conditions (☎511)

Climate

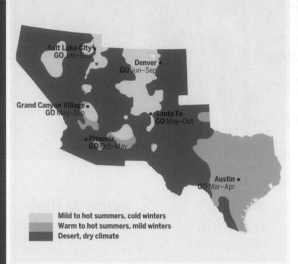

Salt Lake City
GO Jan–Dec

Denver •
GO Jun–Sep

Grand Canyon Village •
GO May–Sep

Santa Fe
GO May–Oct

• Phoenix
GO Oct–May

Austin •
GO Mar–Apr

■ Mild to hot summers, cold winters
■ Warm to hot summers, mild winters
■ Desert, dry climate

When to Go

High Season
» Summer temperatures (June–August) soar well above 100°F (37°C) and national parks are at max capacity; higher elevations bring cool relief.

» In winter (December–March), hit the slopes in Utah, Colorado and New Mexico; giddy-up at southern Arizona dude ranches.

Shoulder Season
» Fall (September–November) is the best season; check out colorful aspens in southern Colorado and northern New Mexico.

» Cooler temperatures and lighter crowds on the Grand Canyon South Rim (April–May, September–November).

Low Season
» National parks in Utah and northern Arizona clear out as the snow arrives (December–March).

» In summer (June–August), locals flee the heat in southern Arizona. Rates plummet at top resorts in Phoenix and Tucson.

Your Daily Budget

Budget: Less than $100

» Campgrounds and hostels: $10–45

» Food at markets, taquerias, sidewalk vendors: $7–12

» Economy car rental: $20 per day

Midrange: $100–250

» Mom-and-pop motels, low-priced chains: $50–100

» Diners, good local restaurants: $10–30

» Museums, national and state parks: $5–25

» Midsize car rental: $30 per day

Top End: More than $250

» Boutique hotels, B&Bs, resorts, park lodges: from $150

» Upscale restaurants: $30–75 plus drinks

» Guided adventures, top shows: from $100

» SUV or convertible rental: from $60 per day

Eating

Roadside diners Simple, cheap places with limited menus.

Taquerias and food stands Outdoor stalls selling tacos, frybread and Sonoran hotdogs.

Farm-to-table In big cities and towns popular with travelers, the focus is increasingly on seasonal and local produce.

Vegetarians Options can be limited in cattle country, but most places have at least some.

Eating price indicators represent the price of a main dish:

$	less than $10
$$	$10–20
$$$	more than $20

Sleeping

B&Bs Quaint accommodations, often in historic houses, usually include an elaborate breakfast.

Motels Affordable roadside accommodations, typically outside downtown; popular along Route 66.

Camping Facilities for tents, often at state and national parks. Some campgrounds also offer simple cabins and RV hookups.

Resorts Popular in warm sunny cities and beautiful backcountry areas; often have spas.

Sleeping price indicators represent the cost of a double room:

$	less than $100
$$	$100–200
$$$	more than $200

Cell Phones

Cell-phone reception can be nonexistent in remote or mountainous areas and map apps can lead you astray. Some models of unlocked cell phones with a US chip or foreign phones with an international plan should work in areas with coverage.

Money

ATMs widely available in cities and towns, but less prevalent on American Indian land. Credit cards accepted in most hotels and restaurants.

Time

Most of the Southwest is on Mountain Time. Arizona does not use daylight savings time (DST), so during that period it's one hour behind. The Navajo Reservation, which lies in Arizona, New Mexico and Utah *does* observe DST.

Useful Websites

National Park Service (www.nps.gov) Current information about national parks.

Lonely Planet (www.lonelyplanet.com/usa/southwest) Destination information and more.

Recreation.gov (www.recreation.gov) Camping and tour reservations on federally managed lands.

Grand Canyon Association (www.grandcanyon.org) Online bookstore with helpful links.

Public Lands Information Center (www.publiclands.org) Provides descriptions, maps and book recommendations.

Arizona Scenic Roads (www.arizonascenicroads.com) Routes and summaries for state and federal scenic roads in Arizona.

Opening Hours

Opening hours vary throughout the year. Many attractions open longer in high season. We've provided high-season hours.

Banks 8:30am to 4:30pm Monday to Thursday, to 5:30pm Friday; some open 9am to 12:30pm Saturday

Bars 5pm to midnight, to 2am Friday and Saturday

Restaurants breakfast 7am to 10:30am Monday to Friday, brunch 9am to 2pm Saturday and Sunday, lunch 11:30am to 2:30pm Monday to Friday, dinner 5pm to 9:30pm, later Friday and Saturday

Stores 10am to 6pm Monday to Saturday, noon to 5pm Sunday

For more, see Road Trip Essentials (p344).

CITY GUIDE

LAS VEGAS

Vegas has been reinventing itself since the days of the Rat Pack. To grab your attention and cash, the old makes way for the new. An oasis of indulgence dazzling in the desert, Vegas' seduction is unrivaled. The Strip shimmers hypnotically, promising excitement, entertainment, fortune and fame. Seeing is believing.

Las Vegas Aerial view of the Strip

Getting Around

Driving on the Strip can be stressful, and at 4.2 miles long it's not always feasible to walk. There are 24-hour bus and shuttle services, and a monorail, which is expensive and inconveniently located but has great views and regular services. Rideshare services are by far the best way to get around Vegas in most circumstances.

Parking

The golden days of free parking at Strip casino hotels and shopping malls are over. Find up-to-date rates at www.vegas.com/transportation/parking-garages.

Where to Eat

The volume and concentration of the Strip's celebrity chefs, hatted fine-dining restaurants and America's favorite food franchises is hard to fathom. If you're a foodie on a pilgrimage, do your research and narrow your selection before you arrive, lest you be unable to secure a reservation.

Where to Stay

The Strip stretches south on S Las Vegas Blvd from Circus Circus to Mandalay Bay. This is where the action is, and rooms are priced accordingly. Many hotels along the Strip charge an additional daily resort fee ($20 to $30). If you dig, you can find deals at older properties. Bargains can be had in summer, midweek and after holidays. Rates are typically lower downtown or just off the Strip.

Useful Websites

Eater Las Vegas (www.vegas.eater.com) News about chefs and restaurants.

Las Vegas Weekly (www.lasvegasweekly.com) Popular weekly magazine with events listings.

lasvegas.com (www.lasvegas.com) Online travel agent dealing solely with Vegas-related bookings.

Lonely Planet (lonelyplanet.com/las-vegas) Where to eat, sleep, shop and hit the town.

Trip through Las Vegas ❶

TOP EXPERIENCES

➡ **Cruise the Strip**
Take in Luxor's glowing beacon, New York–New York's Statue of Liberty, Bellagio's dancing fountains, Paris' Eiffel Tower, Mirage's erupting volcano and the gleaming beacon of the Stratosphere Tower. Phew!

➡ **Catch a Show**
Vegas is synonymous with world-class entertainment. Longtime casino residencies range from Queen Celine to Cher and Ricky Martin, but the real spectacle is Cirque du Soleil, whose resident shows remain the hottest tickets in town.

➡ **Eat like a King**
Per square mile, Vegas must be home to more celebrity chefs and hyped-up restaurants than any other city on earth.

➡ **Bar-Hop Downtown**
After cocktails on the Strip have stripped you of some serious cash, head to Downtown's buzzing Fremont East Entertainment District.

➡ **Shop Yourself to a Standstill**
Whether it's high-end fashion boutiques, please-'em-all malls or kitschy souvenirs, Vegas has myriad ways to lighten your wallet.

➡ **Meander Through Museums**
Sin City isn't the first place you'd expect to find galleries and cultural collections, but the Mob Museum, Bellagio Gallery of Fine Art and others are all worth an hour or two.

➡ **Explore the Surrounding Countryside**
If you have time, don't forget that Red Rock Canyon, Lake Mead and other jaw dropping sights lie outside the city limits.

For more, check out our city and country guides. www.lonelyplanet.com

CITY GUIDE

Santa Fe Outside the Palace of the Governors

SANTA FE

Welcome to 'the city different,' a place that makes its own rules without ever forgetting its long and storied past. Walking through its adobe neighborhoods, or around the busy Plaza that remains its core, there's no denying that Santa Fe has a timeless, earthy soul. Indeed, its artistic inclinations are a principal attraction – there are more quality museums and galleries here then you could possibly see in just one visit.

Getting Around

The Plaza area is easily covered on foot, but you will want a car for exploring outside downtown.

Parking

Near the Plaza there are parking garages at 216 W San Francisco St and 100 E Water St. Both are $1 to $2 per hour with a $12 daily maximum.

Where to Eat

Food is another art form in Santa Fe, and some restaurants are as world-class as the galleries. From spicy, traditional Southwest favorites to cutting-edge cuisine, it's all here. Reservations are always recommended for the more expensive venues, especially during summer and ski season.

There are a number of good restaurants near the Plaza, but some of the tastiest food is found at the city-licensed takeaway stalls on the Plaza lawn – try the beef fajitas with fresh guacamole. Many of Santa Fe's best eateries are in the Railyard District and along the adjacent Guadalupe St.

Where to Stay

When it comes to luxury accommodations, Santa Fe has a number of opulent hotels and posh B&Bs, with some unforgettable historic options within a block of the Plaza. Rates steadily diminish the further you go from downtown, with budget and national chain options strung out along Cerrillos Rd towards I-25.

Book well in advance in summer, particularly during the Indian Market and on opera nights, and also in December. Generally, January and February offer the lowest rates.

Useful Websites

New Mexican (www. santafenewmexican.com) Daily paper with breaking news.

SantaFe.com (www.santafe. com) Listings for upcoming concerts, readings and openings in northern New Mexico.

Santa Fe Reporter (www. sfreporter.com) Free alternative weekly with thorough cultural listings.

Trips through Santa Fe

1 11 12

Austin 'Live Music Capital of the World'

AUSTIN

With its quirky, laid-back vibe and its standing in the music world, Austin is one of the decade's definitive 'it' cities. Watch live music every night, stroll funky South Congress, dig into spicy Tex-Mex and tangy barbecue, and meet some of the friendliest people you'll find.

Getting Around

Downtown is easy to get around, and since Austin is pretty spread out, most everybody drives. However, you can always catch a Capital Metro bus (single ride $1.25) or take a taxi ($2.40 per mile).

Parking

Aside from downtown and campus, parking is usually plentiful and free. Downtown meters ($1.20 per hour) run late on weekends. The parking garage at 1201 San Jacinto is free for two hours and $2 per hour after that, maxing out at $12.

Where to Eat

Barbecue and Tex-Mex are the mainstays, but Austin also has many fine-dining restaurants and a broadening array of world cuisines. For hot tips on new restaurants, pick up the free alternative weekly *Austin Chronicle*, published on Thursday.

Top restaurants are scattered all over town, but South Congress (SoCo) has the best concentration of interesting eateries. For cheap meals on the go, try the food trailer enclaves on SoCo, East 6th and Waller Sts, or S First and Elizabeth Sts.

Where to Stay

Downtown has everything from high-end chains to the historic Driskill Hotel to the Firehouse Hostel. Chains in every price range are found along I-35, and while they may not offer the best Austin experience, great deals can be found. SoCo has some quirky and cool digs. Look for bed and breakfasts in the Hyde Park area.

Useful Websites

Austin CVB (www.austintexas. org) Detailed travel planning.

Austin 360 (www.austin360. com) Listings, listings and more listings.

Austin Chronicle (www. austinchronicle.com) Events calendar from the local weekly.

Trip through Austin

PHOENIX

Arizona's indubitable cultural and economic powerhouse, Phoenix is a thriving desert metropolis boasting some of the best Southwestern and Mexican food you'll find anywhere. And with more than 300 days of sunshine a year, exploring the 'Valley of the Sun' is an agreeable proposition (except in the sapping heat from June to August). Swanky Scottsdale shines with upscale malls, art galleries and posh resorts. Camelback Mountain watches over it all.

Getting Around

A car is the best way to navigate the sprawl, but always allow for traffic jams in your sightseeing schedule. Valley Metro operates buses all over and a 20-mile light-rail line linking north Phoenix with downtown, Tempe/ASU and downtown Mesa. The free Orbit Bus loops around downtown Tempe, and the Scottsdale Trolley is also free of charge.

Parking

Meters cost $1.50 per hour in downtown Phoenix (9am to 5pm weekdays). On-street parking in downtown Scottdsale is free, with time limits. At resorts, parking is usually included in the daily resort fee. Parking is plentiful outside of the downtown area.

TOP EXPERIENCES

➡ Eat Southwestern Cuisine
Phoenix is one of the hotspots of one of America's spiciest, most varied and beloved cuisines – the Mexican-inspired food of the Southwest.

➡ Hike the Surrounding Peaks
Camelback Mountain, Piestawa Peak and South Mountain provide a rugged, saguaro-studded playground for Phoenicians.

➡ Stay in Swanky Resorts
Greater Phoenix is home to top-notch desert oases, like the Biltmore, the chosen lodging of presidents and movie stars.

➡ Catch Local Sport
From the Phoenix Suns (basketball) to the Arizona Diamondbacks (baseball), Phoenix is home to the state's biggest teams.

➡ Potter Around Museums
From the Heard's peerless collection of Southwestern Indian artifacts to the fascinating Musical Instrument Museum, Phoenix has rare rainy days covered.

Phoenix Skyline at dawn

Where to Eat

Phoenix has the biggest selection of restaurants in the Southwest. Reservations are recommended at the more fashionable places.

Good restaurants are scattered across the metropolitan area, with clusters of tasty eats in downtown Phoenix, and in the Arts District and Southbridge in Scottsdale. Mexican restaurants, steakhouses and chic cafes are popular.

Where to Stay

Greater Phoenix is well-stocked with hotels and resorts, with a large concentration of resorts in Scottsdale. What you won't find is many B&Bs, cozy inns or charming mom-and-pop motels. Overall, the lowest rates can be found at national chain hotels. Prices plummet in summer, and you'll see plenty of Valley residents taking advantage of super-low prices at their favorite resorts when the mercury rises.

Useful Websites

Arizona Republic (www.azcentral.com) Arizona's largest newspaper.

Phoenix New Times (www.phoenixnewtimes.com) The major free weekly; lots of event and restaurant listings.

Visit Phoenix (www.visitphoenix.com) Greater Phoenix tourism website.

Trip through Phoenix 🔟

SOUTHWEST USA
BY REGION

The brick-red mesas, plunging canyons, verdant sky islands and endless horizon of the American Southwest make for classic driving country. Add vibrant cities and great centers of American Indian culture, and you could happily lose yourself under these endless skies.

Utah, Colorado & Nevada (p269)

The full gamut of spectacles the Southwest can offer – from petrified dinosaur tracks to the endless neon of the Las Vegas Strip – is up for grabs across these three stunning states.

Gape in wonder at Zion and Bryce Canyon National Parks on Trip 25

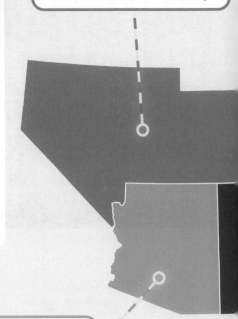

Arizona (p59)

Quintessentially Southwestern, Arizona offers nature at its most spectacular alongside a cutural legacy that stretches deep into American prehistory. From vibrant cities to true wilderness, the Grand Canyon State has it all.

Marvel at the Grand Canyon on Trip 5

See forests of saguaro cacti on Trip 7

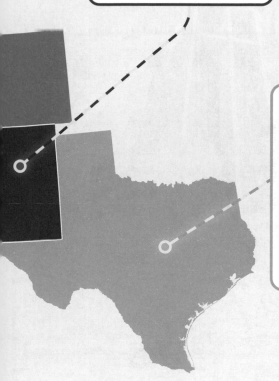

New Mexico (p137)

Whether it is fascinating visits to centuries-old Puebloan sites or losing yourself in the juniper woods of the high sierra, this enchanted state beguiles all who come its way.

Taste piquant New Mexican cuisine in Santa Fe on Trip 11

Scale the Sangre de Cristos Mountains on Trip 15

Texas (p227)

The endless skies of true cowboy country greet all who come to this seemingly boundless land. Deserts studded with quirky small towns, stunning national parks and one of the world's great music cities await.

Feel the music in Austin on Trip 21

Hike Big Bend National Park on Trip 22

SOUTHWEST USA

Classic Trips

SKY NOIR PHOTOGRAPHY BY BILL DICKINSON / SHUTTERSTOCK ©

2

What is a Classic Trip?

All the trips in this book show you the best of Southwest USA, but we've chosen seven as our all-time favorites. These are our Classic Trips – the ones that lead you to the best of the iconic sights, the top activities and the unique Southwest USA experiences. Turn the page to see our cross-regional Classic Trips, and look out for more Classic Trips throughout the book.

Above: Motorcycle riders on Route 66
Left: Chapel of the Holy Cross, Sedona

1

Four Corners Cruise

Everything about this trip demands superlatives – from the Grand Canyon to Vegas, Zion and beyond, it's a procession of some of the biggest, boldest items on many a bucket list.

TRIP HIGHLIGHTS

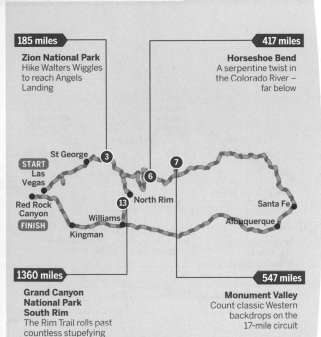

185 miles

Zion National Park
Hike Walters Wiggles to reach Angels Landing

417 miles

Horseshoe Bend
A serpentine twist in the Colorado River – far below

St George — 3

START
Las Vegas

6

7

Red Rock Canyon

13 North Rim

FINISH

Williams

Santa Fe

Albuquerque

Kingman

1360 miles

Grand Canyon National Park South Rim
The Rim Trail rolls past countless stupefying views

547 miles

Monument Valley
Count classic Western backdrops on the 17-mile circuit

---

10 DAYS
1593 MILES/
2564KM

GREAT FOR ...

BEST TIME TO GO
Spring and fall for thinner crowds and pleasant temperatures.

ESSENTIAL PHOTO
The glory of the Grand Canyon from the Rim Trail.

BEST FOR OUTDOORS
Angels Landing Trail in Zion National Park.

Zion National Park The path to Angels Landing

Classic Trip

1 Four Corners Cruise

From a distance, the rugged buttes and mesas of Monument Valley resemble the remains of a prehistoric fortress, red-gold ramparts protecting ancient secrets. Up close, you'll find these rocks mesmerizing, an alluring mix of the familiar and otherworldly. Yes, they're recognizable from multitudes of Westerns, but the big screen doesn't capture the changing light patterns, imposing height or sense of fathomless antiquity. It's a captivating spell — but by no means the only one cast along this Four Corners Cruise.

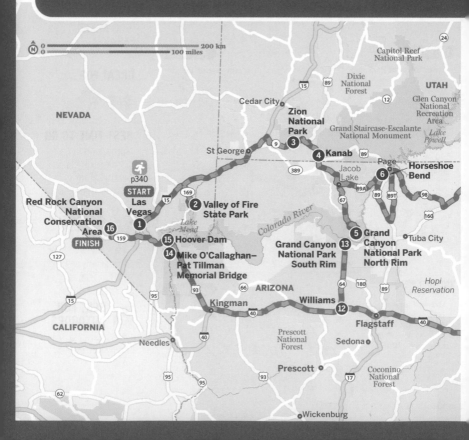

❶ Las Vegas

Take in Sin City's synthetic charms on a morning walk past the iconic casinos and hotels of the **Strip** (p340), then spend the afternoon downtown at the **Mob Museum** (📞702-229-2734; www.themobmuseum.org; 300 Stewart Ave; adult/child $24/14; 🕑9am-9pm; **P**; 🚌Deuce), a three-story collection examining organized crime in America and its connection to Las Vegas. One block south, zip-line over **Fremont St** from the 11th-story launchpad of **Slotzilla** (www.vegasexperience.com/slotzilla-zip-line; Fremont St Mall, Fremont Street Experience; lower line $25, upper line $45; 🕑1pm-1am Sun-Thu, to 2am Fri & Sat; 🚹; 🚌Deuce, SDX), then end the night with an illuminated stroll at the **Neon Museum** (📞702-387-6366; www.neonmuseum.org; 770 N Las Vegas Blvd; 1hr tour adult/child $19/15, after dark $26/22; 🕑tours daily, schedules vary; 🚌113).

The giant pink stiletto in the lobby of Vegas' **Cosmopolitan**

LINK YOUR TRIP

11 High & Low Roads to Taos

Take the high or the low road between Santa Fe and Taos, with fine craftwork, historic churches and mountain scenery.

27 Moab & Southeastern National Parks

From Monument Valley drive north on US 163 to US 191, continuing north to Moab and sandstone arches.

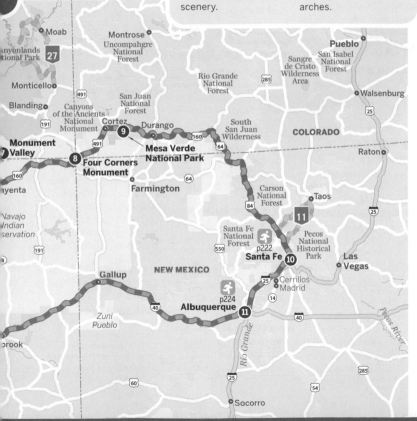

Classic Trip

(☎702-698-7000; www.
cosmopolitanlasvegas.com;
3708 S Las Vegas Blvd; ⏰24hr;
🅿) is an eye-catcher.
Designed by Roark
Gourley, the 9ft-tall
shoe was supposed to be
treated with the reverence due a piece of art,
but its protective ropes
were soon pushed aside
by partygoers seeking 'unique' selfies. In
response, the Cosmopolitan removed the ropes
and in 16 months the
outsized footwear got so
much love it needed to be
sent out for repairs.

 p45

The Drive ›› Follow I-15 north
for 34 miles then take exit 75.
From here, Hwy 169/Valley of Fire
Hwy travels 18 miles to the park.

---

❷ Valley of Fire State Park

Before losing yourself in
the sandstone sculpture-
gardens of Utah, swing
through this masterwork
of desert scenery to prime
yourself for what's ahead.
It's an easy detour, with
the Valley of Fire Hwy
and Hwy 169 running
through the **park** (☎702-
397-2088; www.parks.nv.gov/
parks/valley-of-fire; 29450
Valley of Fire Hwy, Overton;
per vehicle $10; ⏰visitor
center 8:30am-4:30pm, park
7am-7pm) and passing

close to the psyche-
delically shaped red rock
formations. From the
visitor center, take the
winding, scenic side road
out to **White Domes**, an
11-mile round-trip. En
route you'll pass **Rainbow
Vista**, followed by the
turn-off to **Fire Canyon**
and **Silica Dome** (where
Captain Kirk perished in
Star Trek: Generations).

Spring and fall are the
best times to visit; avoid
summer when temperatures typically exceed
100°F (37°C).

The Drive ›› Return to I-15
north, cruising through Arizona
and into Utah. Leave the
highway at exit 16 and follow
Hwy 9 east for 32 miles.

TRIP HIGHLIGHT

❸ Zion National Park

The climb up **Angels
Landing** in **Zion National
Park** (www.nps.gov/zion;
Hwy 9; 7-day pass per vehicle
$30; ⏰24hr, visitor center
8am-7:30pm Jun-Aug, closes
earlier Sep-May) may be the
best day hike in North
America. From **Grotto
Trailhead**, the 5.4-mile
round-trip crosses
the Virgin River, hugs
a towering cliffside,
squeezes through a narrow canyon, snakes up
Walters Wiggles, then
traverses a razor-thin
ridge where steel chains
and the encouraging
words of strangers are
your only safety net. Your
reward after the final
scramble to the 5790ft
summit? A bird's-eye

view of Zion Canyon. The
hike reflects what's best
about the park: beauty,
adventure and the shared
community of people
who love the outdoors.

The Drive ›› Twist out of the
park on Hwy 9 east, driving
almost 25 miles to Hwy 89.
Follow Hwy 89 south to the vast
open-air movie set that is Kanab.

---

❹ Kanab

Sitting between Zion,
Grand Staircase–
Escalante (p286) and
the Grand Canyon North
Rim, Kanab is a good
spot for a base camp.
Hundreds of Western
movies were filmed
here – John Wayne and
other gunslingin' celebs
really put the town on
the map. Today, animal
lovers know that the
town is home to the **Best
Friends Animal Sanctuary** (☎435-644-2001; www.
bestfriends.org; Hwy 89, Angel
Canyon; ⏰9:30am-5:30pm;
♿), the country's largest
no-kill animal shelter.
Tours of the facility –
home to dogs, cats, pigs,
birds and more – are
free, but call ahead to
confirm times and to
make a reservation. The
sanctuary is located in
Angel Canyon, also called
Kanab Canyon by locals.

 p45

The Drive ›› Continue into
Arizona – now on Hwy 89A –
and climb the Kaibab Plateau.
Turn south onto Hwy 67 at
Jacob Lake and drive 44 miles
to Grand Canyon Lodge.

❺ Grand Canyon National Park North Rim

While driving through the ponderosa forest that opens onto rolling meadows in Kaibab National Forest, keep an eye out for mule deer as you approach the entrance to the **park** (www.nps.gov/grca; per vehicle $30, per motorcycle $25, per bicycle, pedestrian or shuttle-bus passenger $15; ⊙mid-May–mid-Oct). Stop by the **North Rim Visitor Center** (☎928-638-7888; www.nps.gov/grca; ⊙8am-6pm mid-May–mid-Oct), beside Grand Canyon Lodge (p75; both closed during the snows of October to May), for information and to join ranger-led nature walks and nighttime programs. If it's five o'clock somewhere, enjoy a cocktail from the lodge terrace of the **Rough Rider Saloon** (www.grandcanyonforever.com; Grand Canyon Lodge; ⊙5:30-10:30am & 11:30am-10:30pm) while soaking up the view.

For an easy but scenic half-day hike, follow the 4-mile **Cape Final Trail** (round-trip) through ponderosa pine forests with great canyon views. The steep and difficult 14-mile **North Kaibab Trail** is the only maintained rim-to-river trail and connects with trails to the South Rim near Phantom Ranch. The trailhead is 2 miles north of Grand Canyon Lodge. For a taste

✓ TOP TIP: NO BOTTLED WATER

As a conservation measure, Grand Canyon National Park no longer sells bottled water. Instead, fill your thermos at water filling stations along the rim or at Canyon View Marketplace. Water bottles had constituted 20% of the waste generated in the park.

of inner-canyon hiking, walk 0.75 miles down to **Coconino Overlook** or 2 miles to the **Supai Tunnel**.

The Drive » Track back to Jacob Lake, then head east on Hwy 89A, down the Kaibab Plateau, past blink-and-miss-it Marble Canyon and to the junction with Hwy 89. Turn left and drive 26 miles north to Page.

TRIP HIGHLIGHT

❻ Horseshoe Bend

The clifftop view at Horseshoe Bend will sear itself onto your memory. One thousand feet below, the **Colorado River** carves a perfect U through a colossal thickness of Navajo sandstone. It's simultaneously beautiful and terrifying. There are no railings – it's just you, a sheer drop and dozens of people you don't know, taking selfies on the treacherous rim. Free-range toddlers are not a good idea. From the parking lot it's a 0.75-mile one-way hike to the rim. There's a moderate hill along the way, and the trail is unshaded, so the walk can be a little strenuous in summer – but it's worth it. The

trailhead is on Hwy 89, south of Page and just south of mile marker 541.

The Drive » Rejoin Hwy 89 and drive north a short distance to Hwy 98. Turn right and follow 98 southeast to Hwy 160. Turn left and drive 34 miles north, passing the entrance to Navajo National Monument. In Kayenta, turn left onto Hwy 163 North and drive almost 22 miles to Monument Valley, on the Arizona–Utah border.

TRIP HIGHLIGHT

❼ Monument Valley

'May I walk in beauty' is the final line of a famous Navajo prayer. Beauty comes in countless forms on this vast reservation, but Monument Valley's majestic array of rugged buttes and wind-worn mesas must be its most sensational. For up-close views of the formations, drive into the **Monument Valley Navajo Tribal Park** (☎435-727-5870; www.navajonationparks.org; per 4-person vehicle $20; ⊙drive 6am-7pm Apr-Sep, 8am-4:30pm Oct-Mar, visitor center 6am-8pm Apr-Sep, 8am-5pm Oct-Mar; P) and follow the unpaved 17-mile scenic loop that

Classic Trip

WHY THIS IS A CLASSIC TRIP
HUGH MCNAUGHTAN, WRITER

Epic, grandiose and utterly beguiling, this trip is nothing less than a crash course in the glories of America's Southwest. While Vegas is a global byword for sin and frivolity, there are plenty of opportunities to make peace with your soul in the wilds of the Grand Canyon's North Rim, in the peerless splendor of Zion National Park's canyons and in the sacred places of the vast Navajo Reservation.

Above left: Grand Canyon National Park
Above right: Riding the South Kaibab Trail

passes some of the most dramatic formations, such as the **East and West Mitten Buttes** and the **Three Sisters**. For a guided tour (1½/2½ hours $65/85), which will take you into areas where private vehicles cannot go, stop by one of the kiosks in the parking lot beside the View Hotel.

🍴 🛏 p45, p305

The Drive » Follow Hwy 163 back to Kayenta. Turn left and take Hwy 160 east about 73 miles to tiny Tee Noc Pos. Take a sharp left to stay on Hwy 160 and drive 6 miles to Four Corners Rd and the Monument.

----

⑧ Four Corners Monument

It's seriously remote, but you can't skip the **Four Corners Monument**

(☎928-871-6647; www. navajonationparks.org; $5; ⏰8am-7pm May-Sep, to 5pm Oct-Apr) on a road trip through the epicenter of the Southwest! Once you arrive, don't be shy: put a foot into Arizona and plant the other in New Mexico. Slap a hand in Utah and place the other in Colorado. Smile for the camera. It makes a good photo, even if it's not 100% accurate – government

surveyors have admitted that the marker is almost 2000ft east of where it should be (although it remains a legally recognized border point). Half the fun here is watching the contortions performed by happy-snappers determined to straddle all four states.

The Drive » Return to Hwy 160 and turn left. It's a 50-mile drive across the northwestern

tip of New Mexico and through Colorado to Mesa Verde. Hwy 160 becomes Hwy 491 for around 20 miles of this journey.

----

9 Mesa Verde National Park

Ancestral Puebloan sites are found throughout the canyons and mesas of **Mesa Verde** (☎970 529 4465; www.nps.gov/meve; 7-day car/motorcycle pass Jun-Aug $20/10, Sep-May $15/7; P 🚭 🐾), perched on a high plateau south of Cortez and Mancos. According to the experts, the Ancestral Puebloans didn't 'disappear' 700 years ago, they simply migrated south, developing into the American Indian tribes that live in the Southwest to this day. If you only have time for a short visit, check out the **Chapin Mesa Museum** and walk through the **Spruce Tree House**, where you can climb down a wooden ladder into a kiva.

Mesa Verde rewards travelers who set aside a day or more to take the ranger-led tours of **Cliff Palace** and **Balcony House**, explore **Wetherill Mesa** (the quieter side of canyon), linger around the museum, or participate in one of the campfire programs at

Morefield Campground (☎970-529-4465; www. visitmesaverde.com; Mile 4; tent/RV site $30/40; ☺May-early Oct; 🐾). The park also provides plenty of hiking, skiing, snow-shoeing and mountain-biking options. Visitors can camp out or stay in luxury at the lodge.

The Drive » Hop back onto US 160, following it 36 miles east to Durango and then another 61 miles to join US 84 south for the 151-mile run to Santa Fe. You'll pass through Abiquiú, home of artist Georgia O'Keeffe from 1949 until her death in 1986. Continue toward Santa Fe, exiting onto N Guadalupe St to head toward the Plaza.

----

10 Santa Fe

This 400-year-old city is pretty darn inviting. You've got the juxtaposition of art and landscape, with cow skulls hanging from sky-blue walls and slender crosses topping centuries-old missions. And then there's the comfortable mingling of American Indian, Hispanic and Anglo cultures, with ancient pueblos, 300-year-old haciendas and stylish modern buildings standing in easy proximity.

The beauty of the region was captured by New Mexico's most famous artist, Georgia O'Keeffe. Possessing the world's largest collection of her work, the **Georgia O'Keeffe Museum** (☎505-946-1000; www.

okeeffemuseum.org; 217 Johnson St; adult/child $12/free; ☺10am-5pm Sat-Thu, to 7pm Fri) showcases the thick brushwork and luminous colors that don't always come through on the ubiquitous posters. Take your time to relish them here firsthand. The museum is housed in a former Spanish Baptist church with adobe walls that has been renovated to form 10 skylit galleries.

The city is anchored by the **Plaza** (p222), which was the end of the Santa Fe Trail between 1822 and 1880.

🍴 🛏 p45, p149, p157

The Drive » The historic route to Albuquerque is the Turquoise Trail, which follows Hwy 14 south for 50 miles through Los Cerrillos and Madrid. If you're in a hurry, take I-25 south.

----

11 Albuquerque

Most of Albuquerque's top sites are concentrated in **Old Town**, which is a straight shot west on Central Ave from Nob Hill and the University of New Mexico (UNM). Soak up the ambience on a walking tour (p224).

The most extravagant route to the top of 10,378ft Sandia Crest is via the **Sandia Peak Tramway** (☎505-856-7325; www.sandiapeak.com; 30 Tramway Rd NE; adult/youth 13-20yr/child $25/20/15, parking $2; ☺9am-9pm Jun-Aug, 9am-8pm Wed-Mon, from 5pm Tue Sep-May). The 2.7-mile tram ride starts in the desert realm of cholla cactus and soars to the pine-topped summit. For exercise, take the beautiful 8-mile (one-way) **La Luz Trail** (www.laluztrail.com; FR 444; parking $3) back down, connecting with the 2-mile **Tramway Trail** to return to your car. The La Luz Trail passes a small waterfall, pine forests and spectacular views. It gets hot, so start early. Take Tramway Blvd east from I-25 to get to the tramway.

✕ ⊨ p45, p57, p157, p173

The Drive ›› From Albuquerque to Williams, in Arizona, I-40 overlaps or parallels Route 66. It's 359 miles to Williams.

----

⑫ Williams

Train buffs, Route 66 enthusiasts and Grand Canyon–bound vacationers all cross paths in Williams, an inviting small town with all the charm and authenticity of 'Main Street America.' If you only have time for a day visit to the park, the **Grand Canyon Railway** (☎reservations 800-843-8724; www.thetrain.com; 233 N Grand Canyon Blvd, Railway Depot; round-trip adult/child from $79/47) is a fun and hassle-free way to get there and back. After a **Wild West show** beside the tracks, the train departs for its 2½-hour ride to the South Rim, where you can explore by foot or shuttle.

Late March through October passengers can ride in reconditioned open-air Pullman cabooses.

On Route 66 the divey **World Famous Sultana Bar** (☎928-635-2021; 301 W Route 66; ⊘10am-2am, shorter hours in winter), which once housed a speakeasy, is a great place to sink some suds beneath a menagerie of stuffed wildlife.

TRIP HIGHLIGHT

⑬ Grand Canyon National Park South Rim

A walk along the **Rim Trail** (www.nps.gov/grca; ⊛; ⊒Hermits Rest, ⊒Village, ⊒Kaibab/Rim) in **Grand Canyon Village** brings stunning views of the iconic canyon, as well as historic buildings, American Indian crafts and geological displays.

Starting from the plaza at **Bright Angel Trail**, walk east on the

Rim Trail to **Kolb Studio** (☎928-638-2771; www.nps. gov/grca; National Historic Landmark District; ⊘8am-7pm Mar-May & Sep-Nov, to 6pm Dec-Feb, to 8pm Jun-Aug; ⊒Village), which holds a small bookstore and an art gallery. Next door is **Lookout Studio** (www.nps. gov/grca; ⊘8am-sunset mid-May–Aug, 9am-5pm Sep–mid-May; ⊒Village), designed by noted architect Mary Jane Colter to look like the stone dwellings of the Southwest's Puebloans.

Step into the 1905 El Tovar hotel (p89) to see its replica Remington bronzes, stained glass, stuffed mounts and exposed beams, or to admire the canyon views from its porches.

Next door, the **Hopi House** (www.nps.gov/grca; Grand Canyon Village; ⊘8am-8pm mid-May–Aug, 9am-6pm Sep–mid-Oct, 9am-5pm mid-Oct–mid-May; ⊒Village), another Colter-designed structure, has sold

PHOTO FINISH: KOLB STUDIO

Before digital photography, brothers Ellsworth and Emery Kolb were shooting souvenir photos of mule-riding Grand Canyon visitors as they began their descent down the Bright Angel Trail. The brothers would sell finished prints to the tourists returning to the rim at the end of the day. But in the early 1900s there was no running water on the South Rim – so how did they process their prints?

After snapping photos from their studio window that overlooked a bend in the trail, one of the brothers would run 4.6 miles down to the waters of Indian Garden with the negatives, print the photos in their lab there and then run, or perhaps hike briskly, back up the Bright Angel to meet visitors with their prints.

high-quality American Indian jewelry and other crafts since 1904. Just east, the **Trail of Time** (www.nps.gov/grca; Grand Canyon Village; ♿; 🚌 Village) interpretive display traces the history of the canyon's formation. End with the intriguing exhibits and gorgeous views of the **Yavapai Geology Museum** (☎928-638-7890; www.nps.gov/grca; Grand Canyon Village; ⊙8am-7pm Mar-May & Sep-Nov, to 6pm Dec-Feb, to 8pm Jun-Aug; ♿; 🚌Kaibab/Rim).

The Drive » Having returned to Williams, take the I-40 113 miles west to Kingman, then join US 93 north. Head north for 75 miles, crossing into Nevada, where exit 2 leads on to Hwy 172 and Hoover Dam.

⑭ Mike O'Callaghan–Pat Tillman Memorial Bridge

This graceful span, dedicated in 2010, was named for Mike O'Callaghan, governor of Nevada from 1971 to 1979, and for NFL star Pat Tillman, who was a safety for the Arizona Cardinals when he enlisted as a US Army Ranger after September 11. Tillman was killed by friendly fire during a battle in Afghanistan in 2004.

Open to pedestrians along a walkway separated from traffic on Hwy 93, the bridge sits 900ft above the Colorado River. It's the second-highest bridge in the US, and provides a bird's-eye view of Hoover Dam and Lake Mead (p120) behind it.

The Drive » Turn right onto the access road and drive a short distance down to Hoover Dam.

⑮ Hoover Dam

A statue of bronze winged figures stands atop **Hoover Dam** (☎702-494-2517; www.usbr. gov/lc/hooverdam; off Hwy 93; admission visitor center incl parking $10; ⊙9am-6pm Apr-Oct, to 5pm Nov-Mar; ♿), memorializing those who built the massive 726ft concrete structure, one of the world's tallest dams. This New Deal public works project, completed ahead of schedule and under budget in 1936, was the first major dam of the **Colorado River**. Thousands of men and their families, eager for work in the height of the Depression, came to Black Canyon and worked in excruciating conditions – dangling hundreds of feet above the canyon in desert heat of up to 120°F (49°C). Over 100 lost their lives.

Today, guided tours begin at the visitor center, where a video screening features original footage of the construction. After the movie take an elevator

ride 50 stories below to view the dam's massive power generators, each of which alone could power a city of 100,000 people.

The Drive » Return to US 93, following it west then north as it joins I-515. Take exit 61 for I-215 north. After 11 miles I-215 becomes Clark County 215. Follow it just over 13 miles to Charleston Blvd/Hwy 159 at exit 26 and follow it west.

⑯ Red Rock Canyon National Conservation Area

The evidence of awesome natural forces in this **national conservation area** (☎702-515-5350; www. redrockcanyonlv.org; 1000 Scenic Loop Dr; car/bicycle $7/3; ⊙scenic loop 6am-8pm Apr-Sep, to 7pm Mar & Oct, to 5pm Nov-Feb; ♿) can't be exaggerated. Created about 65 million years ago, the canyon is more like a valley, with a steep, rugged red rock escarpment rising 3000ft on its western edge, dramatic evidence of tectonic-plate collisions.

The 13-mile, one-way scenic drive passes some of the canyon's most striking features, where you can access hiking trails and rock-climbing routes. The 2.5-mile round-trip hike to **Calico Tanks** climbs through the sandstone and ends atop rocks offering a grand view of the desert and mountains, with Vegas thrown in for sizzle.

National park passes are accepted for admission.

Eating & Sleeping

Las Vegas ❶

✕ Joël Robuchon French $$$

(📞702-891-7925; www.joel-robuchon.com; MGM Grand, 3799 S Las Vegas Blvd; tasting menus $120-425; ⏱5-10pm) The acclaimed 'Chef of the Century' leads the pack in the French culinary invasion of the Strip. Adjacent to the MGM Grand's high-rollers' gaming area, Robuchon's plush dining rooms, done up in leather and velvet, feel like a dinner party at a 1930s Paris mansion. Complex seasonal tasting menus promise the meal of a lifetime – and they often deliver.

Kanab ❹

✕ Sego
Restaurant Modern American $$

(📞435-644-5680; 190 N 300 W, Canyons Boutique Hotel; mains $14-23; ⏱5-9pm Tue-Sat) If Kanab is aspiring to be the next Sedona, this boutique hotel-restaurant will fast track things. Gorgeous eats range from foraged mushrooms with goat's cheese to noodles with red-crab curry and a decadent flourless torte for dessert. There are also craft cocktails and local beers. Hours may be expanding. Reserve ahead: there are few tables.

🛏 Canyons Lodge Motel $$

(📞435-644-3069; www.canyonslodge.com; 236 N 300 W; r $169-179; ❄ @ 🤶 🐾 🐕) A renovated motel with an art-house Western feel. There's a warm welcome, free cruiser bikes and good traveler assistance. In summer, guests enjoy twice-weekly live music and wine and cheese by the fire pit. Rooms feature original artwork and whimsical touches. Recycles soaps and containers.

Monument Valley ❼

🛏 View Hotel Hotel $$$

(📞435-727-5555; www.monumentvalleyview. com; Indian Rte 42; r/ste from $247/349; ❄ @ 🤶) You'll never turn on the TV during the day at this aptly named hotel. Spread over three floors, the 95 Southwestern-themed rooms are pleasant, but nothing compared to the show from the balconies. Rooms that end in numbers higher than 15 (eg 216) have unobstructed panoramas of the valley below; the best, on the 3rd floor, cost $20 more.

Santa Fe ❿

✕ Cafe Pasqual's New Mexican $$$

(📞505-983-9340; www.pasquals.com; 121 Don Gaspar Ave; breakfast & lunch $14-19, dinner $15-39; ⏱8am-3pm & 5:30-10pm; 🌿 🐾) Whatever time you visit this exuberantly colorful, utterly unpretentious place, the food, most of which has a definite south-of-the-border flavor, is worth every penny of the high prices. The breakfast menu is famous for dishes such as *huevos motuleños*, made with sautéed bananas, feta cheese and more; later on, the meat and fish mains are superb. Reservations taken for dinner only.

Albuquerque ⓫

✕ Pop Fizz Mexican $

(📞505-508-1082; www.pop-fizz.net; 1701 4th St SW, National Hispanic Cultural Center; mains $5-8; ⏱11am-8pm; 🤶 🐾) These all-natural *paletas* (popsicles) straight up rock: cool off with flavors such as cucumber chile lime, mango or pineapple habanero – or perhaps you'd rather splurge on a cinnamon-churro ice-cream taco? Not to be outdone by the desserts, the kitchen also whips up all sorts of messy goodness, including carne asada fries, Sonoran dogs and Frito pies.

Classic Trip

Route 66: The Southwest

2

Concrete wigwams; neon cowboys; lumbering dinosaurs: you'll get your kitsch on Route 66 following this storied stretch of the 'Mother Road' through Texas, New Mexico and Arizona.

TRIP HIGHLIGHTS

735 miles
Seligman
As quirky and lovable as it gets on Route 66

90 miles
Cadillac Ranch
Ten colorful Cadillacs take a nosedive into the dirt

START
McLean

(10) Williams
(8)
(6)
(3)

Oatman
FINISH

615 miles
Meteor Crater
Peer over the edge of a mile-wide meteor crash site

560 miles
Petrified Forest National Park
Enjoy a sweeping park view at the Route 66 memorial

5–7 DAYS
900 MILES/ 1448KM

GREAT FOR...

BEST TIME TO GO
April through September for the best conditions on the Colorado Plateau.

ESSENTIAL PHOTO
Capture the quirky concrete tipis at the Wigwam Motel in Holbrook, AZ.

✓ **BEST 2 DAYS**
The natural wonders at Petrified Forest National Park and Meteor Crater.

Classic Trip

2 | Route 66: The Southwest

The Snow Cap Drive-In encapsulates everything that's cool about Route 66. There's personal interaction – did the guy behind the counter just squirt me with fake mustard? It's old-fashioned – why yes, I will get a malt. And it draws a diverse sampling of humanity – from a busload of bleary-eyed tourists to a horde of tough-looking biker dudes, all linked at the Snow Cap by the simple joy of an ice-cream cone.

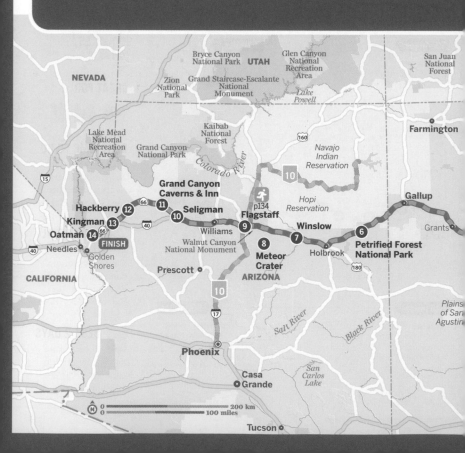

① McLean

Beyond the towns, the great wide open of the Texas Panhandle is punctuated only by the occasional windmill, and the distinct odor of cattle feedlots. The Mother Road cuts across this emptiness for 178 miles, and the entire route has been superseded by I-40 – but there are a few noteworthy attractions.

The sprawling grasslands of Texas and other western cattle states were once open range, where steers and cowboys could wander where they darn well pleased. That all changed in the 1880s when the devil's rope – more commonly known as barbed wire – began dividing up the land into private parcels. The **Devil's Rope Museum** (www.barbwiremuseum.com; 100 Kingsley St; ⊘9am-4pm Mon-Sat Mar-Nov) in the battered town of McLean off exit 141 has vast barbed-wire displays and a quirky little room devoted to Route 66. The detailed map of the road in Texas is fascinating.

LINK YOUR TRIP

10 **Southwest Indian Nations Sojourn**

Swap kitsch for cliff dwellings at Walnut Canyon, west of Meteor Crater.

24 **Heart of Texas**

Swing south to the colorful Palo Duro Canyon from Amarillo.

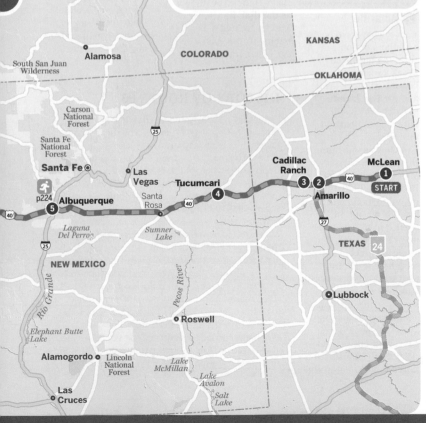

Classic Trip

Also worth a look are the moving portraits of Dust Bowl damage and refugees from human-made environmental disaster.

The Drive » I-40 west of McLean glides over low-rolling hills. The landscape flattens at Groom, home of the tilting water tower and a 19-story cross at exit 112. Take exit 96 for Conway to snap a photo of the forlorn VW Beetle Ranch, aka the Bug Ranch, on the south side of the interstate. 75 miles all told.

----

❷ Amarillo

This cowboy town holds a plethora of Route 66 sites: the **Big Texan Steak Ranch** (p263), the historic livestock auction and the **San Jacinto District**, which still has original Route 66 businesses.

As for the Big Texan, this hokey but classic attraction opened on Route 66 in 1960. It moved to its current location when I-40 opened in 1971 and has never looked back. The attention-grabbing gimmick here is the 'free 72oz steak' offer – you have to eat this enormous portion of cow plus a multitude of sides in under one hour, or you pay for the entire meal ($72). Contestants sit at a raised table to 'entertain'

the other diners. Less than 10% pass the challenge. Insane eating aside, the ranch is a fine place to eat, and the steaks are excellent.

The Drive » Continue west on I-40. Take exit 67, about 5 miles west of the edge of downtown Amarillo, then take S Western St under the interstate to Cadillac Ranch.

TRIP HIGHLIGHT

❸ Cadillac Ranch

Controversial local millionaire Stanley Marsh planted the shells of 10 Cadillacs in the deserted ground west of Amarillo in 1974 – an installation that's come to be known as Cadillac Ranch. He said he created it as a tribute to the golden age of car travel. The

cars date from 1948 to 1959 – a period in which tail fins just kept getting bigger and bigger. Come prepared: the accepted practice is to leave your own mark by spray painting on the cars. It can also get quite windy.

The Drive » Follow I-40 west 68 miles to the New Mexico border. Tucumcari – and its abundance of motel rooms – is 42 miles further.

----

❹ Tucumcari

A ranching and farming town sandwiched between the mesas and the plains, Tucumcari is home to one of the best-preserved sections of Route 66. It's a great place to drive through at night, when dozens

HISTORY OF ROUTE 66

Launched in 1926, Route 66 stretched from Chicago to Los Angeles, linking a ribbon of small towns and country byways as it rolled across eight states. The road gained notoriety during the Great Depression, when migrant farmers followed it west from the Dust Bowl across the Great Plains. The nickname 'The Mother Road' first appeared in John Steinbeck's 1939 novel about the era, *The Grapes of Wrath*. Meanwhile, unemployed young men were hired to pave the final stretches of muddy road. They completed the job, as it turns out, just in time for WWII and the flood of soldiers and factory workers that took the road to fortune and despair. Things got a little more fun in the 1950s, when newfound prosperity prompted Americans to hit the open road. Sadly, just as things got going, the Feds rolled out the interstate system, which eventually caused the Mother Road's demise. The very last town to be bypassed by an interstate was Arizona's Williams, in 1984.

of neon signs – relics of the town's Mother Road heyday – cast a crazy rainbow-colored glow. Tucumcari's Route 66 motoring legacy and other regional highlights are recorded on 35 murals in downtown and the surrounding area. Pick up a map for the murals at the **visitor center** (📞575-461-1694; www.tucumcarinm.com; 404 W Route 66; ⏰8:30am-5pm Mon-Fri).

The engaging **Mesalands Dinosaur Museum** (📞575-461-3466; www.mesalands.edu; 222 E Laughlin St; adult/child $6.50/4; ⏰10am-6pm Tue-Sat Mar-Aug, noon-5pm Tue-Sat Sep-Feb; 🚹) showcases real dinosaur bones and has hands-on exhibits for kids. Casts of dinosaur bones are done in bronze (not the usual plaster of paris), which shows fine detail.

🛏 p57

The Drive » West on I-40, dry and windy plains spread into the distance, the horizon interrupted by flat-topped mesas. To stretch your legs, take exit 277 from I-40 to Route 66, downtown Santa Rosa and the Route 66 Auto Museum, which has upward of 35 cars from the 1920s through the 1960s, all in beautiful condition. It's 174 miles.

- - - - - - - - - - - - - - - - -

⑤ Albuquerque

After 1936, Route 66 was re-aligned from its original path, which linked north through Santa Fe, to a direct line west into

GALLUP MURAL WALK

Take a walk around Gallup, an old Route 66 town on I-40 between Albuquerque and the Arizona border, and experience its 136-year-old story through art. Starting from City Hall on the corner of W Aztec Ave and S 2nd St you'll see plenty of buildings sporting giant murals, both abstract and realist, that memorialize special events in Gallup's roller-coaster history. The city's mural painting tradition started in the 1930s as part of President Franklin D Roosevelt's Great Depression Work Projects Administration (WPA) program. It continues to this day, with 21st-century artists reimagining the story of Gallup through contemporary eyes.

Albuquerque. Today, the city's **Central Ave** follows the post-1937 route. It passes through **Nob Hill**, the university, downtown and **Old Town**. Stop for a walking tour of Old Town if you have time (p224).

The patioed **Kelly's Brewery** (www.kellysbrewpub.com; 3222 Central Ave SE; ⏰8am-10:30pm Sun-Thu, to midnight Fri & Sat), in now-trendy Nob Hill, was an Art Moderne gas station on the Route, commissioned in 1939. West of I-25, look for the spectacular tile-and-wood artistry of the **KiMo Theatre** (📞505-768-3544; www.cabq.gov/kimo; 423 Central Ave NW), across from the old **Indian Trading Post**. This 1927 icon of pueblo-deco architecture blends American Indian and art deco design. It also screens classic movies like *Singin' in the Rain* and *2001: A Space Odyssey*. For prehistoric designs, take exit 154,

just west of downtown, and drive north 3 miles to Petroglyph National Monument (p172), which has more than 20,000 ancient rock etchings.

🍴🛏 p45, p57, p157, p173

The Drive » Route 66 dips from I-40 into Gallup, becoming the main drag, lined with beautifully renovated buildings, including the 1928 Spanish Colonial El Morro Theatre. From Gallup, it's 21 miles to Arizona. Once in Arizona, take exit 311 for Petrified Forest National Park. It's 211 miles all up.

- - - - - - - - - - - - - - - - -

TRIP HIGHLIGHT

⑥ Petrified Forest National Park

The 'trees' of the **Petrified Forest** (📞928-524-6228; www.nps.gov/pefo; vehicle $20, walk-in/bicycle/motorcycle $10; ⏰7am-7pm Mar-Sep, shorter hours Oct-Feb) are fragmented, fossilized 225-million-year-old logs scattered over a vast

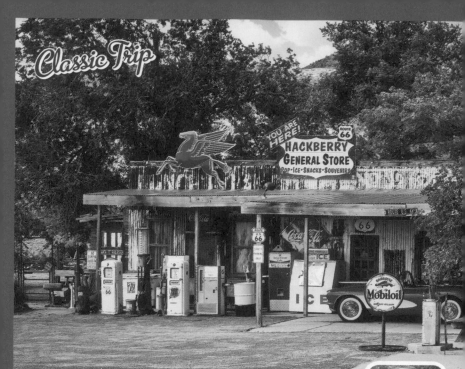

YOU ARE HERE!

ROUTE 66
HACKBERRY
GENERAL STORE
POP•ICE•SNACKS•SOUVENIRS

RAWF8/SHUTTERSTOCK ©

Blue Swallow
MOTEL

VACANCY
TV

17-0-3382

WHY THIS IS A CLASSIC TRIP
HUGH MCNAUGHTAN, WRITER

The stretch of the world's most famous motorway from Seligman to Kingman takes you to the heart of Route 66. From the quirky Burma Shave signs outside Seligman to the nostalgia-steeped Hackberry General Store and the heritage-listed motels of Kingman, it's the Mother Road as it once was, and hopefully will be for years to come.

Above: Hackberry General Store
Left: Blue Swallow Motel, Tucumcari
Right: Wigwam Motel, Holbrook

ANDREY BAYDA / SHUTTERSTOCK ©

CASS TIPPIT/SHUTTERSTOCK ©

area of arid grassland. Many are huge – up to 6ft in diameter – and at least one spans a ravine to form a natural bridge. The trees arrived via major floods, only to be buried beneath silica-rich volcanic ash before they could decompose. Groundwater dissolved the silica, carried it through the logs and crystallized into solid, sparkly quartz mashed up with iron, carbon, manganese and other minerals. Uplift and erosion eventually exposed the logs.

The park, which straddles I-40, has an entrance at exit 311 in the north and another off Hwy 180 in the south. A 28-mile paved scenic road, Park Rd (p54), links the two. To avoid backtracking, westbound travelers should start in the north, eastbound travelers in the south.

The Drive » Drive west 26 miles to Holbrook, a former Wild West town now home to rock shops and the photo-ready Wigwam Motel (p57), which was added to the National Register of Historic Places in 2002. If someone is on the grounds before the 4pm check-in, they'll probably let you peek inside one of the wigwams. Continue west on I-40; it's another 33 miles.

---

7 Winslow

Thanks to the Eagles' 1972 hit 'Take It Easy' (their first single release), lonesome little Winslow is now a popular stop on the tourist track. Pose with the life-sized bronze statue of a hitchhiker backed by a charmingly hokey trompe l'oeil mural of that famous girl in a flatbed Ford at the corner of 2nd St and Kinsley Ave.

✖ 🍽 p57

The Drive » Twenty miles west of Winslow, take exit 233 off I-40 and drive 6 miles south through cattle country, following the signs for Meteor Crater.

TRIP HIGHLIGHT

❽ Meteor Crater

Some 50,000 years ago an asteroid traveling at 26,000mph crashed here, blasting a hole more than 550ft deep and nearly 1 mile across. Today the privately owned **crater** (📞928-289-5898; www.meteorcrater.com; Meteor Crater Rd; adult/senior/child 6-17yr $18/16/9; ⏲7am-7pm Jun–mid-Sep, 8am-5pm mid-Sep–May; 🅿 ♿) is a major tourist attraction with exhibits about meteorites, crater geology and the Apollo astronauts who used its lunar-like surface to train for their moon missions. You're not allowed to go down into

the crater, but there are a few lookout points as well as guided one-hour rim-walking tours (free with admission). Look for the glinting piece of a plane that crashed inside the crater.

The Drive » Follow I-40 to exit 204 and pick up Route 66 into Flagstaff. This is also the exit for Walnut Canyon National Monument. From the east, Route 66 passes a lengthy swath of cheap indie motels as well as the Museum Club (3404 E Rte 66), a log-cabin-style roadhouse that's been refreshing road-trippers since 1936.

---

❾ Flagstaff

This cultured college town still has an Old West heart. At the **visitor center** (📞928-7293-2951; www.flagstaffarizona.org; 1 E Rte 66; ⏲8am-5pm Mon-Sat, 9am-4pm Sun), inside the historic train station, pick up the free Route 66 walking-tour guide. One building of note on the tour is the **Downtowner Motel**, formerly a brothel and now the Grand Canyon International Youth Hostel. Just north of Route 66 are two century-old hotels: the Hotel Monte Vista and the Weatherford Hotel. Both have plenty of character, not to mention convivial watering holes and lively ghosts. See them as part of a Flagstaff walking tour (p134).

If you're interested in architecture, stop by

SCENIC DRIVE: PETRIFIED FOREST NATIONAL PARK

The leisurely Park Rd, which travels through the park (p51), has about 15 pullouts with interpretive signs and some short trails. North of I-40, enjoy sweeping views of the Painted Desert, where nature presents a hauntingly beautiful palette, especially at sunset. After Park Rd turns south, keep a lookout for the roadside display about Route 66, just north of the interstate.

The 3-mile loop drive out to Blue Mesa has 360-degree views of spectacular badlands, log falls and logs balancing atop hills with the leathery texture of elephant skin.

Two trails near the southern entrance provide the best access for close-ups of the petrified logs: the 0.6-mile Long Logs Trail, which has the largest concentration, and the 0.4-mile Giant Logs Trail, which is entered through the **Rainbow Forest Museum** (📞928-524-6822; www.nps.gov; 6618 Petrified Forest Rd; ⏲7am-7pm Mar-Sep, shorter hours Oct-Feb) and sports the park's largest log.

Riordan Mansion State Historic Park (☎928-779-4395; azstateparks.com/riordan-mansion; 409 W Riordan Rd; tour adult/child 7-13yr $10/5; ☺9:30am-5pm May-Oct, 10:30am-5pm Thu-Mon Nov-Apr), practically part of the Northern Arizona University campus. Having made a fortune from their Arizona Lumber Company, brothers Michael and Timothy Riordan built this striking log-slab mansion in 1904. Its Craftsman-style design is the work of architect Charles Whittlesey, who also designed El Tovar on the Grand Canyon's South Rim.

 p57, p89

The Drive » Continue west on I-40 and Route 66 to Williams, home of the Grand Canyon Railway and the last community along Route 66 to be bypassed by I-40. Route 66 runs one way through town, from west to east – you'll need to take parallel Railroad Ave, rejoin I-40, then leave it again at exit 139. All up, a 76-mile drive.

TRIP HIGHLIGHT

⑩ Seligman

This town takes its Route 66 heritage seriously – or with a squirt of fake mustard, thanks to the Delgadillo brothers, who for decades were the Mother Road's biggest boosters. Juan sadly passed away in 2004, but evergreen Angel and his wife still run **Angel & Vilma's Original Route 66**

Gift Shop (☎928-422-3352; www.route66giftshop.com; 22265 E Rte 66; ☺9am-5pm winter, 8am-6pm rest of the year), where you can poke around for souvenirs and admire license plates sent in by fans from all over the world. The much-lamented Juan used to rule prankishly supreme over **Delgadillo's Snow Cap Drive-In** (☎928-422-3291; 301 Rte 66; mains $5-6.50; ☺10am-6pm Mar-Nov), a Route 66 institution serving burgers, ice cream and pranks that's now run by his children Cecilia and John.

The Drive » The Mother Road rolls northwest through dry, scrub-covered country, passing Burma Shave signs and lonely trains. After a drive of 25 miles, look for the kitsch dinosaur at mile marker 115.

----

⑪ Grand Canyon Caverns & Inn

An elevator drops 210ft underground to artificially lit limestone caverns and the skeletal remains of a prehistoric ground sloth at **Grand Canyon Caverns** (☎928-422-3223; www.grandcanyoncaverns.com; Mile 115, Rte 66; tour adult/child from $16/11; ☺8am-6pm May-Sep, call for off-season hours). While there's no connection with the Grand Canyon beyond the name, this can be a cool and diverting escape from the summer heat, and is always

popular with kids. And if you really want to make a night of it, $850 buys repose in the Cavern Suite. This underground 'room' has two double beds, a sitting area and multicolored lamps. If you ever wanted to cast yourself in one of those postapocalyptic survival movies, here's your chance!

The Drive » Continue west through Peach Springs, Truxton and Valentine, for 35 miles.

⑫ Hackberry

Tiny, sleepy Hackberry is one of the few still-kicking settlements on this segment of the Mother Road's original alignment. Inside an eccentrically remodeled gas station dating to 1934 is the **Hackberry General Store** (☎928-769-2605; www.hackberrygeneralstore.com; 11255 E Route 66; ☺9am-6pm Apr-Oct, 10am-5pm Nov-Mar). Originated by highway memorialist Robert Waldmire, the store is a great place to stop for a cold drink and Route 66 memorabilia. Check out the vintage petrol pumps, cars faded by decades of hot desert light, old toilet seats and rusted-out ironwork.

The Drive » From here, Route 66 arcs southwest, back toward I-40, then barrels into Kingman, which is 27 miles away.

Classic Trip

ROUTE 66 READS

John Steinbeck's 1939 novel *The Grapes of Wrath* is the definitive tale of travel on the Mother Road during the Dust Bowl era. Woody Guthrie's *Bound for Glory*, first published in 1943, is the road-trip autobiography of the revered folk singer during the Depression. Several museums and bookshops along Route 66 stock American Indian, Old West and pioneer writing with ties to the old highway.

⓭ Kingman

Founded in the heady 1880s railway days, Kingman is a quiet place today, but popular with Route 66 buffs for its well-preserved motels and other heyday architecture. A 1907 powerhouse holds the **visitor center** (☎928-753-6106; www.gokingman. com; 120 W Andy Devine Ave; ⊗8am-5pm) **and the small but engaging Route 66 Museum** (☎928-753-9889; www.gokingman.com; 120 W Andy Devine Ave; adult/senior/ child 12yr & under $4/3/free; ⊗9am-5pm, last entry at 4pm), **which really brings the glory days of the Mother Road to life. You could also check out the former Methodist church** at 5th and Spring St, where Clark Gable and Carole Lombard eloped in 1939.

In Kingman Route 66 is also called Andy Devine Ave, named after the hometown hero who acted in Hollywood classics like *Stagecoach*, in which he played the perpetually befuddled stagecoach driver.

The Drive » Route 66/Hwy 10 corkscrews 29 miles up through the rugged Black Mountains, passing falling rocks, cacti and tumbleweeds on its way over Sitgreaves Pass (3523ft) to the old mining town of Oatman.

⓮ Oatman

Since the veins of ore ran dry in 1942, crusty Oatman has reinvented itself as a movie set and Wild West tourist trap, complete with staged gun fights (daily at 1:30pm, and sometimes 3:30pm) and gift stores with names like **Fast Fanny's Place** and the **Classy Ass**.

Speaking of asses, there are plenty of them (the four-legged kind, that is) roaming the streets. Placid and endearing, they're the descendants of pack animals left by the early miners. These burros may beg for food, but do not feed them your lunch leftovers; instead, buy healthier hay cubes from nearby stores. Squeezed among the shops is the 1902 **Oatman Hotel** (☎928-768-4408; 181 Main St; ⊗10am-6pm Mon-Fri, 8am-6pm Sat & Sun), a surprisingly modest shack (no longer renting rooms) where Clark Gable and Carole Lombard spent their wedding night in 1939. On July 4 the town holds a sidewalk egg-frying contest. It gets quite warm here in summer.

From here, Route 66 twists down to Golden Shores and the I-40.

Eating & Sleeping

Tucumcari ❹

🛏 **Blue Swallow Motel** Motel **$**
(📞575-461-9849; www.blueswallowmotel.com;
815 E Tucumcari Blvd; r from $75; ❄ 🛜) Spend
the night in this beautifully restored Route 66
motel listed on the State and National Registers
of Historic Places, and feel the decades melt
away. The place has uniquely decorated rooms
with little chairs out on the forecourt, plus a
James Dean mural, and a classic neon sign.

Albuquerque ❺

🍴 **Artichoke Cafe** Modern American **$$$**
(📞505-243-0200; www.artichokecafe.com;
424 Central Ave SE; lunch mains $12-19, dinner
mains $16-39; ⏰11am-2:30pm & 5-9pm Mon-Fri,
5-10pm Sat) Elegant and unpretentious, this
popular bistro prepares creative gourmet
cuisine with panache. It's on the eastern edge of
downtown, between the bus station and I-40.

🛏 **Andaluz** Boutique Hotel **$$**
(📞505-242-9090; www.hotelandaluz.com;
125 2nd St NW; r from $174; 🅿 ❄ @ 🛜 🐾)
Albuquerque's finest historic hotel, built in
the heart of downtown in 1939, has been
comprehensively modernized while retaining
period details. Rooms feature hypoallergenic
bedding and carpets, the restaurant is notable,
and there's a rooftop bar.

Holbrook

🛏 **Wigwam Motel** Motel **$**
(📞928-524-3048; www.galerie-kokopelli.com/
wigwam; 811 W Hopi Dr; r $56-62; ❄) Embrace
the kitschy extremes of Route 66 at this 1937
motel, where each room is a self-contained
concrete tipi. Each is outfitted with restored
1950s hickory log-pole furniture and retro TVs.

Winslow ❼

🍴 **Turquoise Room** Southern US **$$$**
(📞928-289-2888; www.theturquoiseroom.net;
305 E 2nd St, La Posada; breakfast $11-12, lunch
$10-13, dinner $28-31; ⏰7am-4pm & 5-9pm)
Treat yourself to the best meal between Flagstaff
and Albuquerque at La Posada's unique in-house
restaurant. Dishes have a neo-Southwestern flair
and the placemats are handpainted works of art.

🛏 **La Posada** Historic Hotel **$$**
(📞928-289-4366; www.laposada.org; 303 E 2nd
St; d/deluxe $139/169; ❄ 🛜 🐾) An impressively
restored 1930 hacienda designed by the star
architect *du jour* Mary Jane Colter, this was the
last great railroad hotel built for the Fred Harvey
Company along the Santa Fe Railroad. Elaborate
tilework, glass-and-tin chandeliers, Navajo rugs
and other details accent its palatial elegance.

Flagstaff ❾

🍴 **Brix Restaurant
& Wine Bar** International **$$$**
(📞928-213-1021; www.brixflagstaff.com; 413
N San Francisco St; mains $30-32; ⏰5-9pm
Sun & Tue-Thu, to 10pm Fri & Sat; 🍴) Brix offers
seasonal, locally sourced and generally top-notch
fare in a handsome room with exposed brick
walls and an intimate copper bar. Lip-smacking
dishes include cavatelli with Calabrese sausage,
kale and preserved lemon. The wine list is well
curated, and reservations are recommended.

🛏 **Motel Dubeau** Hostel **$**
(📞928-774-6731; www.modubeau.com; 19
W Phoenix Ave; dm/r from $27/53; 🅿 ❄ @ 🛜)
Built in 1929 as Flagstaff's first motel, this
independent hostel offers friendly service and
clean, well-run accommodations. The private
rooms are similar to basic, but handsome, hotel
rooms, with refrigerators, cable TV and private
bathrooms. On-site Nomads serves beer, wine
and light snacks. There are also kitchen and
laundry facilities.

Arizona

ARIZONA IS MADE FOR ROADRUNNERS.
The sixth-largest state in the Union is not
only blessed with jaw-dropping landscapes,
its excellent road network holds some iconic
stretches of tarmac, linking towns, forests,
canyons and waterways that demand
exploration.

And, of course, this is outlaw country. Just
look at the ornery characters and give-'em-hell
stops along these drives: Wyatt Earp took no
prisoners at the OK Corral; wily Geronimo gave
the US Army fits in the Chiricahua Mountains;
the sinful old mining town of Jerome clings
tightly to a crumbling hillside; an ambitious
developer dropped London Bridge into the
empty desert; and finally, there's the relentless
Colorado River, which has been gouging out
the Grand Canyon for 6 million years. So get
your motor runnin'...

Grand Canyon National Park Sunrise at Mather Point (Trip 5)
JAY YUAN / SHUTTERSTOCK ©

59

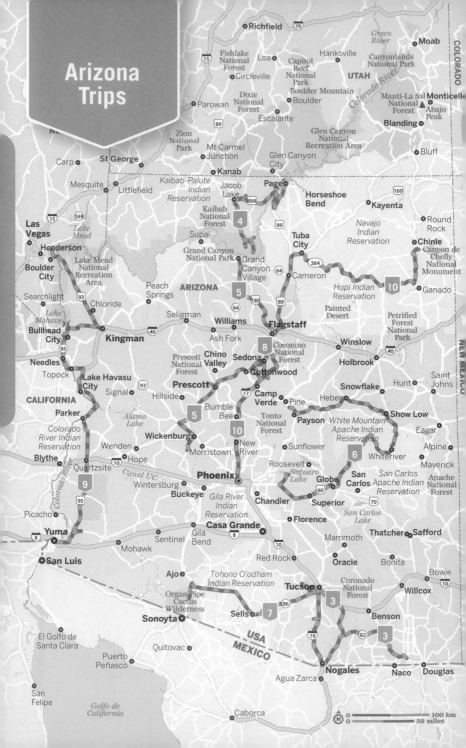

Arizona
Trips

3 **A Taste of the Old West 3 days**
Watch the gunfight at the OK Corral then explore the Queen Mine. (p63)

4 **Grand Canyon North Rim & Lake Powell 3 days**
Follow the Colorado River on its course from Glen Canyon Dam. (p71)

Classic Trip
5 **Fantastic Canyon Voyage 4–5 days**
Cowboy up in Wickenburg, enjoy views in Jerome, then applaud the Grand Canyon. (p79)

6 **Mogollon Rim Country 3–5 days**
The Colorado Plateau crashes against the desert, and this trip cruises the edge. (p91)

7 **Southern Desert Wanderings 3–4 days**
Parks and museums reveal the wonders of the Sonoran Desert. (p99)

8 **Highway 89A: Red Rock Country 2 days**
Hike the red rocks then polish up for galleries, shops and upscale eateries. (p107)

9 **Highway 95: Yuma to Lake Mead 3 days**
Every bend of the Colorado River brings another quirky surprise. (p115)

10 **Southwest Indian Nations Sojourn 3–4 days**
Travel north from prehistoric cliff dwellings to today's Navajo and Hopi reservations. (p123)

 DON'T MISS

Audrey Headframe Park
Stand on a piece of glass over a 1910ft mining shaft. Look down, if you dare, on Trip **5**

Pondering Petroglyphs
Solar calendars? The art of shamans? Or simply prehistoric graffiti? See for yourself in central Arizona on Trips **2** **8**

Horseshoe Bend
If you're a sucker for a gobsmacking view, stroll to this cliffside perch to peer down at the Colorado River – 1100ft below – on Trips **1** **4**

Superstition Mountain Museum
Small and old-school, but a charmer; check out its wacky wildlife dioramas, treasure maps and the likely looting gear of a stagecoach robber on Trip **6**

Airport Mesa
It's an easy scramble to a sweeping 360-degree view of Sedona's monolithic red rocks on Trips **5** **8**

A Taste of the Old West

3

There are three certainties in southern Arizona: big skies, boisterous saloons and endless forests of the iconic saguaro cactus, marching away to the horizon and Mexico.

TRIP HIGHLIGHTS

93 miles

Fairbank Historic Site
For an easy-to-reach ghost town, stop here

102 miles

Tombstone
Watch the 2pm shoot-out at the OK Corral

START
Tucson

2

4

6

FINISH

9

129 miles

Bisbee
This former mining town has reinvented itself as a bohemian enclave

Gates Pass Scenic Overlook
Mountain-flanked view of western Arizona

9 miles

3 DAYS
129 MILES/207KM

GREAT FOR...

BEST TIME TO GO
While the higher stops are cooler, and accessible year-round, Tucson really roasts in the summer months.

 ESSENTIAL PHOTO

A mountain-framed view of the Sonoran Desert at Gates Pass Scenic Overlook.

 BEST FOR WESTERN FANTASIES

The saguaro-swaddled outdoor movie set that is Old Tucson Studios.

3 A Taste of the Old West

Murdered. Shot. Stabbed. Drowned. Killed by Indians. Cowboy Killed in Stampede. The epitaphs at Boothill Graveyard outside Tombstone are brutally specific. One quick stroll around tells you everything you need to know about living – and dying – in Western mining towns in the late 1800s. Though legend may exceed reality, the discovery of gold, silver and copper deposits lured prospectors, gunslingers and outlaws – the entire cast of characters that made the 'Arizona Territory' a true frontier.

1 Tucson

Tucson's Old Western roots go deep: the **Presidio Historic District** (www.nps.gov/nr/travel/amsw/sw7.htm) is a throwback to the Spanish military presence in the 18th century. For an engaging primer on Arizona's Old West history, visit the **Arizona History Museum** (☏520-628-5774; www.arizonahistoricalsociety.org; 949 E 2nd St; adult/senior/child 12-16yr $8/6/4; ☉9am-4pm Mon-Thu, 9am-8pm Fri, 11am-4pm Sat; 🚻) beside the University of Arizona's 1885 campus.

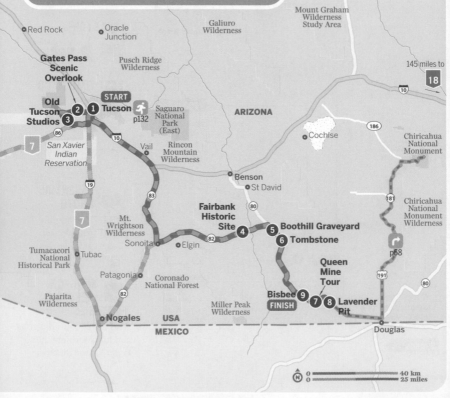

The Arizona Mining Hall exhibit is a walk-through replica of an old copper mine. The Geronimo exhibit displays the Apache warrior's rifle and an 1880s photograph of his negotiations with United States Army General George Crook, taken by Tombstone photographer CS Fly. Lined with charismatic bars and indie businesses, **4th Avenue** (www.fourthavenue.org) is 1 mile west of here.

For more art and history, try the Tucson walking tour (p132).

 p69, 105

The Drive » Drive north two blocks to E Speedway Blvd and turn left. Continue 9 miles as Speedway becomes W Gates Pass Rd and swoops into Tucson Mountain Park. Watch for cops and cyclists. As you climb toward the pass, look for a one-way sign. Turn right here. If you miss it, turn around at the next parking lot.

LINK YOUR TRIP

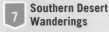

7 Southern Desert Wanderings

From Fairbank travel west on Hwy 82 to Sonoita for wine tasting and high-country wandering.

18 Into the Gila

Drive north from Tombstone to I-10 east for some green chile in southwestern New Mexico.

TRIP HIGHLIGHT

❷ Gates Pass Scenic Overlook

Named for Thomas Gates, who was looking for a short cut through the Tucson Mountains to his carbonate mine, this **overlook** (W Gates Pass Rd) offers a mountain-flanked view of western Arizona. On a clear day you can see 36 miles across the desert to 6875ft **Kitt Peak**, home of the Kitt Peak National Observatory (p104). There are trails, interpretive signs and stunning forests of saguaro. It's a delightful place to watch the sunset.

The Drive » Continue west until Gates Pass Rd ends. Turn left onto S Kinney Rd.

❸ Old Tucson Studios

Nicknamed 'Hollywood in the Desert,' this **old movie set** (☎520-883-0100; www.oldtucson.com; 201 S Kinney Rd; adult/child 4-11yr $19/11; ⏰10am-5pm daily Feb-Apr, 10am-5pm Fri-Sun May, 10am-5pm Sat & Sun Jun-early Sep; 🅿️ 🚻) of 1860s Tucson was built in 1939 for the filming of *Arizona* (1940). Hundreds of flicks followed, bringing in a galaxy of stars. Now a Wild West theme park, it caters mainly to families hankering for shoot-outs, stagecoach rides, saloons, sheriffs and stunts (but no roller coasters

or similar rides). The **museum** displays movie and TV memorabilia, including clothing worn by Clint Eastwood in *Joe Kidd* (1972) and Michael Landon in *Little House on the Prairie* (1974). The surrounding saguaro-studded mountainsides are a stunning spectacle in their own right.

The Drive » Follow S Kinney Rd south to Hwy 86 E. Drive east to I-19, following it north to I-10 east. Continue 21 miles to exit 281 for Hwy 83 south. Pick up Hwy 82 east and cross the San Pedro River. The Fairbank turnoff is just ahead on the left. The total drive is around 87 miles.

TRIP HIGHLIGHT

❹ Fairbank Historic Site

It's the silence that grabs you on a stroll through the ghost town of **Fairbank** (☎520-457-3062; ⏰dawn-dusk), on Hwy 82, just east of San Pedro River, where a handful of old buildings cluster near the road and the river. Established in 1881 to serve the New Mexico & Arizona Railroad, Fairbank was a transportation hub for nearby mining towns, quickly reaching a population of 15,000. The last residents left in the 1970s. Today, there's a **visitor center** (Hwy 82; ⏰9:30am-5:30pm Fri-Sun, hours vary) with displays in the restored 1920s schoolhouse; if it's closed, pick up the walking-tour brochure from the kiosk. The tour loops past abandoned houses, a stable and an 1882 mercantile building.

The Drive » Drive east on Hwy 82 to Hwy 80. Turn right and drive south about 3 miles.

❺ Boothill Graveyard

Boot Hill was a name commonly given to graveyards for gunslingers and those who died violent deaths, ie they died with their boots on. For a list of the graves – and causes of death – of those buried in this **cemetery** (☎520-457-3300; 408 Hwy 80; adult/child 15yr & under $3/ free; ⏰8am-6pm), buy the brochure at the entrance. The graves of Billy Clanton and Tom and Frank McLaury, all killed at the shoot-out at the OK Corral, are on Row 2. The marker for Lester Moore, a Wells Fargo agent, may be the most famous: 'Here lies Lester Moore, Four slugs from a .44, No Les, no More.'

The Drive » Turn left onto Hwy 80, which becomes E Fremont St in Tombstone, about 0.25 miles ahead.

TRIP HIGHLIGHT

❻ Tombstone

On October 26, 1881, Wyatt Earp, brothers Virgil and Morgan and their friend Doc Holliday gunned down outlaws Billy Clanton and Tom and Frank McLaury at

the **OK Corral** (☎520-457-3456; www.ok-corral.com; Allen St, btwn 3rd & 4th Sts; entry $10, without gunfight $6; ⏰9am-5pm). Today, the corral is the heart of Tombstone. It has models of the gunfighters and other exhibits, including CS Fly's early photography studio and a recreated 'crib,' the term for rooms used by hardworking, low-paid prostitutes. The town earned its name from first-on-the-scene prospector Ed Schieffelin, who was told all he would find in the dangerous region was his own tombstone.

The **Bird Cage Theater** (☎520-457-3421; www. tombstonebirdcage.com; 517 E Allen St; adult/senior/child 8-18yr $10/9/8; ⏰9am-6pm) was a saloon, dance hall, gambling parlor and home for 'negotiable affections' in the 1880s. Today it's filled with bullet holes and dusty artifacts like Doc Holliday's old Faro gaming table. Doc Holliday's girlfriend's bar **Big Nose Kate's** (☎520-457-3107; www.bignosekates. info; 417 E Allen St; ⏰10am-midnight) is also full of Wild West character.

For a less sensational look at the town's past, visit the informative **Tombstone Courthouse State Historic Park** (☎520-457-3311; azstateparks.com/tombstone; 223 E Toughnut St; adult/child 7-13yr $7/2; ⏰9am-5pm).

🛏 p69

The Drive » Follow Hwy 80 southeast for 25 miles through desert scrub and the Mule Mountains.

❼ Queen Mine Tour

Could you have worked in the dark confines of an Arizona copper mine? Test your mental toughness on a tour of the **Queen Mine** (☎520-432-2071; www.queenminetour. com; 478 Dart Rd, off Hwy 80; adult/child 4-12yr $13/5.50; 👶) near downtown Bisbee. Visitors wear miners' garb, carry lanterns and ride a mine train 1500ft into one of the area's deepest copper mines. In the early 20th century this was the most productive mine in Arizona, famous for particularly deep-shaded turquoise rocks known as Bisbee Blue. The tour, which lasts about an hour, is fun for kids.

The **Bisbee Visitor Center** (☎866-224-7233, 520-432-3554; www. discoverbisbee.com; 478 Dart Rd; ⏰8am-5pm Mon-Fri, 10am-4pm Sat & Sun) is also here.

The Drive » Drive half a mile south on Hwy 80.

❽ Lavender Pit

The 'Scenic View' sign that points toward this immense stair-stepped gash in the earth might not seem accurate to all sightseers when confronted with this violent

Old Tucson Studios

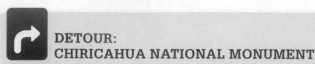

DETOUR:
CHIRICAHUA NATIONAL MONUMENT

Start: 9 Bisbee

Pronounced 'cheery-cow-wha,' this remote **national monument** (☎520-824-3560; www.nps.gov/chir; 12856 E Rhyolite Creek Rd; ⏰ visitor center 8:30am-4:30pm; P 🐾) is a wonderland of whimsical rock formations and ponderosa-fringed gulches. Rearing up from the surrounding seas of arid grassland, it's a 'sky island' of volcanic rocks shaped by the elements into fluted pinnacles, mighty bridges, balancing boulders and soaring spires. The remoteness made Chiricahua a favorite hiding place of Apache warrior Cochise and his men. Today, the same quality attracts birds and wildlife.

From Bisbee, take Hwy 80 then Double Adobe Rd west, turn north on Central Hwy to join Hwy 191, then take 181 to Chiricahua: all up 71 miles. The paved **Bonita Canyon Scenic Drive** climbs 8 miles to Massai Point at 6870ft, where you'll see thousands of spires positioned on the slopes like some petrified army. To explore in greater depth, hit the trails. A free hikers' shuttle bus leaves daily from the **visitor center** (☎520-824-3560; www.nps.gov; 12856 E Rhyolite Creek Rd; ⏰8:30am-4.30pm) at 8:30am or 9am, heading up to Massai Point. Hikers usually return by foot.

If you're short on time, hike the **Echo Canyon Trail** at least half a mile to the **Grottoes**, an amazing 'cathedral' of giant boulders.

but undeniably impressive scar in the earth. An open-pit mine, it produced about 600,000 tons of copper between 1950 and 1974.

The Drive ≫ Follow Hwy 80 north to Tombstone Canyon Rd, which leads into downtown Bisbee.

---

9 Bisbee

Bisbee built its fortune on ore found in the surrounding **Mule Mountains**. Between 1880 and 1975, underground and open-pit mines coughed up copper in sumptuous proportions, generating more than $6 billion worth of metals.

By 1910 the population had climbed to 25,000, and nearly 50 saloons and bordellos crammed notorious **Brewery Gulch**.

As the local copper mines began to fizzle in the 1970s, hippies and artists arrived. The interweaving of the new creative types and the old miners has produced a welcoming bunch of eccentrics clinging to the mountainside.

The **Bisbee Mining & Historical Museum** (☎520-432-7071; www.bisbeemuseum.org; 5 Copper Queen Plaza; adult/senior/child 15yr & under $8/7/3; ⏰10am-4pm) does an excellent job documenting the

town's past and the changing face of mining. From there, wander the galleries and indie shops on **Main St**, with a side trip into Brewery Gulch, where the 100-year-old **St Elmo's** (☎520-432-5578; 36 Brewery Ave; ⏰10am-2am) always attracts a boisterous crowd. Or try the nearby **Old Bisbee Brewing Company** (☎520-432-2739; www.oldbisbeebrewingcompany.com; 200 Review Alley; ⏰noon-10:30pm Sun-Thu, to 11:30pm Fri & Sat), an easy-going watering hole that crafts a lip-smacking variety of brews, including root beer.

✕ 🛏 p69

Eating & Sleeping

Tucson ①

✗ Cafe Poca Cosa — Mexican $$

(📞520-622-6400; www.cafepocacosatucson.
com; 110 E Pennington St; lunch $13-15, dinner
$20-24; ⏱11am-9pm Tue-Thu, to 10pm Fri &
Sat) Chef Suzana Davila's award-winning nuevo-
Mexican bistro is a must for fans of Mexican
food in Tucson. A Spanish-English blackboard
menu circulates between tables because dishes
change twice daily – it's all freshly prepared,
innovative and beautifully presented. The
undecided can't go wrong by ordering the 'Plato
Poca Cosa' and letting Suzana decide what's
best. Great margaritas, too.

🛏 Hotel Congress — Historic Hotel $$

(📞520-622-8848; www.hotelcongress.com;
311 E Congress St; d from $109; 🅿 ❄ 🛜 🐾)
Perhaps Tucson's most famous hotel, this is
where infamous bank robber John Dillinger
and his gang were captured during their 1934
stay, when a fire broke out. Built in 1919 and
beautifully restored, this charismatic place feels
very modern, despite period furnishings such as
rotary phones and wooden radios (but no TVs).
There's a popular cafe, bar and club on-site.

🛏 Hacienda del Sol — Ranch $$$

(📞520-299-1501; www.haciendadelsol.
com; 5501 N Hacienda del Sol Rd; d/ste from
$209/339; ❄ @ 🛜 🐾) An elite hilltop girls'
school built in the 1920s, this relaxing refuge
has artist-designed Southwest-style rooms and
teems with unique touches like carved ceiling
beams and louvered exterior doors to catch
the courtyard breeze. The Hacienda del Sol has
sheltered Spencer Tracy, Katharine Hepburn,
John Wayne and other legends, so you'll be
sleeping with history. The restaurant, The Grill,
is fabulous too.

Tombstone ⑥

🛏 Larian Motel — Motel $

(📞520-457-2272; www.tombstonemotels.com;
410 E Fremont St; r from $79; ❄ 🛜) This one's
a rare breed: a motel with soul, thanks to the
personalized attention from the proprietor, cute
retro rooms named for historical characters
(Doc Holliday, Curly Bill, Wyatt Earp) and a high
standard of cleanliness. It's also close to the
downtown action. Children aged 12 and under
stay free.

Bisbee ⑨

✗ Cafe Roka — American $$

(📞520-432-5153; www.caferoka.com; 35 Main
St; dinner $20-30; ⏱5-9pm Thu-Sat, 3-8pm
Sun) Past the art-nouveau steel door awaits this
sensuously lit grown-up spot with innovative
American cuisine that is at once smart and
satisfying. The four-course dinners include
salad, soup, sorbet and a rotating choice of
mains – perhaps lamb albondigas (meatballs)
with chimichurri and wild rice. The welcoming
central bar is great for solo diners, and
reservations are recommended.

🛏 Shady Dell — Caravan Park $

(📞520-432-3567; www.theshadydell.com;
1 Douglas Rd, Lowell; trailers from $85; ⏱closed
high summer & winter; ❄) This vintage trailer
court puts guests up in original '40s or '50s
travel trailers, meticulously restored and
outfitted with period accoutrements such as
vintage radios (playing '50s songs upon arrival)
and record players. All have tiny kitchens and
swamp coolers; some have toilets, but showers
are in the bathhouse. A 1947 Chris Craft yacht
and a tiki bus are also available.

Grand Canyon North Rim & Lake Powell

4

Want the Grand Canyon without the crowds? Discover the secrets of the Colorado River on this lonely, lovely drive from Lake Powell to Lees Ferry and the canyon's North Rim.

TRIP HIGHLIGHTS

78 miles

Vermilion Cliffs Condor Viewing Site
Scan for birds in the morning

0 miles

Glen Canyon Dam
Tours drop deep into the 720ft-tall dam

START ❶

❼

❹

Bitter Springs

12 ❶
FINISH

Cape Royal
At the end of the road enjoy Grand Canyon views

44 miles

Navajo Bridge Interpretive Center
Offers lofty views of the Colorado River

159 miles

3 DAYS
159 MILES / 256KM

GREAT FOR…

BEST TIME TO GO
May to October when the North Rim is open.

ESSENTIAL PHOTO
The titanic U-curve of the Colorado River at Horseshoe Bend.

BEST FOR OUTDOORS
Hiking the wooded Widforss Trail along the edge of the Canyon's North Rim.

Grand Canyon North Rim & Lake Powell

The Arizona Strip is the Land that Time Forgot. Just look around as you glide over Navajo Bridge. Below, the Colorado River cracks apart the earth. To the north, the Vermilion Cliffs rear up like the crest of some preternaturally petrified crimson tide. To the south, windblown desert scrub sweeps unendingly toward the horizon. And overhead? California condors swoop from their nests, blocking the sun with their prehistoric wings. Marvel — but hold tight to the family chihuahua.

❶ Glen Canyon Dam & Lake Powell

The 720ft-tall **Glen Canyon Dam** (☎928-608-6072; www.glencanyonnha.org; Hwy 89; tour adult/child 7-16yr $5/2.50; ⊙tours 8am-6pm Mon, Tue, Thu, Sun, to 5pm Fri & Sat, to 4pm Wed) is a concrete ode to America's ingenuity and can-do spirit. Completed in 1963, it's the nation's highest concrete arch dam (Hoover Dam to the west is 16ft taller, but is technically a different kind

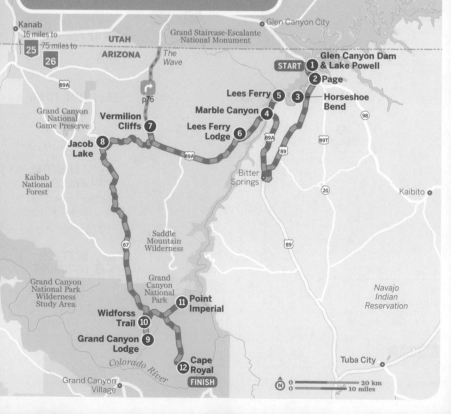

of structure). Guided 45-minute tours, departing from the **Carl Hayden Visitor Center** (📷store 928-608-6068, tours 928-608-6072; www.nps.gov/glca; Hwy 89; ⏰8am-4pm mid-May–mid-Sep, shorter hours mid-Sep–mid-May), drop deep inside the dam via elevators. Displays and videos in the visitor center tell the story of the dam's construction and provide technical insights into its operation.

The adjacent sparkling swath of blue is **Lake Powell**, part of the **Glen Canyon National Recreation Area** (📷928-608-6200; www.nps.gov/glca; 7-day pass per vehicle $25, per pedestrian or cyclist $12). The 186-mile-long lake was named for John Wesley Powell, the one-armed Union veteran who led the groundbreaking Colorado River expedition

LINK YOUR TRIP

25 Zion & Bryce National Parks

Leave the Kaibab Plateau on Hwy 89A and continue to Hwy 9, which makes a stunning red rock descent into Zion.

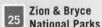

26 Scenic Byway 12

Swing north from Monument Valley for Ancestral Puebloan Ruins.

through the Grand Canyon in 1869. The lake straddles the Utah–Arizona border, its shoreline fringed with striking red rocks. Rent kayaks ($50 per day) at Wahweap Marina at the **Lake Powell Resort** (📷888-528-6154; www.lakepowell.com; 100 Lakeshore Dr; r/ste from $199/344, child under 18yr free; ❄🖤🅿🐾).

The Drive » Page is just three miles southeast. Take Hwy 89 south past Navajo Dr. For an expansive view of the dam, turn right onto Scenic View Rd, following it to the viewpoint parking area.

---

② Page

Established to house the workers who built Glen Canyon Dam, Page today is a great base camp for exploring the area. It's also the place to join a tour of the stunning **Antelope Canyon**, a slot canyon on the Navajo Reservation accessible only on Navajo-led tours. In the more popular upper canyon, about a quarter-mile long, water and wind have carved the sandstone into an astonishingly sensuous temple of nature. Tours can feel like cattle crushes, especially at noon when the perfect light in the canyon makes tours most popular, but the beauty of the site makes it worthwhile. Try **Roger Ekis' Antelope Canyon Tours** (📷928-645-9102; www.antelopecanyon.com;

22 S Lake Powell Blvd; adult/child 5-12yr from $45/35).

🍴 p77

The Drive » Follow Hwy 89 south out of Page. Continue 2 miles south after the junction of Hwy 89 and Hwy 98.

---

③ Horseshoe Bend

For a short hike with a dramatic payoff, it's hard to beat Horseshoe Bend. Here, a 0.75-mile, one-way path leads to a lofty view of the **Colorado River**, where it's cut a 1000ft deep horseshoe bend through sandstone for aeons. Though it's short, the sandy, shadeless trail and moderate incline can be a slog in hot weather. And watch your step – there are no guardrails at the viewpoint and the canyon lip can be treacherous. If you're afraid of heights, or don't trust your toddler-wrangling skills, stop at the covered hilltop shelter – the view is still mighty impressive.

The Drive » Follow Hwy 89 21 miles south to Bitter Springs, where the 89A branches northwest toward the scanty settlement of Marble Canyon, 15 miles further.

TRIP HIGHLIGHT

④ Marble Canyon

Hwy 89A crosses the Navajo Bridge over the Colorado River at Marble Canyon. Actually, there are two bridges: a modern one for motorists that opened in 1995, and the historical one dating to 1929. Walking across the latter you'll enjoy fabulous views down Marble Canyon to the northeast lip of the Grand Canyon. The **Navajo Bridge Interpretive Center** (☎928-355-2319; www.nps.gov/glca; Hwy 89A; ⏰9am-5pm Wed-Sun Mar-early Nov; 🅿) on the west bank has good background information about the bridges and the area. Keep an eye out for California condors.

The Drive ⟫ Return to Hwy 89A and turn right. Turn right again, almost immediately, onto Lees Ferry Rd. Follow it 6 miles.

❺ Lees Ferry

Lees Ferry is the premier put-in for Grand Canyon rafting trips on the Colorado River. It's also a very popular spot for fly-fishing. The area, which is a fee site within Glen Canyon National Recreation Area (p73), was named for John D Lee, the Mormon leader of the 1857 Mountain Meadows Massacre, in which 120 emigrants from Arkansas were murdered by Mormon and Paiute forces. To escape prosecution, Lee moved his wives and children to this remote outpost where they lived at the **Lonely Dell Ranch** and operated the area's only ferry service. Lee was tracked down and

executed in 1877, but the ferry operated until the Navajo Bridge opened in 1929. You can still walk around the ranch, and even sample the fruits of its orchards.

🛏 p77

The Drive ⟫ Take a right onto Hwy 89A and continue about 3 miles. This region, along the Colorado River north of the national park, is called Marble Canyon.

❻ Lees Ferry Lodge

This scrappy roadside bar (p77), not actually at Lees Ferry, is one of those joints where you're never quite sure who's going to roar off the highway and push through the door – rebel motorcyclist, park ranger, retired academic with a passion for lonely places – but they'll surely have a good story. There's a pool table and an impressive selection of beer.

🛏 p77

The Drive ⟫ Take 89A west, and turn right onto the graded House Rock Valley Rd (BLM Rd 1065) at the base of the Kaibab Plateau. Drive 3 miles further for a 25-mile total journey to get to the Condor Viewing Site.

TRIP HIGHLIGHT

❼ Vermilion Cliffs

To increase your chances of spotting a California condor, stop at the **Condor Viewing Site** (www.blm.gov/az; Hwy 89A), near

SOMCHAIJ / SHUTTERSTOCK ©

their release point. The birds, whose ancestors patrolled the skies in prehistoric times, were almost driven to extinction by the 1980s. The remaining condors were placed in captive breeding programs – six were released here in 1996, and more are released each year. Today, a good proportion of the entire global population of wild California condors can be found here.

The Drive ⟫ Return to Hwy 89A as it climbs 5000ft through the Kaibab National Forest to the lakeless outpost of Jacob Lake. All told, a quick 13-mile hop.

Horseshoe Bend

8 Jacob Lake

In these lonesome parts, Jacob Lake is the closest thing to a metropolis – and all it offers is a gas station, a handful of campgrounds, an inn with a bakery and restaurant, and the USFS **Kaibab Plateau Visitor Center** (📞928-643-7298; www.fs.usda.gov; cnr Hwys 89A & 67; ⏰8am-5pm mid-May–mid-Oct). The bakery at the Jacob Lake Inn Restaurant (p77) is known for its homemade cookies.

✗ p77

The Drive » The 44 miles between Jacob Lake and the Grand Canyon Lodge via Hwy 67 south is one of the Southwest's finest drives. It rolls through hills of ponderosa forest that open onto lush meadows in Kaibab National Forest. It is, however, closed between November and May.

9 Grand Canyon Lodge

For immediate inspiration, walk through the stunning sunroom at the Grand Canyon Lodge (p77) to the narrow, quarter-mile path that leads to **Bright Angel Point** (www.nps.gov; North Rim). Here you'll enjoy huge, unobstructed views into the canyon and across to the South Rim. On clear days, look for the San Francisco Peaks, more than 80 miles south.

At 8200ft, the North Rim is about 10°F (6°C) cooler than the South, which is 1000ft lower – even on summer evenings you'll need a sweater. Park admission is $30 per vehicle and the lodge and all services close from mid-October through mid-May.

🛏 p77

DETOUR: THE WAVE

Start: ❼ Vermilion Cliffs

The Wave is a trail-free expanse of slick rock that ends at a smooth, orange-and-white striped rock, shaped into a perfect wave. This sinuous sandstone swirl, which is located in the **Paria Canyon-Vermilion Cliffs Wilderness**, is a favorite of photographers.

A hike to the Wave requires a North Coyote Buttes permit ($7 for man and dog alike), which can be tough to obtain in spring and fall. To order a permit online, visit www.blm.gov and search for 'Coyote Buttes.' They're available four months in advance. The website also provides details about walk-up permits, awarded by lottery at the Grand Staircase–Escalante National Monument Visitor Center in Kanab, UT. If you win a spot, your permit is good for the *following* day. The Wave is around 5.5 miles from the trailhead at Wire Pass, reached by continuing north on House Rock Rd for 18 miles past the Condor Viewing Site, into Utah. Plan for a six-hour hike.

The Drive » Follow Hwy 67 2.7 miles north from the Lodge, passing the North Rim Campground. Continue about 1 mile west on the Point Sublime Access Rd.

----

❿ Widforss Trail

Pick up a sack lunch (remember to order the night before) at the **Grand Canyon Lodge Dining Room** (📞May-Oct 928-638-2611, Nov-Apr 928-645-6865; www.grandcanyonforever.com; breakfast $8-11, lunch $10-13, dinner $18-28; ⏲6:30-10:30am, 11:30am-2:30pm & 4:30-9:30pm mid-May-mid-Oct; 📷 🚻), then spend the morning hiking through meadows and aspen on this 10-mile round-trip trail. Following the edge of a forested plateau, it's a pleasant, pine-shaded walk with great rim-side views. It ends at 7811ft-high **Widforss**

Point, with awe-inspiring canyon views. It's a particularly pretty hike in September and October, when the trees turn golden.

The Drive » Drive north a quarter mile on Hwy 67 to Cape Royal Rd. Turn right, after around 5 miles turn left onto Point Imperial Rd, then continue a further 3 miles.

⓫ Point Imperial

Point Imperial is the highest overlook on the North Rim, at 8803ft. Soak up the view of Nankoweap Creek, the Vermilion Cliffs, Marble Canyon and the Painted Desert.

The Drive » Return to Cape Royal Rd and turn left, passing viewpoints at Vista Encantada, Roosevelt Point and Walhalla Overlook. It's about 12 miles to the Cape Royal Overlook.

TRIP HIGHLIGHT

⓬ Cape Royal

At the end of the road follow the 0.6-mile paved trail that passes **Angel's Window**, a natural arch, before ending at Cape Royal Point and its stupendous views of the canyon.

Eating & Sleeping

Page ❷

✖ Big John's Texas BBQ   Barbecue $

(📞928-645-3300; www.bigjohnstexasbbq.com; 153 S Lake Powell Blvd; mains $13-18; 🕙11am-10pm; 🐾) Cheerfully occupying a partially open-air space that was once a gas station, this barbecue joint is a friendly place to feast on pulled-pork sandwiches and ribs. Pull up a seat at one of the casual picnic tables, and look for live folk and bluegrass music several evenings of the week.

Lees Ferry ❺

🛏 Lees Ferry Campground   Campground $

(📞928-608-6200; www.nps.gov/glca; Lees Ferry, Glen Canyon National Recreation Area; tent & RV sites $20) On a small hill, Lees Ferry Campground has 54 riverview sites along with drinking water and toilets, but no hookups. With views of towering red rocks and the river, it's a strikingly pretty spot to camp. Public coin showers and a laundry are available at Marble Canyon Lodge.

Lees Ferry Lodge ❻

🛏 Lees Ferry Lodge   Lodge $

(📞928-355-2231; www.vermilioncliffs.com; Hwy 89A, Vermilion Cliffs; r/apt $74/125; 🅿❄🐕) Rustic, comfortable, but not actually in Lees Ferry (it's 3 miles west of Marble Canyon), this lodge has 10 rooms, plus a restaurant-bar with a huge array of international beers.

Jacob Lake ❽

✖ Jacob Lake Inn Restaurant   American $$

(📞928-643-7232; www.jacoblake.com; cnr Hwys 89A & 67; mains $19-22; 🕙6:30am-9pm mid-May–mid-Oct, 8am-8pm mid-Oct–mid-May; 🅿) Be surprised by dishes as adventurous as mountain trout almondine, or pork schnitzel in 'Kaibab hunter's sauce.' There's also an ice-cream counter and a great bakery, famed for its cookies. Try the Cookie in a Cloud, a cakey cookie topped with marshmallow and chocolate. During winter, dining is only available at the counter and the kitchen closes a half-hour earlier.

Grand Canyon Lodge ❾

🛏 Grand Canyon Lodge   Historic Hotel $$

(📞advance reservations 877-386-4383, reservations outside USA 480-337-1320, same-day reservations 928-638-2611; www.grandcanyonlodgenorth.com; r/cabin from $130/143; 🕙mid-May-mid-Oct) Walk through the front door of the lodge, and here, framed by picture windows, is the canyon in all its glory. Built in 1937 with wood, Kaibab limestone and glass, the lodge features a spacious rimside dining room and sun porches lined with Adirondack chairs. Guest rooms are not in the lodge itself – most accommodations are cozy log cabins nearby.

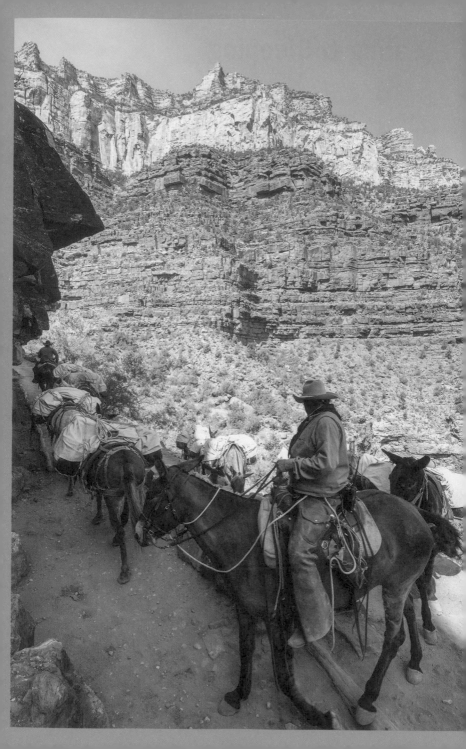

Classic Trip

Fantastic Canyon Voyage

The Old West meets the New on this scenic sojourn to the Grand Canyon. Visit cowboy country and mining towns, wineries and red rocks, before the grand finale at the Big Ditch.

5

TRIP HIGHLIGHTS

235 miles

FINISH
Grand Canyon Village
15

Bright Angel Trail
The descent? It's easy. The climb out? Very wheezy

132 miles

Flagstaff
6 9
3

Arizona Stronghold
Get cozy at this welcoming wine-tasting room

113 miles

Jerome
This cliff-hugging former mine town now peddles good wine, food and art

Congress **Yarnell**
Wickenburg
START

Prescott
Drink like Wyatt Earp on Whiskey Row

90 miles

4–5 DAYS
235 MILES/378KM

GREAT FOR...

BEST TIME TO GO
Visit in fall and spring, to beat the heat and summer crowds.

ESSENTIAL PHOTO

The Grand Canyon from Mather Point.

✓ **BEST FOR HISTORY & CULTURE**

Push through the swinging doors of history in Wickenburg, Prescott and Jerome.

Classic Trip

5 Fantastic Canyon Voyage

This road trip steers you through the greatest hits of Central Arizona, en route to the incomparable Grand Canyon. It's pretty, it's wild and it carries a decent whack of Arizona's rough-and-tumble history. Scenic trails wind past sandstone buttes, ponderosa pines and canyon views. Wild West adventures include horseback rides, saloon crawls and fathomless mine shafts. But this route isn't all about the past: a burgeoning wine scene and great contemporary dining add 21st-century allure.

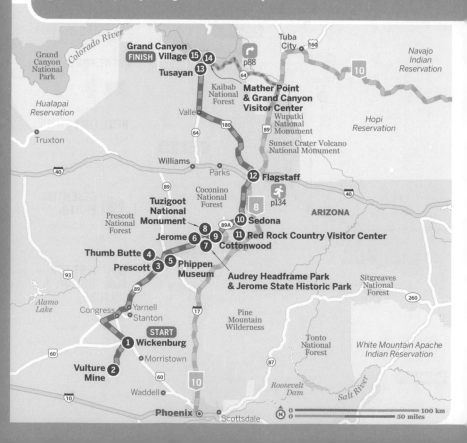

❶ Wickenburg

With its saddle shops and Old West storefronts, Wickenburg looks like it fell out of the sky – directly from the 1890s. At the ever-popular **Desert Caballeros Western Museum** (☎928-684-2272; www.westernmuseum.org; 21 N Frontier St; adult/senior/child 17yr & under $12/10/free; ⏰10am-5pm Mon-Sat, noon-4pm Sun, closed Mon Jun-Aug), the artwork celebrates the West and the lives of those that won it. The Hays *Spirit of the Cowboy* collection examines the raw materials behind the cowboy myth, showcasing rifles, ropes and saddles. The *Cowgirl Up!* exhibit and sale in March and April is a fun and impressive tribute to an eclectic array of Western women artists.

LINK YOUR TRIP

8 Highway 89A: Red Rock Country

For close-up views of stunning red rock scenery, explore Sedona along Hwy 89A.

10 Southwest Indian Nations Sojourn

From Grand Canyon National Park, follow Hwy 64 east to Wupatki National Monument to learn about early residents.

Scattered across downtown are statues of the town's founders and colorful characters. One of the latter was George Sayers, a 'bibulous reprobate' who was chained to the **Jail Tree** on Tegner St in the late 1800s. Press the button to hear his tale, then head over the road to the locally loved Nana's Sandwich Shoppe (p89) for a feed.

Wickenburg is pleasant anytime but summer, when temperatures regularly top 110°F (43°C).

 p89

The Drive » Head west on Hwy 60, turn left onto Vulture Mine Rd. Saguaros and cattle guards mark the lonely 14-mile drive to the mine.

---

❷ Vulture Mine Road

At the remote and dusty **Vulture Mine** (www.vultureminetours.com; 36610 N 355 Ave, off Vulture Mine Rd; donation $10; ⏰tours 8:30am Sat early May–mid-Oct, 10am Sat mid-Oct–early May), Austrian immigrant Henry Wickenburg staked his claim and made his fortune. The site holds the main shaft, where $30 million worth of gold was mined, the blacksmith shop and other decrepit old buildings, and the Hanging Tree. You can visit by guided tour on Saturday mornings between late October and May.

On the way back into town, consider spending the night at the Flying E dude ranch (p89), where guests can sign up for two-hour trail rides.

🛏 p89

The Drive » From downtown Wickenburg, pick up Hwy 93 north and drive 5 miles to 89N. Continuing north, the route leaves the Sonoran Desert and tackles the Weaver Mountains, climbing 2500ft in 4 miles. It's 59 miles to Prescott.

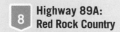

❸ Prescott

Fire raged through Whiskey Row in downtown Prescott ('press-kit') on July 14, 1900. Quick-thinking locals saved the town's most prized possession: the 24ft-long Brunswick Bar that anchored the **Palace Saloon** (☎928-541-1996; www.historicpalace.com; 120 S Montezuma St; ⏰11am-10pm Sun-Thu, to 11pm Fri & Sat). After lugging the solid oak bar onto **Courthouse Plaza**, they grabbed their drinks and continued the party. Prescott's cooperative spirit lives on, infusing the city with a welcoming vibe.

The Palace is at the centre of Prescott's **Historic Downtown** and **Whiskey Row**, where 40 drinking establishments once supplied suds and sour mash to rough-hewn cowboys, miners and wastrels.

Classic Trip

To learn more about Prescott, which was Arizona's first territorial capital, visit the engaging **Sharlot Hall Museum** (☎928-445-3122; www.sharlot.org; 415 W Gurley St; adult/child 13-17yr $9/5; ⏱10am-5pm Mon-Sat, noon-4pm Sun May-Sep, shorter hours Oct-Apr), named for its 1928 founder, pioneer woman Sharlot Hall. The city is also home to the **World's Oldest Rodeo** (☎928-445-3103; www.worldsoldestrodeo.com; 840 Rodeo Dr; tickets $12-25; ⏱Jul), which dates to 1888 and is held the week before July 4.

✖ 🛏 p89

The Drive ≫ From the County Courthouse downtown, drive west on Gurley St, which turns into Thumb Butte Rd, an overall drive of just 4 miles.

❹ Thumb Butte

Prescott sits in the middle of the Prescott National Forest, a 1.2-million-acre playground bursting with scenic slopes, lakes and ponderosa pines. The **Prescott National Forest Office** (☎928-443-8000; www.fs.usda.gov/prescott; 344 S Cortez St; ⏱8am-4:30pm Mon-Fri) has information about local hikes, drives, picnic areas and campgrounds. A day-use fee is required – and

payable – at many area trailheads. Intra-agency passes, including the America the Beautiful pass, cover this fee.

For a short hike, head to the hard-to-miss Thumb Butte. The 1.75-mile **Thumb Butte Trail #33** is a moderate workout and offers nice views of the town and mountains. Leashed dogs are OK.

The Drive ≫ Follow Hwy 89N out of Prescott, passing the Granite Dells rock formations on the 11-mile drive. Granite Dells Rd leads to a trail through the granite boulders on the Mile High Trail System (cityofprescott.net/services/parks/trails).

❺ Phippen Museum

Strutting its stuff like a rodeo champ, the thoroughly engaging **Phippen Museum** (☎928-778-1385; www.phippenartmuseum.org; 4701 Hwy 89 N; adult/student/child 12yr & under $7/5/free; ⏱10am-4pm Tue-Sat, 1-4pm Sun) ropes in visitors with an entertaining mix of special exhibits spotlighting cowboy and Western art. Named for the late George Phippen, a local self-taught artist who helped put Western art on the map, it's worth a stop to see what's brewing. As you'll discover, Western art is broader than oil paintings of weather-beaten faces under broad hat brims – although you might see some of those, as well.

The Drive ≫ Just north, leave Hwy 89 for Hwy 89A. This 27-mile serpentine road brooks no distraction as it approaches hillside Jerome, tucked in the Mingus Mountains. If you dare, glance east for stunning glimpses of the Verde Valley.

TRIP HIGHLIGHT

❻ Jerome

As the road snakes down steep **Cleopatra Hill**, it can be hard to tell whether the buildings are winning or losing their battle with gravity. Just take the **Sliding Jail** – it's waaaay down there at the bottom of town.

Now shabbily chic, this resurrected ghost town was known as the 'Wickedest Town in the West' during its late-1800s copper-mining heyday. In those days it teemed with brothels, saloons and opium dens. When the mines petered out in 1953, Jerome's population plummeted. Then came the '60s, when scores of hippies snapped up crumbling, atmospheric buildings for pennies, more or less restored them and injected the town with a groovy joie de vivre.

Join the party with a stroll past the galleries, indie shops, old buildings and wine-tasting rooms that are scattered up and down the hillside. Local artists sell their work at the **Jerome Artists Cooperative Gallery** (☎928-639-4276; www.

jeromecoop.com; 502 N Main St; ☺10am-6pm) while burly but friendly-enough bikers gather at the **Spirit Room Bar** (☏928-634-8809; www.spiritroom.com; 166 Main St; ☺11am-1am).

🛏 p89

The Drive ❯❯ Follow Main St/Hwy 89A out of downtown then turn left onto Douglas Rd.

---

❼ Audrey Headframe Park & Jerome State Historic Park

Jerome's darkly humorous embrace of its industrial past is clear at this former minehead, which boasts the largest surviving timber framehead in the state. The glass platform covering the mining shaft at **Audrey Headframe Park** (www.jeromehistoricalsociety.com; 55 Douglas Rd; ☺8am-5pm) isn't your everyday roadside attraction: it's death staring you in the face. If the cover shattered, the drop is 1910ft – a mere 650ft longer than from atop the Empire State Building.

Sufficiently disturbed? Chill out next door at the excellent **Jerome State Historic Park** (☏928-634-5381; www.azstateparks.com; 100 Douglas Rd; adult/child 7-13yr $7/4; ☺8:30am-5pm), which explores the town's mining past. The museum is inside the 1916 mansion of eccentric mining mogul Jimmy 'Rawhide' Douglas. The folksy video is worth watching before you explore the museum.

The Drive ❯❯ Hwy 89A drops to tranquil Clarkdale. At the traffic circle, take the second exit onto the Clarkdale Pkwy and into town. Follow Main St east to S Broadway then turn left onto Tuzigoot Rd, a total drive of just 7 miles.

---

❽ Tuzigoot National Monument

Squatting atop a ridge east of Clarkdale, **Tuzigoot National Monument** (☏928-634-5564; www.nps.gov/tuzi; adult/child 15yr & under $10/free; ☺8am-5pm; 🅿 ♿), a pueblo built by the prehistoric Sinaguan people (Spanish for 'without water'), is believed to have been inhabited from AD 1000 to 1400. At its peak as many as 225 people lived in its 110 rooms. Stop by the informative visitor center to examine tools, pottery and arrowheads, then climb a short, steep trail (not suitable for wheelchairs) for memorable views of the Verde River Valley.

The Drive ❯❯ Return to S Broadway and follow it south into Old Town Cottonwood, just 3 miles south of Tuzigoot.

TRIP HIGHLIGHT

❾ Cottonwood

Cottonwood has kicked up its cool quotient, particularly around the pedestrian-friendly **Old Town District**. On this low-key strip there are loads of good restaurants and wine-tasting rooms, and several interesting indie stores. The inviting tasting room **Arizona Stronghold** (☏928-639-2789; www.azstronghold.com; 1023 N Main St; wine tasting $9; ☺noon-7pm Sun-Thu, to 9pm Fri & Sat) has welcoming staff, comfy couches, and live music on Friday nights. Enjoy a few more wine samples across the street at the chocolate-and-wine-pairing **Pillsbury Wine Company** (☏928-639-0646; www.pillsburywine.com; 1012 N Main St; wine tasting $10-12; ☺11am-6pm Sun-Thu, to 9pm Fri & Sat). For wet-and-wild wine tasting in Cottonwood, join a Water to Wine kayak tour ($97) with **Sedona Adventure Tours** (☏877-673-3661; www.sedonaadventuretours.com; ♿) on the Verde River to **Alcantara Vineyards** (☏928-649-8463; www.alcantaravineyard.com; 3445 S Grapevine Way; wine tasting $10-15; ☺11am-5pm).

The Drive ❯❯ Follow Main St south to reconnect with Hwy 89A, then drive a further 20 miles to Sedona. At the roundabout at the junction of Hwy 89A and Hwy 179, called the Y, continue into uptown Sedona. The main visitor center sits at the junction of Hwy 89A and Forest Rd.

Classic Trip

WHY THIS IS A CLASSIC TRIP
HUGH MCNAUGHTAN, WRITER

Yes, the landscape's spectacular, but much of this state's charm lies in how it's translated a rough-and-ready past into a characterful and appealing present. Central Arizona is packed with former mining, railroad and lumber towns that have taken the demise of traditional industries in their stride, developing wine, food and cultural scenes that keep the lifeblood pumping. Enjoy Prescott, Jerome, Cottonwood, Flagstaff and Sedona on your way to the canyon.

Above: Sunset over Sedona
Left: The atmospheric Jerome
Right: Desert View Watchtower, Grand Canyon

DIANA GRAMLICH / SHUTTERSTOCK ©

⑩ Sedona

The stunning red rocks here have an intensely spiritual pull for many visitors. Some New Age believers even think that the sandstone formations hold 'vortices' that vibrate to the frequencies of the 'deepest earth energies.' Judge for yourself atop **Airport Mesa** (Airport Rd), the vortex most convenient to downtown. Here, a short scramble leads to a lofty view of the surrounding sandstone monoliths, which blaze a psychedelic red and orange at sunset. To get to the viewpoint, drive up Airport Rd for half a mile and look for a small parking area ($3) on the left.

Another arresting site is the **Chapel of the Holy Cross** (☎928-282-4069; www.chapeloftheholycross. com; 780 Chapel Rd; ⊙9am-5pm Dec-Feb, to 6pm Mar-Nov), a church tucked between spectacular red-rock columns 3 miles south of town. This modern Catholic chapel was built by Marguerite Brunwig Staude in the tradition of Frank Lloyd Wright.

The Drive ≫ Follow Hwy 179 9 miles south, past Bell Rock, through the village of Oak Creek to the Red Rock Country Visitor Center.

Classic Trip

⑪ Red Rock Country Visitor Center

Outdoor adventurers love the super-scenic hiking and biking trails in and around Sedona. The US Forest Service provides the helpful and free *Recreation Guide to Your National Forest*, which has brief descriptions of popular trails and a map pinpointing their routes and trailheads. Pick one up at the **Red Rock Country Visitor Center** (📞928-203-2900; www.redrockcountry.org; 8375 Hwy 179; 🕙9am-4:30pm), just south of the village of Oak Creek. Staff can guide you to less populated trails, or those best suited to your interests.

The Drive » Hwy 89A rolls north through the riparian greenery of scenic Oak Creek Canyon, where red cliffs and pine forest rear spectacularly from either side of the road. Once out of the canyon pick up I-17 north. The total drive to Flagstaff is 39 miles.

⑫ Flagstaff

Flagstaff's charms are myriad, from its pedestrian-friendly historic downtown to high-altitude pursuits like skiing and hiking. **Humphrey's Peak** (www.fs.usda. gov), the highest point in the state, provides an inspiring backdrop. Start at the downtown visitor center (📞928-7293-2951; www.flagstaffarizona.org; 1 E Rte 66; 🕙8am-5pm Mon-Sat, 9am-4pm Sun), which has free brochures for walking tours, including a guide to Flagstaff's haunted places.

The fascinating **Lowell Observatory** (📞main phone 928-774-3358, recorded information 928-233-3211; www.lowell.edu; 1400 W Mars Hill Rd; adult/senior/child 5-17yr $15/14/8; 🕙10am-10pm Mon-Sat, to 5pm Sun; 🅿), built in 1894 and site of the first official sighting of Pluto (in 1930), sits on a hill just outside downtown. During the day you can take a guided tour, while at night, weather permitting, there's stargazing. Flagstaff's microbreweries are the stars on the one-mile **Flagstaff Ale Trail** (www.flagstaffaletrail. com). But if walking seems too pedestrian, climb aboard the **Alpine Pedaler** (📞928-213-9233; www.alpinepedaler.com; seats from $17; 🕙11am-11pm), a 14-passenger 'party on wheels' that brakes for bars and breweries.

🍴 🛏 p57, 89

The Drive » The next morning – and mornings are best for the 90-mile trip – take Hwy 180 west and enjoy the views of the San Francisco Peaks through the treetops. When you reach Hwy 64 at the town of Valle, turn right and drive the remainder of the journey north on the broad uplands of the Coconino Plateau.

⑬ Tusayan

This little town, sitting 1 mile south of the Grand Canyon's South Entrance on Hwy 64, is basically a half-mile strip of canyon-focused hotels and restaurants. Stop at the **National Geographic Visitor Center & IMAX Theater** (📞928-638-2203; www.explorethecanyon. com; 450 Hwy 64; adult/child $14/11; 🕙visitor center 8am-10pm Mar-Oct, 10am-8pm Nov-Feb, theater 8:30am-8:30pm Mar-Oct, 9:30am-6:30pm Nov-Feb; 🖥Tusayan) to pre-pay the $30 per-vehicle park fee and save yourself what could be a long wait at the entrance. Always screening in the IMAX theater is the terrific 34-minute film *Grand Canyon – The Hidden Secrets*. With exhilarating river-running scenes and virtual-reality drops off canyon rims, the film plunges you into the history and geology of the canyon through the eyes of ancient American Indians, first explorer John Wesley Powell and a soaring eagle.

In summer, you can leave your car here and catch the Tusayan shuttle into the park.

The Drive » Follow Hwy 64 1 mile north to the park entrance. Admission to the national park is $30 per vehicle, $25 for motorcycles or $15 for pedestrians or bikes, and is good for seven days. All up, it's a serene 7 miles to Mather Point.

Grand Canyon National Park Mather Point

⑭ Mather Point & Grand Canyon Visitor Center

Park at the **visitor center** (☏928-638-7888; www.nps. gov/grca; Visitor Center Plaza, Grand Canyon Village; ⊙9am-5pm; 🚌Village, 🚌Kaibab/ Rim) but don't go inside. Not yet. Walk (or run) directly to **Mather Point**, the first overlook after the South Entrance. It's usually packed elbow-to-elbow with a global array of tourists, but even with the crowds there's a sense of communal wonder that keeps things civil. You'll see – the sheer immensity of the canyon just grabs you, then holds you as you scan the endless details – rugged mesas, sculpted spires, and an almost overwhelming sense of scale.

Once your sense of wonder is surfeited, head back to the main visitor center, with its theater and bookstore. On the plaza, bulletin boards and kiosks display information about ranger programs, the weather, tours and hikes. Inside is a ranger-staffed information desk and a lecture hall, where rangers offer daily talks on a variety of subjects. The theater screens a 20-minute movie, *Grand Canyon: A Journey of Wonder*, on the hour and half-hour.

From here, explore the park via park shuttle, a **bike** (📞928-638-3055, 928-814-8704; www.bikegrandcanyon.com; 10 S Entrance Rd, Visitor Center Plaza; 24hr rental adult/child 16yr & under $40/30, 5hr rental $30/20, wheelchair $10, s/d stroller up to 8hr $18/27; ⏰7am-5pm Mar-Oct; 🚌Village, 🚌Kaibab/Rim), or your own four wheels. In summer, parking can be a challenge in Grand Canyon Village.

The Drive » The Village Loop Rd leads into Grand Canyon Village. Pass El Tovar, Kachina and Thunderbird Lodges on the 2-mile drive to Bright Angel Lodge. The Bright Angel Trailhead is just west of the lodge.

- - - - - - - - - - - - - - - -

TRIP HIGHLIGHT

15 Grand Canyon Village

The **Bright Angel Trail** is the most popular of the South Rim corridor trails, and its steep and scenic 8-mile descent to the Colorado River has four logical turn-around

DETOUR: DESERT VIEW DRIVE

Start: 14 Mather Point & Grand Canyon Visitor Center

This scenic road meanders 25 miles to the East Entrance on Hwy 64, passing some of the park's finest viewpoints, picnic areas and historic sites. **Grand View Point** marks the trailhead where miner Peter Berry opened the aptly named Grand View Hotel in 1897 – it really is one of the Grand Canyon's most stunning viewpoints. Another captivating view awaits at **Moran Point** (www.nps.gov/grca; Desert View Dr; 🚻 ♿), named for the landscape painter whose work helped secure the Grand Canyon national monument status in 1908. Further along is **Tusayan Museum & Ruin** (www.nps.gov/grca; Desert View Dr; ⏰9am-5pm), where you can walk around the remains of an excavated Puebloan village dating to 1185. At the end of the road is the **Desert View Watchtower** (www.nps.gov/grca; Desert View, East Enrance; ⏰8am-sunset mid-May–Aug, 9am-6pm Sep–mid-Oct, 9am-5pm mid-Oct–Feb, 8am-6pm Mar–mid-May), designed by Mary Jane Colter and inspired by ancient Puebloan structures – the terrace provides panoramic views of the canyon and river. The circular staircase inside leads past Hopi murals to 360-degree views on the top floor.

points: Mile-and-a-Half Resthouse, Three Mile Resthouse, Indian Garden and Plateau Point. Summer heat can be crippling and the climb is steep. Day hikers should turn around at one of the two resthouses (a 3- to 6-mile round-trip).

If you're more interested in history and geography than strenuous hiking, follow the easy **Rim Trail** east from here. Heading west, the Rim Trail passes every overlook on the way to **Hermits Rest** (www.nps.gov/grca; Hermit Rd; 🚌Hermits Rest), offering spectacular views. The Hermits Rest shuttle runs parallel to the trail, so hike until you're tired, then hop aboard to continue or return. But be sure to hop off for the sunset, which is best at **Hopi Point** (which draws crowds) or **Pima Point**.

🛏 p89

Eating & Sleeping

Wickenburg ❶

🍴 Nana's
Sandwich Shoppe · Sandwiches $

(📞928-684-5539; nanassandwichsaloon.com;
48 N Tegner St; sandwiches $7-9; 🕐7:30am-3pm
Mon-Sat; 🛜) Order at the counter of this busy
sandwich shop in the heart of Wickenburg. The
god-fearing folks here load 'em up right, from
the Mustang (hot pastrami, Swiss cheese,
house dressing, lettuce, tomato and red onion)
to the Cowboy (roast beef, Swiss cheese and
horseradish).

Vulture Mine ❷

🛏 Flying E Ranch · Ranch $$$

(📞928-684-2690; www.flyingeranch.com;
2801 W Wickenburg Way; s/d/house from
$205/280/330; 🕐Nov-Apr; 🛜🏊) The coolest
place at this down-home working cattle ranch
is the boot room, which is lined with scuffed-up
cowboy boots and hats that guests can borrow
on their rides. Sitting on 20,000 acres in the
Hassayampa Valley, the ranch is a big hit with
families and also works well for groups. Two-
hour horseback rides cost $50 (or $80 for two).

Prescott ❸

🍴 Iron
Springs Cafe · American, Cajun $$

(📞928-443-8848; www.ironspringscafe.com;
1501 Iron Springs Rd; brunch & lunch $11-13,
dinner $16-20; 🕐11am-8pm Wed-Sat, 9am-2pm
Sun) Cajun and Southwestern specialties mingle
delightfully inside this former train station –
from the N'awlins muffuletta with sliced ham,
salami and mortadella to the crab cakes and
thick, spicy sausage and okra gumbo, it's all
delicious, and served with real warmth. Train
decor, colorful blankets and easy-bantering
waitstaff enliven three tiny rooms.

🛏 Motor Lodge · Bungalow $$

(📞928-717-0157; www.themotorlodge.com; 503
S Montezuma St; r/ste/apt from $109/129/139;
❄🛜) Set three blocks south of Courthouse
Plaza, the 12 snazzy bungalows here form a

bright and welcoming horseshoe around a
central driveway. Inside, the rooms, whimsical
prints and comfy bedding add to the overall
appeal, making the Motor Lodge a top choice.
Rooms and bathrooms, built in 1936, can be
snug, but many have kitchens and porches.

Jerome ❻

🛏 Jerome Grand Hotel · Hotel $$

(📞928-634-8200; www.jeromegrandhotel.
com; 200 Hill St; r/ste $225/325; ❄🛜) This
former hospital looks like the perfect setting
for a sequel to *The Shining*. Built in 1926 for the
mining community, the sturdy fortress plays
up its unusual history. The halls are filled with
relics of the past, from incinerator chutes to
patient call lights. There's even a key-operated
Otis elevator. Victorian-style rooms are more
traditionally furnished.

Flagstaff ⓬

🛏 Hotel Monte Vista · Historic Hotel $$

(📞928-779-6971; www.hotelmontevista.com;
100 N San Francisco St; r/ste from $115/145;
❄🛜) A huge, old-fashioned neon sign towers
over this 1926 landmark hotel, hinting at what's
inside: feather lampshades, vintage furniture,
bold colors and eclectic decor. Rooms are
named for the movie stars who stayed here,
including the 'Humphrey Bogart,' with dramatic
black walls, yellow ceiling and gold-satin
bedding. Several resident ghosts supposedly
make regular appearances.

Grand Canyon Village ⓯

🛏 El Tovar · Lodge $$$

(📞888-297-2757, ext 6380, front desk &
reservations within 48hrs 928-638-2631; www.
grandcanyonlodges.com; Village Loop Dr; r/
ste from $187/381; 🕐year-round; 🅿❄🛜;
🚌Village) Stuffed mounts. Thick pine walls.
Sturdy fireplaces. Is this the fanciest hotel on
the South Rim or a backcountry hunting lodge?
Despite renovations, this rambling 1905 wooden
lodge hasn't lost a lick of its genteel historic
patina, or its charm.

Mogollon Rim Country

6

Natural wonders and quirky towns dot the Mogollon Rim, an oft-overlooked 200-mile swath of forested cliffs at the southern edge of the Colorado Plateau.

TRIP HIGHLIGHTS

0 miles

Tonto Natural Bridge
Walk across the world's largest natural travertine bridge

START
1

44 miles

Mogollon Rim Visitor Center
From the deck, look over the edge of the Colorado Plateau

3

● Heber

Pinetop-Lakeside

7

Lost Dutchman State Park

9 **FINISH**

● Superior

270 miles

Superstition Mountain Museum
Learn the story of the Lost Dutchman Mine

170 miles

Becker Butte Lookout
Leave the twisty road and savor the view

3–5 DAYS
271 MILES/436KM

GREAT FOR...

BEST TIME TO GO
Spring for wildflowers and fall for the colorful cottonwoods and aspens.

 ESSENTIAL PHOTO
The grandeur of the Salt River Canyon from along Hwy 60.

 BEST FOR HISTORY
Learn the tragic history of the Indian Wars at Fort Apache Historic Park.

6 Mogollon Rim Country

I will keep my eyes on the road. I will keep my eyes on . . . wow! Look at that canyon! Where did those buttes come from? Why is the road dropping so fast? What's happening?! Yep, after the verdant hush of the pines atop the Mogollon Rim (pronounced 'muggy-own'), the stark, twisting drop into Salt River Canyon comes as a shock. But it's these dramatic changes that make this trip such a varied feast for the senses.

TRIP HIGHLIGHT

❶ Tonto Natural Bridge State Park

The drive from Flagstaff to Hwy 87 on S Lake Mary Rd is gorgeous, passing pondersosa pines and glinting lakes as it mounts the Mogollon Rim at the southern edge of the Colorado Plateau. The Rim was named for Don Juan Ignacio Flores Mogollon, a Spanish governor of the province of New Mexico in the 1700s. When you reach Hwy 87, turn right and continue

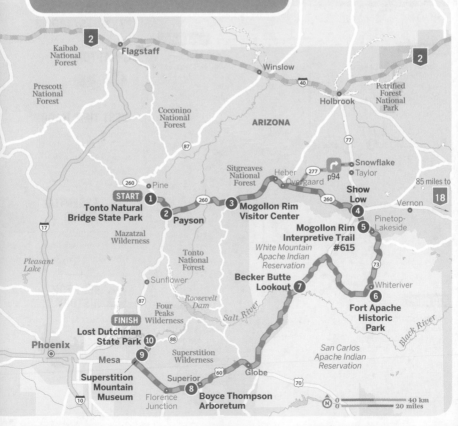

to **Tonto Natural Bridge State Park** (☎928-476-4202; www.azstateparks.com/tonto; off Hwy 87; adult/child 7-13yr $7/4; ⏰8am-6pm Jun-Aug, 9am-5pm Sep-May). The Park's precipitous entrance road ends at the eponymous bridge – at 183ft high and straddling a 150ft-wide canyon, it's the world's largest natural travertine bridge. It formed through countless centuries of attrition, as Pine Creek gradually worked its way through a massive dam of calcium carbonate. You can view it from multiple angles, and steep trails descend into the canyon for close-ups.

The Drive ⟫ Return to Hwy 87 and head south to Payson, all up a drive of 14 miles.

----

❷ Payson

Founded by gold miners in 1882, Payson's real riches turned out to be

LINK YOUR TRIP

Route 66: The Southwest

From Payson, follow Hwy 87 north to Take-It-Easy Corner in Winslow.

Into the Gila
Hankerin' for pie? Drive east on Hwy 60 to Pie Town, NM.

above ground. Vast pine forests fed a booming timber industry, ranchers ran cattle along the Mogollon Rim and down to the Tonto Basin, and wild game was plentiful. Today, Payson is a recreation and retirement destination for Phoenix citizens, with hunting and fishing in the nearby forests, lakes and streams.

Exhibits at the **Rim Country Museum** (☎928-474-3483; www.rimcountrymuseums.com; 700 S Green Valley Pkwy; adult/senior/student/child under 12yr $5/4/3/free; ⏰10am-4pm Mon & Wed-Sat, 1-4pm Sun; P), viewed on docent-led tours, illustrate the native, pioneer and mining history of the region. Highlights include a replica of a blacksmith shop and a walk-through of the Zane Grey Cabin, faithfully rebuilt here after the author's original homestead burned in the tragic 1990 conflagration known as the Dude Fire. Docents can shorten the tour if you have limited time.

✖ ⌂ p97

The Drive ⟫ Heading east, Hwy 260 cuts through a vast blanket of lofty pines, where 'Elk Crossing' and 'Watch for Elk' signs will keep you on your toes as you drive the 30 miles to the next stop.

❸ Mogollon Rim Visitor Center

For expansive views of southern forests and lakes, stop at the **Mogollon Rim Visitor Center** (☎928-333-4301; www.fs.usda.gov; Rim Rd, Tonto National Forest; ⏰9am-3pm Thu-Sun Memorial Day-Labor Day). Its deck looks over the Mogollon Rim, a dramatic geological break a couple of thousand feet high between the high desert of the Colorado Plateau and the low desert to the south. The Rim contains the world's largest contiguous forests of ponderosa pine.

Inside the visitor center you'll find information about local flora, fauna and recreation. There are also animal mounts, including a full-grown bear. Several trails leave from the **Rim Top Trailhead** across Hwy 260. Of these, the **Rim Lakes Vista Trail** crosses back over the highway and travels along the rim for 3 miles to the **Woods Canyon Vista**.

The Drive ⟫ Continue east on Hwy 260. Look south after passing Forest Lakes to see a fire scar from the 2002 Rodeo-Chediski fire, one of the largest fires in Arizona history. After the town of Heber, stay right to follow 260 for 60 miles to Show Low.

④ Show Low

Back in 1876, a 100,000-acre ranch was at stake in a marathon card game. As daybreak approached, the players agreed that whoever could 'show low' would take the prize. One player flipped over the deuce of clubs. The town that arose here took the name Show Low and its main drag was named Deuce of Clubs St. A life-size statue memorializing the players and the card game sits on a small plaza on the south side of E Deuce of Clubs.

The Drive » Continue east on Hwy 260. About 6 miles ahead, look for the pull-off for the Mogollon Rim Interpretive Trail, before mile marker 348. It's just within the city limits for Pinetop-Lakeside, where you'll find restaurants and hotels (p97).

⑤ Mogollon Rim Interpretive Trail #615

This easy 1-mile trail meanders through ponderosa pines in the Apache-Sitgreaves National Forest, along the edge of the Mogollon Rim. The trail passes through forest of great botanical variety; you may see mule deer, and will definitely hear (and hopefully see) a variety of birds. You'll also pass an unusual sight: a Douglas fir beside an alligator juniper, two plants rarely seen together because they have different climatic requirements. And the view from the Rim? Picture rolling waves of trees. The first half mile of the trail is paved and wheelchair accessible.

The Drive » Follow Hwy 260 east to Hon-Dah Resort-Casino on the northern edge of the White Mountain Apache Tribe Reservation. Turn right onto Hwy 73, driving south through ponderosa forest and mountain meadows. The view opens up at Whiteriver. About 5 miles south of town, turn left onto Indian Rte 46 to complete the 33-mile leg.

DETOUR: SNOWFLAKE

Start: ③ Mogollon Rim Visitor Center

Snowflake is the northernmost city of Rim Country. The town gets an occasional light dusting of snow, but is really named after the founders: a Mr Snow and a Mr Flake. Seriously. Settled by Mormon pioneers in the late 1800s, there are more than 100 historic homes here, many with handsome red brick and white trim. From Heber-Overgaard, take Hwy 277 east.

⑥ Fort Apache National Historic Park

Bounded by the Mogollon Rim to the north and the Salt River to the south, the White Mountain Apache Tribe Reservation covers 2627 sq miles, most of which is forest. Head for the Nohwike' Bágowa Cultural Center and Museum at **Fort Apache Historic Park** (information 928-338-4525, museum 928-338-4625; www.wmat.nsn.us; 127 Scout St; adult/senior/child $5/3/free; park 7am-sunset, cultural center & museum 8am-5pm Mon-Sat summer, closed Sat winter), an Army post between 1870 and 1922, where you'll find a thorough introduction to the White Mountain Apache world.

A self-guided tour leads to the fort's historic buildings. An exhibit inside an 1871 officers' quarters highlights Apache scouts and explains why tribal members helped the US Army subdue other native tribes in the Indian Wars. The **Theodore Roosevelt Boarding School** was established here in 1923 and is still in operation.

Admission includes entry to the **Kinishba Ruins**, a pre-Columbian stone pueblo that once had hundreds of rooms. At the museum, pick up a guide to the ruins,

Superstition Mountain Museum Elvis Memorial Chapel

which are at the end of a well-graded dirt road that begins 4 miles west off Hwy 73: they're well worth a stop.

The Drive » From the ruins, turn right onto Hwy 73 and drive 24 miles to US 60. Turn left for a twisting descent through the stunning Salt River Canyon. As you drop into the canyon, watch for the overlook parking lot between mile markers 298 and 297.

TRIP HIGHLIGHT

⑦ Becker Butte Lookout

Pull over, pull over, pull over! You've got to see the view from this stone-walled overlook, which is perched above the majestic **Salt River Canyon**, a 2000ft gash carving its way through the imposing landscape. The river,

unhampered by dams, runs wild below the juniper-covered buttes. Hwy 60 runs through the **White Mountain Apache Tribe Reservation** north of the Salt River, and a recreational permit is required to explore beyond the overlooks (see www.wmatoutdoors.org). South of the river, the highway runs through the **San Carlos Apache**

THE TRUTH IS OUT THERE

One of the USA's most famous cases of putative alien abduction took place in Rim Country. Logger Travis Walton claims he was abducted near Snowflake by an alien craft in 1975. What makes his story interesting is that there were eyewitnesses, and a police manhunt failed to turn up Walton for two days – time on the mother ship, he says. According to the Forest Service, the telephone booth is still there and makes a nice photo op. For more details, visit Walton's website, www.travis-walton.com, or check out the 1993 movie *Fire in the Sky*, based on his story.

Tribe Reservation. For recreational permit information here, see www.sancarlosapache.com.

The Drive » Hwy 60 passes more viewpoints as it drops to the Salt River. After crossing the river the highway climbs out of the canyon. Continue west through Globe, which makes a good lunch stop (p97), and Superior, where copper country rises toward rim country. It's 92 miles from the Hwy 60 junction to the next stop.

8 Boyce Thompson Arboretum

This lovely **arboretum** (☏520-689-2811; ag.arizona.edu/bta; 37615 US Hwy 60, Superior; adult/child $12.50/5; ☺6am-3pm May-Sep, 8am-5pm Oct-Apr; P) covers nearly 400 acres and is a living museum with flora species from arid regions around the world. During the spring bloom, which peaks March though early May, the park is vibrant with color and smells as sweet as a candy factory.

Saguaros bloom in May and June. Leashed pets are welcome.

The Drive » Follow US 60 west around 24 miles to W Mountain View Rd. Turn right and drive north about 4.5 miles to North Apache Trail/AZ 88 and turn right again.

TRIP HIGHLIGHT

9 Superstition Mountain Museum

The thoroughly delightful **Superstition Mountain Museum** (☏480-983-4888; www.superstitionmountainmuseum.org; 4087 N Apache Trail, Apache Junction; adult/senior/child $5/4/free; ☺9am-4pm; P) welcomes guests with mesmerizing dioramas of wild animals trying to kill each other – again. But most impressive is the wall of treasure maps, all purporting to lead to the Lost Dutchman Mine, where 19th-century German prospector Jacob Waltz, the 'Dutchman,'

allegedly struck gold in these parts. On his deathbed, Waltz supposedly revealed the whereabouts of the source of ore, but it's never been found – despite the efforts of thousands.

Outside, you'll find the Elvis Memorial Chapel from the Elvis movie *Charro!* (1969). It was moved here after surviving a devastating fire at Apacheland Movie Ranch.

The Drive » Drive 1 mile northeast on N Apache Trail, passing the Goldfield Ghost Town (goldfieldghosttown.com), an unabashed tourist trap that is also, well, kind of fun.

10 Lost Dutchman State Park

The sought-after gold mine it's named after is the main claim to fame of this **state park** (☏480-982-4485; www.azstateparks.com; 6109 N Apache Trail, Apache Junction; per vehicle/bicycle $7/3; ☺sunrise-10pm), but this striking place is really a treasure itself, with a surreal massif of the Superstition Mountains dominating the terrain. Enjoy easy and moderate trails and perhaps pitch for the night in the very pretty campground. Look for vast blooms of desert wildflowers here, especially after a wet winter.

🛏 p97

Eating & Sleeping

Payson ❷

🍴 Beeline Cafe Diner $

(📞928-474-9960; 815 S Beeline Hwy; mains $8-12; ⏰5am-9pm) This home-style diner, with its padded stools and booths, could be called the bee*hive*, so busy are its mornings, with locals swarming in for massive breakfasts. Cash only.

🍴 Ayothaya Thai Cafe Thai $

(📞928-474-1112; www.ayothayathaicafe.com; 404 E Hwy 60; mains $11-15; ⏰11am-9pm Sun-Thu, to 10pm Fri & Sat) This bright and airy eatery doesn't deviate from the international template for Thai restaurants (you'll find no exotic surprises here), but you can tell the owner and chef cut his teeth in the mother country.

🛏 Majestic Mountain Inn Motel $

(📞928-474-0185; www.majesticmountaininn.com; 602 E Hwy 260; d from $69; 🅿 ❄ 🛜 🐾) Set among landscaped pines and grassy lawns, this is easily the nicest lodging in Payson – and a good-value one, too. The two-story property is more of a motel than a lodge-like inn, but the luxury rooms have double-sided gas fireplaces, sloped wooden ceilings and spa tubs.

🛏 Ponderosa Campground Campground $

(📞877-444-6777; www.recreation.gov; Hwy 260; campsites $18; ⏰Apr-Oct) This USFS spot is 12 miles northeast of Payson on Hwy 260 and has 48 single sites and two group sites as well as drinking water and toilets, but no showers. Inquire at the ranger station for other campgrounds in the Tonto National Forest.

Pinetop-Lakeside

🍴 Darbi's Cafe American $

(📞928-367-6556; darbiscafe.com; 235 E White Mountain Blvd; breakfast $7-9, lunch & dinner $9-13; ⏰6am-2pm Sun-Tue, to 8pm Wed-Sat) This might be the most popular restaurant along the Mogollon Rim. It's hard to tell what locals love more, the yummy, stylized American food or owner Darbi Massey, who grew up around here. Breakfast gets especially fervent raves.

🛏 Nine Pines Motel Motel $

(📞928-367-2999; www.ninepinesmotel.com; 2089 E White Mountain Blvd; s/d from $57/87; 🅿 🛜 🐾) Beds in the cozy rooms here are set in natural pine frames and the decor is tastefully homey. Larger rooms have fireplaces and foldout futon couches. All have refrigerators and microwaves, and the owner is welcoming.

Globe

🍴 La Luz Del Dia Cafe Diner $

(📞928-425-8400; 304 N Broad St; mains $7-10; ⏰6:30am-2:30pm Mon-Sat) This real locals' diner, run by the same family since 1973, has six tables and a counter with stools. Regulars sip coffee while browsing the newspaper and chatting with the cook.

Lost Dutchman State Park ❿

🛏 Lost Dutchman State Park Campground Campground $

(📞reservations 520-586-2283; www.azstateparks.com; 6109 N Apache Trail, Apache Junction; tent/hookup from $15/25; ⏰reservations 8am-5pm; 🅿) With saguaros up close and a craggy offshoot of the Superstition Mountains as a backdrop, this is one of the prettiest campgrounds in eastern Arizona. It has 134 campsites, 68 powered, and 24/7 online booking is available all year.

Southern Desert Wanderings

You'll swoosh past saguaros on this loop through the Sonoran Desert, where Spanish missions mingle with missile sites, wineries work their magic and a lofty observatory looks to the stars.

TRIP HIGHLIGHTS

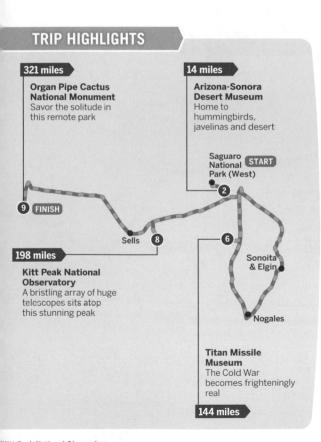

321 miles

Organ Pipe Cactus National Monument
Savor the solitude in this remote park

14 miles

Arizona-Sonora Desert Museum
Home to hummingbirds, javelinas and desert

Saguaro National Park (West) **START**

2

9 **FINISH**

Sells **8**

6

Sonoita & Elgin

198 miles

Kitt Peak National Observatory
A bristling array of huge telescopes sits atop this stunning peak

Nogales

Titan Missile Museum
The Cold War becomes frighteningly real

144 miles

3–4 DAYS
321 MILES/517KM

GREAT FOR...

BEST TIME TO GO
October to March, to avoid the desert heat.

ESSENTIAL PHOTO
Frame a towering saguaro against the sky in the western section of the cacti's namesake park.

BEST FOR FLORA & FAUNA
Wander past coyotes and cacti at the Arizona-Sonora Desert Museum.

<table>
<tr><td>7</td><td>

Southern Desert Wanderings

Along with the Grand Canyon, the saguaro forests of southern Arizona must be the state's most iconic sites. Striding in serried ranks across broad, cloud-dappled plains and up sweeping mountain flanks, these giant cacti make a stunning impression on the eye. But giant cacti aren't the only attractions of this delightful desert drive: mountaintop observatories, rippling wine country and moody Spanish missions await.

</td></tr>
</table>

❶ **Saguaro National Park (West)**

If you're standing beside a docent at this cacti-filled **park** (☎Rincon 520-733-5153, Tucson 520-733-5158, park information 520-733-5100; www.nps.gov/sagu; 7-day pass per vehicle/bicycle $10/5; ☼ sunrise-sunset), do not refer to the limbs of the saguaro (sah-wah-ro) as branches. As you'll quickly learn, a saguaro has 'arms,' not mere branches – a distinction that makes sense when you consider the human-like features

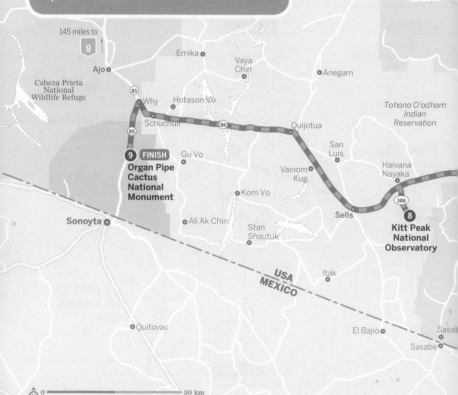

of these silent scarecrows of the Sonoran Desert. A vast army of these majestic ribbed sentinels is protected within the park.

The park is divided into two halves, separated by 30 miles and the city of Tucson. In the western Tucson Mountain District, the **visitor center** (📞520-733-5158; www.nps.gov/sagu; 2700 N Kinney Rd; 🕐9am-5pm) sits beside the short **Cactus Garden Trail** where signage identifies desert plants. The nearby **Coonie Bajada Loop Drive** is a 6-mile graded dirt road through cactus forest.

The Drive » Watch for cyclists on N Kinney Rd as you drive 3 miles south.

- - - - - - - - - - - - - - - - -

TRIP HIGHLIGHT

② Arizona-Sonora Desert Museum

Home to cacti, coyotes and tiny hummingbirds, this fascinating **place** (📞520-883-2702; www.desertmuseum.org; 2021 N Kinney Rd; adult/senior/child 3-12yr $20.50/18.50/8; 🕐8:30am-9pm Oct-Feb, 7:30am-5pm Mar-Sep, incl 10pm Sat Jun-Aug) is one part zoo, one part botanical garden and one part museum – a trifecta that can keep young and old entertained for easily half a day. All sorts of desert denizens, from cantankerous coatis to playful prairie dogs, make their home in natural enclosures hemmed in by invisible fences. The grounds are thick with desert plants, and docents are on hand to answer questions and give demonstrations.

Wear a hat and walking shoes, and remember that the big cats are most active in the morning.

The Drive » Continue south to Hwy 86. Drive east to I-19, taking it north to I-10 east. Leave I-10 east at exit 281 for Hwy 83 south to Sonoita at Hwy 82, a total journey of 61 miles. To get to Elgin, cross Hwy 82 and continue on Hwy 83 a further 4 miles to Elgin Rd.

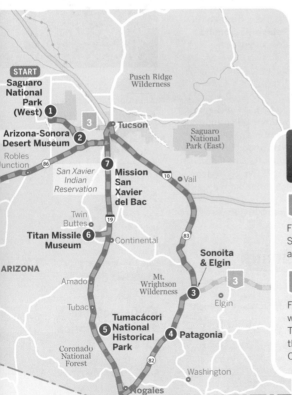

START
Saguaro National Park (West) ①

Arizona-Sonora Desert Museum ②

Robles Junction

San Xavier Indian Reservation

Tucson

Pusch Ridge Wilderness

Saguaro National Park (East)

Mission San Xavier del Bac ⑦

Vail

Twin Buttes

Titan Missile Museum ⑥

ARIZONA

Continental

Amado

Tubac

Tumacácori National Historical Park ⑤

Coronado National Forest

Mt. Wrightson Wilderness

Sonoita & Elgin

③

Elgin

Patagonia ④

Washington

Nogales

LINK YOUR TRIP

3 **A Taste of the Old West**

Follow Hwy 82 east from Sonoita to a ghost town and the OK Corral.

9 **Highway 95: Yuma to Lake Mead**

Feeling the need to see water after all that desert? Take Hwy 85 north to I-10 then head west to the Colorado River.

❸ Sonoita & Elgin

Ah, what a view: long vistas of lush, windswept high grassland; dark, knobby forest mountains; and slow upland streams in the creases in between. Sonoita and tiny Elgin, in the southern grasslands, were once important railway stops, but since the line closed in 1962, tourism, viticulture and the arts have been their bread and butter.

The valleys here occupy a special microclimate amenable to wine grapes, making the region a center for Arizona's burgeoning wine industry. For tastings, start at **Callaghan Vineyards** (☏520-455-5322; www.callaghanvineyards.com; 336 Elgin Rd; tasting $10; ⏲11am-4pm Thu-Sun) in Elgin, traditionally one of the most highly regarded wineries in the state. Return to Sonoita for **Dos Cabezas Wineworks** (☏520-455-5141; www.doscabezas.com; 3248 Hwy 82; tasting $8-13; ⏲10:30am-4:30pm Thu-Sun), a rustically pretty,

family-run operation near the crossroads of Hwys 82 and 83.

The Drive ❯❯ Return to Hwy 82 and follow it west to Patagonia, which is sandwiched between the Mexican border, the Santa Rita Mountains and the Patagonia Mountains: a drive of 22 miles all up.

❹ Patagonia

Sitting almost 5000ft above sea level, Patagonia is cool and breezy. The town borders Sonoita Creek, part of a riparian green zone that draws migrating birds and sharp-eyed birders.

A few gentle trails meander through the **Patagonia-Sonoita Creek Preserve** (☏520-394-2400; www.nature.org/arizona; 150 Blue Heaven Rd; $6; ⏲6:30am-4pm Wed-Sun Apr-Sep, 7:30am-4pm Wed-Sun Oct-Mar), an enchanting willow and cottonwood forest managed by the Nature Conservancy. It supports seven distinct vegetative ecosystems, four endangered species of native fish and more than 300 species of birds,

including rarities from Mexico. The peak migratory seasons are April and May, and late August to September. Join guided nature walks on Saturday mornings at 9am.

✖ 🛏 p105

The Drive ❯❯ Follow Hwy 82 southwest, passing Patagonia Lake State Park on the 18 miles to the border town of Nogales. Here, pick up I-19 north to complete the 36-mile leg.

❺ Tumacácori National Historical Park

This pink-and-cream **edifice** (☏520-398-2341; www.nps.gov/tuma; I-19, exit 29;

TELLES FAMILY SHRINE

On Hwy 82 south of Patagonia, just beyond mile marker 16, look east for a pull-off and historic plaque. The latter spotlights **John Ward's Ranch**, established here in 1858. Behind the plaque, stairs climb to a protected shrine built inside a rock face. The shrine was created in the 1940s by Juanita and Juan Telles, who promised to keep its candles burning if their sons returned safely from WWII. Their sons came home, and the candles still burn.

adult/child 15yr & under $5/2; ⊙9am-5pm; P) shimmers on the desert air like a missionary's dream. In 1691 Father Eusebio Kino and his cohort arrived at the Tumacácori settlement and quickly founded a mission to convert the local American Indians. However, repeated Apache raids and the harsh winter of 1848 drove the priests out, leaving the complex to crumble for decades. Start self-guided tours of the hauntingly beautiful ruins at the visitor center.

Just south, pick up spices, salsa and fantastic homemade chile pastes at **Santa Cruz Chili & Spice**

(☎520-398-2591; www.santa cruzchili.com; 1868 E Frontage Rd; ⊙8am-5pm Mon-Fri, 10am-5pm Sat, to 3pm Sat summer), in business since the 1950s.

The Drive » Continue north on I-19. Exit 34 leads to Tubac, a former Spanish garrison town now home to a cluster of 100 or so galleries and shops selling art and high-end crafts. Continue north to exit 69 to complete the 26-mile leg.

TRIP HIGHLIGHT

❻ Titan Missile Museum

The **Titan Missile Museum** (☎520-625-7736, www.titanmissilemuseum.org; 1580 Duval Mine Rd, Sahuarita;

adult/senior/child 7-12yr $9.50/8.50/6; ⊙9:45am-5pm Sun-Fri, 8:45am-5pm Sat, last tour 3:45pm) is where the obliteration of humanity becomes frighteningly real. At this original Titan II missile site, a crew stood ready 24/7 to launch a nuclear warhead within seconds of receiving a presidential order. The Titan II was the first liquid-propelled intercontinental ballistic missile (ICBM) that could be fired from below ground and could reach its target – halfway around the world – in 30 minutes or less. The facility was on constant alert from 1963 to 1986. The 75-minute tours are both creepy and fascinating, and reservations are advised.

The Drive » Rejoin I-19 north and drive to exit 92 for the next 18-mile hop.

- - - - - - - - - - - - - - - - - -

❼ Mission San Xavier del Bac

The dazzling white towers of this **mission** (☎520-294-2624; www. patronatosanxavier.org; 1950 W San Xavier Rd; donations appreciated; ☾ museum 8:30am-4:30pm, church 7am-5pm) bring an otherworldly glow to the desert. Nicknamed 'White Dove of the Desert,' the original mission was founded by Jesuit missionary Father Eusebio Kino in 1700, but was mostly destroyed in the Pima uprising of 1751. Its successor was gracefully rebuilt in the late 1700s in a harmonious blend of Moorish, Byzantine and Mexican Renaissance styles. Carefully restored in the 1990s and still religiously active, it's one of the best-preserved and most beautiful Spanish missions in the country.

The wall-sized carved, painted and gilded retable behind the altar, in the moody, candlelit interior, tells the story of creation in dizzying detail. The faithful line up to pray to a reclining wooden figure of St Francis, the mission's patron saint.

The Drive » Follow San Xavier Rd west to S Mission Rd, go north to W Valencia Rd, then west 9 miles to Hwy 86 south. Continue just over 25 miles. Turn left onto Hwy 386 and climb to Kitt Peak – a twisty drive with ravishing views across the desert. It's a total of 49 miles.

- - - - - - - - - - - - - - - - - -

TRIP HIGHLIGHT

❽ Kitt Peak National Observatory

Dark and clear night skies make **Kitt Peak** (☎520-318-8726; www. noao.edu/kpno; Hwy 86; tours adult/child $9.75/3.25; ☾9am-4pm; 👪) a perfect site for one of the world's largest observatories. Just east of **Sells**, this 6875ft-high mountaintop is stacked with two radio telescopes and 22 optical telescopes. Guided tours (at 10am, 11:30am and 1:30pm) last 60 minutes. Make reservations two to four weeks in advance for the wonderful Nightly Observing Program ($50; no programs from mid-July to the end of August). The small visitor center has exhibits and a gift shop, but no food.

The Drive » Take Hwy 386 north back to Hwy 86. Drive 81 miles west on Hwy 86 to Why and the junction with Hwy 85. Follow Hwy 85 south 22 miles to the Kris Eggle Visitor Center in Organ Pipe Cactus National Monument.

TRIP HIGHLIGHT

❾ Organ Pipe Cactus National Monument

Along the Mexican border, this remote **national park** (☎520-387-6849; www. nps.gov/orpi; Hwy 85; per vehicle $12; ☾ visitor center 8:30am-5pm) is a gorgeous, forbidding land. It's home to an astonishing number of animals and plants, including 28 species of cacti, first and foremost its namesake organ-pipe. A giant columnar cactus, it differs from the more prevalent saguaro in that its arms radiate from the base. Organ-pipes are common in Mexico but very rare north of the border. Animals that have adapted to this arid climate include bighorn sheep, coyotes, kangaroo rats, mountain lions and the pig-like javelina.

Winter and early spring, when Mexican gold poppies and purple lupines blanket the barren ground, are the most pleasant seasons to visit. Summers are shimmering hot (routinely above 100°F/37°C) and bring monsoon rains between July and September.

The 21-mile **Ajo Mountain Drive** leads northeast from the visitor center through a spectacular landscape of steep-sided jagged cliffs and burned-red rocks.

🛏 p105

Eating & Sleeping

Tucson

✖ El Charro Café · · · · · · · · · · · · · · · · · Mexican $$
(📞520-622-1922; www.elcharrocafe.com;
311 N Court Ave; lunch $10-12, dinner $16-20;
🕙10am-9pm) This rambling, buzzing hacienda
has been making great Mexican food on this
site since 1922. They're particularly famous for
the *carne seca*, sundried lean beef that's been
reconstituted, shredded and grilled with green
chile and onions. The fabulous margaritas pack
a burro-stunning punch, and help while away
the time as you wait for your table.

✖ Lovin' Spoonfuls · · · · · · · · · · · · · · · · · · Vegan $
(📞520-325-7766; www.lovinspoonfuls.com;
2990 N Campbell Ave; breakfast $6-9, lunch
$5.25-8, dinner $7.25-11.25; 🕙9:30am-9pm
Mon-Sat, 10am-3pm Sun; 🖋) Burgers, country-
fried chicken and club sandwiches – the menu
reads like one at your typical diner but there's a
big difference: no animal products will ever find
their way into this vegan haven. Outstandingly
creative choices include the Old Pueblo bean
burrito and Buddha's Delight – a gingery stir-fry
of cabbage, shiitake and other goodies over
brown rice.

🛏 Arizona Inn · Resort $$
(📞520-325-1541; www.arizonainn.com; 2200
E Elm St; d/ste from $229/299; 🗱🖋🗱) High
tea in the library, complete with scones and
finger sandwiches, is a highlight here. Croquet
might be too, if only we knew the rules. Historic
and aristocratic touches such as these provide
a definite sense of privilege – and we like it.
Mature gardens and old-Arizona grace provide a
respite from city life and the 21st century.

Patagonia ❹

✖ Velvet Elvis · Pizza $
(📞520-394-2102; www.velvetelvispizza.com;
292 Naugle Ave; mains $8-24; 🕙11:30am-8pm;
📶) Yes, a velvet Elvis does indeed hang on the
wall at this gourmet pizza joint in Patagonia.
Motorcyclists, foreign visitors and date-night
couples – everybody visiting the area – roll in
at some point for one of the 14 designer pies, or
perhaps rigatoni with spicy sausage. These diet-
spoilers will make you feel like Elvis in Vegas: fat
and happy.

🛏 Duquesne House · · · · · · · · · · · · · · · · · · · B&B $$
(📞520-394-2732; www.theduquesnehouse.
com; 357 Duquesne Ave; r $140; @) This
photogenic, sky-blue adobe B&B was once a
boarding house for miners. Today there are
three spacious, eclectically appointed suites
with garden areas where you can watch the sun
set, listen to the birds chirp, smell the rosemary
and generally bliss out. Mondays through
Thursdays the B&B offers a 'Bed, No Bread'
special – $105 per night with no breakfast.

Organ Pipe Cactus National Monument ❾

🛏 Twin Peaks Campground · · · · · · · · · · · Campground $
(📞520-387-6849, ext 7302; www.nps.gov/
orpi; 10 Organ Pipe Dr; tent & RV sites $16) The
208 first-come, first-served sites at Twin Peaks
Campground by the Kris Eggle Visitor Center
are often full by noon from mid-January through
March. There are toilets, three solar-heated
showers and drinking water, but no hookups.
Call on the day of travel to confirm campsite
availability.

Highway 89A: Red Rock Country

8

This gorgeous drive is like entering an animated landscape painting, from the lush greenery of Oak Creek to the fiery brilliance of the Red Rock Scenic Byway.

TRIP HIGHLIGHTS

0 miles

Oak Creek Vista
Scope out your drive from this cliff-top perch

1 START

2

9 miles

Slide Rock State Park
Swoosh through Mother Nature's water park

FINISH

9

8

61 miles

Bell Rock Pathway
Re-invigorate with a pedal past a vortex

49 miles

V-Bar-V Heritage Site
A rare female shaman is etched on the rock

**2 DAYS
61 MILES/98KM**

GREAT FOR...

BEST TIME TO GO
Temperatures are most pleasant fall through spring.

 ESSENTIAL PHOTO

Cathedral Rock looks mighty majestic from Red Rock Crossing.

✓ **BEST FOR OUTDOORS**

Wheee! Whoosh over red rock waterfalls at Slide Rock State Park.

Oak Creek Cathedral Rock

Highway 89A: Red Rock Country

Sunday drivers, this trip is for you. A 61-mile lasso loop, it was designed to maximize gawping, punctuated with a few easy stops that get you close to those magnetic red rocks. Plus, there's shopping and dining along the way. Once you've driven the main loop, choose a path, join a tour or pinpoint another petroglyph site for further exploration.

TRIP HIGHLIGHT

❶ Oak Creek Vista

With its dramatic canyon walls and riparian lushness, **Oak Creek Canyon** is certainly stunning. But what makes this 14-mile stretch of Hwy 89A really special is the hint of the untamed, the lure of nature's bounty not yet captured and commodified. See for yourself at Oak Creek Vista, about 14 miles south of Flagstaff. From this towering perch, the pine-draped canyon whooshes ahead like an unruly child just

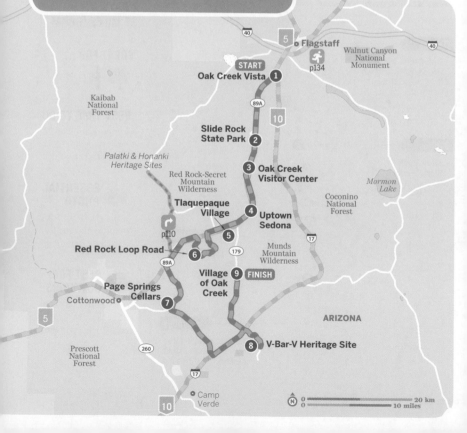

released from Mother Nature's time out. American Indian vendors sell jewelry beside the parking lot.

🛏 p113

The Drive ❯❯ Hwy 89A twists into the canyon then rolls along Oak Creek past Pine Flat and Cave Springs campgrounds in the Coconino National Forest. The trailhead for the popular West Fork Trail, which follows the creek for 7 miles, soon beckons on the right.

TRIP HIGHLIGHT

❷ Slide Rock State Park

On a hot summer day you're likely to get caught in a traffic jam at **Slide Rock State Park** (📞928-282-3034, information line 602-542-0202; www.azstateparks.com/parks/slro; 6871 N Hwy 89A, Oak Creek Canyon; per car Jun-Sep $20, Oct-May $10;

LINK YOUR TRIP

5 **Fantastic Canyon Voyage**

Continue north on Hwy 89A from Oak Creek Vista to charismatic Flagstaff.

10 **Southwest Indian Nations Sojourn**

From V-Bar-V drive north on I-17 to the cliff dwellings at Walnut Canyon National Monument.

⏱8am-7pm Jun-Aug, shorter hours rest of the year; 🚻), where swimmers come in droves to swoosh down the creek on rock-lined chutes and watery slides. Come early or late in the day to avoid the worst congestion. If things get too crowded, you can always wait until you reach **Grasshopper Point** (📞928-203-2900; www.fs.usda.gov; vehicle/pedestrian $8/3; ⏱9am-6pm Mon-Thu, 8am-6pm Fri-Sun), south of Oak Creek Visitor Center.

The Drive ❯❯ Continue south past Manzanita Campground; it's three sinuous, scenic miles to the next stop.

❸ Oak Creek Visitor Center

The pull-off for this small **visitor center** (📞928-203-0624; www.fs.usda.gov; Hwy 89A, Indian Gardens; ⏱9am-4pm Apr-Oct) is a nice place to stretch your legs. A lovely little coffee and sandwich shop, **Indian Gardens Cafe & Market** (📞928-282-7702; www.indiangardens.com; 3951 N Hwy 89A; breakfast $8-9, lunch $9-11; ⏱7:30am-5pm Mon-Thu, to 6pm Fri-Sun; 🅿), can be found here, as well as the long-established **Garland's Indian Jewelry** (📞928-282-6632; www.garlandsjewelry.com; 3953 Hwy 89A; ⏱10am-5pm) selling jewelry, kachinas, baskets and pottery.

The Drive ❯❯ Continue south on Hwy 89A, passing a great swimming hole, Grasshopper

Point (car-day use fee $8), before rolling into Sedona's 'city' center, called Uptown. Four miles in total.

❹ Uptown Sedona

Compact and busy (particularly around March and April), Uptown is where you'll find reservation desks for tour companies hoping to take you deeper into the stunning red rock country around Sedona. Jeep tours here are a fun, if bumpy, way to see the sights, but it can be hard to distinguish between the companies. One thing to check is backcountry accessibility; the companies have permits for different routes and sites, so if there's a specific formation you want to see, check around. The hard-to-miss **Pink Jeep Tours** (📞928-282-5000; www.pinkjeeptours.com; 204 N Hwy 89A; ⏱6am-10pm; 🚻) run 15 different thrilling and funny off-road and hiking tours lasting from about two hours to four hours (from $154/139).

Sedona's **visitor center** (📞928-282-7722, www.visitsedona.com; 331 Forest Rd; ⏱8.30am-5pm), great for info on hikes and other activities in red rock country, is at the corner of Hwy 89A and Forest Rd.

🍴🛏 p113

The Drive » Take Hwy 89A a short distance south to the roundabout at its junction with Hwy 179, known locally as the Y. Take 179 south and turn right almost immediately.

- - - - - - - - - - - - - - - - - -

❺ Tlaquepaque Village

This **shopping village** (☎928-282-4838; www.tlaq.com; 336 Hwy 179; ☺10am-5pm) is a series of Mexican-style interconnected plazas that are home to dozens of high-end art galleries, shops and restaurants. It's easy to lose a couple of hours meandering through this maze. If you're peckish, head a little further down Hwy 179 to the lip-smacking Mexican Elote Cafe (p113).

The Drive » Return to the Y and pick up Hwy 89A south. Chimney Rock and Coffee Pot Rock glow to the north. After passing Arroyo Pinon Dr, turn left onto upper Red Rock Loop Rd. The junction is 4 miles west of the Y.

- - - - - - - - - - - - - - - - - -

❻ Red Rock Loop Road

Any time is a good time to drive the winding 7-mile Red Rock Loop Rd, which is paved except for one short section. If you're in a mood to take photographs, turn left after 1.5 miles for the **Red Rock Crossing/Crescent Moon Recreation Area** (Upper Red Rock Loop Rd; day-use per vehicle $10, cash only; ☻). A small army of photographers usually gathers at the

crossing at sunset to record the dramatic light show unfolding on iconic **Cathedral Rock**.

Continue driving through the blaze of sandstone glory to the aptly named **Red Rock State Park** (☎928-282-6907; azstateparks.com/red-rock; 4050 Red Rock Loop Rd; adult $7, child 7-13yr $4, 6yr & under free; ☺8am-5pm, visitor center 9am-4:30pm; ☻). Not to be confused with Slide Rock State Park, this far more low-key place includes an environmental education center, a visitor center, picnic areas and 5 miles of well-marked trails in a riparian environment boasting gorgeous scenery. Ranger-led activities include nature walks, bird walks and full-moon hikes during warmer months.

The Drive » Rejoin Hwy 89A, turn left and drive 7 miles southwest to N Page Springs Rd.

- - - - - - - - - - - - - - - - - -

❼ Page Springs Cellars

The vineyards, wineries and tasting rooms lining Hwy 89A and I-17 are bringing a dash of energy and style to central Arizona's Verde Valley. Several wineries with tasting rooms hug a scrubby stretch of Page Springs Rd, east of Cornville – one of the best is **Page Springs Cellars** (☎928-639-3004; pagespringscellars.com; 1500

DETOUR: PALATKI & HONANKI HERITAGE SITES

Start: ❹ Uptown Sedona

Thousand-year-old Sinaguan cliff dwellings and rock art are great reasons to brave a 9-mile dirt road leading to two archaeological sites on the edge of the wilderness. At **Palatki Heritage Site** (☎reservations 928-282-3854; www.fs.usda.gov; Red Rock or Federal Interagency Pass $5; ☺9:30am-3pm) there's a small visitor center and three easy trails (not amenable to wheelchairs, unfortunately). To manage crowds, reservations are required. True ruin groupies should ask here about the ruins at **Honanki Heritage Site** (www.fs.usda.gov; Red Rock Pass $5; ☺9:30am-3pm), another 3 miles north. To get to Palatki, follow Hwy 89A west 10 miles from the Y then turn right onto dirt FR 525 (Red Canyon Rd) and follow it about 6 miles to FR 795. Take FR 795 for 1.5 miles. Both sites require a Red Rock Pass.

Slide Rock State Park

TOP TIP: RED ROCK PASSES

To park at many trailheads and recreational areas in the Coconino National Forest, you'll need to buy a **Red Rock Pass** ($5/15 per day/week) from visitor centers, ranger stations or vending machines at some trailheads and picnic areas. Passes go on your dashboard. Federal Interagency passes are valid. Applicable areas are plastered with signs, which you can ignore if stopping briefly for a photograph. Check the *Recreation Guide to Your National Forest*, available at National Forest visitor centers or online, to determine where the passes are required. Currently, passes are required at most recreational sites beside Hwy 89A in Oak Creek Canyon and beside Hwy 179 between Chapel Rd and the Bell Rock Pathway trailhead in the village of Oak Creek.

Page Springs Rd, Cornville; tours $10; ⊙11am-7pm Sun-Wed, to 9pm Thu-Sat). This busy spot has welcoming, knowledgeable staff and a cozy back porch overlooking Oak Creek. It's a thoroughly enjoyable place to savor the bruschetta and Rhône-style Arizona wines.

The Drive ≫ Turn right onto Page Springs Rd and drive south to Cornville Rd, which you'll follow south 8 miles to I-17. Drive north to exit 298 and FR 618. Drive east about 3 miles, passing Beaver Creek Campground. The total drive is just over 20 miles.

- - - - - - - - - - - - - - - - - -

TRIP HIGHLIGHT

⑧ V-Bar-V Heritage Site

More than 1000 petroglyphs – most attributed to the southern Sinaguan people who lived at nearby **Montezuma Castle** – have been identified at this well-protected Forest Service **site** (☑928-203-2900; www.redrockcountry.org/recreation/cultural/v-v; 6750 N Forest Ranger Rd, Rimrock; ⊙9:30am-3pm Fri-Mon). A short trail from the **visitor center** to the rock site runs parallel to a tributary of the **Verde River**. During the Sinaguan period (between AD 1150 and 1400) the site was probably used by shamans and in part as a solar calendar. See if you can find the depiction of a female shaman. And the embracing stick-figure couple? Not dancing. A Red Rock Pass is required.

The Drive ≫ Follow FR 618 west, crossing I-17. The Red Rock Scenic Byway (Hwy 179) begins three miles from here and continues for the rest of the final, 10-mile leg. Enjoy the show.

- - - - - - - - - - - - - - - - - -

TRIP HIGHLIGHT

⑨ Village of Oak Creek

Now that the scenic driving is done, stop at the Red Rock Country Visitor Center (p86), just south of the village of Oak Creek, for more information about places you want to explore further. Pick up the free *Recreation Guide to Your National Forest*, which has a great map of hiking and biking trails in greater Sedona and along Oak Creek. The map also shows camping spots and picnic areas.

A great cycling route is the easy but beautiful **Bell Rock Pathway** just north on Hwy 179. The pathway is across the street from **Bike & Bean** (☑928-284-0210; www.bike-bean.com; 30 Bell Rock Plaza; bike rental per hour/day from $19/55; ⊙8am-5pm), a blissful combo of coffee bar and bike-rental place. The 7-mile round-trip crosses lots of other hiking and biking paths, and it's easy to spend a day exploring. Hwy 179 takes you north back to Uptown Sedona.

🛏 p113

Eating & Sleeping

Oak Creek Vista ❶

🛏 Briar Patch Inn
Cabin $$$

(📞928-282-2342; www.briarpatchinn.com; 3190 N Hwy 89A; cabins from $265; 🛜) Nestled in nine wooded and grassy acres above Oak Creek, this bucolic and peaceful B&B hideaway offers 19 handsome cabins with Southwestern decor and American Indian art. All include patios and kitchens, many have fireplaces and several sit just above the gurgling waters. The buffet breakfast, served on the creekside patio, includes fruit, quiche, eggs, muffins and yogurt.

Uptown Sedona ❹

✕ Coffee Pot Restaurant
Breakfast $

(📞928-282-6626; www.coffeepotsedona.com; 2050 W Hwy 89A; breakfast $8-9, lunch $9-10; 🕐6am-2pm; 👪) A go-to breakfast and lunch joint since the 1950s, the Pot is nothing fancy but gets the refueling job done, with massive plates of reasonably priced fare and a huge selection. There is a bewildering 101 types of omelet, including what may be the world's only peanut butter, jelly and banana special.

✕ Elote Cafe
Mexican $$$

(📞928-203-0105; www.elotecafe.com; Arabella Hotel, 771 Hwy 179; mains $22-28; 🕐5-10pm Tue-Sat) Come here for some of the best, most authentic Mexican food in the region. Elote Cafe serves unusual and traditional dishes you won't find elsewhere, like the namesake *elote* (fire-roasted corn with spicy mayo, lime and cotija cheese) or smoked chicken in guajillo chiles. Reservations are not accepted and the line can be off-putting: come early, bring a book, order a margarita.

✕ Dahl & DiLuca Ristorante
Italian $$$

(📞928-282-5219; www.dahldaliluca.com; 2321 Hwy 89A; mains $27-38; 🕐5-10pm) Though this lovely Italian place fits perfectly into the groove and color scheme of Sedona, at the same time it feels like the kind of place you'd find in a small Italian seaside town. It's a bustling, welcoming spot serving excellent, authentic Italian food. Try the pork chop and asparagus from the grill or the four-cheese ravioli in truffle cream.

🛏 Lantern Light Inn
Inn $$

(📞928-282-3419; www.lanternlightinn.com; 3085 W Hwy 89A; r/guesthouse $159/309; 🛜) Kris and Ed, the lovely couple running this small inn in West Sedona, will put you right at ease. The antique-filled rooms range from small and cozy, overlooking the back deck and garden, to the huge guesthouse out back, and all feel comfortably overstuffed.

Village of Oak Creek ❾

🛏 Cozy Cactus
B&B $$

(📞928-284-0082; www.cozycactus.com; 80 Canyon Circle Dr; d from $210; ❄🛜) This five-room B&B, run by Carrie and Mark, works well for adventure-loving types – the Southwest-style house bumps up against Agave Trail, and is just around the bend from cyclist-friendly Bell Rock Pathway. Post-adventuring, get comfy beside the firepit on the back patio, perfect for wildlife watching and stargazing, and enjoy the three-course breakfast that awaits you the next morning.

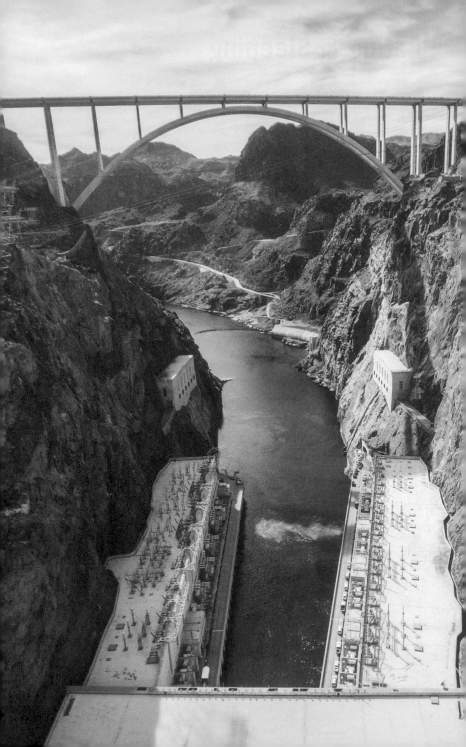

Highway 95: Yuma to Lake Mead

9

In western Arizona the scenery comes with a few quirky sides: a notorious prison, a tiny chapel, a lonely ghost town and the actual London Bridge.

TRIP HIGHLIGHTS

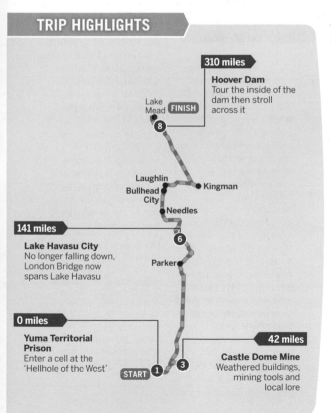

310 miles

Hoover Dam
Tour the inside of the dam then stroll across it

Lake Mead **FINISH**

8

Laughlin
Bullhead City
Kingman

Needles

141 miles

6

Lake Havasu City
No longer falling down, London Bridge now spans Lake Havasu

Parker

0 miles

Yuma Territorial Prison
Enter a cell at the 'Hellhole of the West'

START **1**

3

42 miles

Castle Dome Mine
Weathered buildings, mining tools and local lore

3 DAYS
312 MILES/502KM

GREAT FOR...

BEST TIME TO GO
Fall to spring for gem shows and to avoid the searing summer heat.

 ESSENTIAL PHOTO

Hoover Dam from the Mike O'Callaghan–Pat Tillman Memorial Bridge.

 BEST FOR ENGINEERING

Drop deep into Hoover Dam to learn how it was built.

Hoover Dam Mike O'Callaghan–Pat Tillman Memorial Bridge, viewed from the dam

9 Highway 95: Yuma to Lake Mead

There are some lonely stretches in this dessicated part of the state, it can't be denied. But, in between, there's plenty to savor, and some classic southwestern highway towns in which to hang your hat and kick up your heels. Plus, you can marvel at one of the greatest engineering feats in the USA.

TRIP HIGHLIGHT

❶ Yuma

This sprawling city at the confluence of the Gila and Colorado Rivers was home to Arizona's notorious **territorial prison** (☎928-783-4771; www.azstateparks.com; 1 Prison Hill Rd; adult/child 7-13yr $6/3; ☺9am-5pm daily, closed Tue & Wed Jun-Sep), which was nicknamed the 'Hellhole of the West,' in part because of the city's blazing temperatures. Between 1876 and 1909, 3069 convicts were incarcerated here for crimes ranging from murder to 'seduction under the promise of marriage.'

Today, the prison is Yuma's star attraction. Walking around the yard, behind iron-grille doors and into cells crowded with stacked bunks, you might get retroactively scared straight. And that's without mentioning the Dark Cell, a cave-like room where troublesome prisoners were locked together in a 5ft-high metal cage. Step inside and tremble. To delve deeper into Yuma's frontier history make time for the nearby **Yuma Quartermaster Depot State Park** (☎928-783-0071; www.azstateparks.com/yuma-quartermaster; 201 N 4th Ave; adult/child 7-13yr $4/2; ☺9am-5pm daily, closed Mon Jun–Sep).

A new trail system along the adjacent Colorado River links the prison with downtown's **Gateway Park** and the restored **Yuma East Wetlands**.

 p121

The Drive ❯❯ Jump onto US 95 N, following the railroad tracks and sandy hills to complete the 17-mile drive to the next stop.

❷ Pause-Rest-Worship Church

Northeast of Yuma, a tiny white-and-blue **chapel** (S Ave 13E) sits modestly on a patch of nondescript farmland. The 8ft-by-12ft structure seats about 12 and has stained-glass windows. A local farmer built the original in 1995 as a memorial to his wife, Loren Pratts; when a freak storm destroyed it in 2011, the local community rallied to rebuild it. If you're feeling contemplative, pull over, step inside and ponder the meaning of neighborliness.

The Drive ❯❯ Continue north on Hwy 95. After 25 miles turn right onto Castle Dome Mine Rd (mile marker 55) and drive 10 miles, the last seven of which are unpaved but well maintained. The drive takes you south of the Yuma Proving Ground, where the US Army tests weapon systems and munitions, and then into the Kofa National Wildlife Refuge.

TRIP HIGHLIGHT

❸ Castle Dome Mine

Meticulously reconstructed using as many original artifacts as possible, the remote **museum** (☎928-920-3062; castledomemuseum.org; Castle Dome Mine Rd; adult/child 7-11yr $10/5; ⏰10am-5pm, call for hours mid-Apr-Sep) here showcases an impressively evocative mining town that was founded in 1864 during a silver boom.

There are about 50 buildings in all, many of them retrieved from nearby mines. As you walk from the saloon to the blacksmith shop you can read about the people who used to live here. Also displayed is the world's oldest pair of Levi's, dating from 1890.

🔗 LINK YOUR TRIP

1 Four Corners Cruise

From Hoover Dam, drive northwest 33 miles on Hwy 93 to Sin City to kick off a classic Southwest loop.

2 Route 66: The Southwest

North of Lake Havasu, leave I-40W at exit 1, join Route 66 then climb to see the begging burros of Oatman.

A separate walking tour passes mine shafts and an old cemetery. Cash or check only.

The Drive ›› Return to Hwy 95 and continue north 50 miles to the I-10. Cross the interstate, turn left on W Main St and follow it about a mile.

❹ Quartzsite

The desert here floods with RVs in January and February, when visitors arrive for rock and mineral shows. Quartzsite's most curious monument is a small stone pyramid topped by a metal camel in the town graveyard. This memorial is for Haiji Ali, a Syrian camel driver who arrived in 1856 to help with a US Army experiment using camels to transport goods across the desert. The experiment didn't work but Ali, nicknamed Hi Jolly, became a prospector. He died here in 1902.

The Drive ›› Hwy 95 N enters the Colorado River Indian Reservation 25 miles north of Quartzsite. Buy gas and fast food in Parker. To drive over Parker Dam (the world's deepest dam, with 73% of its 320ft height beneath the riverbed) turn left onto Parker Dam Rd about 15 miles north. Return to Hwy 95 N to finish the 57-mile leg.

❺ Bill Williams National Wildlife Refuge

Abutting **Cattail Cove**, where the Bill Williams

River meets Lake Havasu, is this calm **wildlife refuge** (☎928-667-4144; www.fws.gov/refuge/Bill_Williams_River; 60911 Hwy 95; ☉visitor center 8am-4pm Mon-Fri, 10am-2pm Sat & Sun), which helps protect the unique transition zone between the Mojave and Sonoran desert ecosystems. On a finger of land pointing into the lake, there's a 1.4-mile interpretive trail through a botanic garden of native flora, with shaded benches and access to fishing platforms. Endangered birds like to roost in the largest cottonwood/willow grove along the entire length of the Colorado River. The entrance is between miles 161 and 162.

The Drive ›› With Lake Havasu to the west, drive north 24 miles to Lake Havasu City.

TRIP HIGHLIGHT

❻ Lake Havasu City

Gracefully arched, Georgian-era **London Bridge** may be one of Arizona's most incongruous tourist sites, but it's also among its most popular. It's a bona fide original, having spanned the Thames from 1831 to 1967, when it was quite literally falling down (as predicted in the nursery rhyme). Purchased by a developer, it was dismantled and reassembled in the Arizona desert. Day-trippers come by the

busload to walk across it and soak up faux British 'heritage' in the kitschy-quaint **English Village**.

The lake is the other major draw. Formed in 1938 by the construction of Parker Dam, it's beloved by water rats, especially students on spring break (roughly March to April) and summer-heat refugees from Phoenix and beyond.

Lake Havasu City London Bridge

The helpful **visitor center** (📞928-855-5655; www.golakehavasu.com; 422 English Village; 🕒9am-5pm) sits at the northeastern corner of the bridge.

🍴 🛏 p121

The Drive » Drive north to I-40 W. From I-40, continue west to Needles, just over the California border, and join Hwy 95 to complete the 66-mile northern run.

❼ Bullhead City & Laughlin

Named for a rock that resembled the head of a snoozing bull (now under Lake Mojave), Bullhead City began as a construction camp for Davis Dam, built in the 1940s. The town survives today primarily because of the casinos across the Colorado River in Laughlin, which has a little more sizzle. The twin town was founded in 1964 by gaming impresario Don Laughlin (a high-school dropout from Minnesota) and is a good stop for a cheap sleep and a little gambling action.

🍴 🛏 p121

The Drive » Follow Hwy 95 N to Hwy 68 E. It's not the quickest route but it leads through a

DETOUR: VALLEY OF FIRE STATE PARK

Start: ⑨ Lake Mead

For a scenic drive with an even more scenic end point, follow **Lakeshore Scenic Dr** northwest from the Alan Bible Visitor Center to Northshore Rd, heading northeast along Lake Mead.

At Hwy 169, turn left for the **Valley of Fire State Park** (📞702-397-2088; www.parks.nv.gov/parks/valley-of-fire; 29450 Valley of Fire Hwy, Overton; per vehicle $10; ☻visitor center 8:30am-4:30pm, park 7am-7pm), a fantasyland of wondrous shapes carved in vibrant red sandstone by the erosive forces of wind and water. Hwy 169 runs past the visitor center, which displays excellent desert-life exhibits, sells books and maps, and has information about hikes and ranger-led activities.

glorious, rocky pass to Route 66 hot spot Kingman, where museums, vintage motels and good food await. From Kingman, take Hwy 93 N. After crossing into Nevada, take exit 2 for NV 172, the dam-access road. The distance is 103 miles all up.

- - - - - - - - - - - - - - -

TRIP HIGHLIGHT

⑧ Hoover Dam

Completed in 1936, this mighty **dam** (📞702-494-2517; www.usbr.gov/lc/hooverdam; off Hwy 93; admission visitor center incl parking $10; ☻9am-6pm Apr-Oct, to 5pm Nov-Mar; ♿), on the Arizona–Nevada border, created Lake Mead, which has 700 miles of shoreline. The 726ft concrete structure was

the Colorado River's first major dam, and its graceful curve and art-deco style contrast superbly with the stark landscape.

Guided-tour options include the 30-minute power-plant tour or the more in-depth, one-hour Hoover Dam tour. Tickets for both are sold at the visitor center. If you're interested in history and construction facts, spring for the longer tour. Tickets for the power-plant tour can also be purchased online.

The nearby Mike O'Callaghan–Pat Tillman Memorial Bridge (p44) features a pedestrian walkway with perfect views upstream of

Hoover Dam. Nearby **Boulder City** is a pleasant place to spend the night.

🛏 p121

The Drive » Return to Hwy 93 W. Drive about 1.5 miles to Lakeshore Dr and turn right.

- - - - - - - - - - - - - - -

⑨ Lake Mead

Lake Mead and Hoover Dam are the most visited sites within the **Lake Mead National Recreation Area** (📞info desk 702-293-8906, visitor center 702-293-8990; www.nps.gov/lake; Lakeshore Scenic Dr; 7-day entry per vehicle $10; ☻24hr; ♿), which encompasses 110-mile-long Lake Mead, 67-mile-long Lake Mohave and many miles of desert around the lakes. The excellent **Lake Mead Visitor Center** (Alan Bible Visitor Center; 📞702-293-8990; www.nps.gov/lake; Lakeshore Scenic Dr, off US Hwy 93; ☻9am-4:30pm), halfway between Boulder City and Hoover Dam, has information on recreation and desert life. Here, hikers and cyclists can pick up a map of the **River Mountains Loop Trail** (www.rivermountainstrail.com), which offers 32 miles of trails around the lake. From there, North Shore Rd winds around the lake and makes a great scenic drive.

Eating & Sleeping

Yuma ❶

🍴 Lutes Casino · American $

(📞928-782-2192; www.lutescasino.com; 221 S Main St; mains $7-8; ⏰10am-8pm Mon-Thu, to 9pm Fri & Sat, to 6pm Sun) You won't find any roulette or slots at this charismatic 1920s-era hangout, just a warehouse-sized gathering spot. What's here? Attic-like treasures hanging from the ceiling, movie memorabilia, maybe a dude playing the piano and a true cross section of the town. Expect diner-style, nuthin' fancy fare. The 'especial' is a burger topped with a sliced hot dog (antacid not included).

🛏 Historic Coronado Motor Hotel · Motel $$

(📞928-783-4453; www.coronadomotorhotel. com; 233 4th Ave; r $134; ❄ @ 🛜 🏊 🐾) The template for motels to come (it was Best Western's first property), the Coronado is a must for motel-history buffs. Featuring red-tile roofs, bright turquoise doors, two swimming pools and newly upgraded rooms, it's a handsome and historic example of the genre. Some rooms have kitchenettes, there are three laundry rooms, and kids under 13 stay free.

Lake Havasu City ❻

🍴 Angelina's Italian Kitchen · Italian $$

(📞928-680-3868; 1530 El Camino Dr; mains $12-28; ⏰4-10pm) This is Italian American food done the right way: plenty of garlic, plenty of red sauce, and big portions. But it's also easy to venture beyond the red-check tablecloth standards: seafood (not from the lake, of course) is the star in dishes such as shrimp risotto, and the marsala-braised beef calls out for cooler weather than Lake Havasu normally offers.

🛏 Heat · Boutique Hotel $$

(📞928-854-2833; www.heathotel.com; 1420 N McCulloch Blvd; r/ste from $209/249; ❄ 🛜) Perhaps the slickest hotel on Arizona's 'West Coast,' Heat offers a majority of rooms with private patios that have views of London Bridge. In the 'inferno' rooms, bathtubs fill from the ceiling. An outdoor cocktail lounge overlooking the bridge and the lake feels almost like the deck of a cruise ship.

Bullhead City & Laughlin ❼

🍴 Laughlin Ranch Grill · American $$

(📞928-754-1322; www.laughlinranch.com; 1360 William Hardy Dr, Bullhead City; mains $22-27; ⏰10am-9pm Mon-Sat, to 6pm Sun; 🛜) Actually in Bullhead, yet part of the Laughlin Ranch Golf Club, the Grill aims for mountain-lodge chic, with stone walls, high ceilings, a fireplace and views over the links. Choose from burgers, steaks and pasta or, on Fridays, fish specials.

🛏 Aquarius Casino Resort · Hotel $$

(📞702-298-5111; www.aquariuscasinoresort. com; 1900 S Casino Dr; r/ ste from $59/179; 🅿 ❄ @ 🛜 🏊) The Aquarius hits the jackpot: chic, welcoming and budget-friendly. The lobby has art-deco touches, while rooms are modern with big windows and flat-screen TVs. The Splash Cabaret has free entertainment on Friday and Saturday nights, and the pool and tennis court area is up on a rooftop mezzanine.

Boulder City

🛏 Boulder Dam Hotel · Hotel $

(📞702-293-3510; www.boulderdamhotel. com; 1305 Arizona St; r from $89) This simple and gracious Dutch Colonial–style hotel has welcomed illustrious guests since 1933. Rate includes made-to-order breakfast and entry to the on-site Boulder City/Hoover Dam Museum.

Southwest Indian Nations Sojourn

10

American Indian history is the draw on this busy trip that rolls north from Phoenix to cliff dwellings, a lava field and trading posts before ending at remote and beautiful Canyon de Chelly.

TRIP HIGHLIGHTS

345 miles

Canyon de Chelly National Monument
Marvel at massive Spider Rock in the sacred Navajo heartland

8 FINISH

Cameron

168 miles

Sunset Crater Volcano National Monument
Buckled lava flows, whispering pines and rearing peaks make this wilderness unforgettable

4

Camp Verde **2**

85 miles

Montezuma Castle National Monument
This sheer cliff face shelters Sinaguan dwellings that have endured for centuries

Phoenix **1**
START

Heard Museum
The ancient and current lives of the Southwestern Indians take vivid shape here

0 miles

3–4 DAYS
345 MILES/555KM

GREAT FOR...

BEST TIME TO GO
Navajo rodeos are held most weekends May through September; the Navajo Nation Fair is in September.

ESSENTIAL PHOTO

The ancient cliff-hugging adobe houses of Montezuma Castle.

BEST FOR HISTORY

Phoenix's Heard Museum – a glorious trove of Southwestern Indian artifacts.

Hopi dancers

10 Southwest Indian Nations Sojourn

The flourishing of indigenous cultures in the Southwest between AD 100 and 1400 included the Hohokam, Sinaguan, Mogollon and Ancestral Puebloans. Their cliff dwellings, irrigation canals and petroglyphs stretch from the Phoenix area north into the Navajo Nation. While archaeologists and historians can only guess at why these cultures abandoned their elaborate settlements, it's thought climate variation played a huge part. The descendants of these mysterious peoples occupy their land to this day.

TRIP HIGHLIGHT

❶ Phoenix

For a fascinating introduction to the American Indian nations of the Southwest, visit Phoenix's wonderful **Heard Museum** (☑602-252-8848; www.heard.org; 2301 N Central Ave; adult $18, child 6-17yr & student $7.50, senior $13.50; ☉9:30am-5pm Mon-Sat, 11am-5pm Sun; [P] [♿]). The sheer imagination and craftsmanship of the kachina (Hopi spirit doll) collection is particularly memorable. More somber but equally unforgettable is the 'Boarding School Experience,' a permanent display recounting the controversial federal policy of removing American Indian children from their families and sending them to remote boarding schools to 'Americanize' them.

Explore Phoenix's Scottsdale neighbourhood on a walking tour (p130).

✕ 🏠 p129

The Drive » Take I-17 93 miles north on the first leg. Fort Verde State Historic Park at exit 287 is the site of an 1873 US Army fort, built during the Indian Wars. Further north, exit 289 and W Middle Verde Rd lead half a mile east to Montezuma Castle Rd.

TRIP HIGHLIGHT

❷ Montezuma Castle National Monument

This stunningly well-preserved Sinagua **cliff**

dwelling (📞928-567-3322; www.nps.gov/moca; Montezuma Castle Rd, Camp Verde; combination pass with Tuzigoot National Monument adult/child 15yr & under $10/free; ⏰8am-5pm; P 🚻) dates back 1000 years. The name refers to its castle-like location high on a cliff – early explorers thought the five-story-high pueblo was Aztec and dubbed it Montezuma. A museum interprets the archaeology of the site, which is visible from a short, wheelchair-accessible trail (which doesn't lead up to the protected site itself).

If you're interested in prehistoric irrigation techniques (and who isn't?) drive north to exit 293 to see the **Montezuma Well** (📞928-567-4521; www. nps.gov/moca; ⏰8am-5pm), a 470ft-wide sinkhole surrounded by Sinaguan and Hohokam dwellings.

LINK YOUR TRIP

1 Four Corners Cruise

On the Navajo Reservation, take Hwy 160 east from Tuba City to link to the incomparable Monument Valley.

5 Fantastic Canyon Voyage

From Cameron, Hwy 64 rolls west to the South Rim of the Grand Canyon National Park.

The Drive >> Return to I-17 and drive north. At exit 298, FR 618 leads east to petroglyphs at V-Bar-V Heritage Site. Just south of Flagstaff, on the brink of the lushly wooded Colorado Plateau, turn right onto I-40 and drive to exit 204, then follow Walnut Canyon Rd for 3 miles. All up, a 70-mile drive.

❸ Walnut Canyon National Monument

With so many big-name attractions nearby, the beautiful and strangely peaceful **Walnut Canyon** (📞928-526-3367; www. nps.gov/waca; I-40 exit 204; adult/child under 16yr $8/free; ⊙8am-5pm Jun-Oct, 9am-5pm Nov-May, trails close 1hr earlier; 🅿) calmly sidesteps the limelight. The Sinaguan cliff dwellings here are set in the nearly vertical walls of a small limestone butte amid a forested canyon of supreme beauty. The mile-long **Island Trail** steeply descends 185ft (beware – this means more than 200 stairs) and passes 25 rooms built under the natural overhangs of the curvaceous butte. The shorter, wheelchair-accessible **Rim Trail** is still worth the effort, offering several views of the cliff dwellings from across the canyon.

The Drive >> Follow Walnut Canyon Rd across I-40 and turn left onto Route 66. Follow Route 66 west to Hwy 89, from where it's about 12 miles to Park Loop Rd, and only a little further to Sunset Crater.

TRIP HIGHLIGHT

❹ Sunset Crater Volcano National Monument

Some time around AD 1064 a volcano erupted here, spewing ash over 800 sq miles, spawning the Kana-A lava flow and leaving behind the 8029ft, soot-black Sunset Crater. The eruption forced farmers to vacate lands they had cultivated for 400 years, as subsequent fulminations continued for more than 200 years.

Covered by a single entrance fee ($20 for one car, valid for seven days), both Sunset Crater Volcano and Wupatki National Monument lie along Park Loop Rd, a well-marked 35-mile circuit east of Hwy 89.

The **Sunset Crater Volcano National Monument Visitor Center** (📞928-526-0502; www.nps.gov/sucr; Loop Rd; car/motorcycle/bicycle or pedestrian $20/15/10; ⊙8am-5pm Jun–Oct, 9am-5pm Nov–May) houses a seismograph and other exhibits pertaining to volcanology. Viewpoints and a 1-mile interpretive trail through the buckled landscape of the **Bonito lava flow** (formed c 1180) spotlight volcanic features. There's also a 0.3-mile, wheelchair-accessible loop.

📖 p129

The Drive >> Continue 16 miles north on Park Loop Rd to the Wupatki National Monument Visitor Center.

❺ Wupatki National Monument

The first eruptions here enriched the soil, and ancestors of today's Hopi and Zuni people returned to farm the land in the early 1100s. By 1180, thousands were living here in advanced multistory buildings, but by 1250 their pueblos stood abandoned.

About 2700 of these structures lie within **Wupatki** (📞928-679-2365; www.nps.gov/wupa; Park Loop Rd 545; car/motorcycle/bicycle or pedestrian $20/15/10; ⊙visitor center 9am-5pm, trails sunrise-sunset; 🅿 🚻), though only a few are open to the public (others can be visited by those organized enough to secure a place on one of the National Park Service tours). A short self-guided tour of the largest dwelling, **Wupatki Pueblo**, begins behind the visitor center.

The Drive >> Return to Hwy 89 N, which enters the Navajo Reservation just beyond Gray Mountain. Cameron Trading Post, which has a huge selection of American Indian crafts, is just north of the junction with Hwy 64. Continue on Hwy 89 N for almost 16 miles. Turn right onto Hwy 160 and drive another 10 miles to Tuba City.

MARYANNE NELSON / GETTY IMAGES ©

Canyon de Chelly National Monument

6 Tuba City & Moenkopi

Tuba City, named for 19th-century Hopi chief Tuve (or Toova) is the largest single community in the Navajo Nation. To the southeast is the village of Moenkopi, a small Hopi enclave surrounded by Navajo land. For details about cultural protocol, visit www. explorenavajo.com, and remember that alcohol is not permitted on the reservation.

Tuba City is home to the interesting **Explore Navajo Interactive Museum** (📞928-640-0684; www.explorenavajo.com; 10 N Main St; adult/senior/child 7-12yr $4.50/3.50/3; ⏱8am-6pm Mon-Sat, noon-6pm Sun), where you'll discover why the Navajo call themselves the 'People of the Fourth World,' and learn about the tragic Long Walk. Contemporary Navajo life is also explored.

Next door, and included in your entry fee, is a small museum about the Navajo Code Talkers, who provided invaluable service to the American effort in WWII. Visits wrap up in the historic Tuba City Trading Post, which dates to the 1870s. For more information about exploring the Navajo Reservation and obtaining the permits required for hiking and camping, visit www. navajonationparks.org.

🛏 p129

The Drive ⟫ Drive east 64 miles on Hwy 264 to Second Mesa.

7 Hopi Nation

Three rocky, sand-colored hilltops, named First, Second and Third Mesa, form the heart of the Hopi Nation, which is completely surrounded by the much

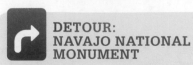

DETOUR: NAVAJO NATIONAL MONUMENT

Start: ⑥ Tuba City & Moenkopi

The sublimely well-preserved Ancestral Puebloan cliff dwellings of **Betatkin** and **Keet Seel** are protected at the **Navajo National Monument** (📞928-672-2700; www.nps.gov/nava; Hwy 564; ⊙ visitor center 8am-5:30pm Jun-early Sep, 9am-5pm early Sep-May) and can only be reached on foot. The site, administered by the National Park Service, is 9 miles north of Hwy 160 at the end of paved Hwy 564.

For a distant glimpse of Betatkin follow the easy **Sandal Trail** about half a mile from the visitor center. Betatkin is reached on a ranger-led 3-mile round-trip hike from the visitor center. Carry plenty of water, especially if setting off on the steep and strenuous 17-mile round-trip hike to the beautiful Keet Seel. The trail, open late May to early September, is limited to 20 people daily and requires a backcountry permit. Make reservations starting in late January.

larger **Navajo Nation**. Descendants of the Ancestral Puebloans, the Hopi are one of the most untouched tribes in the US. Their village of **Old Oraibi** may be the oldest continuously inhabited settlement in North America.

On Second Mesa, the Hopi Cultural Center (p129) provides food and lodging, and is the home of the small **Hopi Museum** (📞928-734-6650; Hwy 264, Mile 379; adult/child 12yr & under $3/1; ⊙8am-5pm Mon-Fri, 9am-3pm Sat; 🅿)), with walls full of historical photographs and cultural exhibits.

The Hopi have a deep and distinguished tradition of decorative arts and crafts: for a list of galleries and artists, visit www.hopiartstrail.com.

Be aware that photographs, sketching and recording are not allowed on the reservation.

🛏 p129

The Drive » Drive 57 miles east on Hwy 264 to Hwy 191. The junction is in the Navajo capital of Window Rock, where you should make time for the excellent tribal museum. For Canyon de Chelly, follow Hwy 191 north to Chinle and turn right onto Indian Rte 7 to complete this 91-mile leg.

⑧ Canyon de Chelly National Monument

Inhabited for 5000 years, the sacred and beautiful Canyon de Chelly (pronounced 'd-shay') shelters prehistoric rock art and 1000-year-old Ancestral Puebloan dwellings. Navajo families still farm the narrow strip of land at the canyon's base.

The national monument is on private Navajo land, but is run by the National Park Service. The 16-mile **South Rim Drive** runs along the canyon's scenic lip and has the most dramatic viewpoints. It dead-ends at the spectacular **Spider Rock Overlook**. For the most part the **North Rim Drive** follows a side canyon called **Canyon del Muerto**. Viewpoints at the **Antelope House Overlook** offer lofty cliff-top views of a natural rock fortress and cliff dwellings.

Only enter hogans (traditional homes) with a guide and don't take photographs without permission. To travel inside the canyon, choose a guide from the list provided by the **visitor center** (📞928-674-5500; www.nps.gov/cach; ⊙8am-5pm) and found on the park website.

🛏 p129

Eating & Sleeping

Phoenix ❶

✕ Fry Bread House   American Indian $
(☎602-351-2345; 4140 N 7th Ave; mains $6-7; ⊕10am-8pm Mon-Thu, to 9pm Fri & Sat) The American Indian treat known as an elephant ear or Navajo taco is a flat piece of fried dough topped with meat, beans and veggies, or, for dessert, smeared with honey. This small place gets packed to the gills with nearby office workers at lunchtime, so try to avoid the rush.

🛏 Sheraton Wild Horse Pass Resort & Spa   Resort $$$
(☎602-225-0100, www.wildhorsepassresort.com; 5594 W Wild Horse Pass Blvd, Chandler; r/ste from $339/534; P ❊ 🛜 ☲) At sunset, scan the lonely horizon for the eponymous wild horses silhouetted against the South Mountains. Owned by the Gila River tribe and nestled on their sweeping reservation south of Tempe, this 500-room resort is a stunning alchemy of modern luxury and American Indian tradition. The domed lobby is a mural-festooned roundhouse, and rooms reflect the traditions of local tribes. The award-winning Kai Restaurant serves indigenous Southwestern cuisine.

Sunset Crater Volcano National Monument ❹

🛏 Bonito Campground   Campground $
(☎928-526-0866; www.fs.usda.gov/recmain/coconino/recreation; Loop Rd; tent & RV sites $24; ⊕May–mid-Oct) Across from the Sunset Crater Volcano National Monument Visitor Center (p126), the USFS-run Bonito Campground provides 44 sites with running water and restrooms but no showers or hookups. There's a 14-day limit on stays and no reservations.

Moenkopi ❻

🛏 Moenkopi Legacy Inn & Suites   Hotel $$
(☎928-283-4500; www.experiencehopi.com; cnr Hwys 160 & 264; r/ste from $160/171; ❊ 🛜 ☲) Unquestionably the most luxurious digs in Moenkopi, the Legacy Inn is built in a stylized version of traditional Hopi village architecture – the lobby, with its soaring ceiling supported by pine pillars, is particularly effective. Rooms have marble and granite bathrooms and reproductions of historical photographs from the Hopi archives at Northern Arizona University.

Hopi Nation ❼

🛏 Hopi Cultural Center Restaurant & Inn   Hotel $$
(☎928-734-2401; www.hopiculturalcenter.com; Hwy 264, Mile 379; r $115; ⊕restaurant 7am-9pm summer, to 8pm winter) Reservations are essential for the hotel at the Hopi Cultural Center, especially in summer when its 33 modern, undistinguished rooms usually book out. The restaurant (meals $9 to $12) serves interesting, if quite bland, Hopi dishes such as *noqkwivi* (lamb and hominy stew) served with blue-corn frybread. Less adventurous palates will find a salad bar and the usual American fare.

Canyon de Chelly National Monument ❽

🛏 Spider Rock Campground   Campground $
(☎928-781-2014/16; www.spiderrockcampground.com; Navajo Hwy 7; tent/RV sites $11/16, hogans $31-47; ☲) This Navajo-run campground 12 miles from the visitor center on South Rim Drive is surrounded by piñon and juniper trees. No tent? Rent one for $9 or spend the night in a traditional Navajo hogan. Solar-heated showers cost $3, credit cards aren't accepted, and basic drinks and snacks are sold.

STRETCH YOUR LEGS
SCOTTSDALE

Start/Finish Experience Scottsdale visitor center

Distance 2 miles/3.2km

Duration Three hours

History, art and food are highlights on this stroll through the heart of downtown Scottsdale, taking in the Wild West shtick of the Old Town and the chic galleries and upscale eateries of the Arts District and Southbridge.

Take this walk on Trip

Experience Scottsdale

The helpful staff at this **visitor center** (☎480-421-1004; www.experiencescottsdale. com; 7014 E Camelback Rd; ☺9am-6pm Mon-Sat, 10am-5pm Sun) can give you the full low-down on Scottsdale's sights and services. The *Scottsdale Official Visitors' Guide* is a compact, glossy key to the remaining historic buildings and other noteworthy attractions of this formerly small town.

The Walk ≫ Walk south down Scottsdale Rd, crossing Indian School Rd then 1st Ave. On your left is the Sugar Bowl, an ice-cream parlor that's been pleasing crowds since 1958. Stop for a sundae, or keep going and take the next left, onto Main St.

Old Town Scottsdale

This slightly twee Wild West–themed enclave is filled with cutesy buildings, covered sidewalks and stores hawking mass-produced American Indian jewelry and Western art. But if you're prepared to go with it you'll generally find some fun-loving folks kicking back in the **Rusty Spur Saloon** (☎480-425-7787; www.rustyspursaloon.com; 7245 E Main St; ☺10am-1am Sun-Thu, to 2am Fri & Sat), a pack-'em-in-tight urban 'Western' bar where the grizzled Budweiser crowd gathers for cheap drinks and gritty country bands. It's in an old bank that closed during the Depression – the vault now holds liquor instead of greenbacks, although you'll see lots of dollar bills hanging from the ceiling.

The Walk ≫ Walk east on Main St, crossing Brown Ave, and continue east a short distance on the pedestrianized Civic Center Park Path.

Scottsdale Civic Center Mall

Old school meets new school in the blocks near the **Civic Center**. Learn about Scottsdale's first settlers through the intriguing period artifacts and photographs collected at the **Scottsdale Historical Museum** (☎480-945-4499; www. scottsdalemuseum.org; 7333 E Scottsdale Mall; ☺10am-5pm Wed-Sun Oct-May, to 2pm Wed-Sun Jun & Sep) – it's inside the picturesque **Little Red Schoolhouse**, built in 1909.

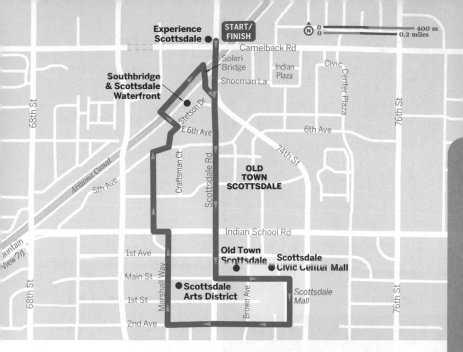

Things get more sophisticated just south at the **Scottsdale Museum of Contemporary Arts** (☏480-874-4666; www.smoca. org; 7374 E 2nd St; adult/student/child 15yr & under $10/5/free, free Thu & after 5pm Fri & Sat; ◷noon-5pm Sun, Tue & Wed, noon-9pm Thu-Sat), which sits inside a cleverly adapted former movie theater and showcases global art, architecture and design.

The Walk ›› Turn right out of the museum, take another immediate right onto E 2nd St and cross Brown Ave and Scottsdale Rd. Turn right at Marshall Way and walk two blocks north to rejoin Main St.

Scottsdale Arts District

The Arts District is bursting with galleries laden with everything from epic Western oil paintings to cutting-edge sculpture and moody Southwestern landscapes. Every Thursday evening art lovers gather for the **Art Walk** (www. scottsdalegalleries.com; ◷7-9pm), which centers on Marshall and Main.

The Walk ›› Continue north on Marshall Way, crossing Indian School Rd. At the Horse Fountain, turn right onto 5th Ave, which is lined with boutiques and eateries.

Southbridge & Scottsdale Waterfront

Restaurants with inviting patios border the **Arizona Canal**, which separates Southbridge from the Waterfront District to the north. Enjoy lunch and the happy bustle at the **Herb Box** (☏480-289-6160; www.theherbbox.com; 7134 E Stetson Dr; brunch $13-15, lunch $14-17, dinner $17-22; ◷11am-9pm Mon-Thu, 11am-10pm Fri, 9am-10pm Sat, 9am-4pm Sun; 🛜🖊), a sleek bistro with great people-watching potential, beloved of the Scottsdale brunch set. From here, cross the **Marshall Way Bridge** and follow the pedestrian walkway east to the 100ft-long **Soleri Bridge**, a stainless-steel wonder by the late artist and architect Paolo Soleri. Walk north back to the visitor center and to browse the upscale boutiques of **Scottsdale Fashion Square** (www.fashionsquare.com; 7014 E Camelback Rd; ◷10am-9pm Mon-Sat, 11am-6pm Sun; 🛜).

The Walk ›› Walk to Scottsdale Rd and head back north to the Experience Scottsdale visitor center.

STRETCH YOUR LEGS TUCSON

Start/Finish El Presidio Park

Distance 1.7 miles/2.7km

Duration Three hours

Set in a broad desert valley beneath snaggle-toothed, saguaro-swaddled slopes, Arizona's second-largest city effortlessly blends its American Indian, Spanish, Mexican and Anglo traditions. Western art sets an inspirational tone for this stroll through downtown Tucson. The walk winds through the Presidio then heads to the antique Hotel Congress.

Take this walk on Trips

3 7

El Presidio Park

Pick up the free *Turquoise Trail* map from the **Tucson Visitors Center** (520-624-1817; www.visittucson.org; 811 N Euclid Ave; 9am-5pm Mon-Fri, to 4pm Sat & Sun), then drive downtown to explore. Park at the Presidio underground garage (160 W Alameda; 6am to 8pm Monday to Friday; $8 maximum) then head above ground to your starting point, El Presidio Park – named for the Spanish fort from which the city grew. First used by Europeans in 1539, this open space was also employed by the 18th-century Spanish garrison, and later saw the Mormon Battalion first plant the American flag in 1846.

The Walk >> Cross to the north side of Alameda St, then head west to the museum.

Tucson Museum of Art

The museum is part of the historically significant but low-key **Presidio Historic District**, the site of the original Spanish fort from which Tucson grew, and now an expensive residential area sometimes known as 'Snob Hollow.' Bounded by W Alameda St, N Stone Ave, W 6th St and Granada Ave, the Presidio teems with adobe town houses and restored 19th-century mansions and is thought to be one of the oldest inhabited places in North America. For a small city, the principal art museum – the **Tucson Museum of Art** (520-624-2333; www.tucsonmuseumofart.org; 140 N Main Ave; adult $12, senior & student $10, child 13-17yr $7; 10am-5pm Tue-Sat, noon-5pm Sun) – is impressive. There's a noteworthy collection of Western and contemporary art, and the permanent exhibition of pre-Columbian artifacts opens a fascinating window into deep-rooted American cultures.

The Walk >> Walk north, then east onto Washington St, crossing Meyer Ave.

Old Town Artisans

The arts-and-crafts enclave at the heart of the Presidio, **Old Town Artisans** (www.

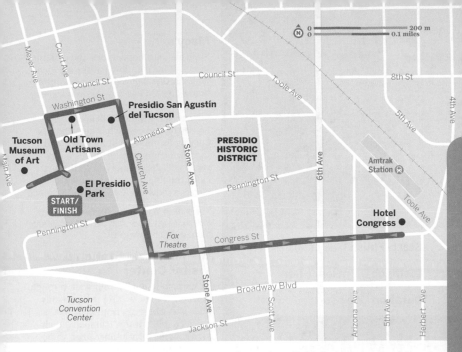

oldtownartisans.com; 201 N Court Ave; ⊙10am-5:30pm Mon-Sat, 11am-5pm Sun Sep-May, to 4pm daily Jun-Aug) is a block-long warren of adobe apartments filled with galleries and crafts stores centred on a lush and lovely courtyard cafe. It's a good destination for quality arts and crafts produced in the Southwest and Mexico.

The Walk >> Keep walking east on Washington St to reach the re-created vestiges of the Spanish fort bordering Church Ave.

Presidio San Agustín del Tucson

The Spanish Presidio San Agustín del Tucson dates back to 1775, but the fort itself was built over a Hohokam site that has been dated to AD 700 to 900. The original fort is completely gone, although there's a small reconstructed section at the corner of Church Ave and Washington St.

The Walk >> Follow Church Ave south to Congress St. Turn left and walk east, passing the Fox Theatre, a renovated 1930s art-deco

dream palace with fluted golden columns, water fountains and a giant sunburst mural radiating from the ceiling. Keep walking east to the Hotel Congress.

Hotel Congress

The beautifully restored 1919 Hotel Congress (p69) is a bohemian vintage beauty and a beehive of activity, stimulated by its popular cafe, bar and club. Infamous bank robber John Dillinger and his gang were captured here during their 1934 stay, when a fire broke out at the hotel. Off the lobby, peruse newspaper clippings and photos about Dillinger's capture. The popular **Cup Cafe** (☎520-798-1618; www.hotelcongress.com/food; 311 E Congress St, Hotel Congress; breakfast $11-12, lunch $12-13, dinner $19-24; ⊙7am-10pm Sun-Thu, to 11pm Fri & Sat; 🛜🅿) serves a global array of dishes, with a decent selection of vegetarian mains.

The Walk >> Retrace Congress, Church and Pennington back to El Presidio Park, or walk south to amble through more of Tucson's historic heart.

STRETCH YOUR LEGS
FLAGSTAFF

Start/Finish Macy's

Distance 0.7 miles/1.1km

Duration One hour

Flagstaff's lumber-town pedigree and student-fueled bonhomie make this meander through downtown a delight. Vintage neon, grand, ghost-riddled hotels and cheery local bars abound on this leisurely stroll through Flag's compact heart.

Take this walk on Trips

Macy's

Students, outdoorsy types and caffeine lovers all hunker down at the wooden tables at this beloved bohemian **coffeehouse** (☎928-774-2243; www.macyscoffee. net; 14 S Beaver St; breakfast/lunch $6/7; ◷6am-6pm; 🛜🖉). The delicious house-roasted coffee has kept the city buzzing for more than 30 years, and the vegetarian menu includes many vegan choices, along with traditional cafe grub like pastries, steamed eggs, bagels, sandwiches, yogurt and granola.

The Walk ≫ Walk north on Beaver St, crossing Phoenix Ave and the railroad tracks. Turn right into the train-station parking lot.

Historic Train Station & Visitor Center

At some point during your walk through downtown 'Flag,' a train will probably glide past. For years from their first arrival in 1882, trains trumpeted their arrival in the lofty lumber town with ear-splitting horns; now the city officials, mindful of slumbering tourists anxious to get their rest before tackling the Grand Canyon, have banned the noisy ritual. The handsome red-brick stationhouse, vestige of Flagstaff's early boom years, now contains the Amtrak office and the **visitor center** (☎928-7293-2951; www.flagstaffarizona.org; 1 E Rte 66; ◷8am-5pm Mon-Sat, 9am-4pm Sun). Pop in here for free downtown walking guides that will steer you to notable and haunted sites, including stops on the old **Route 66**.

The Walk ≫ From the station, turn right on Route 66 and walk to San Francisco St. Turn left, cross the main road and walk one block north and across Aspen Ave.

Hotel Monte Vista

An old-fashioned neon sign towers over this allegedly haunted 1926 hotel (p89), hinting at the antique delights inside: feather lampshades, vintage furniture, bold colors and eclectic decor. Rooms are named for the movie stars and musicians who spent a night here.

The hotel is famous for its ghosts, and the front desk keeps a list of

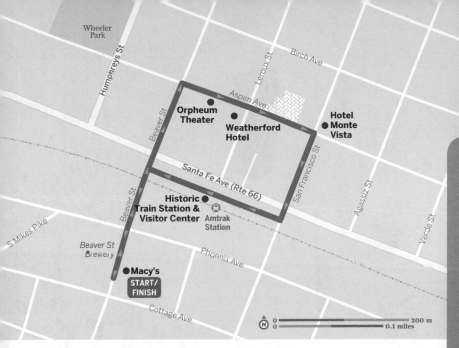

resident spirits. According to one story, a woman died in the rocking chair of the Jon Bon Jovi Room and is said to now haunt the room. Creepier still is the Gary Cooper Room, supposedly haunted by two prostitutes who were stabbed and thrown out the window in the 1930s. And if you're in room 210, listen out for the Phantom Bellboy.

The Walk » Cross San Francisco St and walk northwest on Aspen Ave, passing Heritage Sq. Cross Leroux St and head to the dignified old hotel on the northwestern corner.

Weatherford Hotel

There's something undeniably appealing about this Old West **hotel** (☎928-779-1919; www.weatherfordhotel.com; 23 N Leroux St; s/d from $115/155; ❄ 🛜), which opened on New Year's Day in 1900. Maybe it's the fact that it manages to pack in no fewer than three bars: two on the 1st floor and one on the 3rd. It's also cool that two icons of the west, artist Thomas Moran and author Zane Grey, were guests. Moran drew sketches of the Western landscape while staying here, and Grey worked on his book *Call of the Canyon.*

Ever since 1999 an illuminated 6ft-tall pine cone drops here twice on New Year's Eve, at 10pm EST and midnight Mountain Time.

The Walk » Head back to W Aspen Ave, turn left and walk a half block.

The Orpheum

John Weatherford, the eponymous founder of the Weatherford Hotel, also built this nearby **theater** (☎928-556-1580; www.orpheumflagstaff.com; 15 W Aspen Ave; tickets from $15), which opened as a movie house in 1911. Closing in 1915 after a violent snowstorm collapsed the roof, the Orpheum reopened in 1917. Today the handsome building is a live-music venue showcasing regional and indie bands.

The Walk » Continue to Beaver St and turn left, crossing Route 66 and Phoenix Ave. Toast your successful completion of the walk with a microbrew at Beaver St Brewery, or cross Beaver St to return to Macy's.

New Mexico

NEW MEXICO IS CALLED THE LAND OF ENCHANTMENT for a reason, and you'll find out why as you drive through the technicolor landscapes that inspired Georgia O'Keeffe, past traditional adobe villages tucked beneath the 13,000ft Sangre de Cristo range and over juniper-speckled plains that seem to roll to infinity. Along the way you'll stop at old mud-brick *santuarios* filled with sacred folk art, visit ancient and living pueblos, explore surreal underground caverns and soak in soothing hot springs.

You'll travel what might be the oldest road in America and follow in the footsteps of Geronimo and Billy the Kid. You're never far from great hiking and camping – or platters of local cuisine smothered in the state's signature green or red chile sauce.

Santa Fe New Mexico Museum of Art (Trips 1, 11 & 12)
LIZCOUGHLAN / SHUTTERSTOCK ©

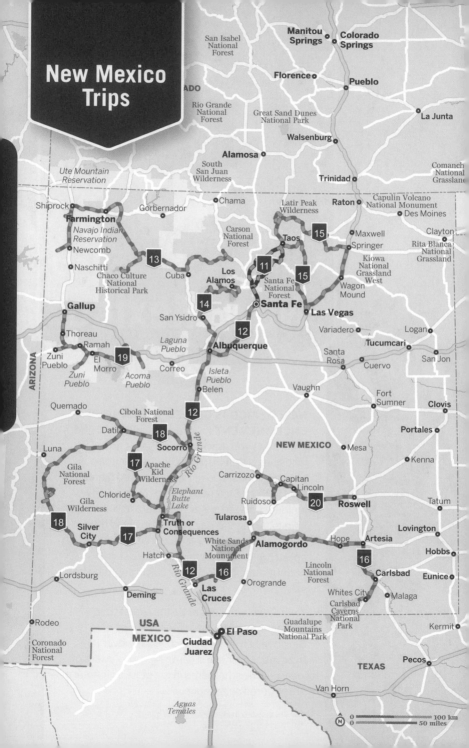

New Mexico Trips

DON'T MISS

Lincoln

The entire town is a historical monument, including the courthouse from which Billy the Kid shot his way to freedom; on Trip **20**

Ghost Ranch

Hike, ride horseback or take a van tour through the colorful terrain immortalized in the paintings of Georgia O'Keeffe, on Trip **13**

Santuario de Chimayó

This adobe church built in 1816 is home to miracle healings and is the site of the largest Catholic pilgrimage in the US. Find it on Trip **11**

Canyon Road

The heart of the Santa Fe art scene, with over 100 galleries plus fine dining and the oldest tavern in town (El Farol). Dive in on Trips **11** **12**

Pueblos

Find some of the oldest continuously inhabited places in North America, rich in culture including dances and crafts, on Trips **11** **15** **19**

Classic Trip

High & Low Roads to Taos

11

Santa Fe. Taos. The Rio Grande. The Sangre de Cristos. And all the adobe villages, galleries, Spanish Colonial churches and burrito stands in between make this loop a classic.

TRIP HIGHLIGHTS

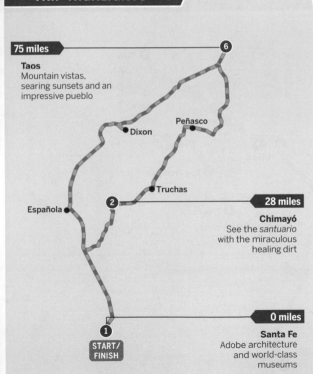

75 miles — ⑥

Taos
Mountain vistas, searing sunsets and an impressive pueblo

Dixon

Peñasco

Truchas

Española ②

28 miles
Chimayó
See the *santuario* with the miraculous healing dirt

0 miles
Santa Fe
Adobe architecture and world-class museums

①
START/ FINISH

1–4 DAYS
150 MILES/241KM

GREAT FOR...

BEST TIME TO GO
June to March, when temps are not too hot.

ESSENTIAL PHOTO

Capture the gorge and mountains at once, from Hwy 68 near Taos.

BEST FOR CULTURE

The 'miracle church' – and the chile – in Chimayó.

Chimayó El Santuario de Chimayó

Classic Trip

11 High & Low Roads to Taos

Starting in hip, historic Santa Fe, you'll rise from scrub-and-sandstone desert into ponderosa forests, snaking between the villages at the base of the 13,000ft Sangre de Cristos, until you reach the Taos Plateau. After checking out this little place that's lured artists, writers and hippies for the past century, head back south through the ruggedly sculpted Rio Grande Gorge, with the river coursing alongside you.

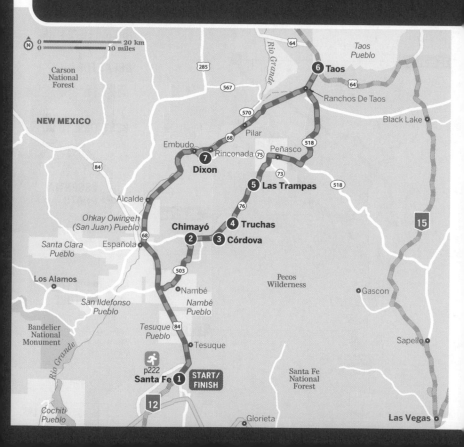

TRIP HIGHLIGHT

❶ Santa Fe

Walking among the historic adobe neighborhoods, and even around the tourist-filled plaza, there's no denying that 400-year-old Santa Fe has a timeless, earthy soul. Known as 'the city different,' it seamlessly blends historical and contemporary styles and casts a spell that's hard to resist: it's the second-oldest city in the US, the oldest state capital, and throws the oldest annual party (Fiesta) while boasting the second-largest art market in the nation, plus gourmet restaurants, world-class museums, opera, spas and more. At 7000ft above sea level, Santa Fe is also the highest state capital in the US, and a fantastic base for hiking, mountain biking,

LINK YOUR TRIP

 12 El Camino Real & Turquoise Trail

A natural segue south from Santa Fe along the historic Rio Grande road.

 15 Enchanted Circle & Eastern Sangres

Loop north from Taos, over the mountains and back again.

HIGH/LOW ROAD FESTIVALS

Try to catch – or avoid, if you hate crowds – some of the highlights from around the year on the High and Low Roads. Check websites for exact dates each year:

Easter (Chimayó) – March/April

Taos Pueblo Pow-Wow (www.taospueblopowwow.com) – July

International Folk Art Market (www.folkartmarket.org; Santa Fe) – July

Spanish Market (www.spanishcolonial.org; Santa Fe) – July

Indian Market (www.swaia.org; Santa Fe) – August

Santa Fe Fiesta (www.santafefiesta.org) – September

High Road Art Tour (www.highroadnewmexico.com; Hwy 76 to Peñasco) – September

Dixon Studio Tour (www.dixonarts.org) – November

Christmas on Canyon Rd – December

backpacking and skiing. The plaza area (p222) has the highest concentration of sights but it's also worth a trip to Museum Hill, where you'll find the fantastical **Museum of International Folk Art** (☎505-827-6344; www.internationalfolkart.org; 706 Camino Lejo; adult/child $12/free; ⏰10am-5pm, closed Mon Nov-Apr) and the excellent **Museum of Indian Arts & Culture** (☎505-476-1250; www.indianartsandculture.org; 710 Camino Lejo; adult/child $12/free; ⏰10am-5pm, closed Mon Sep-May), among others.

🍴 🛏 p45, p149, p157

The Drive » For this 28-mile leg, take Hwy 84/285 north, then exit right onto Hwy 503 towards Nambé. Turn left onto Juan Medina Rd, toward the Santaurio de Chimayó.

TRIP HIGHLIGHT

❷ Chimayó

Tucked into this little village is the so-called 'Lourdes of America,' **El Santuario de Chimayó** (☎505-351-9961; www.elsantuariodechimayo.us; ⏰9am-6pm May-Sep, to 5pm Oct-Apr), one of the most important cultural sites in New Mexico. In 1816, this two-towered adobe chapel was built over a spot of earth said to have miraculous healing properties. Even today, the faithful come to rub the *tierra bendita* (holy dirt) from a small pit inside the church on whatever hurts; some mix it with water

and drink it. The walls of the dirt room are covered with crutches, left behind by those healed by the dirt. During Holy Week, about 30,000 pilgrims walk to Chimayó from Santa Fe, Albuquerque and beyond in the largest Catholic pilgrimage in the US. The artwork in the *santuario* is worth a trip on its own.

Chimayó also has a centuries-old tradition of producing some of the finest weavings in the area and has a handful of family-run galleries. Irvin Trujillo, a seventh-generation weaver, whose carpets are in collections at the Smithsonian in Washington, DC, and the Museum of Fine Arts in Santa Fe, works out of his gallery **Centinela Traditional Arts** (☎505-351-2180; www.chimayoweavers.com; Hwy 76; ☻9am-6pm Mon-Sat, 10am-5pm Sun). Naturally dyed blankets, vests and pillows are sold, and you can watch the artists weaving on handlooms.

✗ ⌂ p149

The Drive ≫ Follow Hwy 76 north for a few miles, and take the right-side turnoff to Córdova.

- - - - - - - - - - - - - - - - - -

❸ Córdova

Down in the Rio Quemado Valley, this little town is best known for its unpainted, austere *santos* (saint) carvings created by local masters such as George Lopez, Jose Delores Lopez and Sabinita Lopez Ortiz – all members of the same artistic family. Stop and see their work at the **Sabinita Lopez Ortiz shop** (☎505-351-4572; County Rd 1317; ☻hours vary) – one of a few galleries in town.

The Drive ≫ Hop back on Hwy 76 north, and climb higher into the Sangre de Cristo Mountains, for about 4 miles.

WINTER THRILLS

One of the biggest winter draws to this part of New Mexico is the skiing and snowboarding, and **Taos Ski Valley** (☎866-968-7386; www.skitaos.org; lift ticket adult/teen/child $98/81/61; ☻9am-4pm) is the premier place to hit the slopes. There's just something about the abundant powder, wicked steeps and laid-back atmosphere that makes this mountain a wintery heaven-on-earth – that is, if heaven has a 3274ft vertical drop.

Offering some of the most difficult terrain in the US, it's a fantastic place to zip down steep tree glades into untouched powder bowls. Seasoned skiers luck out, with more than half of the 70-plus trails at the Taos Ski Valley ranked expert; but there's also an award-winning ski school, so complete beginners thrive here too. The resort has a peak elevation of 12,481ft and gets an average of more than 300in of snowfall annually. The resort also has a skier-cross obstacle course at its popular terrain park.

That said, **Ski Santa Fe** (☎505-982-4429, snow report 505-983-9155; www.skisantafe.com; lift ticket adult/teen/child $75/60/52; ☻9am-4pm Dec-Mar) is no slouch. Less than 30 minutes from the Santa Fe plaza, it boasts the same fluffy powder (though usually a little less), with an even higher base elevation (10,350ft). Briefly admire the awesome desert and mountain vistas, then fly down chutes, steep bump runs or long groomers. The resort caters to families and expert skiers alike with its varied terrain. The quality and length of the ski season can vary wildly from year to year depending on how much snow the mountain gets (you can almost always count on a good storm in late March).

❹ Truchas

Rural New Mexico at its most sincere is showcased in Truchas, originally settled by the Spaniards in the 18th century. Robert Redford's *The Milagro Beanfield War* was filmed here (but don't bother with the movie – the book it's based on, by John Nichols, is waaaay better). Narrow roads, many unpaved, wend between century-old adobes. Fields of grass and alfalfa spread toward the sheer walls and plunging ridges that define the western flank of the Truchas Peaks. Between the rundown homes are some wonderful art galleries, which double as workshops for local weavers, painters, sculptors and other artists. The best place to get an overview of who's painting/sculpting/carving/weaving what is the **High Road Marketplace** (📞505-689-2689; 1642 Hwy 76; ⏰10am-5pm, to 4pm winter), a cooperative art gallery with a huge variety of work by area artists.

The Drive » Continue north on Hwy 76 for around 8 miles, transecting the little valleys of Ojo Sarco and Cañada de los Alamos.

❺ Las Trampas

Completed in 1780 and constantly defended

LOCAL KNOWLEDGE: NATURE CALLS

Want to see the scenery without a pane of glass in front of your face? Off the High Road, take a stroll on the **Santa Barbara Trail**, which follows a trout-filled creek through mixed forest into the Pecos Wilderness; it's pretty flat and easygoing. To reach the trailhead, take Hwy 73 from Peñasco and follow the signs.

Off the Low Road, turn onto Hwy 570 at Pilar and check out the **Orilla Verde Recreation Area** (📞575-758-8851; Hwy 570; day-use $3, tent/RV sites $7/15), where you can hang out or camp along the Rio Grande (or tube or fish in it). Hike up to the rim on Old 570, a dirt road blocked by a landslide, with expansive vistas of the Taos Plateau and the Sangre de Cristos.

Some of the best views in the state are from the top of **Lake Peak** (12,409ft), which can be reached on a day hike starting at the Santa Fe Ski Basin.

From Taos Ski Valley, you can day hike to the top of **Wheeler Peak** (13,161ft), New Mexico's highest summit (the views are pretty good up there, too). For trail maps and more information, go to the **Travel Bug** (📞505-992-0418; www.mapsofnewmexico.com; 839 Paseo de Peralta; ⏰7:30am-5:30pm Mon-Sat, 11am-4pm Sun; 📶) bookshop in Santa Fe or the **Taos Visitor Center** (📞575-758-3873; taos.org; 1139 Paseo del Pueblo Sur; ⏰9am-5pm; 📶).

against Apache raids, the **Church of San José de Gracia** (📞505-351-4360; Hwy 76; ⏰by appointment, call ahead) is considered one of the finest surviving 18th-century churches in the USA and is a National Historic Landmark. Original paintings and carvings remain in excellent condition, and self-flagellation bloodstains from Los Hermanos Penitentes (a 19th-century religious order with a

strong following in the northern mountains of New Mexico) are still visible. On your way out of town, look right to see the amazing irrigation aqueduct, carved from tree trunks!

The Drive » Continue north on Hwy 76, through lovely Chamisal. At the T, turn right onto Hwy 75 and stay on it through Peñasco and Vadito. At Hwy 518, turn left toward Taos. At the end of the road, turn right on Paseo del Pueblo Sur/Hwy 68 and take it on into Taos – around 32 miles in total.

WHY THIS IS A CLASSIC TRIP
CHRISTOPHER PITTS, WRITER

If you had to pick one trip that would make you want to immediately pack your bags and move to New Mexico, this would be it: the state's two most enchanting cities, the historic Taos Pueblo, the cultural legacy of El Santuario de Chimayó and the unique, piquant flavor of rural life and New Mexican cuisine – all set against a continuous panorama of spellbinding landscapes.

Above: Taos Pueblo
Left: Food stand in Santa Fe
Right: El Santuario de Chimayó

❻ Taos

Taos is a place undeniably dominated by the power of its landscape: 12,300ft often-snowcapped peaks rise behind town, a sage-speckled plateau unrolls to the west before plunging 800ft straight down into the Rio Grande Gorge. The sky can be a searing sapphire blue or an ominous parade of rumbling thunderheads. And then there are the sunsets...

The pueblo here is one of the oldest continuously inhabited communities in the United States and it roots the town in a long history with a rich cultural legacy – including conquistadors, Catholicism and cowboys. Taos remains a relaxed and eccentric place, with classic mud-brick buildings, quirky cafes and excellent restaurants. It's both rural and worldly, and a little bit otherworldly.

The best thing to do is to walk around the plaza area soaking in the aura of the place. But you also won't want to miss **Taos Pueblo** (📞575-758-1028; www.taospueblo.com; Taos Pueblo Rd; adult/child $16/free; ⏱8am-4:30pm Mon-Sat, 8:30am-4:30pm Sun, closed mid-Feb–mid-Apr). Built around 1450 and continuously inhabited ever since, it's the largest existing multistoried pueblo structure in the USA and one of the best surviving examples of traditional adobe construction. Also well worth a visit is the **Millicent Rogers Museum** (📞575-758-2462; www.millicentrogers.org; 1504 Millicent Rogers Rd; adult/child $10/2; ⏱10:10am-5pm Apr-Oct, closed Mon Nov-Mar), filled with pottery, jewelry, baskets and textiles from the private collection of a model and oil heiress who moved to Taos in 1947 and acquired one of the best collections of American Indian and Spanish Colonial art in the USA.

🍴 🛏 p149

The Drive ❯❯ On this 26-mile leg, cruise the Low Road back toward Santa Fe by taking Hwy 68 south. Just before the road drops downhill, there's a large pullout with huge views, so hop out and see what you're leaving behind. Then head down into the Rio Grande Gorge. Go left on Hwy 75 to Dixon.

❼ Dixon

This small agricultural and artistic community is spread along the gorgeous Rio Embudo valley. It's famous for its apples but plenty of other crops are grown here too, including some of the grapes used by two award-winning local wineries, **Vivac** (📞505-579-4441; www.vivacwinery.com; 2075 Hwy 68; tasting $8; ⏱10am-6pm Mon-Sat, from noon Sun) and **La Chiripada** (📞505-579-4437; www.lachiripada.com; Hwy 75; tasting $10; ⏱11am-5pm Mon-Sat, from noon Sun), both of which have tasting rooms. In summer and fall, there's a farmers market on Wednesday afternoons, with food fresh from the fields. Our favorite art gallery is actually on Hwy 68, in Rinconada, just north of Hwy 75: **Rift Gallery** (📞505-579-9179; www.saxstonecarving.com; 2249 Hwy 68; ⏱10am-5pm Wed-Sun May-Sep, shorter hours rest of year) features masterful ceramics and stonework. On the first weekend in November, local artists open their homes and studios to the public in New Mexico's oldest studio tour. In summer, ask at the local food co-op and some kind soul might point you to the waterfalls, up a nearby dirt road.

🍴 🛏 p149

The Drive ❯❯ Back on Hwy 68, head south along the river, through Embudo (a great lunch stop) and out of the gorge. Continue through Española, where you'll meet Hwy 84/285, which you can take back to Santa Fe. This leg is around 47 miles.

Eating & Sleeping

Santa Fe ❶

✘ Harry's Roadhouse
American, New Mexican $$

(📞505-989-4629; www.harrysroadhousesantafe.com; 96 Old Las Vegas Hwy; lunch $8-14, dinner $9-23; 🕐7am-9:30pm; 🚼) This casual longtime favorite on the southern edge of town feels like a rambling cottage with its various rooms and patio garden – and there's also a full bar. And, seriously, *everything* here is good. Especially the desserts.

🛏 El Paradero
B&B $$

(📞505-988-1177; www.elparadero.com; 220 W Manhattan Ave; r from $155; P 🌐 @ 🛜) Each room in this 200-year-old adobe B&B, south of the river, is unique and loaded with character. Two have their own bathrooms across the hall, the rest are en suite; our favorites are rooms 6 and 12. The full breakfasts satisfy, and rates also include afternoon tea. A separate casita holds two kitchenette suites that can be combined into one.

Chimayó ❷

✘ Rancho de Chimayó
New Mexican $

(📞505-984-2100; www.ranchodechimayo.com; County Rd 98; mains $7-11, dinner $10-25; 🕐11:30am-9pm, closed Mon Nov-Apr) Half a mile north of the Santuario, this bright, spacious garden-set restaurant serves classic New Mexican cuisine, courtesy of the Jaramillo family's famed recipes. Best of all is the basket of warm, fluffy *sopaipillas* (puffed-up pastries) that comes with each dish. The same management offers cozy B&B rooms (from $79) across the street.

🛏 Casa Escondida
B&B $$

(📞505-351-4805; www.casaescondida.com; 64 County Rd 100; r from $130; 🌐🛜🛁) Set on 6 acres, a mile or so north of Chimayó, this unpretentious and highly recommended B&B features eight beautiful rooms, all en suite and furnished in Southwestern style. Some have outdoor decks, all share use of a communal covered porch and a hot tub.

Taos ❻

✘ Lambert's
Modern American $$$

(📞505-758-1009; www.lambertsoftaos.com; 123 Bent St; lunch $11-14, dinner $23-38; 🕐11:30am-close; ✒ 🚼) Consistently hailed as the 'Best of Taos,' this charming old adobe just north of the Plaza remains what it's always been – a cozy, romantic local hangout where patrons relax and enjoy sumptuous contemporary cuisine, with mains ranging from lunchtime's barbecue pork sliders to dinner dishes such as chicken mango enchiladas or Colorado rack of lamb.

🛏 Historic Taos Inn
Historic Hotel $$

(📞575-758-2233; www.taosinn.com; 125 Paseo del Pueblo Norte; r from $119; P 🌐🛜) Lovely and always lively old inn, where the 45 characterful rooms have Southwest trimmings such as heavy-duty wooden furnishings and adobe fireplaces (some functioning, some for show). The famed **Adobe Bar** (🕐11am-11pm, music 6:30-10pm) spills into the cozy central atrium, and features live music every night – for a quieter stay, opt for one of the detached separate wings – and there's also a good **restaurant** (breakfast & lunch $7-15, dinner $15-28; 🕐11am-3pm & 5-9pm Mon-Fri, 7:30am-2:30pm & 5-9pm Sat & Sun).

Dixon ❼

✘ Zuly's Cafe
Cafe $

(📞505-579-4001; 234 Hwy 75; mains $6-14; 🕐7:30am-3pm Tue-Thu, 7:30am-8pm Fri, 9am-8pm Sat) This superfriendly place, run by Dixon native Chalako Chilton, serves some of the best green chile you'll find anywhere, plus espresso coffees.

🛏 Tower Guest House
Guesthouse $

(📞505-579-4288; www.vrbo.com/118083; cottage $95; 🛜🛁) Located on a garlic farm, this lovely cottage is close to the Rio Embudo. Sleeps three.

El Camino Real & Turquoise Trail

Historic sights, hot springs, wildlife sanctuaries and well-known cities line this route first established over 400 years ago – the Royal Road, which linked Mexico City to Santa Fe.

12

TRIP HIGHLIGHTS

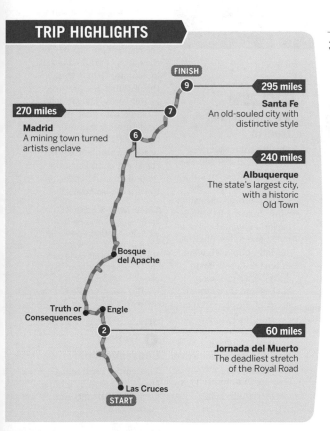

FINISH

9

295 miles

Santa Fe
An old-souled city with distinctive style

270 miles

7

Madrid
A mining town turned artists enclave

6

240 miles

Albuquerque
The state's largest city, with a historic Old Town

Bosque del Apache

Truth or Consequences   **Engle**

2

60 miles

Jornada del Muerto
The deadliest stretch of the Royal Road

Las Cruces
START

3–4 DAYS
295 MILES/475KM

GREAT FOR ...

BEST TIME TO GO
September until December is best for festivals.

ESSENTIAL PHOTO
Late-afternoon glow on an adobe wall in Santa Fe.

BEST FOR BIRDERS
Cranes and more at Bosque del Apache.

12 El Camino Real & Turquoise Trail

Leaving Las Cruces, this trip mostly follows New Mexico's main arteries – the Rio Grande and I-25 – north. Except when you're driving a dirt road through a section of desert called the Jornada del Muerto (Journey of Death). Or meandering through a bird sanctuary. Or winding past the Ortiz Mountains and through old mining towns along the legendary Turquoise Trail on your way into Santa Fe.

❶ Las Cruces

New Mexico's second-largest city, Las Cruces isn't much of a charmer, but before you hit the road take a stroll around the **Old Mesilla plaza**, which still exudes a sense of history even if it's only 160 years old. Billy the Kid was sentenced to death in the courthouse here.

✖ 🛏 p157, p189

The Drive » Take I-25 north to exit 32, then turn right onto dirt County Rd 71/72 and follow it for 5.2 miles. Then, turn left at an intersection, heading north on CR E 070 toward Engle. Go 14 miles, driving around the aptly named Point of Rocks, to Yost Escarpment. It's 45 miles in all.

TRIP HIGHLIGHT

❷ Jornada del Muerto

This 90-mile waterless stretch of desert was the most feared section of the Camino Real. Over the years, hundreds perished while crossing it. Travelers back then would cover as much ground as possible at night, but you'll want to see the desert basin dotted with creosote bushes and the angular uplift of the San Andres Mountains. Pull over at Yost Escarpment and walk an easy 1.5-mile (one-way) trail into the Jornada that takes you along the actual Camino Real route. There are interpretive signs along the way. In summer, try to avoid midday.

The Drive » Continue north from the Yost Escarpment parking lot for just over 4 miles to the entrance to Spaceport America at County Rd A39.

❸ Genesis Statue at Spaceport America

You can't just drop by **Spaceport America** (📞844-727-7223; www.spaceportamerica.com; adult/child $45/30), the world's first commercial spaceport, for a look around – guided tours are the only way to visit. But you can check out the simple but striking **Genesis statue** in the roundabout just before the entrance gate. Created by sculptor Otto Rigan, the arc-shaped sculpture is 40ft across and 5ft deep. Studded with glass in a configuration that mimics the constellations overhead on a summer night, the statue sparkles in the moonlight as it bends toward the heavens.

The Drive » Return to A13 and continue north. At Engle, turn left to Truth or Consequences on Hwy 51 – which curves around 300ft-high Elephant Butte Dam and the drought-shrunken lake behind it. It's about 30 miles from the statue to Truth or Consequences..

❹ Truth or Consequences

This quirky town met a challenge posed by a radio game show in 1950 and

changed its name to that of the show, hoping to raise publicity for itself. Popular with retirees and with a growing New Age subculture, T or C is best known for two things: its hot springs and the Spaceport. Hot spring spas with pools for day-use cluster near the Rio Grande.

If the Genesis statue sparked your curiosity about the Spaceport, head to the **Geronimo Trail Scenic Byway Visitor Center** (☎575-894-1968; www.geronimotrail.com; 301 S Foch St; ⏱9am-4:30pm Mon-Sat, to 2:30pm Sun) downtown to sign up for a guided tour of the facility – but note that reservations should be made well in advance and tours typically depart only on weekends. Spaceport America was funded in part by Sir Richard Branson, who, at the time of research, was planning to launch his Virgin Galactic

---

LINK YOUR TRIP

11 **High & Low Roads to Taos**

Continue north from Santa Fe on this classic route into the soul of New Mexico.

13 **Georgia O'Keeffe Country**

From Santa Fe, head 48 miles northwest on Hwy 84 to Abiquiú for the state's most colorful trip.

LOCAL KNOWLEDGE: TURQUOISE TRAIL GEMS

Along with the main stops on the Turquoise Trail, you won't want to miss the **Tinkertown Museum** (☎505-281-5233; www.tinkertown.com; 121 Sandia Crest Rd; adult/child $3.50/1; ⏰9am-6pm Apr-Oct; 👪) – one of the weirdest in the state. Huge, detailed hand-carved dioramas of Western towns, circuses and other bizarre scenes come alive with a quarter and signs encourage visitors to 'eat more mangoes naked.' It's just outside Cedar Crest on Hwy 536.

But wait, there's more: one of our favorite restaurants ever. The **San Marcos Cafe** (☎505-471-9298; 3877 Hwy 14; mains $8-12; ⏰8am-2pm; 👪) feels like a country home. Aside from some of the best red chile you'll ever taste, turkeys strut and squabble outside and the whole place is connected to a feed store, giving it genuine Western soul.

passenger rockets from this isolated patch of desert within months. Tour hIghlights include a ride in a swirling G-force machine, an opportunity to climb aboard hi-tech fire trucks and posing for photos on the 2.7-mile-long 'spaceway.' Tours leave from the visitor center, and the round-trip experience takes about three hours.

✕ 🛏 p157

The Drive » Take I-25 north from T or C for 35 miles to exit 115, then turn right onto Hwy 1, following it north for 20 or so hilly miles..

❺ Bosque del Apache National Wildlife Refuge

A surprising oasis of water and wildlife, the

Bosque del Apache

(www.fws.gov/refuge/ bosque_del_apache; Hwy 1; per vehicle $5; ⏰dawn-dusk) covers over 57,000 acres along the Rio Grande, with forested wetlands at its heart. Though a menagerie of mammals, reptiles and amphibians can be spotted, birds are the big draw: 371 species roost here by the tens of thousands, mainly from November to February. The stars of the avian show are the sandhill cranes, who even get their own festival (mid-November). It's worth driving the 12-mile loop through the refuge any time of year.

The Drive » Head north on Hwy 1 to San Antonio, then west on Hwy 380, then north on I-25, 98 miles in total.

DENNIS W DONOHUE/SHUTTERSTOCK ©

TRIP HIGHLIGHT

❻ Albuquerque

New Mexico's largest city was founded in 1706 and for centuries centered on the Old Town Plaza, which is where you'll find many of Albuquerque's sights and attractions. The

Bosque del Apache National Wildlife Refuge Sandhill cranes

area around the plaza is worth a stroll (p224). Though its gritty charm can sometimes be hard to spot, the neighborhoods around the University of New Mexico and Nob Hill are hipper than ever. And some fantastic museums can be found here, including the **National Museum of Nuclear Science &**

History (☎505-245-2137; www.nuclearmuseum.org; 601 Eubank Blvd SE; adult/child & senior $12/10; ☺9am-5pm; 🖼), with engaging exhibits on the development of nuclear weapons, energy, medical technology and more.

🍴 🛏 p45, p57, p157, p173

The Drive » On this 43-mile leg we diverge from the Camino Real to hop on the more scenic Turquoise Trail. Take I-40 east to exit 175, where you'll take Hwy 14 north.

- - - - - - - - - - - - - - - - - -

❼ Madrid
This former company-owned mining village has transformed into a quirky gallery town

DETOUR: HATCH

Start: ❶ Las Cruces

The town of Hatch, 40 miles north of Las Cruces up I-25, is known as the 'Chile Capital of the World,' sitting at the heart of New Mexico's chile-growing country. New Mexican chiles didn't originate here – most have centuries-old roots in the northern farming villages around Chimayó and Española – but the earth and irrigation in these parts proved perfect for mass production. Recent harvests have declined sharply, as imported chile is encroaching on the market, but the town still clings to its title. Even if you miss the Labor Day Weekend **Chile Festival** (www.hatchchilefest.com; ☺Sep), pull off the interstate at exit 41 and pop into **Sparky's Burgers** (📞575-267-4222; www.sparkysburgers.com; 115 Franklin St; mains $6-11; ☺10:30am-7pm Thu-Sun) for what might be the best green chile cheeseburger in the state, served with casual pride.

To get there, when driving north from Las Cruces, skip exit 32 to the Jornada del Muerto and continue another 8.5 miles on I-25 to Hatch. Then, after getting your chile fix, head back to the Jornada exit and continue along the route – or blow off the desert road and continue on I-25 to rejoin the drive in Truth or Consequences.

that looks cute on the surface but still has an unruly edge underneath. Hop out and browse a while.

The Drive » Continue north on Hwy 14 for 3 miles, then turn left into Cerrillos.

❽ Cerrillos

This little village was at the center of the turquoise trade in Spanish colonial times. To see an erratic display of historical memorabilia, stop into the **Turquoise Mining Museum** (📞505-438-3008; www.casagrandetradingpost.com; 17 Waldo St; $2; ☺9am-5pm). A mile north of town, amid scrubby desert hills pockmarked with historic mining sites, **Cerrillos Hills State Park** (📞505-474-0196; www.nmparks.com; per vehicle $5; ☺sunrise-sunset) holds 5 miles of hiking trails.

The Drive » Continue north on Hwy 14, which will turn into one of Santa Fe's main commercial drags, Cerrillos Rd, 24 miles total.

TRIP HIGHLIGHT

❾ Santa Fe

Though spurs of El Camino Real continued on up to Taos and beyond, the main trail ended here, at the Santa Fe plaza, once the Spanish chose this spot as the capital of New Mexico in 1610. It's worth taking the time to walk around the plaza (p222), but to get the best sense of what life might have been like during the days when El Camino Real was the main route into the city, head to Santa Fe's southern outskirts, where you'll find **Rancho de las Golondrinas** (📞505-471-2261; www.golondrinas.org; 334 Los Pinos Rd, La Cienega; adult/child $6/free; ☺10am-4pm Wed-Sun Jun-Sep, tours by reservation only in Apr, May & Oct; 🚻). Once an overnight stopping place on the trail, it's now a 200-acre living museum, carefully reconstructed and populated with historical re-enactors. You can watch bread baking in an *horno* (traditional adobe oven), and visit the blacksmith, the molasses mill or traditional crafts workshops. There are orchards, vineyards and livestock, and festivals are held throughout the summer. To get there, take I-25 south to exit 276, then follow the signs.

🍴 🛏 p45, p149, p157

Eating & Sleeping

Las Cruces ❶

🛏 Lundeen Inn of the Arts   B&B $$

(📞505-526-3326; www.innofthearts.com; 618 S Alameda Blvd, Las Cruces; r/ste $125/155; 🅿❄🛜🐾) Each of the 20 guest rooms in this large and very lovely century-old Mexican Territorial–style inn is unique and decorated in the style of a New Mexico artist. Check out the soaring pressed-tin ceilings in the great room. Owners Linda and Jerry offer the kind of genteel hospitality you seldom find these days.

Truth or Consequences ❸

✕ Passion Pie Cafe   Cafe $

(📞575-894-0008; www.deepwaterfarm.com; 406 Main St; breakfast & lunch mains $4-10; 🕙7am-3pm; 🛜) Watch T or C get its morning groove on through the windows of this espresso cafe, and set yourself up with a breakfast waffle; the Elvis (with peanut butter) or the Fat Elvis (with bacon too) should do the job. Later on there are plenty of healthy salads and sandwiches.

🛏 Riverbend Hot Springs   Boutique Hotel $$

(📞575-894-7625; www.riverbendhotsprings.com; 100 Austin St; r $97-218, RV sites $60; ❄🛜🐾) This delightful place, occupying a fantastic perch beside the Rio Grande, is the only T or C hotel to feature outdoor, riverside hot tubs – tiled, decked and totally irresistible. Accommodations, colorfully decorated by local artists, ranges from motel-style rooms to a three-bedroom suite. Guests can use the public pools for free, and private tubs for $10. No children under 12.

Albuquerque ❻

✕ Golden Crown Panaderia   Bakery $

(📞505-243-2424; www.goldencrown.biz; 1103 Mountain Rd NW; mains $7-20; 🕙7am-8pm Tue-Sat, 10am-8pm Sun) Who doesn't love a friendly neighborhood cafe-bakery? Especially one in a cozy old adobe, with gracious staff, oven-fresh bread and pizza (with green chile or blue-corn crusts), fruity empanadas, smooth espresso coffees and cookies all round? Call ahead to reserve a loaf of quick-selling green chile bread – then eat it hot, out on the patio.

🛏 Böttger Mansion   B&B $$

(📞505-243-3639, www.bottger.com; 110 San Felipe St NW; r $115-159; 🅿❄@🛜) The friendly proprietor gives this well-appointed B&B, built in 1912 and one minute's walk from the plaza, an edge over tough competition. Three of its seven themed, antique-furnished rooms have pressed-tin ceilings, one has a Jacuzzi tub, and sumptuous breakfasts are served in a honeysuckle-lined courtyard loved by bird-watchers. Past guests include Elvis, Janis Joplin and Machine Gun Kelly.

Santa Fe ❾

🛏 Santa Fe Motel & Inn   Hotel $$

(📞505-982-1039; www.santafemotel.com; 510 Cerrillos Rd; r from $149, casitas from $169; 🅿❄@🛜🐾) Even the motel rooms in this downtown option, close to the Railyard and a real bargain in low season, have the flavor of a Southwestern B&B, with colorful tiles, clay sunbursts and tin mirrors. The courtyard casitas cost a little more and come with kiva fireplaces and little patios. Rates include a full hot breakfast, served outdoors in summer.

Georgia O'Keeffe Country

From Chaco Canyon's ancient architecture and the multicolored cliffs that inspired O'Keeffe to the intricate textiles of Navajo weavers, topography and creativity are inseparable here.

13

TRIP HIGHLIGHTS

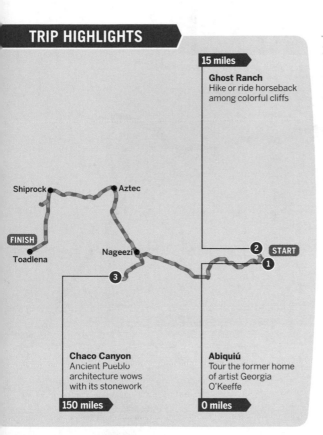

15 miles

Ghost Ranch
Hike or ride horseback among colorful cliffs

Shiprock

Aztec

FINISH
Toadlena

Nageezi

2 **START**
1

3

Chaco Canyon
Ancient Pueblo architecture wows with its stonework

150 miles

Abiquiú
Tour the former home of artist Georgia O'Keeffe

0 miles

2–3 DAYS
327 MILES/526KM

GREAT FOR...

BEST TIME TO GO
May to October, for the best light.

ESSENTIAL PHOTO
Capture the perspective of doorways and stonework at Chaco.

BEST FOR DRIVERS
Hwy 96 is one of the most beautiful roads in the state.

13 Georgia O'Keeffe Country

The first part of this trip just might cover our favorite stretches of road in the state, around Abiquiú Lake, up the Chama River, through a rainbow-hued gap in the Jemez Mountains – the colors and the light blend into pure eye-candy. Then strike out through the badlands of the Navajo Nation, across barren desert flats and under the shadow of Shiprock, where the earth and sky converge with raw, elemental intensity.

TRIP HIGHLIGHT

❶ Abiquiú

Founded in 1754 through a Spanish land grant, the tiny town of Abiquiú near the Chama River has a few galleries and a lovely church, but is most famous as the home of painter Georgia O'Keeffe. After returning to the area many times in the 1930s and '40s, she bought an old adobe fixer-upper in 1945, restored it, and moved in in 1949. She lived between there

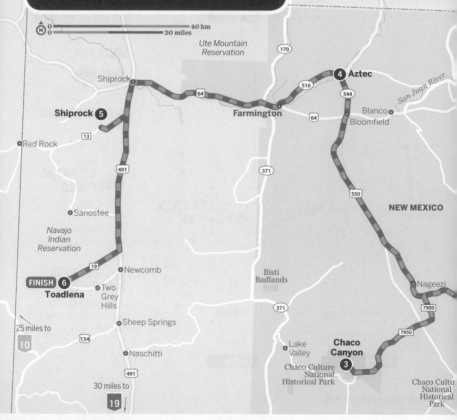

and her place up the road at Ghost Ranch for the next 35 years. You can visit her Abiquiú house on the **Georgia O'Keeffe Home & Studio Tour** (☎505-685-4539; www.okeeffemuseum.org; 21120 Hwy 84; tours $35-65; ⏱Tue-Sat mid-Mar–mid-Nov). Enclosed by a mudbrick wall, this Spanish Colonial hacienda blends into the landscape and remains much as it was when she lived here. You must make reservations for the tour, which leaves from the Tour Office next to the Abiquiú Inn. Of course, if you're in Santa Fe you should also check out the **Georgia O'Keeffe Museum** (p42).

🛏 p165

The Drive » Taking Hwy 84 north for 14 miles, force yourself to keep your eyes on the road as you drive around the jewel-like Abiquiú Lake ringed by multicolored cliffs. Turn right at the sign for Ghost Ranch.

LINK YOUR TRIP

10 **Southwest Indian Nations Sojourn**

From Toadlena, skip state lines to check out more of the Navajo Nation, crossing the Chuska Mountains via Hwy 134 to Canyon de Chelly.

19 **Highway 53 to Acoma**

From Toadlena, head south to Gallup on Hwy 491 to check out ancient pueblos, lava flows and wolves.

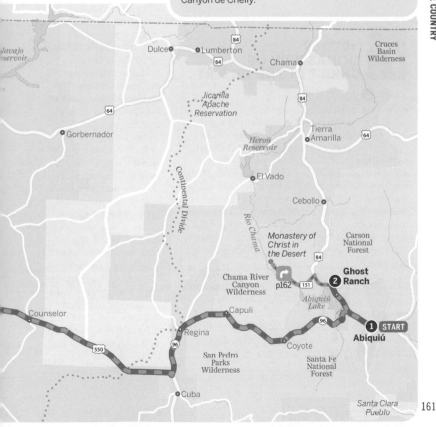

TRIP HIGHLIGHT

❷ Ghost Ranch

If you're familiar with O'Keeffe's work, you may feel like you've been here before. Some of her most celebrated pieces were inspired by the sensual forms and colors of the cliffs, canyons and mesalands around **Ghost Ranch** (📞505-685-1000; www.ghostranch.org; Hwy 84; day pass adult/child $5/3; 🚻). Though her home here is closed to the public, you can explore the area on hiking trails, guided horseback adventures or a van tour that includes stops at vistas immortalized in O'Keeffe's paintings. There are also small museums and various lodging options.

🛏 p165

The Drive » Backtrack 6 miles south on Hwy 84, then turn right onto Hwy 96, which takes you through a pastel geological wonderland. When you reach Hwy 550, near Cuba, turn right (north); before Nageezi turn left onto County Rd 7900, then right onto the washed-out dirt County Rd 7950, following signs for Chaco Culture National Historical Park. It's 130 miles total.

DETOUR: MONASTERY OF CHRIST IN THE DESERT

Start: ❷ Ghost Ranch

It's hard to imagine a more peaceful place for spiritual contemplation. Set 13 miles down a dirt road, surrounded by the majestic Chama River Wilderness, you'll find the **Monastery of Christ in the Desert** (📞505-990-8581; www.christdesert.org; off Hwy 84; ⏰8am-6pm). This Benedictine Abbey welcomes visitors as day or overnight guests; you can go into the unique church that combines elements of Japanese and New Mexican design, attend prayer services, or stay in a small, simple guesthouse (average suggested donation $90 per night). In tune with the aura of the place, quiet is requested.

To get here from Ghost Ranch, head north on Hwy 84 for 2.5 miles, then turn left onto Forest Rd 151. The drive is spectacular: some of the cliffs are purple! There are plenty of places to hang out by the river, and a few campsites (p165). When you're done with this detour, retrace your steps back to Hwy 96 and pick up the drive there.

TRIP HIGHLIGHT

❸ Chaco Canyon

About 1000 years ago, Chaco Canyon was the center of an Ancestral Puebloan (Anasazi) civilization that spread across the San Juan Basin and beyond, linked together by a carefully engineered network of 30ft-wide roads. Today, Chacoan culture is famed for the impressive architecture it left behind: Great Houses intricately pieced together, stone by stone, and oriented with remarkable accuracy to solar and lunar events as well as the cardinal directions.

You can walk through some Great Houses and other structures at **Chaco Culture National Historical Park** (📞505-786-7014; www.nps.gov/chcu; per vehicle $20; ⏰7am-sunset). The biggest attraction is Pueblo Bonito, which towered four to five stories tall and may have had 600 to 800 rooms and kivas. Though none of Chaco's sites have been reconstructed, plenty of rockwork is still intact. A loop road connects the main archaeological sites, hiking trails head off into the surrounding area, and there's an informative visitor center and a campground. But there's no food, gas or other supplies (water is

Ghost Ranch Multicolored cliffs

available only at the visitor center). The closest towns with accommodations are Farmington, Aztec and Cuba. The last stretch of dirt road on the way here is in very poor shape – do not attempt to drive it in muddy or snowy conditions.

🛏 p165

The Drive » Head back to Hwy 550 and head north. At Bloomfield, turn right onto Hwy 64, then make a pretty quick left onto Hwy 544. It's 75 miles total.

----

④ Aztec

Although little Aztec has a handful of interesting turn-of-the-19th-century buildings on the National Register of Historic Places, the

town's main draw is the 27-acre **Aztec Ruins National Monument** (📞505-334-6174; www.nps.gov/azru; 84 Ruins Rd; adult/child $5/free; 🕑8am-5pm Sep-May, to 6pm Jun-Aug). This ancient Puebloan settlement features the largest reconstructed kiva in the country, with an internal diameter of almost 50ft, originally built around AD 1100.

Though the site itself isn't as amazing or extensive as Chaco, the Great Kiva is pretty impressive. During summer, rangers give early-afternoon talks about ancient architecture, trade routes and astronomy.

🛏 p165

The Drive » Take Hwy 516 to Farmington, which makes a good lunch stop, then Hwy 64 west to the town of Shiprock. Cross the San Juan River and continue straight ahead on Hwy 491 (formerly Hwy 666, nicknamed the Devil's Hwy). At mile marker 85, turn right onto Indian Rte 13. It's about 60 miles total.

- - - - - - - - - - - - - - - -

❺ Shiprock

The most striking sight in New Mexico's northwestern corner is Shiprock, a 1700ft volcanic plug that is eerily eroded into what looks like a schooner – at least to white people. The Navajo name for it, Tsé Bit'a'i, means 'rock with wings.' According to one Navajo history, the tribe had been under attack in a place far to the north when the ground beneath them became a giant bird that flew them to safety, delivering them to their homeland; the bird then turned back into earth, but kept its shape. It's also said that for some time Navajos dwelt atop the great rock, coming down to farm and tend

LOCAL KNOWLEDGE: BISTI BADLANDS

One of the weirdest micro-environments in New Mexico is 38 miles south of Farmington, off Hwy 371. The Bisti Badlands, part of the Bisti/De-Na-Zin Wilderness Area, is an undeveloped realm of multicolored hoodoos, sculpted cliffs and balancing rocks. From the parking area, you have to follow the unmaintained path for at least a mile before getting to the heart of the formations, then wander as you will, taking care not to damage the fragile geology or to get lost. The hours just after sunrise and before sunset are most spectacular.

sheep, but that one day the trail to the desert floor was destroyed by lightning; those up at the summit couldn't descend and died there. Climbing Shiprock is strictly forbidden (yes, illegal), in part for fear that the spirits of the dead will be disturbed. Unfortunately, you can't even hike over to it, but there are some great views about 5 miles west along Indian Rte 13.

The Drive » Head back to Hwy 491 and turn right, heading south. When you reach the Shell station at mile marker 61, turn right onto Indian Rte 19 and go about 12 miles. In all, it's 44 miles.

- - - - - - - - - - - - - - - -

❻ Toadlena

Tucked against the Chuska Mountains, Toadlena and neighboring Two Grey Hills are renowned as the sources of the finest rugs anywhere in Navajo

country. Some weavers from this area continue to reject commercially produced wool and synthetic dyes, preferring the wool of their own churro sheep in its natural hues. They card white, brown, grey and black hairs together, blending the colors to the desired effect, then they spin and weave the wool – tightly – into mesmerizing geometric patterns. The **Toadlena Trading Post** (📞888-420-0005; www.toadlenatradingpost.com; ⊘9am-6pm Mon-Sat, noon-5pm Sun May-Sep, closed Sun rest of year), run by textile expert Mark Winter, is the local market where many of these world-class artisans sell their work. Prices range from about $125 to $7000 or more. The Trading Post has a small museum with extraordinarily fine exhibits.

Eating & Sleeping

Abiquiú ❶

🛏 Abiquiú Inn   Hotel $$
(📞505-685-4378; www.abiquiuinn.com; US
Hwy 84; r from $110, casitas from $120; P 🛜)
This sprawling riverside collection of shaded
faux-dobes is peaceful and lovely; some of the
spacious rooms have kitchenettes.

Ghost Ranch ❷

🛏 Ghost Ranch Lodging   Cabin $
(tent & RV sites $25, dm $69, r with/without
bathroom from $119/109; ❄ @) A retreat
center on 21,000 acres at the foot of the
Sangre de Cristo Mountains, Ghost Ranch is
a spectacular spot with basic lodging – you're
here for the serenity, not comfort. Meals are
cafeteria-style and pricey ($14 for dinner),
though breakfast is included. No phones or TVs
in the rooms; wi-fi in the visitor center only.

Chama River Canyon

🛏 Rio Chama
Campground   Campground $
(Forest Service Rd 151; campsites free; ⏰ mid-
Apr–Oct; 🐾) Riverside camping with eleven
sites surrounded by brilliant colored cliffs, birds
and the silence of the Chama River Canyon
Wilderness. It's 1 mile south of the Monastery of
Christ in the Desert (p162). There's no drinking
water available. First-come, first-serve.

Cuba

✖ El Bruno's   Mexican $$
(📞575-289-9429; www.elbrunos.com; Hwy
550; mains $8-24; ⏰11am-10pm) The best
place to eat for many miles, this riverside
restaurant, close to the bridge, serves high-
class Mexican specialties from *carne asada*
to steak, and has a shaded outdoor patio. The
green chile here is tops.

🛏 Sueños Encantados
y Casa Vieja   B&B $
(📞505-249-7597; www.suenosencantados.com;
San Pablo Rd; r $80-125; 🛜) Set on the grounds
of a still-operating 19th-century ranch, this rural
B&B conveys the full-on Southwest experience,
complete with three rooms in the adobe casa (one
with full kitchen). Continental breakfast included;
full breakfast is $10 per person. It's located
8 miles south of Cuba, off County Rd 11.

Chaco Canyon ❸

🛏 Gallo Campground   Campground $
(📞877-444-6777; www.recreation.gov; tent
& RV sites $15) This lovely but isolated spot is
1 mile east of the visitor center (the only place
with water). Reserve ahead or check availability
online to ensure you can get a spot.

Aztec ❹

🛏 Step Back Inn   Hotel $
(📞505-334-1200; www.stepbackinn.com; 123 W
Aztec Blvd; r $98; ❄ 🛜) The best place to stay
in Aztec, this friendly and unexpectedly smart
little motel, on the highway across from Main St
and looking more like something you'd expect
to find in New England than New Mexico, offers
tasteful antique-furnished rooms.

Farmington

✖ Three Rivers
Eatery & Brewhouse   American $
(📞505-324-2187; www.threeriversbrewery.com;
101 E Main St; mains $9-27, pizza $7-14; ⏰11am-
9pm; 🛜 👶) Managing to be both trendy *and*
kid-friendly, this hip spot spreads through three
different buildings along one block, serving
pub grub, pizzas and its own microbrews.
Try the homemade potato skins or artichoke
and spinach dip; burgers are just okay. Spiffy
sandwiches (Thai turkey wrap) and soups
(broccoli cheddar) are served at lunchtime. Pool
tables in the taproom.

Highway 4: Jemez Mountains

14

One minute you're in the cutting-edge scientific community where the atomic bomb was built, the next you're exploring ancient cliff dwellings. And by day's end, you're soaking in hot springs.

TRIP HIGHLIGHTS

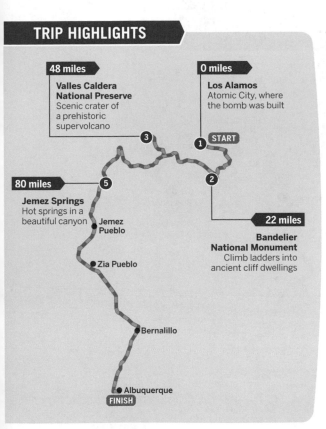

48 miles
Valles Caldera National Preserve
Scenic crater of a prehistoric supervolcano

0 miles
Los Alamos
Atomic City, where the bomb was built

START

80 miles
Jemez Springs
Hot springs in a beautiful canyon

Jemez Pueblo

Zia Pueblo

22 miles
Bandelier National Monument
Climb ladders into ancient cliff dwellings

Bernalillo

Albuquerque
FINISH

2 DAYS
128 MILES/206KM

GREAT FOR...

BEST TIME TO GO
May to October, when the weather is best.

ESSENTIAL PHOTO
Climbing a ladder to a cave dwelling in Bandelier National Monument.

BEST FOR RELAXING
Soak up the waters in Jemez Springs.

Highway 4: Jemez Mountains

From Los Alamos, this route takes you across the finger-like mesas to Bandelier National Monument, where cliff dwellings line beautiful Frijoles Canyon. Then wend your way into the Jemez Mountains (pronounced 'hem-ez'), passing through the caldera of an ancient supervolcano that's now home to huge herds of elk. Descend through the red-walled Jemez River canyon, where hot springs abound, then into the horse pastures of Albuquerque's north valley.

TRIP HIGHLIGHT

❶ Los Alamos

The top-secret Manhattan Project sprang to life in Los Alamos in 1943, turning a sleepy mesa-top village into a laboratory of secluded geniuses busy developing the first atomic bomb. Los Alamos National Laboratory still develops weapons, but it's also been at the cutting edge of other scientific advances, including mapping the human genome and

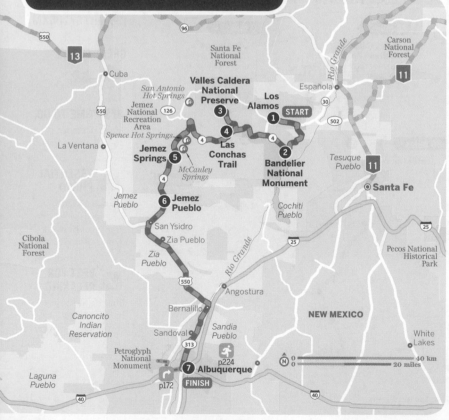

supercomputing. The Lab dominates everything here and gives Los Alamos County the highest concentration of PhDs per capita in the US, along with the highest per-capita income in the state. It's set atop a series of mesas and hugged by national forest, much of which unfortunately burned in the 48,000-acre Cerro Grande fire of 2000, leaving the hills behind town eerily barren. More of the surrounding forest was ablaze in 2011, as the fire around Las Conchas scorched over 150,000 acres – the largest ever recorded in New Mexico. Fortunately, it narrowly missed the Lab.

The **Los Alamos Historical Museum** (📞505-662-6272; www. losalamoshistory.org; 1050

LINK YOUR TRIP

11 **High & Low Roads to Taos**

While driving the Low Road south from Taos, take Hwy 30 to Hwy 502 to Los Alamos to start your Jemez trip.

13 **Georgia O'Keeffe Country**

Take Hwy 550 north to join this colorful route near Chaco Canyon.

LOCAL KNOWLEDGE: MORE HOT SPRINGS

Along Hwy 4 just north of Jemez Springs, there are a number of natural hot springs that you can hike into. One of the most accessible is **Spence Hot Springs**, between miles 25 and 24. The temperature's only about 95°F (35°C), but it's a gorgeous setting and the inevitable weird naked guy adds authenticity to the experience. The nearby **McCauley Springs**, with a trailhead at Battleship Rock Picnic Area, is also lukewarm. For something more ambitious, seek out **San Antonio Hot Springs** – it's a 5-mile hike in to the pools – but worth it! From Hwy 4, take Hwy 126 and watch for signs for Forest Rd 376 and the trailhead.

Bathtub Row; ⏰9:30am-4:30pm Mon-Fri, 11am-4pm Sat & Sun) has interesting exhibits on what daily life was like in 'the town that didn't exist' during the Manhattan Project era. The **Bradbury Science Museum** (📞505-667-4444; www.lanl.gov/museum; 1350 Central Ave; ⏰10am-5pm Tue-Sat, 1-5pm Sun & Mon) has compelling displays on the bomb's development and the political context of the time, along with modern research in medical and computer sciences. A short film introduces the history of the Manhattan Project.

🍴 🛏 p173

The Drive » Drive 12 miles, taking East Jemez Rd to Hwy 4 West, which curves around finger-like mesas. Turn left onto the entrance road for Bandelier.

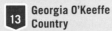
TRIP HIGHLIGHT

❷ Bandelier National Monument

The sublime, peach-colored cliffs of Frijoles Canyon are pocked with caves and alcoves that were home to Ancestral Puebloans until the mid-1500s. Today, they're the main attraction at **Bandelier National Monument** (📞505-672-3861; www.nps.gov/band; Hwy 4; per vehicle $20; ⏰dawn-dusk; 🦽) – a rewarding stop whether you're interested in ancient Southwestern cultures or just want to walk among pines and watch the light glowing off the canyon walls.

The **Alcove House**, 140ft above the ground and reached by climbing four ladders, is a highlight (though it's not for those with vertigo). The more adventurous can strike out on rugged trails that traverse 50 sq miles of canyon and mesa wilderness dotted with archaeological sites; backpackers should pick up a free backcountry permit from the visitor center. Kids love it here.

🛏 p173

The Drive » Head back out of Bandelier and turn left on Hwy 4, heading west as the road twists its way 16 miles into the heart of the Jemez.

TRAVELLER70/SHUTTERSTOCK ©

TRIP HIGHLIGHT

❸ Valles Caldera National Preserve

Ever wonder what the crater of a dormant supervolcano looks like 1,250,000 years after it first blows? Just check out **Valles Caldera National Preserve** (📞575-829-4100; www.nps.gov/vall; Hwy 4; per vehicle $20; ⏰8am-6pm mid-May–Oct, 9am-5pm Nov–mid-May) – the prehistoric explosion here was so massive that chunks were thrown as far away as Kansas. The 89,000-acre bowl – home to New Mexico's largest elk herd – is simply breathtaking, with vast meadows from which hills rise like pine-covered islands. There are miles of hiking and mountain-biking trails in summer and snowshoeing and cross-country skiing trails (groomed and backcountry) in winter. There are no paved roads; a 4WD vehicle is recommended when weather is bad. In summer, 35 free daily permits are available for vehicles. There's an information center in Jemez Springs.

The Drive » Continue on Hwy 4 west, until you come to the trailhead for Las Conchas – about 0.25 miles past the fishing/picnic area of the same name – between mile markers 37 and 36.

❹ Las Conchas Trail

A perfect spot to get out of the car and stretch your legs, the Las Conchas Trail follows the East Fork of the Jemez River as it meanders through grassy meadows and rocky canyons. For the first couple of miles, it's a blissful, easy hike. Las Conchas is also a popular climbing area,

Bandelier National Monument Alcove House

with a number of routes bolted into the volcanic rhyolite. Note that the weather can change quickly here, especially during the summer monsoon season.

The Drive » There's only one main road here, so follow Hwy 4 west then south for 19 miles, as it descends into the tight Jemez River Canyon.

TRIP HIGHLIGHT

5 Jemez Springs

The little village of Jemez Springs was built around a cluster of hot springs, as was the ruined pueblo that's preserved at the **Jemez Historic Site** (☑575-829-3530; www.nmmonuments.org; Hwy 4; adult/child $5/free, joint Coronado ticket $7;

⊘8:30am-5pm Wed-Sun). Today, most visitors come for the waters, which you can experience yourself at the rustic **Jemez Springs Bath House** (☑575-829-3303; www.jemezspringsbathhouse.com; 62 Jemez Springs Plaza; per 25/50min $12/18; ⊘10am-5pm Sun-Tue, to 6pm Thu-Sat), which has private tubs, massages and more. There's also the friendly, outdoor **Giggling Springs** (☏575-829-9175; www.gigglingsprings.com; 40 Abousleman Loop; per 1/2hr $25/40; ☺11am-5pm Wed-Mon), rich in scenic atmosphere.

 p173

The Drive » Keep heading down canyon on Hwy 4 for 12 miles, between the red rock walls and past popular fishing pullouts. All the locals advise against speeding here – you will get a ticket.

----

❻ Jemez Pueblo

Ten miles south of Jemez Springs, in a Martian-red landscape, the **Walatowa Visitor Center** (☏575-834-7235; www.jemezpueblo.com; 7413 Hwy 4; ☺8am-5pm Apr-Oct, 10am-4pm Wed-Sun Nov-Mar) at Jemez Pueblo houses the small, sort-of-interesting Museum of Pueblo Culture. The gift shop sells the pottery for which the pueblo's artisans are renowned.

The Drive » Follow Hwy 4 to the end, turn left on Hwy 550 south, then right onto Hwy 313. After 8 miles, at the roundabout, take 4th St, then go right on Hwy 528. Turn left on S Rio Grande Blvd, through surprisingly rural North Valley horse country as you head downtown. It's 48 miles total.

----

❼ Albuquerque

The largest city in the state, Albuquerque offers some unique introductions to Hispanic and American Indian culture. The **Indian Pueblo Cultural Center** (IPCC; ☏505-843-7270; www.indianpueblo.org; 2401 12th St NW; adult/child $8.40/5.40; ☺9am-5pm) is a must-see even on the shortest of Albuquerque itineraries. The history exhibits are fascinating, and the arts wing features the finest examples of each pueblo's work. The IPCC also houses a large gift shop and retail gallery. Along with serving Pueblo-style cuisine, the on-site **Pueblo Harvest Cafe** (☏505-724-3510; www.indianpueblo.org; 2401 12th St NW; lunch $12-16, dinner $13-28; ☺7am-9pm Mon-Sat, 7am-4pm Sun; 🚗 👪) holds weekend art demonstrations, bread-baking demos and dances.

South of downtown, the **National Hispanic Cultural Center** (☏505-246-2261; www.nhccnm.org; 1701 4th St SW; museum adult/child $6/free; ☺10am-5pm Tue-Sun) for visual, performing and literary arts has three galleries and the nation's premier Hispanic genealogy library. The work in the permanent collection is exciting and provocative, with many pieces by Albuquerque-based artists. Each June the center hosts the **Festival Flamenco**. The Old Town Plaza is a good spot to go for a stroll (p224).

🍴 🛏 p45, p57, p157, p173

DETOUR: PETROGLYPH NATIONAL MONUMENT

Start: ❼ **Albuquerque**

Along the edge of an ancient lava field on Albuquerque's west side are more than 20,000 petroglyphs on basalt slabs at **Petroglyph National Monument** (☏505-899-0205; www.nps.gov/petr; 6001 Unser Blvd NW; ☺ visitor center 8am-5pm). It's easy to spot the rock art in the park's three viewing areas: **Rinconada Canyon** has the longest trail (2.2 miles round-trip) and is best if you want some solitude; **Boca Negra Canyon** features three short trails; **Piedras Marcadas** has 300 petroglyphs along a 1.5-mile trail. For powerful views but no rock art, hit the **Volcanoes Trail**, where you'll hike among cinder cones. Note: smash-and-grab thefts have been reported at some trailhead parking lots, so don't leave valuables in your vehicle.

The visitor center, on Western Trail at Unser Blvd, is 7.5 miles north of Old Town; head west on I-40 across the Rio Grande and take exit 154 north.

Eating & Sleeping

Los Alamos ❶

✖ Pyramid Cafe   Mediterranean $

(📞505-661-1717; www.pyramidcafesf.com; 751 Central Ave; mains $7-18; ⏱11am-3pm & 4:30-8:30pm Mon-Fri, from noon Sat) Middle Eastern food keeps hungry locals happy here: gyros, felafel, shwarma and moussaka bring in the crowds – or maybe it's the Turkish coffee.

Bandelier National Monument ❷

🛏 Juniper Campground   Campground $

(📞877-444-6777; www.recreation.gov; campsites $12) Set among the pines near the monument entrance, the park campground holds about 100 campsites, drinking water, toilets, picnic tables and fire grates, but no showers or hookups.

Jemez Springs ❺

✖ Hwy 4 Coffee   Cafe $

(📞575-829-4655; www.hwy4coffee.com; 17502 Hwy 4; mains $6-12; ⏱8am-2pm Mon & Tue, to 4pm Thu, Fri & Sun, to 7pm Sat) Locals rave about this little spot that specializes in sandwiches, pizzas and pastries. Breakfast choices include oatmeal and breakfast burritos. And espresso!

✖ Los Ojos
Restaurant & Saloon   Tex-Mex $

(📞575-829-3547; www.losojossaloon.com; Hwy 4; mains $9-13; ⏱11am-10pm Mon-Sat, 8am-10pm Sun) An atmospheric saloon with a surprising variety of vegetarian burritos and chile considering the number of animal heads on the walls.

🛏 Cañon del Rio B&B   B&B $$

(📞575-829-4377; www.canondelrio.com; 16445 Hwy 4; r $129-139; 🛜🐾) If you're looking for gorgeous canyon views, a pool, a hot tub and a day spa, killer breakfasts and terrific hosts, this is your place. No kids or pets allowed.

🛏 Jemez Mountain Inn   Inn $

(📞575-829-3926; www.jemezmtninn.com; 17555 Hwy 4; r $85-125; 🅿🛜) Each room at this peaceful place has a different New Mexican theme and all are comfortably appointed. No kids or pets allowed.

🛏 Laughing Lizard Inn   Motel $

(📞575-829-3410; www.thelaughinglizard.com; 17526 Hwy 4; r $70, ste $100-125; ❄🛜🐾) This simple motel is nuthin' fancy, but has been renovated with care and has a real homey feel. Mattresses are springy, and each room is unique. All open onto a covered porch. The newer suite can include a kitchen (optional) and sleeps up to four.

Albuquerque ❼

✖ Artichoke Cafe   Modern American $$$

(📞505-243-0200; www.artichokecafe.com; 424 Central Ave SE; lunch mains $12-19, dinner mains $16-39; ⏱11am-2:30pm & 5-9pm Mon-Fri, 5-10pm Sat) Elegant and unpretentious, this popular bistro prepares creative gourmet cuisine with panache and is always high on foodies' lists of Albuquerque's best. It's on the eastern edge of downtown, between the bus station and I-40.

🛏 Hotel Chaco   Hotel $$$

(📞866-505-7829; www.hotelchaco.com; 2000 Bellamah Ave NW; r from $230; 🅿❄🛜🐾🐾) Albuquerque's newest addition takes its inspiration from the ancient site of Chaco Canyon in northwestern New Mexico. Rooms blend modern expectations with traditional motifs, each featuring a Navajo weaving from Toadlena and soothing earth-colored tones. Great views from the rooftop restaurant and bar.

🛏 Casas de Sueños   B&B $$

(📞505-247-4560; www.casasdesuenos.com; 310 Rio Grande Blvd SW; r $119-179; 🅿❄@🛜) Set in luscious gardens a short walk from Old Town, this lovely and peaceful place holds 21 adobe casitas (small cottages). All feature handcrafted furniture and original artwork, while some have kitchenettes, fireplaces and/or private hot tubs. Full breakfasts are cooked to order.

Enchanted Circle & Eastern Sangres

15

Hike the Rio Grande Gorge, stay at a haunted hotel, hit some hot springs, spot pronghorns and feed alpacas on this scenic trip up and over the Sangre de Cristos.

TRIP HIGHLIGHTS

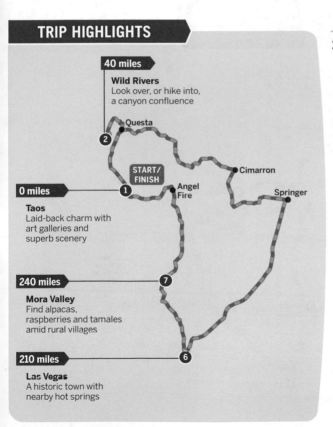

40 miles

Wild Rivers
Look over, or hike into, a canyon confluence

Questa

2

Cimarron

START/ FINISH

1

Angel Fire

Springer

0 miles

Taos
Laid-back charm with art galleries and superb scenery

240 miles

7

Mora Valley
Find alpacas, raspberries and tamales amid rural villages

210 miles

6

Las Vegas
A historic town with nearby hot springs

2 DAYS
297 MILES/479KM

GREAT FOR...

BEST TIME TO GO
August to October: after monsoon season, before winter.

 ESSENTIAL PHOTO

Capture the confluence of the Red River and the Rio Grande from above.

✓ **BEST FOR SEANCES**
Cimarron's St James Hotel.

15 Enchanted Circle & Eastern Sangres

This loop links canyons to forests to mountains to prairies. You'll catch views of 13,107ft Wheeler Peak (the state's highest) and pass through gorgeous valleys with classic New Mexican villages where century-old adobes sit beside modern mobile homes. You'll probably see plenty of wildlife – from elk and antelope to bighorn sheep. Hiking and fishing opportunities abound, and if you're into meditating, we've got the spot for you!

TRIP HIGHLIGHT

1 Taos

For over 100 years, Taos has been a magnet for artists, writers and creative thinkers of all types. Painters were entranced by the light here in 1898 and established an art colony; DH Lawrence hoped to build a utopia outside of town; Carl Jung was deeply affected by visiting Taos Pueblo, the place that also inspired Aldous Huxley's *Brave New World*; Georgia O'Keeffe and

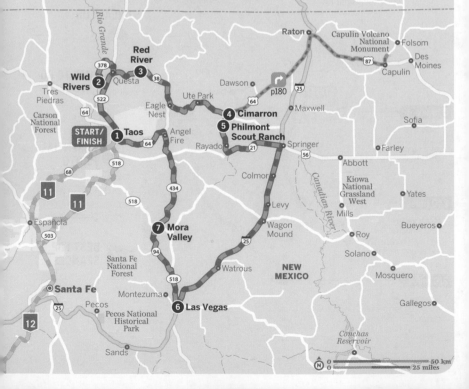

Ansel Adams were here; Dennis Hopper shot key scenes from *Easy Rider* around Taos, then moved here himself. It's easy to see why.

Innovators today include architect Michael Reynolds, designer of Earthships – self-sustaining, environmentally savvy houses built with recycled materials such as used automobile tires and cans. Earthships heat and cool themselves, make their own electricity and catch their own water. You can visit one Earthship community by heading west 1.5 miles past the **Rio Grande Gorge Bridge** – itself well worth seeing – on Hwy 64. Granted, the Earthship **self-guided tour** (J575-613-4409; www.earthship.com; US Hwy 64; self-guided tours $8; 9am-5pm Jun-Aug,10am-4pm Sep-May) is a little

LINK YOUR TRIP

11 High & Low Roads to Taos

Join these two loops at Taos to cover both sides of the Sangre de Cristos.

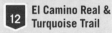

12 El Camino Real & Turquoise Trail

From Las Vegas, continue south on I-25 to hop on these historic routes in Santa Fe.

LOCAL KNOWLEDGE: KTAO: SOLAR-POWERED RADIO

When in Taos, unplug your iPod and turn on the radio. Set the dial to 101.9 KTAO, which claims to be the 'world's largest solar-powered radio station.' The real live DJs play whatever they feel like playing and daily features include horoscope readings (at 10am and 6pm) by local psychic Elissa Heyman. Weekly shows include 'Moccasin Wire' (7pm to 10pm Monday), devoted to American Indian music.

Attached to the station is the **KTAO Solar Center** (J575-758-5826; www.ktao.com; 9 Ski Valley Rd; bar 4-9pm Mon-Thu, to 11pm Fri & Sat), one of the best places in town to see concerts or just have a drink and a meal in the bar-restaurant. It's family-friendly, with a playground on the lawn for kids.

disappointing – you basically watch a short DVD and check out the visitor center. Actually staying in an **Earthship Rental** (J575-751-0462; www.earthship.com; US Hwy 64; earthship $150-430;) overnight is way better.

To see some choice works of the original Taos Society of Artists, visit the **Blumenschein Home & Museum** (J575-758-0505; www.taoshistoricmuseums.org; 222 Ledoux St; adult/child $8/4, Martínez Hacienda joint ticket $12; 10am-5pm Mon-Sat, noon-5pm Sun Apr-Oct, closed Wed & Thu rest of year).

✕ ⊨ p149, p181

The Drive » Take Hwy 522 north just past Questa, then turn left onto Hwy 378. It's 40 miles in total.

TRIP HIGHLIGHT

2 Wild Rivers

One of the most impressive stretches of the Rio Grande Gorge is where it meets the Red River. At **Wild Rivers Recreation Area** (J575-586-1150; Hwy 378; 10am-4pm late May-early Sep) some trails plunge 800ft down into the canyon while others meander along the mesa. If you don't feel like a hike, drive the scenic 13-mile Wild Rivers Backcountry Byway loop and stop at La Junta, the perfect spot for a picnic overlooking the twin gorges. The waters are popular with anglers fishing for trout.

⊨ p181

The Drive » A total of 27 miles; backtrack to Questa, then take Hwy 38 east.

❸ Red River

A blend of Bavaria and the Old West, Red River brings people in with festivals and events year-round – except mid-March to mid-May, when the town is dead. In summer, kids love **Frye's Old Town Shootout** (📞575-754-3028; 100 W Main St; ⏰4pm Tue, Thu & Sat Jun-Sep; 👍), a Wild West drama.

🍴 p181

The Drive » A 40-mile drive, continue east on Hwy 38, over Bobcat Pass (9820ft) and down through the little lakeside village of Eagle Nest. Drive Hwy 64 east through curvaceous Cimarron Canyon, where there's good fishing, camping and rock climbing.

❹ Cimarron

Cimarron has a wild past. It once served as a stop on the Santa Fe Trail, and a hangout for gunslingers, train robbers, desperadoes, lawmen and other Wild West figures including Kit Carson, Buffalo Bill Cody, Annie Oakley, Wyatt Earp, Jesse James and Doc Holliday. The old **St James Hotel** alone saw the deaths of 26 men within its walls. Today, the restored hotel is said to be so haunted that one of its rooms is never rented out. It's really the main reason for stopping in Cimarron, either for the night or a bite to eat.

🛏 p181

The Drive » Head 5 miles south on Hwy 21. You might see herds of Boy Scout burros here!

❺ Philmont Scout Ranch

The largest Boy Scout camp in the country, Philmont Scout Ranch covers 137,000 acres along the breathtaking eastern slope of the Sangre de Cristos. While you need to be a Scout to trek the trails, anyone can drop into the **Philmont Museum** (📞575-376-1136; www.philmontscoutranch.org; 17 Deer Run Rd; ⏰8am-5:30pm Jun-Aug, shorter hours rest of year) or tour **Villa Philmonte**, a Spanish Mediterranean mansion built in 1927 by Waite Phillips, the oil baron who was Philmont's original benefactor. Pick up high-quality outdoor gear and all sorts of Philmont-related souvenirs at **Tooth of Time Traders**.

The Drive » Continue south, then east, on Hwy 21. Look out for antelope! At Springer, pick up I-25 south. Before long, you'll see why Wagon Mound is so-named. Get off the interstate at exit 345. It's a 98-mile drive.

TRIP HIGHLIGHT

❻ Las Vegas

Once a major stop along the Santa Fe Trail and later the Santa Fe Railroad, 19th-century Las Vegas was one of the biggest, baddest boomtowns in the West. Billy the Kid held court here with his pal Vicente Silva (leader

Taos Rio Grande Gorge Bridge

DETOUR:
CAPULIN VOLCANO
NATIONAL MONUMENT

Start: ❹ **Cimarron**

Rising 1300ft above the surrounding plains, Capulin is the most accessible of several volcanoes in the area. From the visitor center at **Capulin Volcano National Monument** (📞575-278-2201; www.nps.gov/cavo; vehicle $7; ⏱8am-5pm Jun-Aug, to 4:30pm Sep-May), a 2-mile road spirals up the mountain to a parking lot at the crater rim (8182ft), where trails lead around and into the crater. From Cimarron, take Hwy 64 north, hop on I-25 for 5 miles, take exit 451, and head east on Hwy 87/64. The park entrance is 3 miles north of Capulin village, off Hwy 325.

of the Society of Bandits – the roughest, toughest gang in New Mexico) and Doc Holliday owned a saloon (although ultimately his business failed because he kept shooting at the customers).

Today, aside from strolling around the plaza, the best reasons to visit Las Vegas are 5 miles northwest of town on Hwy 65, near Montezuma Castle (you'll know it when you see it), which is part of the United World College of the West. Along the road in front of the castle, you can soak in a series of natural **hot spring pools**. Bring a swimsuit and test the water – some are scalding hot! And don't miss the **Dwan Light Sanctuary** (⏱6am-10pm) on the school campus, a meditation chamber where prisms in the walls cast rainbows inside.

🛏 p181

The Drive » Head north on Hwy 518; at mile marker 12, turn left onto Hwy 94, which will take you 30 miles all the way to Mora – but pay attention, as a couple of turns are required. Between mile markers 4 and 5, look south for great views of Hermit Peak.

TRIP HIGHLIGHT

❼ Mora Valley

This scenic agricultural valley, whose hub is the town of Mora, is known throughout northern New Mexico as an enclave where traditional Hispanic ways still remain strong. In 2013, Mora County became the first in the nation to ban fracking, though the ordinance has since been overturned by a federal judge.

At **Tapetes de Lana Weaving Center** (📞575-387-2247; www.moravalleyspinningmill.com; cnr Hwys 518 & 434; ⏱7:30am-5pm Mon-Fri, 8am-4pm Sat, 9am-2pm Sun) you can see handlooms in action, browse for handmade rugs and buy yarns that are spun and dyed on-site, and tour one of the few active wool mills in the US. At the **Victory Ranch** (📞575-387-2254; www.victoryranch.com; Hwy 434; tours $6; ⏱10am-4pm Fri-Sun; 👣), 1 mile north of Mora, hand-feed the cute and fluffy alpacas and shop for alpaca wool gifts.

Two miles west of Mora is the **Cleveland Roller Mill Historical Museum** (📞575-387-2645; www.clevelandrollermillmuseum.org; Hwy 518; ⏱10am-3pm Sat & Sun late May-early Sep), housed in a functional 19th-century adobe-and-stone flour mill, with gears and cogs and pulleys inside. Five miles east of Mora, the **Salman Ranch** (📞866-281-1515; www.salmanraspberryranch.com; Hwy 518, at Hwy 442; ⏱10am-4pm Tue-Sun in season; 👣) is famous for its pesticide-free raspberry fields, where you pick your own from mid-August to mid-October. Off-season, stop by the ranch store and La Cueva Mill, one of New Mexico's best-preserved 19th-century industrial adobe buildings.

🍴 p181

The Drive » Take Hwy 434 north, through Guadalupita and the ski-resort town of Angel Fire. Turn left on Hwy 64 west, which will take you back into Taos. Watch for elk – sometimes in the middle of the road! This last leg is about 60 miles.

Eating & Sleeping

Taos ❶

✗ Taos Diner   Diner $

(📞575-758-2374; www.taosdiner.com;
908 Paseo del Pueblo Norte; mains $7-12;
🕑7:30am-2:30pm; 🚻) Diner grub at its finest,
prepared with a Southwestern, organic spin.
Mountain men, scruffy jocks, solo diners and
happy tourists – everyone's welcome here.
The breakfast burritos rock. There's another
branch (📞575-751-1989; 216B Paseo Del
Pueblo Sur; mains $7.50-11.50; 🕑7am-3pm)
south of the plaza.

🛏 Mabel Dodge Luhan House   Inn $$

(📞505-751-9686; www.mabeldodgeluhan.
com; 240 Morada Lane; r from $116; 🅿) Every
inch of this rambling compound, once home to
Mabel Dodge Luhan, the so-called Patroness
of Taos, exudes elegant-meets-earthy beauty.
Sleep where Georgia O'Keeffe, Willa Cather or
Dennis Hopper once laid their heads, or even
use a bathroom decorated by DH Lawrence.
It also runs arts, crafts, spiritual and creative
workshops. Rates include buffet breakfast.
Wi-fi in public areas only.

Wild Rivers ❷

🛏 Wild Rivers Recreation
Area Campground   Campground $

(day use $3, campsites $5-7) Five small
first-come, first-served campgrounds dot
the scenic drive that loops through the sage-
speckled recreation area. Potable water and
toilets on-site.

Red River ❸

✗ Shotgun Willie's   Diner $

(📞575-754-6505; www.shotgunwilliescafe.
com; 403 W Main St; mains $5-13; 🕑7am-2pm)
Locals love this tiny place, serving the ultimate
hangover sop-up, artery-clogging breakfast
specials of fried eggs, meats and potatoes. The
true house specialty is barbecue, served by the
pound. Order the brisket combo.

Cimarron ❹

🛏 St James Hotel   Historic Hotel $$

(📞575-376-2664; www.exstjames.com; 617
Collison St; r $85-135; ❋ 🛜) The public
spaces here, including a decent midrange
restaurant and a bar with a pool table, are pure
Victoriana, all dark wood and animal heads.
The 12 historic rooms in the main building
have a genuine period feel (no TVs); an annex
holds 10 modern rooms.

Las Vegas ❻

🛏 Plaza Hotel   Historic Hotel $$

(📞505-425-3591; www.plazahotellvnm.com;
230 Old Town Plaza; r $89-149; ❋ @ 🛜 🐾) This
historic hotel, opened in 1882, offers affordable
rates for its 72 spacious, high-ceilinged rooms.
The whole place has an appealing Wild West
flavor, and has rightfully brushed shoulders
with celebrity in films such as *No Country for
Old Men*. Although the floorboards still creak,
rooms are plenty comfortable. A convivial **bar**
(🕑2-9pm) and popular restaurant look out over
the plaza.

Mora Valley ❼

✗ Teresa's Tamales   Mexican $

(📞575-387-2754; 3296 Hwy 518, Cleveland;
dishes $3-7; 🕑8am-5pm Mon-Sat) A tiny cinder-
block building with a wood stove and votive
candles in the corner. Come to this community
hub for some of the best tamales ($3) in the
state. Smothered burritos are huge, served up
gloriously on a Styrofoam plate. It's 4 miles west
of Mora, just past Cleveland.

Las Cruces to Carlsbad Caverns

16

Crossing the southern swath of the state, you can sled down gleaming white sand dunes, walk through stalagmite-columned caves and swim in a waterfall in the desert. It's no mirage...

TRIP HIGHLIGHTS

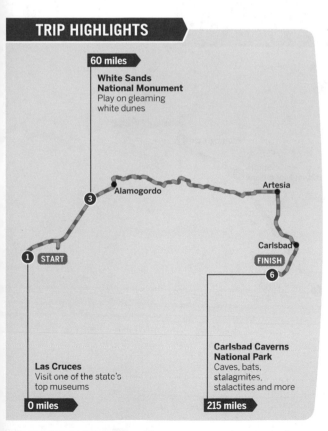

60 miles

White Sands National Monument
Play on gleaming white dunes

Alamogordo

3

Artesia

Carlsbad

1 START

FINISH

6

Las Cruces
Visit one of the state's top museums

0 miles

Carlsbad Caverns National Park
Caves, bats, stalagmites, stalactites and more

215 miles

2–3 DAYS
215 MILES/346KM

GREAT FOR...

BEST TIME TO GO
September till November offers the best weather.

 ESSENTIAL PHOTO
The play of light and shadow on wind-sculpted dunes at White Sands National Monument.

✓ BEST NATURAL SIGHT
Carlsbad Caverns is like nothing else in the Southwest.

White Sands National Monument Ethereal dunes

183

16 Las Cruces to Carlsbad Caverns

White Sands means two things in these parts: the national monument where you can frolic in dunes that look like giant snowdrifts, and the missile range surrounding it that's the largest military installation in the US – within which the first atomic blast ever was unleashed. From this sandy basin, the route climbs into pine-clad forests and, ultimately, descends 755ft underground into the trippy subterranean world of Carlsbad Caverns.

TRIP HIGHLIGHT

❶ Las Cruces

Though this city at the southern crossroads of I-25 and I-10 doesn't have a wealth of attractions, it does have one museum you won't want to miss. The **New Mexico Farm & Ranch Heritage Museum** (📞575-522-4100; www.nmfarmandranchmuseum.org; 4100 Dripping Springs Rd; adult/child $5/3; ⏰9am-5pm Mon-Sat, noon-5pm Sun; 👶) has more than just engaging displays about the agricultural history

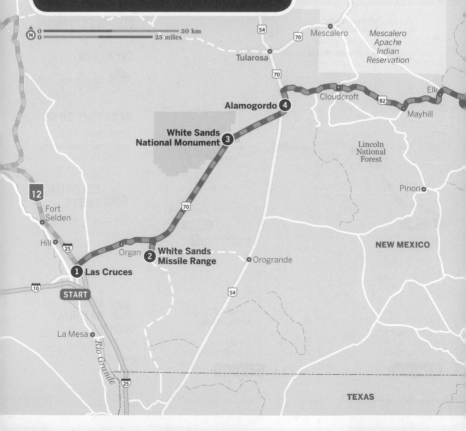

of the state – it's got livestock! There are daily milking demonstrations and an occasional 'parade of breeds' of cattle, along with stalls of horses, donkeys, sheep and goats. Other demonstrations include blacksmithing (Friday to Sunday), spinning and weaving (Wednesday), and heritage cooking (call for times). You'll understand much more about New Mexican life and culture after a visit here.

✗ ⊨ p157, p189

The Drive » Take I-25 north to Hwy 70. Drive east through a notch in the Organ Mountains and drop into the Tularosa Valley. Between mile markers 169 and 170, exit at White Sands Missile Range; it's 26 miles in total.

----

❷ White Sands Missile Range

If it flies, explodes and was made in America, there's a good chance it was tested here. (Occasionally, Hwy 70 even closes to prevent 'collateral damage' during launches.) The **White**

Sands Missile Test Center Museum (☎575-678-3358; www.wsmr-history.org; ⏰8am-4pm Mon-Fri, 10am-3pm Sat) features an outdoor missile garden, a real V-2 rocket and exhibits with lots of defense-related artifacts. Park outside the Test Center gate and check-in at the office before walking to the museum.

The Drive » Continue east on Hwy 70 for 34 miles. Be prepared to stop along the way at a Border Patrol checkpoint, which are sometimes manned with drug-sniffing dogs.

TRIP HIGHLIGHT

❸ White Sands National Monument

Undulating through the Tularosa Basin like something straight out of a dream, the ethereal

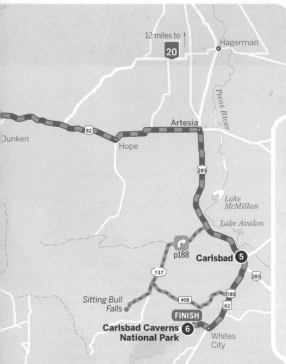

LINK YOUR TRIP

12 **El Camino Real & Turquoise Trail**
From Las Cruces, head north up the Rio Grande Valley along the 400-year-old route that linked Mexico City to Santa Fe.

20 **Billy the Kid Trail**
From Artesia, drive 30 miles north on US 285 to Roswell, for a trip that covers UFOs and outlaws.

dunes at **White Sands National Monument** ([phone] 575-479-6124; www.nps.gov/whsa; adult/child $5/free; [hours] 7am-9pm Jun-Aug, to sunset Sep-May) are a highlight of any trip to New Mexico and a must on every landscape photographer's itinerary. Try to time a visit to White Sands with sunrise or sunset (or both), when it's at its most magical. From the visitor center drive the 16-mile scenic loop into the heart of the dazzlingly white sea of sand that is the world's largest gypsum dune field, covering 275 sq miles. Along the way, get out of the car and romp around a bit. Hike the **Alkali Flat**, a 4.5-mile (round-trip) backcountry trail through the heart of the dunes, or the simple 1-mile loop nature trail. Don't forget your sunglasses – the sand is as bright as snow!

Spring for a $15 plastic saucer at the visitor center gift shop then **sled** one of the back dunes. It's fun, and you can sell the disc back for $5 at day's end (no rentals to avoid liability). Check the park calendar for **sunset strolls** and occasional moonlight **bicycle rides** (adult/child $5/2.50), the latter best reserved in advance.

Backcountry campsites, with no water or toilet facilities, are a mile from the scenic drive. Pick up one of

DOUG MEEK / SHUTTERSTOCK ©

the limited permits ($3, issued first-come, first-served) in person at the visitor center at least one hour before sunset.

The Drive » Keep heading east on Hwy 70 for 16 miles.

----

❹ Alamogordo

Alamogordo (Spanish for 'fat cottonwood') might not be laden with charm, but it's super convenient to White Sands.

The main attraction is the four-story **New Mexico Museum of Space History** ([phone] 575-437-2840; www.nmspacemuseum.org; 3198 Hwy 2001; adult/child $7/5; [hours] 10am-5pm Wed-Sat

& Mon, noon-5pm Sun; [access]). Nicknamed the 'golden cube,' it looms over town and has excellent exhibits on space research and flight. Its **theater and planetarium** shows films on everything from the Grand Canyon to the dark side of the moon, as well as laser shows and multimedia presentations on a huge wraparound screen.

Railroad buffs and kids flock to the **Toy Train Depot** ([phone] 505-437-2855; 1991 N White Sands Blvd; $4; [hours] noon-4:30pm Wed-Sun; [access]), an 1898 railway depot with five rooms of train memorabilia and

Carlsbad Caverns

toy trains, and a 2.5-mile narrow-gauge mini-train you can ride through Alameda Park.

✖ 🛏 p189

The Drive ❯❯ Take Hwy 82 east, and you'll soon find yourself rising from the Chihuahuan Desert into the forested Sacramento Mountains. Pass Cloudcroft – maybe stop to grab a bite or stay overnight (p189) – and continue on, downhill and across open plains. At Artesia, turn south onto Hwy 285. It's 147 miles total.

- - - - - - - - - - - - - - - - - -

❺ Carlsbad

Carlsbad is a convenient base from which to visit the famous caverns south of town, as well as **Guadalupe Mountains National Park** just across state lines in Texas. There's not a whole lot to see in Carlsbad itself, but the **Living Desert State Park** (☎575-887-5516; www. nmparks.com; 1504 Miehls Dr N, off Hwy 285; adult/child $5/3; 🕐8am-5pm Jun-Aug, 9am-5pm Sep-May, last zoo entry 3.30pm) is worth a gander. It's a great place to see and learn about roadrunners, wolves and antelopes, along with desert plants like agave, ocotillo and yucca. The park has a good 1.3-mile trail that showcases different habitats of the Chihuahuan Desert, plus a reptile house.

✖ 🛏 p189

The Drive ❯❯ Take Hwy 62/180 south for 20 miles to White's City, then Hwy 7 into Carlsbad Caverns National Park.

- - - - - - - - - - - - - - - - - -

❻ Carlsbad Caverns National Park

Huge caves hide under the hills at **Carlsbad Caverns National Park** (☎575-785-2232, bat info 505-785-3012; www.nps.gov/cave; Carlsbad Cavern Hwy; adult/child $10/free; 🕐 caves 8:30am-5pm late May-early Sep, 8:30am-3:30pm early

DETOUR: SITTING BULL FALLS

Start: ❺ Carlsbad

An oasis in the desert, **Sitting Bull Falls** (County Rd 409; per vehicle $5; ☉8:30am-5pm) is tucked among the burly canyons of the Guadalupe Mountains, 42 miles southwest of Carlsbad. A spring-fed creek pours 150ft over a limestone cliff, with natural pools below and above the falls that are big enough to splash around in. There are a series of caves behind the waterfalls, which can be explored with a ranger.

Twenty-six miles of trails around the falls offer the best hiking anywhere near Carlsbad. Though there's no camping in the designated recreation area right around the falls, backpackers may hike in and camp further up Sitting Bull Canyon, or up Last Chance Canyon, where you should also find water flowing. It can get brutally hot here in summer, so hiking is generally best from late fall to early spring. Arrange cave walks and pick up trail maps and other info at the **Lincoln National Forest office** (☎575-885-4181; 5203 Buena Vista Dr; ☉7:30am-4:30pm Mon-Fri) in Carlsbad.

To get there, turn west on NM 137 (also called the 'Queen Hwy') from US 285 just north of Carlsbad, or turn west on County Rd 408 (the Dark Canyon Rd) from US 180/62 just south of Carlsbad, and follow the signs to Sitting Bull Falls.

the Big Room – an underground chamber about 8.2 acres in size and over 800ft below the surface – but it's more enjoyable to hike in 1.25 miles from the cave mouth. Wear a sweatshirt: the temperature is 56°F (13°C) year-round.

The cave's other claim to fame is the 300,000-plus Mexican free-tailed bat colony that roosts here from mid-May to mid-October. Be here by sunset, when they cyclone out for an all-evening insect feast.

Guided tours of **additional caves** (☎877-444-6777; www.recreation.gov; adult $7-20, child $3.50-10) are available, and should be reserved well in advance.

Wilderness backpacking – above ground, in the desert – requires a permit (free); the visitor center sells topographical maps of the hiking trails. November to March is the best time for backpacking (no rattlesnakes, better temperatures). To get an up-close glimpse of the desert in air-conditioned comfort, take the 9-mile gravel **Walnut Canyon Desert Drive**.

Sep-late May; 🚹), where you can walk through a weird subterranean wonderland that's covered in stalactites, stalagmites and other fantastical geological features. You can ride an elevator from the visitor center (descending the length of the Empire State Building in under a minute) to

Eating & Sleeping

Las Cruces ❶

✗ Chala's Wood-Fired Grill   New Mexican $

(📞575-652-4143; 2790 Ave de Mesilla, Mesilla; mains $5-10; ⏱8am-9pm Mon-Sat, to 8pm Sun) With house-smoked carnitas and turkey, housemade bacon and chile-pork sausage, plus *calabacitas* (squash and corn), quinoa salad and organic greens, this place rises well above the standard New Mexican diner fare. Located at the southern end of Mesilla, it's kick-back casual and the price is right.

🛏 Best Western Mission Inn   Motel $

(📞575-524-8591; www.bwmissioninn.com; 1765 S Main St; r from $71; ❄🖥⚒) A truly out-of-the-ordinary accommodation option: yes it's a roadside chain motel, but the rooms are beautifully kitted out with attractive tiling, stonework and colorful stenciled designs; they're sizeable and comfortable; and the rates are great.

Alamogordo ❹

✗ Rizo's   Mexican $

(📞575-434-2607; 1480 White Sands Blvd; mains $9-15; ⏱9am-9pm Tue-Sat, to 6pm Sun; 🖥) Service can be a bit brisk at this no-frills place, but it's still one of the town's most reliable eats. In addition to all the usual suspects, you'll find *gorditas* (corn pockets), *carne asada* fries (topped with about everything) and drinks like *agua fresca* and *horchata*.

🛏 Oliver Lee Memorial State Park   Campground $

(📞575-437-8284; www.nmparks.com; 409 Dog Canyon Rd; tent/RV sites $8/14) Spending a night or two in the fully equipped campground in this spring-fed canyon, 12 miles south of Alamogordo, will give you the chance to see ferns and flowers growing in the desert. The 5.5-mile Dog Canyon National Recreational Trail climbs 2000ft over 5.5 miles for terrific views of the Tularosa Basin.

Cloudcroft

🛏 Lodge Resort & Spa   Historic Hotel $$

(📞800-395-6343; www.thelodgeresort.com; 601 Corona Pl; r $125-235; @🖥⚒) Built in 1899 as a getaway for railroad employees, this historic hilltop lodge is now a full-scale resort, with a wonderful restaurant, a golf course, beautiful grounds and a pampering spa. Period-furnished rooms in the main Bavarian-style building can be a bit small but they're cozy, with high beds and showers not baths; less-attractive Pavilion rooms are a few blocks away.

Carlsbad ❺

✗ Trinity Restaurant & Wine Bar   American $$

(📞575-234-9891; www.thetrinityhotel.com; 201 S Canal St; lunch $8-12, dinner $14-34; ⏱7am-9pm Mon-Sat; 🖊) This elegant split-level dining room – the ceiling is so high there's room for a mezzanine floor – offers Carlsbad's finest dining, with a menu of steaks, seafood and Italian specialties, and pasta and salad for vegetarians. Nonkosher carnivores will love the roast pork in a cabernet/green chile reduction. Lightning-fast lunch service makes it a favorite rendezvous for downtown employees.

🛏 Trinity Hotel   Boutique Hotel $$

(📞575-234-9891; www.thetrinityhotel.com; 201 S Canal St; r $149-209; ❄🖥) Carlsbad's best hotel is housed in a grand downtown building that started life as the First National Bank in 1892. Friendly and family-run, it has an excellent restaurant. The sitting room of one suite is inside the old vault; another still has a bullet hole.

Geronimo Trail

Follow the trail of this legendary Apache chief, through old mining towns, over serpentine passes and into the box canyon where he ultimately surrendered.

17

TRIP HIGHLIGHTS

2–3 DAYS
190 MILES/306KM

GREAT FOR...

BEST TIME TO GO
May to October, for warm days that linger into evening.

 ESSENTIAL PHOTO
Frame an antique at Chloride's Pioneer Store.

 BEST FOR VIEWS
Emory Pass: gape at the Rio Grande Basin panorama and beyond.

Very Large Array Radio Telescope · **FINISH**

130 miles ── ⑥
Chloride
One semi-restored old mining town that's worth the trip

⑤ ◀ **88 miles**
Truth or Consequences
Soak in the hot springs

Emory Pass
● **Hillsboro**

START
①

Silver City
Historic downtown is endearingly quirky

0 miles

17 Geronimo Trail

From the former boomtown of Silver City – which is now rich with great cafes – you'll snake your way over precipitous Emory Pass and out to the Rio Grande Valley. Like Geronimo himself, you can soak in the healing mineral springs at Truth or Consequences before heading for the eastern flank of the Gila's Black Range and north to the sublime Plains of San Agustin.

TRIP HIGHLIGHT

❶ Silver City

Way back in the day, the site of Silver City was settled by Apache people. When the Spanish came to the area to mine copper, they opted to set up residence outside this little valley. Less tactful were the American prospectors who arrived in the late 1860s, and flooded in following the silver strike in 1870. They established the town and conflict with the Apache people

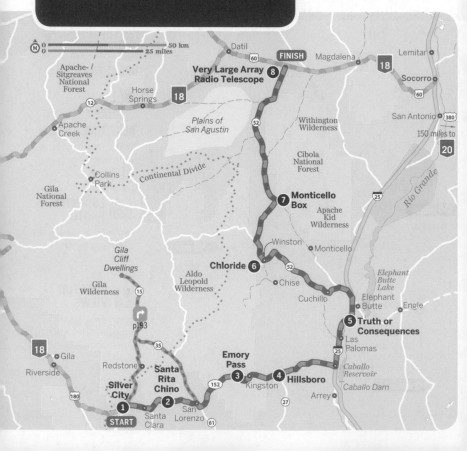

erupted. Silver City's founder, John Bullard, was killed in 1871. Since then, the fortunes of the town have risen and fallen a few times. Today, the economy is largely based on copper mining from the nearby Santa Rita mine.

These days, Silver City is a pretty lively place. The town attracts adventure addicts, who come to work and play in the nearby mountains and rivers. It's also home to a healthy student population – Western New Mexico University is based here. The **University Museum** (📞575-538-6386; www.wnmu.edu/univ/museum.shtml; 1000 W College Ave; 🕐9am-4:30pm Mon-Fri, 10am-4pm Sat & Sun) boasts the world's largest collection of Mimbres pottery and was

DETOUR:
GILA CLIFF DWELLINGS

Start: ❶ Silver City

It's easy to imagine how the mysterious, relatively isolated **Gila Cliff Dwellings National Monument** (📞575-536-9461; www.nps.gov/gicl; Hwy 15; adult/child $5/free; 🕐trail 9am-4pm, visitor center to 4:30pm) might have looked in the 13th century. Here, the influence of the Ancestral Puebloans on the Mogollon culture is writ large. Take the 1-mile round-trip self-guided trail that climbs 180ft to the dwellings, overlooking a lovely forested canyon. Parts of the trail are steep and involve ladders. The trail begins at the end of Hwy 15, 2 miles beyond the visitor center.

To get here, take twisting Hwy 15 north from Silver City (figure on a two-hour drive). Heading back from the cliff dwellings, take Hwy 35 down the pleasant Mimbres Valley for a change of scenery, or to skip onwards to stop 3 on this Trip.

LINK YOUR TRIP

18 **Into the Gila**
Check out the west side of the range on this trip, which connects at Silver City.

20 **Billy the Kid Trail**
From the Very Large Array, take Hwy 60 east, I-25 south, then Hwy 380 east to link up with this outlaw's route at Valley of Fires.

completely renovated in 2017.

🍴 🛏 p197, p205

The Drive » Take Hwy 180 east, then at Santa Clara turn left onto Hwy 152. After about 5.5 miles, look for the Chino Mine Observation Point on your right.

---

❷ Santa Rita Chino Open Pit Copper Mine Observation Point

Worked by American Indians and Spanish and Anglo settlers, this is the oldest active mine in the Southwest. From the observation point along Hwy 152, you can get an eyeful of it. A staggering 1.5 miles wide, the open pit is 1800ft deep, and produces 300 million pounds of copper annually.

The Drive » Continue east on Hwy 152 for 26 miles. After San Lorenzo, the road becomes increasingly serpentine as you climb over the Black Range. There are a number of Forest Service campgrounds along this section.

---

❸ Emory Pass

Your journey over the Black Range tops out at the 8228ft Emory Pass. The lookout point offers expansive views of the Rio Grande basin to the east and the rows of craggy peaks that jut from it like sharp teeth. There's a hiking trailhead here that leads north along the spine of the Black Range.

The Drive » You're not done with the curves yet – you've still got to go 16.5 miles down the other side of the pass!

---

④ Hillsboro

Precious ore, including gold, silver and copper, was discovered around Hillsboro in the mid-1800s, but the boom didn't last long. When the silver market crashed in 1893 so did most of the towns. Today, Hillsboro is one of the largest ones left, with a population of around 300. It's best known for its Apple Festival on the Labor Day weekend (early September), featuring everything apple, including freshly baked pies and delicious cider. See some historical miscellany at the **Black Range Museum** (Hwy 152; admission by donation; ⊙11am-4pm Fri-Sun); if it's closed, go around back and yell for Jim and he'll likely open up.

✖ p197

The Drive » Continue east, out of the foothills and into the Rio Grande Valley. Take I-25 north. It's 31 miles total.

TRIP HIGHLIGHT
⑤ Truth or Consequences

According to local lore, Geronimo himself came to this place to partake of the healing hot

waters – and you should too. Long said to have therapeutic properties, the waters range in temperature from 98°F to 115°F (36°C to 46°C) and have a pH of 7 (neutral). Our favorite spot to soak is **Riverbend Hot Springs** (☎575-894-7625; www.riverbendhotsprings.com; 100 Austin St; shared/private per hour $10/15; ⊙8am-10pm), which has shared and private tubs overlooking a – wait for it – bend in the river. For something more spa-tastic, and way more expensive, hit the **Sierra Grande Lodge & Spa** (☎877-288-7637; www.sierragrandelodge.com; 501 McAdoo St; per 30min $30; ⊙by reservation), with posh private pools and a full menu of massages, facials, scrubs and even private yoga classes.

To engage your brain as well as your body, stop by the **Geronimo Springs Museum** (www.geronimospringsmuseum.com; 211 Main St; adult/student $6/3; ⊙9am-5pm Mon-Sat, noon-5pm Sun), an engaging mishmash of minerals, local art and historical artifacts ranging from prehistoric Mimbres pots to beautifully worked cowboy saddles.

✖ 🛏 p157

The Drive » After filling up with gas, head north out of Truth or Consequences on Hwy 181, then turn left onto Hwy 52, bearing west, toward the Black Range. The road winds around

WIHO1962/SHUTTERSTOCK ©

Cuchillo Mountain, into the little town of Winston. At the T intersection, turn left and follow signs for 2.7 miles to Chloride. In total, it's 40 miles.

TRIP HIGHLIGHT
⑥ Chloride

In the foothills of the Black Range, tiny Chloride (population eight) was abustle in the 19th century with enough

Chloride Historic buildings

silver miners to support eight saloons. By the end of the 20th century, the town was on the verge of disintegration. Fortunately, the historic buildings are being restored by Don and Dona Edmund, who began renovating the old **Pioneer Store** (☎575-743-2736; www.pioneerstoremuseum. com; by donation; ⏰10am-4pm) in 1994. Today, this

general store from 1880 is a museum with a rich collection of miscellany from Chloride's heyday, including wooden dynamite detonators, farm implements, children's coffins, saddles and explosion-proof telephones used in mines. You can see the Hanging Tree to which rowdy drunks were tied until they sobered

up, the Monte Cristo Saloon (now an artist co-op and gift shop) and a few other buildings in various stages of rehabilitation.

🛏 p197

The Drive » Backtrack to Winston and keep going straight, north on Hwy 52. After 9 miles, continue straight onto the dirt road, toward Dusty. After 9 more miles,

LOCAL KNOWLEDGE: KINGSTON

A blink-and-you'll-miss-it community of just 30 people (compared to 7000 in its heyday), Kingston is a small clutch of wooden buildings about a quarter mile off Hwy 152, between Emory Pass and Hillsboro. It's hard to believe this was one of the baddest cities in New Mexico, boasting 28 bars catering to everyone from Chinese fortune seekers to Billy the Kid, Butch Cassidy and Mark Twain. The only building that looks almost like it did during the 19th century is the beautifully restored **Percha Bank** (☏575-895-5652; Main St; ⊙11am-3pm Fri-Sun May-Sep), c 1884. Complete with an enormous working vault, the bank building is now a museum and art gallery. If no one's there, ask over at the **Black Range Lodge** (☏575-895-5652; www.blackrangelodge.com; 119 Main St; r $79-110; 🛜), a comfortably rustic B&B that was once a casino and saloon.

turn right onto Forest Rd 140/CRE 14. Drive to the parking/turnaround area just before the track crosses the stream.

TRIP HIGHLIGHT

❼ Monticello Box

This steep-walled canyon that rises abruptly along Alamosa Creek was frequented by Geronimo and his renegade Chiricahua Apache band during the mid-1870s, in part because of a sacred warm spring inside the gorge. Outside, not far from the junction of Hwy 52 and Forest Rd 140, sat the headquarters of the Warm Springs Apache reservation. It was here, in April 1877, that Geronimo arrived for what he believed would be a peaceful meeting with 'Indian agent' John Clum; instead, Geronimo was captured, shackled and interned at the San Carlos reservation in Arizona (from which he would later escape).

Note that the land surrounding the canyon is private and access has become the subject of fierce debate over the past several years. At the time of research, Monticello Box was closed to the public, though it's possible it may reopen in the future. If you do explore, wear water shoes or sandals, as you'll have to cross the stream a few times even if you're only hiking in a short distance.

The Drive » Heading north on Hwy 52 for about 40 miles, you'll traverse some of New Mexico's most subtly stunning terrain, up intermittent Alamosa Creek and out onto the undulating Plains of San Agustin. Bonus points if you can manage to time this around sunset. You'll hit the Very Large Array just before reaching Hwy 60.

----

❽ Very Large Array Radio Telescope

If you make it to this literally otherworldly looking spread of massive antenna dishes before dark, check out the museum and take a walking tour of the facility (p201). If you arrive too late, it's still worth the trip just to see the silhouettes against the twilight sky. For the museum, turn left on Hwy 166.

Eating & Sleeping

Silver City ❶

✗ Jalisco Cafe
New Mexican $

(☎575-388-2060; 103 S Bullard St; mains
$7-14; ⏰11am-8pm) The most popular place to
get your chile fix in Silver City, spanning three
dining rooms. The red chile con carne plate is an
excellent choice.

🛏 Palace Hotel
Historic Hotel $

(☎575-388-1811; www.silvercitypalacehotel.
com; 106 W Broadway; r incl breakfast $58-94;
❄🛜) A restored 1882 hotel, the Palace is
an atmospheric stopover. All rooms feature
old-fashioned Territorial style decor; they vary
from small (with a double bed) to two-room
suites (king- or queen-size beds). Expect
some historical quirks – water pressure in the
showers is very low (ours was unusable) and
wi-fi is iffy in some rooms. Breakfast is good,
however, and the owners are friendly.

Gila Cliff Dwellings National Monument

🛏 Gila Cliff Dwellings Campgrounds
Campground

(www.nps.gov/gicl; Gila Cliff Dwellings National
Monument; free) There are four campgrounds
in and around Gila Cliff Dwellings National
Monument (p193); all have vault toilets but none
have drinking water – fill up at the visitor center.
All are first-come, first-served, but they rarely
fill up outside of major weekends.

Hillsboro ❹

✗ Hillsboro General Store Café
New Mexican $

(☎575-895-5306; www.hillsborogeneralstore.
com; 100 Main St; mains $5-10; ⏰8am-3pm Fri-
Tue) Housed in Hillsboro's historic general store,
this place is a surprise of the best kind. The New
Mexican plates feature local chile, free-range
locally raised meats, organic veggies – and the
pies are so good they often sell out.

Chloride ❻

🛏 Harry Pye Cabin
Cabin $$

(☎575-743-2736; cabins $125; 🐾) Stay in
Chloride's oldest building, which has been
renovated and modernized into comfortable
two-bedroom accommodations. It's got a mini-
kitchenette with a microwave. Reserve ahead.

Into the Gila

18

From the otherworldly sight of the Very Large Array to the absolutely earthy experience of the burly Gila Mountains, take a trip into New Mexico's wild southwest.

TRIP HIGHLIGHTS

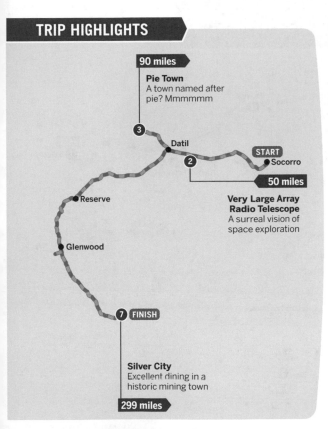

90 miles

Pie Town
A town named after pie? Mmmmmm

3

Datil

2

START
Socorro

50 miles

Very Large Array Radio Telescope
A surreal vision of space exploration

Reserve

Glenwood

7 **FINISH**

Silver City
Excellent dining in a historic mining town

299 miles

---

2 DAYS
299 MILES/481KM

GREAT FOR...

BEST TIME TO GO
May to October, when it's warm enough to enjoy.

 ESSENTIAL PHOTO
Focus on the telescope that's the Very Large Array.

 BEST FOR DESSERTS
Pie Town – c'mon, the town is named for its pie!

Very Large Array Radio Telescope Antenna dishes

18 | Into the Gila

With its huge dish antennas spread across a swath of the Plains of San Agustin and pointing at the sky, the Very Large Array launches this trip to an out-of-this-world beginning. Hwys 12 and 180 curve around the Gila massif, bringing you to the Catwalk, the San Francisco Hot Springs and on into the historic Wild West town of Silver City, now bursting with art galleries.

❶ Socorro

Named in 1598 by conquistador Don Juan de Oñate after local Piro Indians gave him and his men corn, Socorro (which means 'aid' or 'help') has a pleasant plaza, with a couple of good places to grab a bite nearby – but that's about it. The main sight in town is the **San Miguel Mission** (www. sdc.org/~smiguel; 403 San Miguel Rd), sections of which date to the 1600s. Socorro is also close to the Bosque del Apache

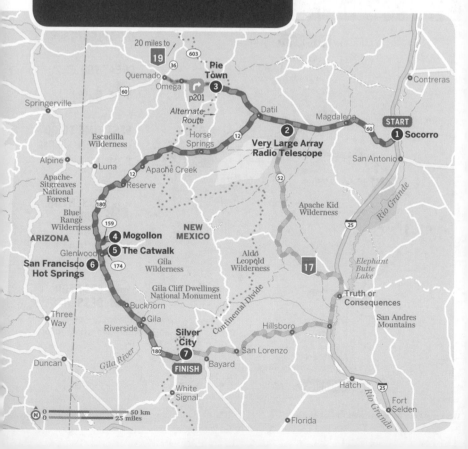

National Wildlife Refuge (p154).

 p205

The Drive >> Head west on Hwy 60 for 45 miles, then turn left onto Hwy 52; go 2.3 miles and turn right on Hwy 166 to the Very Large Array Radio Telescope. Don't expect to have mobile phone service for most of this drive.

TRIP HIGHLIGHT

❷ Very Large Array Radio Telescope

Twenty-seven huge antenna dishes (each weighing 230 tons) together comprise a single superpowered telescope – the **Very Large Array Radio Telescope** (VLA; ☎505-835-7000; www.nrao.edu; off Hwy 52; adult/child $6/free; ⏰8:30am-sunset), run by the National Radio Astronomy Observatory. They move along railroad tracks that

LINK YOUR TRIP

17 Geronimo Trail
At Silver City, just keep on going to follow the path of this Apache legend.

19 Highway 53 to Acoma
Take the scenic back roads north of Pie Town to check out lava flows, pueblos and more.

DETOUR: LIGHTNING FIELD

Start: ❸ Pie Town

Heading on toward the Arizona border on Hwy 60, out in the high desert plains around Quemado, gleams the **Lightning Field** (☎505-898-3335; www.diaart.org/sites/main/lightningfield; adult/child Jul & Aug $250/100, May, Jun, Sep & Oct $150/100), an art installation created by Walter de Maria in 1977. Four hundred polished steel poles stand in a giant grid, with each stainless rod about 20ft high – but the actual lengths vary so the tips are all level with each other. During summer monsoons, the poles seem to draw lightning out of hovering thunderheads. The effect is truly electrifying! You can only visit if you stay overnight in the simple on-site cabin, with only six visitors allowed per night. Advance reservations are required. Check out the website for more details.

crisscross the open plains, their layout reconfigured as needed to study the outer limits of the known universe. To match the resolving power of the VLA, a regular telescope would have to be 22 miles wide!

The VLA has increased our understanding of black holes, space gases and radio emissions, among other celestial phenomena. And it's had starring and cameo roles in Hollywood films, including *Contact, Armageddon* and *Independence Day*. If none of that's enough to interest you, well, they're just unbelievably cool. There's a small museum at the visitor center, where

you can take a free, self-guided tour with a window peek into the control building.

The Drive >> Head west on Hwy 60 for 35 miles; when you see the striking crags of the Sawtooth Mountains to the north, you're getting close. Hope you're hungry!

TRIP HIGHLIGHT

❸ Pie Town

Yes, seriously, a town named after pie. And for good reason. They say you can find the best pies in the universe here (which makes you wonder what they've really been doing at the VLA). The **Pie-O-Neer Café** (☎575-772-2711; www.pie-o-neer.com; Hwy 60; slices from $5; ⏰11:30am-4pm Thu-Sat mid-Mar–Nov) just might prove their case. The pies are dee-lish, the soups and stews are homemade, and you'll be hard pressed to find another host as welcoming as Kathy Knapp – who advises you to call in advance to make sure they won't run out of pie before you get there, and just to check that it's even open!

On the second Saturday of September, Pie Town holds its annual **Pie Festival** (www. pietownfestival.com; ☺Sep), with baking and eating contests, the crowning of the Pie Queen, Wild West gunfight reenactments and horned toad races.

The Drive » Backtrack 20 miles to Datil, then turn south on Hwy 12. Curve into the Gila, past Reserve, which is a good lunch stop (p205), and head south on Hwy 180. Turn left at Hwy 159 and follow

it for nine vertiginous, slow-going miles on a route that's often impassable in winter. It's 130 miles total – let the carsick-prone ride shotgun!

---

❹ Mogollon

Once an important mining town, Mogollon is now a semi–ghost town inhabited by only a few antique and knickknack shops and, as is typical for middle-of-nowhere New Mexico, one proud little restaurant. This one is called the **Purple Onion** (Main St; mains $5-10; ☺9am-5pm Sat & Sun late May–mid-Oct), and it's as good as you'd hope after making the trip. You can poke around in spring and fall, but things here are mostly only open on summer weekends.

The Drive » Wind your way back to Hwy 180 and continue south for 3 miles, then turn left

on Hwy 174 and follow signs for the Catwalk.

---

❺ The Catwalk

Sixty-five miles northwest of Silver City, the Catwalk trail follows a suspended metal walkway through narrow Whitewater Canyon, where you can see the creek rushing beneath your feet. The Catwalk is wheelchair-accessible and great for kids. While some will find it disappointingly short, it offers a painless way to experience a bit of the Gila.

The Drive » Back on Hwy 180, head south for about 7 miles to the turn off for San Francisco Hot Springs (between mile markers 59 and 58) and continue to the parking lot.

---

❻ San Francisco Hot Springs

Down in the bottom of a cottonwood-shaded oasis, right along the gently flowing San Francisco River, are a couple of hot-spring pools. To reach them you've got to hike about 2 miles, gradually descending until you reach the canyon's edge, when the trail becomes steeper – but from there it's only a hundred feet or so down to the bottom. You've got to wade across the river to reach the springs, but poke

THE GILA

The 3.3 million acres of the Gila (hee-lah) cover eight mountain ranges, including the Mogollon, Tularosa, Blue and Black. This rugged country is just right for black bears, mountain lions and the reintroduced Mexican grey wolves (despite what the billboards around Reserve may say), plus four species of endangered fish including Gila trout. Really, it's no surprise that it was here that legendary conservationist Aldo Leopold spearheaded a movement to establish the world's first designated wilderness area, resulting in the creation of the Gila Wilderness in 1924; in 1980, the adjacent terrain to the east was also designated as wilderness and named after Leopold.

Whitewater Canyon

LOCAL KNOWLEDGE: HATE TO BACKTRACK?

If you're in Pie Town, you don't need to retrace your route to Datil to pick up Hwy 12. Instead, from Hwy 60, head south on the dirt road that's directly across from the junction with Hwy 603 North. Go straight on this for 6.2 miles, then take the left fork onto Green Gap Rd/A56. At the next fork 8.8 miles later, continue straight towards Horse Springs. Then 2 miles later, go left at an unsigned fork, down a hill (there's a mailbox at the fork). Stay on that for 28 miles, until you hit Hwy 12 at Horse Springs. (If you're trying to do this route backwards, there's no sign on Hwy 12 at Horse Spring, so look for the dirt road heading north at the windmill between mile markers 48 and 49.) In dry weather, two-wheel-drive vehicles should be OK; in wet weather, you'd definitely want a 4WD, if you attempt it at all.

around a bit and you'll find them. In summer it can be extremely hot at midday – and afternoon skies can suddenly brew with thunderstorms – so be sure to take drinking water and watch the weather.

The Drive » Continue on Hwy 180 south for 57 miles, all the way into Silver City.

- - - - - - - - - - - - - - - - - - -

TRIP HIGHLIGHT

❼ Silver City

The granddaddy of New Mexico's boom-bust-boom town success stories, Silver City's streets are dressed with a lovely mishmash of old brick and cast-iron Victorians and thick-walled red adobe buildings. The place still emits a Wild West air. Billy the Kid spent some of his childhood here, and a few of his haunts can still be found mixed in with the new coffee shops, quirky galleries and Italian ice-cream parlors gracing the historic downtown. Ensconced in an elegant house from 1881, the **Silver City Museum** (www.silvercitymuseum.org; 312 W Broadway; suggested donation $3; ⊘9am-4:30pm Tue-Fri, 10am-4pm Sat & Sun) features mining and household artifacts from Silver City's Victorian heyday, as well as stunning photographs of the aftermaths of some of the flash floods that ripped through town.

✕ ⊨ p197, p205

Eating & Sleeping

Socorro ❶

✕ M Mountain Coffee   Cafe $
(📞575-838-0809; 110 Manzanares St W; ⏰7am-6pm; 📶) A casual, comfy-chair coffee shop, with pastries, bowls of chile and ice cream.

✕ Owl Bar Cafe   Burgers $
(📞575-835-9946; 79 Main St, San Antonio; mains $5-13; ⏰8am-8pm Mon-Sat) Leave I-25 at exit 139, 10 miles south of Socorro, to sample the finest green chile cheeseburgers this side of Hatch. The potent mix of greasy beef, soft bun, sticky cheese, tangy chile, lettuce and tomato drips onto the plate in perfect burger fashion.

🛏 Socorro Old Town B&B   B&B $$
(📞575-418-9454; www.socorrobandb. qwestoffice.net; 114 W Baca St; r $125; ❄📶) Across from San Miguel Mission in the Old Town neighborhood, and housed in an extensively restored old adobe, this B&B has the feeling of a family home, with easygoing hosts and two clean, comfortable rooms.

🛏 Casa Blanca Bed & Breakfast   B&B $
(📞575-835-3027; www.casablanca bedandbreakfast.com; 13 Montoya, San Antonio; r $90-110; ⏰Oct-Mar; 📶) This three-room B&B offers basic rooms close to the Bosque del Apache National Wildlife Refuge (p154), 8 miles south of Socorro.

Reserve

✕ Adobe Café & Bakery   Bakery $
(📞575-533-6146; cnr Hwys 180 & 12; mains $9-12; ⏰7am-8pm Sun & Mon, to 3pm Wed-Fri) A culinary oasis in the middle of nowhere (aka '7 miles west of Reserve'). Aside from creative renditions of typical diner fare, the Adobe features venison burgers, elk sausage and some good vegetarian options.

Silver City ❼

✕ Buckhorn Saloon   Steak $$
(📞575-538-9911; www.buckhornsaloon andoperahouse.com; 32 Main St, Pinos Altos; mains $11-49; ⏰4-10pm Mon-Sat) Once part opera house, this venerable saloon is Silver City's most atmospheric dining option, offering serious steaks and seafood amid 1860s Wild West decor – try the fresh and tasty buffalo burgers. There's live music on weekend nights. It's located in Pinos Altos, 7 miles north of Silver City.

🛏 Murray Hotel   Historic Hotel $$
(📞575-956-9400; www.murray-hotel.com; 200 W Broadway; r $109-219; ❄📶) Built in 1938, this downtown hotel is more about art-deco panache than Wild West history; it's a classy spot, with five stories of tastefully retro-furnished rooms. Breakfast included.

Highway 53 to Acoma

19

Take the back road from Gallup to Acoma Pueblo, where you can meet wolves, explore lava caves and check out a mountain of old-school graffiti.

TRIP HIGHLIGHTS

200 miles

Acoma Pueblo
The ancient Sky City famed for its pottery

START
● Gallup

Ramah

Grants

②

● **El Morro National Monument**

⑤

Wild Spirit Wolf Sanctuary

⑥
FINISH

Zuni Pueblo
Native crafts and dances amid beautiful sandstone scenery

40 miles

El Malpals
Hike across basalt flows and into lava tubes

125 miles

**2 DAYS
200 MILES/322KM**

GREAT FOR...

BEST TIME TO GO
May to October, after the winds and before the snows.

📷 ESSENTIAL PHOTO
A howling wolf at Wild Spirit Wolf Sanctuary.

☑ BEST FOR CULTURE
Dances at Zuni Pueblo.

19 Highway 53 to Acoma

Your GPS may tell you that the best route from Gallup to Acoma is I-40, but humans are still (sometimes) smarter than their devices. Prove it by taking the back road, first to Zuni Pueblo, famous for its fetishes, then across rippling hills and alongside a massive lava field set against sandstone cliffs. Before hitting mesa-top Acoma Pueblo, you'll spend some time on the interstate – but not much.

❶ Gallup

The mother town on New Mexico's Mother Road seems stuck in time. Settled in 1881, when the railroad came through, Gallup had her heyday during the road-tripping 1950s, and many of the dilapidated old hotels, pawn shops and billboards, mixed in with today's galleries and trading posts, seem like they haven't changed much since the Eisenhower administration.

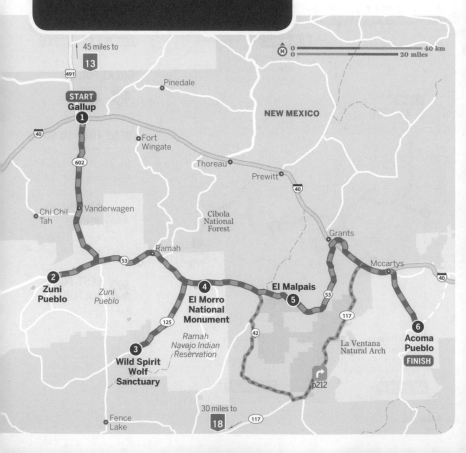

Modern-day Gallup is an interesting mix of Anglos and American Indians; it's not unusual to hear people speaking Navajo on their cell phones while buying groceries at the local Walmart. Tourism is limited mostly to Route 66 road-trippers and those in search of American Indian history and handicrafts: Route 66 runs straight through downtown Gallup's historic district and is lined with pretty, renovated light-red sandstone buildings housing dozens of kitschy souvenir shops as well as high-quality American Indian art.

Downtown, stretch your legs and check out the murals – some from the 1930s – painted on numerous buildings. Then stop into the **Ellis Tanner Trading Company** (📞505-863-4434;

LINK YOUR TRIP

13 **Georgia O'Keeffe Country**

Head north from Gallup along Hwy 491 for Navajo culture and ancient ruins.

18 **Into the Gila**

Take small roads south from Hwy 53 to Hwy 60, for rugged mountains, high-tech telescopes – and pie!

www.etanner.com; 1980 Hwy 602; ⊙8am-7pm Mon-Sat). The shop doubles as a sort of social gathering place for local Navajos and still operates a functional trade counter. If you don't have anything to swap, your dollar is good in the huge pawn room. Dig around for one of the unique pieces of turquoise jewelry tucked away behind a collection of vintage sheep-wool rugs.

✗ 🛏 p213

The Drive » This leg is 38 miles. Take Hwy 602 south, then fork right onto Indian Rte 4. Turn right on Hwy 53, toward Zuni.

- - - - - - - - - - - - - - - - - -

TRIP HIGHLIGHT

❷ Zuni Pueblo

Zuni is the name given by the Spanish to the pueblo known to the tribe that dwells there as Halona-weh, meaning 'red ant hill' – which symbolizes the center of the universe. Its artisans are famed for their jewelry and fetishes, and you can buy beautiful pieces at little shops throughout the town. For a good selection in one place, go to **Turquoise Village** (📞505-782-5521; www.turquoisevillage.com; 1184 Hwy 53; ⊙9:30am-5pm Mon-Sat).

The **A:shiwi A:wan Museum & Heritage Center** (📞505-782-4403; www.ashiwi-museum.org; Ojo Caliente Rd; admission by

donation; ⊙9am-5pm Mon-Fri) traces Zuni history with tribal artifacts and early photos. Nearby, the massive **Our Lady of Guadalupe Mission** features impressive locally painted murals of about 30 life-size kachinas (ancestral spirits). The church dates from 1629, although it has been rebuilt twice since then. The **Zuni Tourism Office** (📞505-782-7238; www.zunitourism.com; 1239 Hwy 53; tours $15; ⊙8:30am-5:30pm Mon-Fri, 10:30am-4pm Sat, noon-4pm Sun) is a good place to start your visit.

The most famous ceremony at Zuni is the all-night **Shalak'o ceremonial dance**, held on the first weekend in December and continuing for the next several days. The **Zuni Tribal Fair** (late August) features a powwow, local food and arts-and-crafts stalls. To observe any ceremony in Zuni, you must attend an orientation; call the tourist office for more information.

🛏 p213

The Drive » Take Hwy 53 east 8 miles past Ramah, which makes a good lunch stop, turn right onto Indian Rte 125, then go 7.8 miles and hang a right on Indian Rte 120. Your next stop is 4 miles up, on your left.

- - - - - - - - - - - - - - - - - -

❸ Wild Spirit Wolf Sanctuary

Animal-lovers won't want to miss the **Wild**

Spirit Wolf Sanctuary

(📞505-775-3032; www.
wildspiritwolfsanctuary.org;
378 Candy Kitchen Rd; tours
adult/child $10/5, tent/cabin
$15/125; 🕐 tours 11am,
12:30pm, 2pm & 3:30pm
Tue-Sun; 🐾). Home to
rescued captive-born
wolves and wolf-dog
mixes, the sanctuary
offers four interactive
walking tours per day,
where you walk with the
wolves – and get closer
than you imagined – that
roam the sanctuary's
large natural-habitat
enclosures. On the
quarter-mile walk you'll
learn everything you ever
wanted to know about
wolves, from behavior to
what they like to eat to
why they make terrible
watchdogs. For a special
'photo tour' ($50 per
person per hour) – when
you can actually get
inside the pens – make
reservations two weeks
in advance. Primitive
camping is available for
$15 per night, with all
the wolf howling you ever
wanted to hear included.
There's also a guest cabin
with two bedrooms, a big
loft and full kitchen.

The Drive » Having got your
wolf fix, get back on Hwy 53 and
head east for 3 miles.

---

④ El Morro National Monument

El Morro National Monument (📞505-783-4226; www.
nps.gov/elmo; Hwy 53; 🕐9am-
6pm Jun-Aug, to 5pm Sep-May),
also called Inscription
Rock, has been auto-
graphed by passers-by
since 1250, when the first
pueblo petroglyphs were
etched near the top of this
200ft hunk of sandstone
rising above a permanent
pool of water. Spanish
conquistadors, Anglo
pioneers and railway
surveyors all paused to
fill their canteens at the
200,000-gallon waterhole,
and when they stopped
many couldn't help
leaving a record of their
visit behind. It's quite a
sight – more than 2000
messages were carved
into the soft rock before
President Teddy Roosevelt
turned El Morro into
America's second national
monument. Of the two
trails that leave the
visitor center, the paved,
half-mile loop to **Inscription Rock** is wheelchair
accessible. The unpaved,
2-mile **Mesa Top loop
trail** requires a steep
climb to the pueblos. Trail
access ends one hour
before closing.

The Drive » Continue east for
about 19 miles on Hwy 53, past
the Cimarron Rose (p213).

TRIP HIGHLIGHT

⑤ El Malpais

The rugged **El Malpais
National Monument**
(www.nps.gov/elma; Hwy 53 &
Hwy 117), pronounced *el-
mahl-pie-ees* and mean-
ing 'bad land' in Spanish,
consists of almost 200
sq miles of lava flows

JOSEMARIA TOSCANO / SHUTTERSTOCK ©

Acoma Pueblo Sky City

bounded by Hwy 53 to the north and Hwy 117 to the east. Five major flows have been identified, the most recent pegged at only 2000 to 3000 years old. Prehistoric American Indians may have witnessed the final eruptions: local legends refer to 'rivers of fire.'

There are numerous trails here, though expect very strenuous, exposed hikes (bring a compass). Stop by the **Information Center** (☎505-783-4774; Hwy 53; ☺8:30am-4:30pm Mar-Sep) to pick up permits to explore nearby lava tubes – some of which are ice caves – or get the lowdown on possible hikes. Alternatively,

stop by the **Northwest New Mexico Visitor Center** (☎505-876-2783; south side of I-40, exit 85; ☺8am-5pm) in Grants.

🛏 p213

The Drive ≫ Hop back on I-40 and head east to exit 96. Turn right on Hwy 124, then left on Indian Rte 27. Go left again on Indian Rte 30 (Pueblo Rd), then right on Indian Rte 38 (Haaku Rd), and keep going for about 6 miles. The total distance is 54 miles.

TRIP HIGHLIGHT

6 Acoma Pueblo

Journeying to the top of Sky City is like climbing into another world. There are few more dramatic mesa-top locations – the

village sits 7000ft above sea level and 367ft above the surrounding plateau. It's one of the oldest continuously inhabited settlements in North America; people have lived at Acoma since the 11th century. In addition to a singular history and a dramatic location, it's also justly famous for its pottery, which is sold by individual artists on the mesa. There is a distinction between 'traditional' pottery (made with clay dug on the reservation) and 'ceramic' pottery (made elsewhere with inferior clay and simply painted by the artist), so ask the vendor.

Visitors can only go to Sky City on **guided tours** (☎800-747-0181; www.acomaskycity.org; Rte 38; tours adult/child $25/17; ☺hourly tours 8:30am-3:30pm Mar-Oct, 9:30am-2:30pm Sat & Sun Nov-Feb), which leave from the visitor center at the bottom of the mesa. Check the website or phone to confirm that it'll be open. Note that between July 10 and July 13 and either the first or second weekend in October, the pueblo is closed to visitors. Though you must ride the shuttle to the top of the mesa, you can choose to walk down the rock path to the visitor center on your own.

 p213

DETOUR: CHAIN OF CRATERS BACKCOUNTRY BYWAY

Start: 5 El Malpais

For a real backcountry adventure, follow the rugged Chain of Craters Backcountry Byway (aka County Rd 42) across the western and southern quadrants of the Malpais. The road connects with Hwy 53 a few miles west of El Malpais Information Center and bounces along for 33 miles until it hits Hwy 117, about 15 miles south of La Ventana arch. Along the way, it passes several craters, caves and lava tubes (reached by signed trails). Unless you paid for full coverage on your rental car, a high-clearance vehicle is highly recommended, but 4WD isn't (usually) necessary; in wet or snowy weather, the road might be impassable.

For further exploration, follow Hwy 117 north. Possible hikes here include the recommend Narrows Trail (8 miles), with views of La Ventana arch, and the Lava Falls Loop (1 mile), which traverses the now-frozen ripples, fissures, vents and craters of a lava flow.

Eating & Sleeping

Gallup ❶

🛏 El Rancho   Historic Hotel $$

(📞505-863-9311; www.elranchohotel.com;
1000 E Hwy 66; r $98-116, motel r $54-74;
P ❄ 🛜 ♿ 🐾) Opened in 1937, with a superb
lobby resembling a rustic hunting lodge,
Gallup's finest historic hotel quickly became
known as the 'home of the movie stars.' Big,
bright and decorated with eclectic Old West
fashions, rooms are named after former guests
including Humphrey Bogart and John Wayne.
There's also a good restaurant and bar, plus a
cheaper, modern motel wing.

🛏 Red Rock
Park Campground   Campground $

(📞505-722-3839; Churchrock, off Hwy 66;
tent/RV sites $10/20; 🐾) Pop your tent up in
this beautiful setting with easy access to tons
of hiking trails. Six miles east of town, it has
showers, flush toilets, drinking water and a
grocery store.

Zuni Pueblo ❷

🛏 Inn at Halona   Inn $

(📞505-782-4547; www.halona.com; 23b Pia
Mesa Rd; r from $75; P 🛜) This exceptionally
friendly inn, across from the museum behind
the Halona Plaza food store, is the only place
in New Mexico where visitors can stay in
the middle of a pueblo. Check out which of
its eight pleasant and very different rooms,
decorated with Zuni arts and crafts, fits your
fancy. Breakfast is served in the flagstone
courtyard in summer.

Highway 53

🛏 Cimarron Rose   B&B $$

(📞800-856-5776; www.cimarronrose.com;
689 Oso Ridge Rd; ste $145-210; 🛜) If you're
looking for a peaceful alternative to the chains
of Grants and Gallup, and want to stay green,
pay a visit to the Cimarron Rose. Conveniently
located on Hwy 53 between El Malpais and El
Morro in the Zuni Mountains, this B&B offers
three Southwestern-style suites, with full
kitchens, pine walls and hardwood floors.

El Malpais ❺

🛏 Joe Skeen
Campground   Campground $

(Hwy 117; camping free) Eleven miles south
of I-40 on Hwy 117, in El Malpais National
Conservation Area, this small, peaceful
campground offers vault toilets and picnic
tables but no water.

Acoma Pueblo ❻

🍴 Y'aak'a Cafe   American Indian $

(mains $6-9; 🕘9am-3pm) Try the Pueblo Taco,
served on fresh frybread. It's located in the Sky
City Cultural Center; grab a bite here before or
after your tour.

Billy the Kid Trail

20

Walk in the bootprints of Billy the Kid, the pawprints of Smokey Bear and the ET-prints (just roll with it...) of the Roswell aliens.

TRIP HIGHLIGHTS

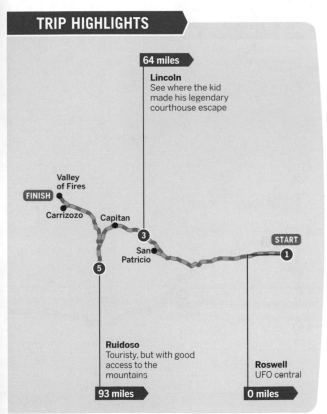

64 miles

Lincoln
See where the kid made his legendary courthouse escape

Valley of Fires

FINISH

Carrizozo

Capitan

3

San Patricio

5

START
1

Ruidoso
Touristy, but with good access to the mountains

93 miles

Roswell
UFO central

0 miles

2 DAYS
128 MILES/206KM

GREAT FOR...

BEST TIME TO GO
July to October, for the UFO Festival, hot summer days and fall foliage.

ESSENTIAL PHOTO
Pose with aliens in Roswell.

BEST FOR HISTORY
The legendary Wild West town, Lincoln.

20 Billy the Kid Trail

Crisscross classic outlaw country in a section of New Mexico that's rife with mystery. Did aliens crash near Roswell? Did Pat Garrett kill Billy the Kid? And how did they get that bear into pants and a hat, anyway? Here, the Rio Hondo carves a sweet canyon through the foothills of the Capitan Mountains, Sierra Blanca Peak towers over the Tularosa Basin and a lava field is open for exploration.

TRIP HIGHLIGHT

❶ Roswell

Whether or not you're a true believer, a visit to Roswell is worthwhile to experience one of America's most enduring, eclectic and fanatical pop-culture phenomena. Sure it's about as cheesy as it gets for some, but conspiracy theorists and *X-Files* fanatics descend from other worlds into Roswell in real seriousness. Oddly famous as both the country's largest producer of wool and its UFO capital, Roswell

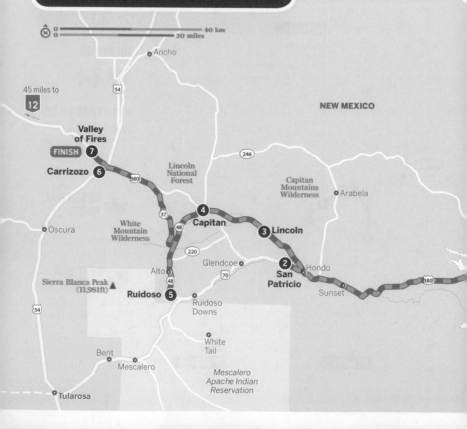

has built a tourist industry around the alleged July 1947 UFO crash, after which the military quickly closed the area and allowed no more information to filter out for several decades. Was it a flying saucer? The local convention and visitors bureau suggest that Roswell's special blend of climate and culture attracted touring space aliens who wanted a closer look. Decide for yourself at the **International UFO Museum & Research Center** (☎575-625-9495; www.roswellufomuseum.com; 114 N Main St; adult/child $5/2; ⏰9am-5pm), where original photographs and witness statements form the 1947 Roswell Incident Timeline and explain the 'great cover-up.' The library claims to have the most comprehensive UFO-related materials in the world, and we have no reason to be skeptical.

✕ 🛏 p221

The Drive » Take Hwy 70/380 west for almost 50 miles, across the plains and into the scenic Hondo Valley. At the fork where Hwys 70 and 380 split, go left onto Hwy 70 and travel about 4 miles.

----

❷ San Patricio

San Patricio, a tranquil country village along the Rio Ruidoso, boasts the kind of golden glow and gentle scenery that's been drawing artists to New Mexico for more than a century. Stop in at the **Hurd-La Rinconada Gallery** (☎800-658-6912; www.wyethartists.com; off Hwy 70; ⏰9am-5pm Mon-Sat), set on a huge spread with an orchard and a polo field, to see (and purchase) the work of classic New Mexican artist Peter Hurd and his son Michael, plus that of their relatives, the Wyeths. You can also stay overnight here in one of five lovely **casitas** ($140-250; 🛜🐾).

The Drive » Backtrack to Hwy 380 and turn left at the fork, heading west for 13 miles.

TRIP HIGHLIGHT

❸ Lincoln

More of a museum than a town, Lincoln is where the gun battle that turned Billy the Kid into a legend took place. Favoring authenticity over Hollywood stereotypes, Lincoln is about as close to 19th-century reality as it gets. Some say it's the best preserved Wild West town in America. Modern influences, such as souvenir stands,

NEW MEXICO **20** BILLY THE KID TRAIL

LINK YOUR TRIP

12 **El Camino Real & Turquoise Trail**

From Valley of Fires, continue west on 380 to hop on this historic route at Bosque del Apache National Wildlife Refuge.

16 **Las Cruces to Carlsbad Caverns**

Connect Roswell and Carlsbad to see the caverns, White Sands and more.

❶ Roswell
START

20
285
p218
70
246
285
35 miles to
16

4

are not allowed, and the main street has been designated the **Lincoln Historic Site** (📞575-653-4082; www.nmmonuments.org/lincoln; adult/child $7/free; 🕐Apr-Oct). It's a pretty cool place to get away from this century for an afternoon. Start at the **Anderson-Freeman Visitors Center** (🕐8:30am-4:30pm), where exhibits on the Buffalo soldiers, Apaches and the Lincoln County War explain the town's history. Then stroll the main street to the **Tunstall Store** (with a remarkable display of late 19th-century merchandise), the courthouse where the Kid famously shot his way to freedom, and **Dr Wood's house**, an intact turn-of-the-century doctor's home and office.

 p221

The Drive » Continue west for 12 miles on Hwy 380.

---

❹ Capitan

You've seen his likeness in state and national forests everywhere around the region. But did you know that Smokey Bear was also a real black bear? Once upon a time (back in 1950), a little cub was found clinging to a tree, paws charred from a 17,000-acre forest fire in the Capitan Mountains. What better name to give him than that of the famous cartoon bear that had been the symbol of fire prevention since 1944? Nursed back to health, Smokey spent the rest of his days in the National Zoo in Washington, DC, and became a living mascot. At the 3-acre **Smokey Bear Historical Park** (📞575-354-2748; 118 W Smokey Bear Blvd; adult/child $2/1; 🕐9am-4:30pm), in the village of Capitan, 12 miles west of Lincoln, you can see the bear's grave and learn all about forest fires. Every 4th of July, a **Smokey the Bear Stampede** features a parade, a rodeo, cookouts and other festivities. **Smokey Bear Days**, celebrated the first weekend in May, includes a street dance, a wood-carving contest, and craft and antique-car shows.

The Drive » Head uphill on Hwy 48 south for 17 miles, which skirts the eastern edge of the million-acre Lincoln National Forest – this is the part of the drive that really rocks in fall when the leaves put on a spectacular color show. The Sacramento Mountain range to the west of the highway adds to the scenic allure.

TRIP HIGHLIGHT

❺ Ruidoso

You want lively in these parts? You want Ruidoso. Downright bustling in the summer and big with punters at the racetrack, resortlike Ruidoso has an utterly pleasant climate thanks to its lofty and forested perch near the Sierra Blanca (11,981ft). Neighboring Texans and local New Mexicans escaping the summer heat of Alamogordo and Roswell are happy campers here (or more precisely, happy cabiners). The lovely Rio Ruidoso, a small creek with good fishing, runs through town. Summertime hiking and wintertime skiing at Ski Apache keep folks busy, as do a number of galleries.

DETOUR: BILLY'S GRAVE

Start: ❶ Roswell

If you're driving this route as a pilgrimage to Billy, then you might want to make the 84-mile trek north from Roswell to **Fort Sumner**, where Sheriff Pat Garret shot and killed Billy the Kid on July 14, 1881, when the outlaw was just 21 years old. Billy's grave is next to the poignant **Bosque Redondo Memorial** (📞575-355-2573; www.bosqueredondomemorial.com; 3647 Billy the Kid Rd; 🕐8:30am-4:30pm Wed-Mon). His tombstone is protected by an iron cage to keep 'souvenir hunters' from stealing it. Again.

Roswell International UFO Museum & Research Center

LOCAL KNOWLEDGE: BEST VISTAS

The best views for many miles are at the summit of **Sierra Blanca Peak** (11,981ft); to claim them, you'll have to leave the car and set out on foot for a day. Park in the smaller lot at Ski Apache, and set out on Trail 15. Follow signs west and south along Trails 25 and 78 to the top of Lookout Mountain (11,580ft). From there, an obvious beaten path continues due south for 1.25 miles up Sierra Blanca. On the way up you'll gain about 2000ft of elevation; the round-trip hike is just over 9 miles long. It's best done from June to October. The **ranger station** (575-257-4095; www.fs.usda.gov/lincoln; 901 Mechem Dr; 8am-4pm Mon-Fri, plus Sat in summer) in Ruidoso has more information.

The **Hubbard Museum of the American West** (575-378-4142; www.hubbardmuseum.org; 26301 Hwy 70; adult/child $7/2; 9am-5pm Thu-Mon;) displays more than 10,000 Western-related items including Old West stagecoaches and American Indian pottery, and works by Frederic Remington and Charles M Russell. An impressive array of horse-related displays, including a collection of saddles and the Racehorse Hall of Fame, lures horse-lovers.

Ruidoso Downs (575-378-4431; www.raceruidoso.com; 26225 Hwy 70; grandstand seats free; Fri-Mon late May-early Sep) has weekend horse racing, including Labor Day's All American Futurity, the world's richest quarter-horse race, with a purse of $3 million.

p221

The Drive » Take Hwy 48 north, then turn left onto Hwy 37. At Hwy 380, hang a left, then another left once you reach Hwy 54/Central Ave in Carrizozo. In total, it's around 30 miles.

---

6 Carrizozo

Sitting where the Sacramento Mountains hit the Tularosa Basin, Carrizozo is worth a quick stop to peruse historic 12th St, once the town's main axis. Take a look into **Gallery 408** (575-648-2598; www.gallery408.com; 408 12th St; 10am-5pm Mon, Fri & Sat, noon-5pm Sun). In addition to the work of a number of regional artists, you can see what remains of the herd of Painted Burros – a local public sculpture project similar to the Cow Parades of Chicago and New York, but on a slightly smaller scale. Some have pun-tastic names, like the Asstronomer, its body decorated with the night sky. Proceeds from donkey sales benefit the local animal shelter, Miracles Paws for Pets.

The Drive » Backtrack to Hwy 380 then head west a few miles to the sprawling slab of basalt. You can't miss it.

---

7 Valley of Fires

Four miles west of Carrizozo, explore the rocky blackness of a 125-sq-mile lava flow that's 160ft deep in the middle. A 0.6-mile nature trail at **Valley of Fires Recreation Area** (575-648-2241; Hwy 380; per vehicle 1/2+ people $3/5) is well paved, easy for kids and marked with informative signs describing the geology of the volcanic remains. You're also allowed to hike off-trail, simply cutting cross-country over the flow as you like to create your own adventure. There are campsites and shaded picnic tables near the visitor center.

p221

Eating & Sleeping

Roswell ❶

✕ Cowboy Cafe
Diner $

(📞575-622-6363; 1120 E 2nd St; mains $6-15; 🕑6am-2pm) One of the few truly local joints left in town, this is a good option for a breakfast before hitting the UFO museum or the road.

🛏 Heritage Inn
Historic Hotel $$

(📞575-748-2552; www.artesiaheritageinn.com; 209 W Main St, Artesia; r incl breakfast from $99; ❄ @ 🛜) The nicest place to stay hereabouts is not in Roswell, but in sleepy downtown Artesia, 36 miles south towards Carlsbad. If you're in the mood for slightly upscale digs – bearing in mind you're in southeastern New Mexico – this Victorian-era establishment offers 11 Old West–style rooms. Half have both bath and shower, the rest a shower only.

🛏 Bottomless Lakes State Park
Campground $

(📞575-624-6058; www.emnrd.state.nm.us; 545A Bottomless Lakes Rd; tent/RV sites $8/14) The seven lakes at this much-loved park – technically they're sinkholes – provide welcome relief in summer (day-use per vehicle $5). Waterfront campgrounds range from primitive campsites to the developed site at Lea Lake, the only place you're allowed to swim, which has bathrooms and showers. They're 10 miles east of Roswell on Hwy 380, then 5 miles south on Hwy 409.

Lincoln ❸

✕ Smokey Bear Restaurant
Diner $

(📞575-354-2257; www.smokeybearrestaurant.com; mains $5-10; 🕑6am-8pm) This little diner next to the Smokey Bear park (p218) serves all of Smokey's personal favorites – who knew bears were partial to chicken quesadillas and breakfast burritos?

Ruidoso ❺

✕ Casa Blanca
New Mexican $$

(📞575-257-2495; 501 Mechem Dr; mains $8-27; 🕑11am-9pm Mon-Thu, to 10pm Fri & Sat, to 8pm Sun) Dine on Southwestern cuisine in a renovated Spanish-style house or on the pleasant patio in the summer. It's hard to go wrong with the New Mexican plates, but it's also got big burgers and chicken-fried steak.

✕ Cornerstone Bakery
Cafe $

(📞575-257-1842; www.cornerstonebakerycafe.com; 1712 Sudderth Dr; mains $5.50-11; 🕑7am-3pm Mon-Fri, to 4pm Sat & Sun; 🖋) Totally irresistible, hugely popular local bakery and cafe, where everything, from the breads, pastries and espresso to the omelets and croissant sandwiches, is just the way it should be. Stick around long enough and the Cornerstone may become your morning touchstone.

🛏 Sitzmark Chalet
Hotel $

(📞575-257-4140; www.sitzmark-chalet.com; 627 Sudderth Dr; r from $87; ❄ 🛜) This ski-themed chalet offers 17 simple but nice rooms. Picnic tables, grills and an eight-person hot tub are welcome perks.

🛏 Inn of the Mountain Gods
Casino Hotel $$

(📞800-545-9011; www.innofthemountaingods.com; 287 Carrizo Canyon Rd; r from $109; ❄ 🛜 🏊) This luxury, lakeside casino resort on the Mescalero Apache Reservation offers surprisingly low online rates. Gamblers can feed slots, while guided fishing, paddleboat rentals, a championship golf course and horseback riding are just a concierge call away. Several restaurants, a nightclub and a sports bar are also on-site. It's fun for a night or two.

Valley of Fires ❼

🛏 Valley of Fires Campground
Campground $

(Hwy 380; tent/RV sites $7/18) Camp beside the lava flow, with easy access to hikes.

STRETCH YOUR LEGS SANTA FE

Start/Finish Santa Fe Plaza

Distance 2.5 miles/4km

Duration Two to four hours

The only way to see the best of Santa Fe is on foot, strolling through its old adobe soul and into its renowned museums, churches, art galleries and historic buildings.

Take this walk on Trips

1 11 12

New Mexico Museum of Art

At the plaza's northwest corner, the **New Mexico Museum of Art** (☎505-476-5072; www.nmartmuseum.org; 107 W Palace Ave; adult/child $12/free; ⏲10am-5pm Tue-Sun) features collections of the Taos Society of Artists, Santa Fe Society of Artists and other legendary collectives – it's a who's who of the geniuses who put this dusty town on par with Paris and New York.

The Walk » Cross Lincoln Ave.

Palace of the Governors

Built in 1610, the **Palace of the Governors** (☎505-476-5100; www.palaceofthegovernors.org; 105 W Palace Ave; adult/child $12/free; ⏲10am-5pm, closed Mon Oct-May) is one of the oldest public buildings in the USA. It displays a handful of historic relics, but most of its holdings are now shown in an adjacent exhibition space called the **New Mexico History Museum**, a glossy, 96,000-sq-ft expansion that opened in 2009.

The Walk » Browse the selection of American Indian pottery and jewelry, talking to the artisans about their work. Then cross Palace Ave.

Shiprock

In a 2nd-floor loft at the northeast corner of the Plaza, **Shiprock** (www.shiprocktrading.com; 53 Old Santa Fe Trail; ⏲10am-5pm Mon-Fri, noon-5pm Sat) has an extraordinary collection of Navajo rugs. Run by a fifth-generation Southwest Indian art trader, its vintage pieces are the real deal.

The Walk » Walk one block south, then turn left on E San Francisco St. If you're hungry, first make a pit stop across the plaza at the casual Plaza Cafe.

St Francis Cathedral

Jean Baptiste Lamy was sent to Santa Fe by the pope with orders to tame the Wild Western outpost town through culture and religion. Convinced that the town needed a focal point for religious life, he began construction of **St Francis Cathedral** (www.cbsfa.org; 131 Cathedral

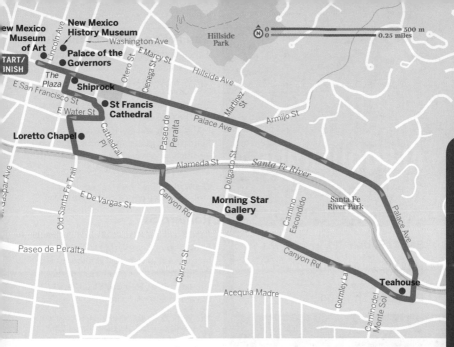

Pl; ⏰8:30am-4:30pm) in 1869. Inside is a small chapel that houses the oldest Madonna statue in North America.

The Walk » Just south of the cathedral, turn right on Water St, to the corner with Old Santa Fe Trail.

Loretto Chapel

Modeled on Sainte-Chapelle in Paris, **Loretto Chapel** (☎505-982-0092; www.lorettochapel.com; 207 Old Santa Fe Trail; $3; ⏰9am-5pm Mon-Sat, 10:30am-5pm Sun) was built between 1873 and 1878 for the Sisters of Loretto, the first nuns to come to New Mexico. Today the chapel is a museum popular for **St Joseph's Miraculous Staircase** – which seems to defy the laws of physics by standing with no visible support.

The Walk » Walk south and turn left on E Alameda St. Turn right on Paseo de Peralta, then left onto Canyon Rd – the legendary heart of Santa Fe's gallery scene.

Morning Star Gallery

Of all the Canyon Rd shops dealing in American Indian antiquities, **Morning Star** (☎505-982-8187; www.morningstargallery.com; 513 Canyon Rd; ⏰9am-5pm Mon-Sat) remains the best: weaving, jewelry, beadwork, kachina (Hopi spirit) dolls and even a few original ledger drawings are just some of the stars at this stunning gallery, which specializes in pre-WWII Plains Indian ephemera. Some artifacts here are finer than those in most museums and sell for hundreds of thousands of dollars.

The Walk » Meander on down Canyon Rd, stopping into whichever galleries catch your eye.

Teahouse

Prepare for a dilemma – at the **Teahouse** (☎505-992-0972; www.teahousesantafe.com; 821 Canyon Rd; ⏰9am-9pm; 📶), you'll be confronted with the list of 150 types of tea. There's coffee too, and a great food menu, from baked polenta with poached eggs to wild mushroom porcini panini to grilled salmon salad. And freshly baked desserts. It's a perfect last stop on Canyon Rd.

The Walk » Turn left on Palace Ave and walk back to the plaza.

STRETCH
YOUR LEGS
ALBUQUERQUE

Start/Finish Old Town Plaza

Distance 1 mile/1.6km

Duration Three hours

Albuquerque's Old Town Plaza is touristy for a reason: it's the one place in the city that's still got a historic ambiance, and it's easy to walk between its excellent museums and galleries (and cheesy souvenir shops, too).

Take this walk on Trips

San Felipe de Neri Church

The adobe **San Felipe de Neri Church** (www.sanfelipedeneri.org; Old Town Plaza; ⏰7am-5:30pm daily, museum 9:30am-5pm Mon-Sat) dates from 1793 and is Old Town's most famous photo op. Check out the pressed-tin ceiling inside. To really catch the spirit here, attend a Spanish-language mass at 8:30am on Sundays or a weekday mass (in English) at 7am, except Thursdays.

The Walk » Stroll down the west side of the plaza to the southwestern corner with Romero St.

Romero St

Peruse the **galleries** that line both sides of the street, featuring arts and crafts by regional artists and Southwestern Indian tribes. For creative ceramics, you can't beat **Romero St Gallery** (106 Romero St; ⏰10am-5pm).

The Walk » Head back to S Plaza St and turn right. You'll pass Treasure House Books, with books on just about any subject related to New Mexico. Then turn right on San Felipe St.

American International Rattlesnake Museum

Probably the most interesting and unique museum in town, the **American International Rattlesnake Museum** (📞505-242-6569; www.rattlesnakes.com; 202 San Felipe St NW; adult/child $5/3; ⏰10am-6pm Mon-Sat, 1-5pm Sun Jun-Aug, 11:30am-5:30pm Mon-Fri, 10am-6pm Sat, 1-5pm Sun Sep-May) hosts more species of rattlesnake than any other single place in the world. Looking at them up close (behind glass), you may be surprised at how beautiful they are.

The Walk » Head north on San Felipe St. Check out the work of the artisans under the portal opposite the plaza, then continue on and turn right into the alley at Old Town Antiques.

Our Lady of Guadalupe Chapel

This chapel is small, and it's not historical, but it's worth going in anyway; the entries in the notebooks are moving testimonies of faith in times of hardship. Some say a ghost or spirit resides here...

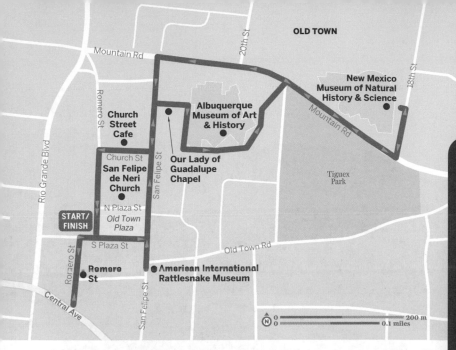

The Walk » Continue down the alley and turn right, circling around to the entrance of the Albuquerque Museum of Art & History.

Albuquerque Museum of Art & History

Conquistador armor and weaponry are highlights at the excellent **Albuquerque Museum of Art & History** (☎505-242-4600; www.cabq.gov/museum; 2000 Mountain Rd NW; adult/child $4/1; ⊙9am-5pm Tue-Sun), where visitors can get a glimpse of the city's tricultural American Indian, Hispanic and Anglo past. There's also an engaging gallery featuring the work of New Mexican artists. Don't forget to wander around the diverse array of sculptures outside.

The Walk » Walk across Mountain Rd and around the corner to the museum's entrance on 18th St.

New Mexico Museum of Natural History & Science

The **New Mexico Museum of Natural History & Science** (☎505-841-2800; www. nmnaturalhistory.org; 1801 Mountain Rd NW; adult/child $8/5; ⊙9am-5pm Wed-Mon; 👪) features an Evolator (evolution elevator), which transports visitors through 38 million years of New Mexico's geologic and evolutionary history. Best is the exhibit about the development of personal computing, focusing on the early days when Bill Gates operated out of Albuquerque – plus a room where you can play Pong projected on a big wall.

The Walk » Walk back across Mountain Rd and down San Felipe. Turn right on Church St.

Church Street Cafe

Grab a table at the **Church St Cafe** (☎505-247-8522; www.churchstreetcafe.com; 2111 Church St NW; mains $9-17; ⊙8am-9pm Mon–Sat, to 4pm Sun) and get your chile fix for the day. The food's the best around the plaza area, and the cafe is historic and huge, with a nice patio. Try the Spanish hot chile dip or the veggie fajitas.

The Walk » The plaza is just a block to the south.

Texas

TEXAS IS BIG – AND WE MEAN BIG.
The only way to truly appreciate its size is to hit the road and discover what's out there in those wide open spaces. The cities have tons to offer, but Texas does 'small town' like few other states, with friendly locals, historic buildings, quirky claims to fame and an easygoing way of life everywhere you look.

So what's your pleasure? Fields of wildflowers and rolling hills in the land of Lady Bird Johnson? Beaches and seafood in coastal towns along the Gulf? An epic journey from the Mexico border to the Texas panhandle? Or intriguing desert landscapes with surprising stops along the way, culminating in an enormous national park? Whatever route you choose, saddle up for adventure on a grand scale.

Big Bend National Park (Trip 22)

Texas Trips

DON'T MISS

Waring–Welfare Drive

When the wildflowers are in bloom, take this short but worthwhile detour on the way to Comfort, TX, in Trip 21

Prada Marfa

This roadside art installation is dramatically set against the backdrop of dusty West Texas; find it on Trip 22

Beer Drinking

Grab an ice-cold Shiner Bock and join the locals at Gruene Hall or on the Terlingua Porch in Trips 21 22

Goliad

Although not as well remembered as the Alamo, this fort has an equally important place in Texas history. See it in Trip 23

Miss Hattie's Bordello Museum

You can tell everyone you visited a notorious Texas brothel at this only slightly risqué stop on Trip 24

Goliad Presidio La Bahia (Trip 23)

Classic Trip

Hill Country

Gently rolling hills are blanketed with wildflowers and dotted with vineyards. Friendly locals enjoy an easy way of life, with dance halls, lazy rivers and local art adding to the fun.

21

TRIP HIGHLIGHTS

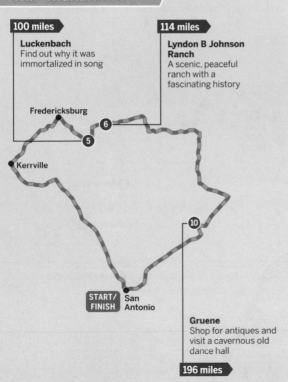

100 miles

Luckenbach
Find out why it was immortalized in song

114 miles

Lyndon B Johnson Ranch
A scenic, peaceful ranch with a fascinating history

Fredericksburg

5 **6**

Kerrville

10

START/ FINISH San Antonio

Gruene
Shop for antiques and visit a cavernous old dance hall

196 miles

2–5 DAYS
229 MILES/369KM

GREAT FOR...

BEST TIME TO GO
In March and April for wildflower season.

📷 ESSENTIAL PHOTO

Bluebonnets – pose your kids or yourself in a field full of wildflowers.

☑ BEST FOR CULTURE

Two-stepping at Texas' oldest dance hall in Gruene.

Texas bluebonnets

231

21 Hill Country

In March and early April when wildflowers are blooming, this is one of the prettiest drives in all of Texas – perfect for a day trip or a meandering and low-stress vacation. Along this route, you can rummage through antique stores, listen to live music, dig in to a plate of barbecue, and learn about the US president who called this area home.

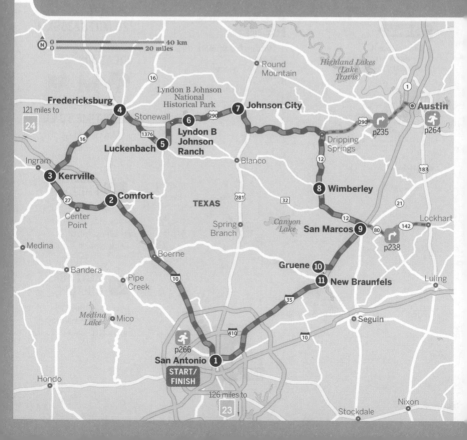

❶ San Antonio

While sprawling San Antonio isn't part of the Hill Country, it's a great launching point for your trip. Don't miss the lovely, European-style River Walk, a paved canal that winds its way through downtown and is lined with colorful cafes, hotel gardens and stone footbridges. It stretches north to the museum district and south to the missions, adding pretty mileage for walking and cycling. For the best overview, hop on a Rio San Antonio cruise (p266).

Whatever you do, pay your respects at the **Alamo** (p266), the beloved historical site where revolutionaries fought for Texas' independence from Mexico.

The Drive ≫ Ready to get out of town? Head northwest on I-10 to get to Comfort, less

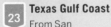

LINK YOUR TRIP

23 **Texas Gulf Coast**
From San Antonio, drive 143 miles south along Hwy 37 to reach the coastal town of Corpus Christi.

24 **Heart of Texas**
From Kerrville, travel 149 miles northwest to San Angelo.

than an hour from downtown San Antonio. When the wildflowers are blooming, detouring north on Waring-Welfare Rd then back on TX 473 makes a nice scenic drive.

❷ Comfort

Remarkably under the tourist radar, Comfort is a 19th-century German settlement and perhaps the most idyllic of the Hill Country bunch, with rough-hewn limestone homes from the late 1800s and a beautifully restored historic center in the area around High and 8th Sts.

Shopping for antiques is the number-one activity, but you'll also find a few good restaurants, a winery and, as the town's name suggests, an easy way of life. Start at the **Comfort Antique Mall** (📞830-995-4678; www.visitcomfortantiquemall.com; 734 High St; ⏰10am-5pm), where you can pick up a map of antique stores, or go to the Comfort chamber of commerce website (www.comfort-texas.com) to discover your options.

🛏 p239

The Drive ≫ The interstate is a straight shot, but we prefer the back road of TX 27 west to Kerrville that takes you through serene farmland.

❸ Kerrville

The Hill Country can feel a bit fussy at times, but

not Kerrville. What it lacks in historic charm, it makes up for in size, offering plenty of services for travelers, as well as easy access to kayaking, canoeing and swimming on the Guadalupe River. Stretch your legs on the new **River Trail** (www.kerrvilletx.gov; ⏰dawn-dusk; 🐾), which runs alongside the Guadalupe River for several miles. The best place to hop in the water is **Kerrville-Schreiner Park** (📞830-257-5300; www.kerrvilletx.gov; 2385 Bandera Hwy; adult/child 3-12yr/senior $4/1/2; ⏰office 8am-5pm, day use to 10pm).

Check out an eye-catching collection of cowboy art at the **Museum of Western Art** (📞830-896-2553; www.museumofwesternart.com; 1550 Bandera Hwy; adult/student/child under 8yr $7/5/free; ⏰10am-4pm Tue-Sat). The building itself is beautiful, with hand-made mesquite parquet floors and unique vaulted domes overhead.

🍴 p239

The Drive ≫ Take TX 16 northeast of town for half an hour to get to Fredericksburg.

❹ Fredericksburg

The unofficial capital of the Hill Country, Fredericksburg is a 19th-century German settlement that specializes in 'quaint.' The town packs a lot of charm into a relatively small amount of space, with a boggling array of welcoming inns and B&Bs and a main street lined with historic buildings housing German restaurants, biergartens, antique stores and shops. The informative **National Museum of the Pacific War** (☎830-997-8600; www. pacificwarmuseum.org; 340 E Main St; adult/child $14/7; ☺9am-5pm) spotlights the Pacific Theater in WWII. Admiral Chester Nimitz, Commander of the US fleet there during the war, grew up in Fredericksburg.

Many of the shops are typical tourist-town offerings, but there are enough interesting stores to make it fun to wander. Plus, the town is a great base for checking out the surrounding

peach orchards and vineyards. A few miles east of town, **Wildseed Farms** (☎830-990-1393; www.wildseedfarms.com; 100 Legacy Dr; ☺9:30am-5pm) has cultivated fields of wildflowers and sells seed packets along with wildflower-related gifts.

🛏 p239

The Drive » Five miles southeast of town on Hwy 290, turn right on Ranch Rd 1376 and follow it 4.5 miles into Luckenbach. There are only a handful of buildings here, so don't worry that the actual town is somewhere else.

- - - - - - - - - - - - - - - - - -

TRIP HIGHLIGHT

❺ Luckenbach

You won't find a more laid-back place than Luckenbach, where the main activity is sitting at a picnic table under an old oak tree with a cold bottle of Shiner Bock and listening to guitar pickers (who are often accompanied by roosters). Come prepared

to relax and get to know some folks while basking in the small-town atmosphere.

Start at the old trading post established back in 1849 – now the **Luckenbach General Store** (☎830-997-3224; www.luckenbachtexas.com; 412 Luckenbach Town Loop; ☺9am-11pm Sun-Thu, to midnight Fri, to 1am Sat), which also serves as the local post office, saloon and community center. Out back you'll find the picking circle, and there's often live music on the weekends in the old dance hall; go online to check out the town's music schedule (www. luckenbachtexas.com).

The Drive » Take Luckenbach Rd back north to Hwy 290. The LBJ Ranch is just 7 miles down and the entrance is right off the highway.

- - - - - - - - - - - - - - - - - -

TRIP HIGHLIGHT

❻ Lyndon B Johnson Ranch

You don't have to be a history buff to appreciate the family home of the 36th president of the United States. Now the **LBJ Ranch** (☎national park visitor center 830-868-7128, state park visitor center 830-644-2252; www.nps.gov/lyjo; Hwy 290, Stonewall; tour adult/child under 18yr $3/free; ☺ranch grounds 9am-5:30pm, house tours 10am-4:30pm), this beautiful piece of Texas land is where Lyndon B Johnson was born, lived and died.

SCENIC DRIVE: WILDFLOWER TRAILS

You know spring has arrived in Texas when you see cars pulling up roadside and families climbing out to take the requisite picture of their kids surrounded by bluebonnets, Texas' state flower. From March to April in Hill Country, Indian paintbrushes, winecups and bluebonnets are at their peak.

Check the **Wildflower Hotline** (☎800-452-9292) to find out what's blooming where. Taking Rte 16 and FM 1323, north from Fredericksburg and east to Willow City, is usually a good route.

The park includes the Johnson birthplace, the one-room schoolhouse where he briefly attended school and a neighboring farm that now serves as a living history museum. The centerpiece of the park is the ranch house where LBJ and Lady Bird lived and where he spent so much time during his presidency that it became known as the 'Texas White House.'

You can also see the Johnson family cemetery, where LBJ and Lady Bird are both buried under sprawling oak trees.

Stop by the visitor center to get your free park permit and a map.

The Drive » LBJ's childhood home is just 15 minutes east on Hwy 290.

⑦ Johnson City

You might assume Johnson City was named after President Johnson, but the bragging rights go to James Polk Johnson, a town settler back in the late 1800s. The fact that James Johnson's grandson went on to become president of the United States was just pure luck.

Here you'll find **Lyndon B Johnson's Boyhood Home** (☏830-868-7128; www.nps.gov/lyjo; 200 E Elm St; ☺tours half hourly 9am-noon & 1-4:30pm), which Johnson himself had restored for personal posterity. Park rangers from the **visitor center**

DETOUR: AUSTIN

Start: ⑦ Johnson City

Since this trip is all about winding your way through the Hill Country, we didn't list Austin as a stop. After all, it warrants its own whole trip, which we hope your central Texas itinerary already includes.

However, we'd be remiss if we didn't mention that when you get to Dripping Springs, you're only half an hour from the Texas state capital. While you're there, do some exploring and stretch your legs with a walking tour (p264).

(☏830 868 7128; www.nps.gov/lyjo; 100 E Ladybird Lane, cnr E Ladybird Lane & Ave G; ☺9am-5pm) – where you can also find local information and exhibits on the president and first lady – offer free guided tours every half-hour that meet on the front porch. On the surface, it's just an old Texas house, but it's fascinating when you think about the boy who grew up there.

The Drive » Follow Hwy 290 south toward Blanco then east toward Dripping Springs. At Dripping Springs, turn right on Ranch Rd 12 towards Wimberley.

⑧ Wimberley

A popular weekend spot for Austinites, this artists community gets absolutely bonkers during summer weekends – especially on the first Saturday of each month from March to December, when

local art galleries, shops and craftspeople set up booths for **Wimberley Market Days**, a bustling collection of live music, food and more than 475 vendors at Lion's Field on RR 2325. Keep an eye out for the 50 painted cowboy boots scattered around town (www.bootifulwimberley.com).

For excellent scenic views of the surrounding limestone hills, take a drive on FM 32, otherwise known as the Devil's Backbone. From Wimberley, head south on RR 12 to FM 32, then turn right toward Canyon Lake. The road gets steeper, then winds out onto a craggy ridge – the 'backbone' – with a 360-degree vista.

Afterwards, cool off at Wimberley's famous **Blue Hole** (☏512-660-9111; www.cityofwimberley.com; 100 Blue Hole Lane; adult/child 4-12yr/under 4 $9/5/free; ☺park 8am-dusk, swimming area 10am-6pm Sat & Sun May, daily

Classic Trip

WHY THIS IS A CLASSIC TRIP
AMY BALFOUR, WRITER

An easy drive from Austin and San Antonio, the Hill Country will lure you in with its natural beauty and easygoing but festive spirit. You can drive this entire loop in under five hours, but what's the rush? The small towns here hide historic treasures and culinary finds, plus there's a new gorgeous view around every bend. You'll be glad if you decide to linger.

Above: Performers at Luckenbach
Left: Old license plates
Right: Country store, Wimberley

Jun-Aug), one of the Hill Country's best swimming holes. It's a privately owned spot in the calm, shady and crystal-clear waters of Cypress Creek.

 p239

The Drive ›› Keep going south on Ranch Rd 12; San Marcos is about 15 minutes southeast through some more (mostly) undeveloped countryside.

----

9 San Marcos

Around central Texas, 'San Marcos' is practically synonymous with 'outlet malls.' Bargain shoppers can make a full day of it at two side-by-side shopping meccas. It's not exactly in keeping with the spirit of the Hill Country, but it's a popular enough activity that we had to point it out.

The fashion-oriented **San Marcos Premium Outlets** (☏512-396-2200; www.premiumoutlets. com; 3939 S IH-35, exit 200; ◷10am-9pm Mon-Sat, to 7pm Sun) is enormous – and enormously popular – with 140 name-brand outlets. Across the street, **Tanger Outlets** (☏512-396-7446; www.tangeroutlet. com/sanmarcos; 4015 S IH-35, exit 200; ◷9am-9pm Mon-Sat, 10am-7pm Sun) has more modest offerings, with brands that aren't that expensive to start with, but it's still fun to hunt for deals.

The Drive ›› Shoot 12 miles down I-35 to the turnoff for

Canyon Lake. Gruene is just a couple of miles off the highway.

TRIP HIGHLIGHT

❿ Gruene

Get a true taste of Texas at **Gruene Hall** (☎830-606-1281; www.gruenehall.com; 1280 Gruene Rd;

🕑11am-midnight Mon-Fri, 10am-1am Sat, 10am-9pm Sun), a dance hall where folks have been congregating since 1878, making it Texas' oldest. It opens early, so you can stop by anytime to toss back a longneck, two-step on the well-worn wooden dance floor or play horseshoes out in the yard. There's only a cover charge on weekend nights and when big acts are playing, so at least stroll through and soak up the vibe.

The town is loaded with antique stores and shops selling housewares, gifts and souvenirs, and **Old Gruene Market Days** are held the third weekend of the month, February through November, and the first weekend of December.

🍴 🛏 p239

The Drive » You don't even have to get back on the interstate; New Braunfels is just 3 miles south.

⓫ New Braunfels

The historic town of New Braunfels was the first German settlement in Texas. In summer, visitors flock here to float down the Guadalupe River in an inner tube – a Texas summer tradition. There are lots of outfitters in town, like **Rockin' R River Rides** (☎830-629-9999; www.rockinr.com; 1405 Gruene Rd; tube rental $20). Their rental prices include shuttle service, and for an additional fee they can also hook you up with an ice chest to keep your drinks cold and a tube to float it on.

🍴 p239

The Drive » From New Braunfels it's 32 miles on I-35 back to San Antonio.

DETOUR: LOCKHART

Start: ❾ San Marcos

People travel from all over the state to dig into brisket, sausage and ribs in Lockhart, officially designated in 1999 as the Barbecue Capital of Texas. Lucky for you, you only have to detour 18 miles to experience the smoky goodness. You can eat very well for under $15 at the following places:

Black's Barbecue (☎512-398-2712; www.blacksbbq.com; 215 N Main St; sandwiches $10-13, brisket per pound $16.50; 🕑10am-8pm Sun-Thu, to 8:30pm Fri & Sat) A longtime Lockhart favorite since 1932, with sausage so good Lyndon Johnson had them cater a party at the nation's capital.

Kreuz Market (☎512-398-2361; www.kreuzmarket.com; 619 N Colorado St; brisket per pound $16.49; 🕑10:30am-8pm Mon-Sat, to 6pm Sun) Serving Lockhart since 1900, the barn-like Kreuz Market uses a dry rub, which means you shouldn't insult them by asking for barbecue sauce – they don't serve it, and the meat doesn't need it.

Smitty's Market (☎512-398-9344; www.smittysmarket.com; 208 S Commerce St; brisket per pound $14.90; 🕑7am-6pm Mon-Fri, to 6:30pm Sat, 9am-6:30pm Sun) The blackened pit room and homely dining room are all original (knives used to be chained to the tables). Ask them to trim off the fat on the brisket if you're particular about that.

Eating & Sleeping

Comfort ❷

🛏 Hotel Faust — B&B $$

(📞830-995-3030; www.hotelfaust.com; 717 High St; r $139-169, 2-bedroom cottage $250; ⊜✳🛜) For some true historic charm, spend the night at Hotel Faust. The limestone building dates from the late 1800s, but the rooms have all been gutted and beautifully restored. For a special treat, stay in their Ingenhuett Log Cabin ($210 per night), built in the 1820s and moved to its present location from Kentucky.

Kerrville ❸

✗ Francisco's — American $$$

(📞830-257-2995; www.franciscos-restaurant. com; 201 Earl Garrett St; lunch mains $7.25-10, dinner mains $13-38; ⏲11am-3pm Mon-Sat & 5:30-9pm Thu-Sat) Colorful, bright and airy, this bistro and sidewalk cafe is housed in an old limestone building in the historic district. It's packed at lunch, and is one of the swankiest places in town for a weekend dinner.

Fredericksburg ❹

🛏 Cotton Gin Village — Cabin $$

(📞830-990-8381; www.cottonginlodging. com; 2805 S Hwy 16; cabins incl breakfast $229; 🅿🛜) Rustic on the outside, posh on the inside. Oh yes, we like it here. Just south of town, this cluster of stone-and-timber cabins offers guests a supremely private stay away from both the crowds and the other guests. Cabins come with a stone wood-burning fireplace. Romantic getaway? Start packing.

Wimberley ❽

✗ Leaning Pear — American $

(📞512-847-7327; www.leaningpear.com; 111 River Rd; lunch mains $7-13, dinner mains $11-24; ⏲11am-9pm Tue-Sat, to 3pm Sun) Get out of the crowded downtown area for a relaxed lunch. This cafe exudes Hill Country charm like a cool glass of iced tea, with salads and sandwiches served in a restored stone house.

Gruene ❿

✗ Gristmill Restaurant — American $$

(📞830-606-1287; www.gristmillrestaurant. com; 1287 Gruene Rd; mains $10-24; ⏲11am-9pm Sun-Thu, to 10pm Fri & Sat, closes 1hr later summer) Conscientious service and juicy steaks topped with lemon-butter are highlights here, where a pre-show dinner (it's behind Gruene Hall, p238) transforms into a memorably pleasant experience. Right under the water tower, the restaurant is located within the brick remnants of a long-gone gristmill. Indoor seating affords a rustic ambience, while outdoor tables get a view of the river.

🛏 Gruene Mansion Inn — Inn $$$

(📞830-629-2641; www.gruenemansioninn. com; 1275 Gruene Rd; r incl breakfast from $225; 🅿✳🛜) This cluster of buildings is practically its own village, with rooms in the mansion, a former carriage house and the old barns. Richly decorated in a style the owners call 'rustic Victorian elegance,' the rooms feature lots of wood, floral prints and pressed-tin ceiling tiles. The hot breakfast buffet is fantastic. Gruene Hall is next door. Two-night minimum.

New Braunfels ⓫

✗ Huisache Grill & Wine Bar — American $$

(📞830-620-9001; www.huisache.com; 303 W San Antonio St; mains $10-25; ⏲11am-10pm) Located in a former home, this cozy, stylish eatery breaks with local tradition by not being even remotely German. An impressively lengthy wine list is one of the draws, as is the variety of choices on the menu – everything from sandwiches to seafood and steaks.

Big Bend Scenic Loop

22

Although it's known for wide open spaces, west Texas is packed with surprising experiences that makes this a supremely well-rounded drive.

TRIP HIGHLIGHTS

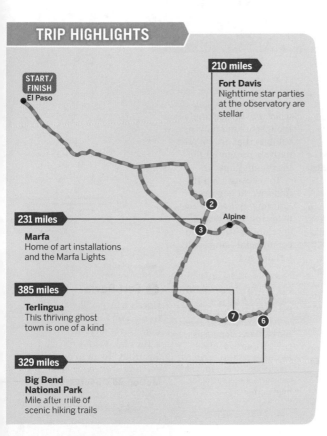

START/FINISH
El Paso

210 miles
Fort Davis
Nighttime star parties at the observatory are stellar

Alpine

231 miles
Marfa
Home of art installations and the Marfa Lights

385 miles
Terlingua
This thriving ghost town is one of a kind

329 miles
Big Bend National Park
Mile after mile of scenic hiking trails

5–7 DAYS
690 MILES/1110KM

GREAT FOR...

BEST TIME TO GO
Best between February and April – before the heat sets in.

 ESSENTIAL PHOTO
Prada Marfa, a quirky roadside art installation.

 BEST FOR OUTDOORS
McDonald Observatory's nighttime star parties.

22 | Big Bend Scenic Loop

Getting to visit Big Bend National Park and experience the endless vistas straight out of an old Western are reason enough to make this trip. But you'll also have plenty of fun along the way, exploring the quirky small towns that are prime road-trip material. Unforgettable experiences in west Texas include minimalist art installations, nighttime astronomy parties and thriving ghost towns.

❶ El Paso

Start your trip in El Paso, a border city that's wedged into a remote corner of west Texas. While here, take advantage of the great Mexican food you can find all over the city – it's right across the river from Mexico – and enjoy El Paso's many free museums. Downtown, the **El Paso Museum of Art** (☎915-212-0300; www.elpasoartmuseum.org; 1 Arts Festival Plaza; ⊙9am-5pm Tue-Sat, to 9pm Thu, noon-5pm Sun) has a terrific Southwestern collection.

And don't miss the **El Paso Holocaust Museum** (☎915-351-0048; www.elpasoholocaustmuseum.org;

715 N Oregon St; ⊙9am-5pm Tue-Fri, 1-5pm Sat & Sun), which hosts amazingly thoughtful and moving exhibits that are imaginatively presented for maximum impact.

To the west, you'll find several good restaurants and watering holes in the new and developing Montecillo commercial and residential district.

The Drive » Head east on I-10 for two hours, then turn onto TX 118 toward Fort Davis. The area is part of both the Chihuahuan Desert and the Davis Mountains, giving it a unique setting where the endless horizons are suddenly interrupted by rock formations springing from the earth.

TRIP HIGHLIGHT

❷ Fort Davis

Here's why you'll want to plan on being in Fort Davis on either a Tuesday, Friday or Saturday: to go to an evening star party at **McDonald Observatory** (☎432-426-3640; www.mcdonaldobservatory.org;

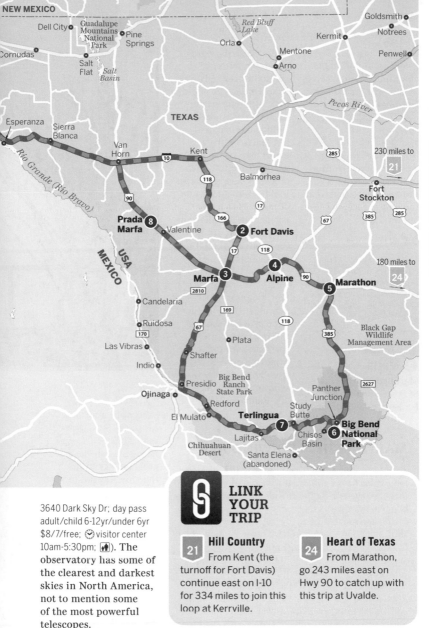

3640 Dark Sky Dr; day pass
adult/child 6-12yr/under 6yr
$8/7/free; ☉ visitor center
10am-5:30pm; ♿). The
observatory has some of
the clearest and darkest
skies in North America,
not to mention some
of the most powerful
telescopes.

Besides that, nature
lovers will enjoy **Davis**

§ LINK YOUR TRIP

21 **Hill Country**
From Kent (the
turnoff for Fort Davis)
continue east on I-10
for 334 miles to join this
loop at Kerrville.

24 **Heart of Texas**
From Marathon,
go 243 miles east on
Hwy 90 to catch up with
this trip at Uvalde.

Mountains State Park
(📞432-426-3337; www.
tpwd.state.tx.us; Hwy 118;
adult/child under 13yr $6/
free), and history buffs
can immerse themselves
at the 1854 **Fort Davis
National Historic Site**
(📞432-426-3224; www.
nps.gov/foda; Hwy 17;
adult/child under 16yr $7/
free; ⏰8am-5pm; 🐾), a
well-preserved frontier
military post that's
impressively situated at
the foot of Sleeping Lion
Mountain.

🛏 p247

The Drive » Marfa is just
20 minutes south on TX 17, a
two-lane country road where
tumbleweeds bounce slowly
by and congregate around the
barbed-wire fences.

TRIP HIGHLIGHT

❸ Marfa

Marfa got its first taste
of fame when Rock
Hudson, Elizabeth Taylor
and James Dean came
to town to film *Giant*
(1956).

But these days, this
tiny town with one
stoplight draws visitors
from around the world
for a different reason:
its art scene. Donald
Judd single-handedly
put Marfa on the art-
world map in the 1980s
when he used a bunch
of abandoned military
buildings to create one
of the world's largest
permanent installations
of minimalist art at
the **Chinati Foundation**
(📞432-729-4362; www.
chinati.org; 1 Calvary Row; Full
Collection Tour adult/student
$25/10, Selections Tour adult/
student $20/10; ⏰ by guided
tour 10am & 2pm Wed-Sun).

Art galleries are
sprinkled around town,
exploring everything
from photography to
sculpture to modern
art. **Ballroom Marfa**

XRADIOPHOTOG/SHUTTERSTOCK ©

(📞432-729-3600; www.
ballroommarfa.org; 108 E
San Antonio St; suggested
donation $5; ⏰10am-6pm
Wed-Sat, to 3pm Sun) is a
great gallery to catch
the vibe. Try not to visit
on a Monday or Tuesday,
when many businesses
are closed.

🍴 🛏 p247

The Drive » Alpine is about
30 minutes east of Marfa on
Hwy 90/67.

❹ Alpine

The biggest little town
in the area, Alpine is the
county seat, a college

MARFA LIGHTS VIEWING AREA

The Marfa Lights that flicker beneath the Chinati
Mountains have captured the imagination of
many a traveler over the decades, with accounts
of mysterious lights that appear and disappear
on the horizon that go all the way back to the
1800s. Numerous studies have been conducted
to explain the phenomenon, but the only thing
scientists all agree on is that they have no idea
what causes the apparition.

Catch the show at the Marfa Lights Viewing
Area, on the south side of the road between Marfa
and Alpine. From the platform, look south and
find the red blinking light (that one's real). Just to
the right is where you will (or won't) see the Marfa
Lights doing their ghostly thing.

Terlingua Starlight Theater

town (Sul Ross University is here) and the best place to stock up on whatever you need before you head down into the Chihuahuan Desert.

Stop by the **Museum of the Big Bend** (☏432-837-8143; www.museumofthebigbend.com; 400 N Harrison St; donations accepted; ⊙9am-5pm Tue-Sat, 1-5pm Sun) to brush up on the history of the Big Bend region. But don't expect it to be dry and dusty. The multimedia exhibits are big and eye-catching, and display-reading is kept to a minimum. Most

impressive? The enormous replica wing bone of the Texas pterosaur found in Big Bend – the largest flying creature ever found, with an estimated wing span of more than 50ft.

🍴 🛏 p247

The Drive » Keep heading east. In 15 miles, look south for the guerilla art installation Target Marathon, a fun nod to Prada Marfa. In another 15 miles you'll reach the seriously tiny town of Marathon (mar-a-thun). The views aren't much during this stretch of the drive, but Big Bend will make up for all that.

❺ Marathon

This tiny railroad town has two claims to fame. It's the closest town to Big Bend's north entrance – providing a last chance to fill up your car and your stomach – and it's got the **Gage Hotel** (☏432-386-4205; www.gagehotel.com; 102 NW 1st St/Hwy 90; r $229-279; ❋ @ 🛜 ☒), a true Texas treasure that's worth a peek, if not an overnight stay.

The Drive » Heading south on Hwy 385, it's 40 miles to the northern edge of Big

Bend, and 40 more to get to the Chisos Basin, the heart of the park. The flat road affords miles and miles of views for most of the drive.

TRIP HIGHLIGHT

6 Big Bend National Park

At 1252 sq miles, this national park is almost the size of Rhode Island. Some people duck in for an afternoon, hike a quick trail and leave, but we recommend staying at least two nights to hit the highlights.

Seventeen miles south of the Persimmon Gap Visitor Center, pull over for the **Fossil Discovery Exhibit** (www.nps.gov/bibe), which spotlights the dinosaurs and other creatures that inhabited this region beginning 130 million years ago.

With more than 200 miles of trails to explore, it's no wonder hiking is one of the most popular activities, with many of the best hikes leaving from the Chisos Basin. Hit the short, paved **Window View Trail** at sunset, then hike the 4.4-mile **Window Trail** the next morning before it gets too hot. Spend the afternoon hiking the shady 4.8-mile **Lost Mine Trail**, or take a scenic drive to see the eerily abandoned **Sam Nail Ranch** or the scenic **Santa Elena Canyon**.

🛏 p247

The Drive » From the west park entrance, turn left after 3 miles then follow the signs for Terlingua Ghost Town, just past Terlingua proper. It's about a 45-minute drive from the middle of the park.

TRIP HIGHLIGHT

7 Terlingua

Quirky Terlingua is a unique combination: it's both a ghost town and a social hub. When the local cinnabar mines closed down in the 1940s, the town dried up and blew away like a tumbleweed, leaving buildings that fell into ruins.

But the area has slowly repopulated, businesses have been built on top of the ruins, and locals gather here for two daily rituals. In the late afternoon, everyone drinks beer on the porch of **Terlingua Trading Company** (📞432-371-2234; terlinguatradingco.homestead.com; 100 Ivey St; ⏲10am-9pm). And after the sun goes down, the party moves next door to Starlight Theater (p247), where there's live music every night.

🍴 p247

The Drive » Continue west on Rte 170, also known as the River Road, for a gorgeous drive along the Rio Grande inside Big Bend Ranch State Park. In 60 miles or so you'll reach Presidio. Head north on Hwy 67 to return to Marfa, then cut west on Hwy 90.

------

8 Prada Marfa

So you're driving along a two-lane highway out in the middle of nowhere, when suddenly a small building appears in the distance like a mirage. You glance over and see ... a Prada store? Known as the 'Prada Marfa' (although it's really closer to Valentine) this art installation set against the backdrop of dusty west Texas is a tongue-in-cheek commentary on consumerism.

The Drive » Take Hwy 90 back to I-10 and head west to El Paso.

Eating & Sleeping

Fort Davis ❷

🛏 Indian Lodge   Inn $$

(📞lodge 432-426-3254, reservations 512-389-8982; www.tpwd.texas.gov; Hwy 118; r $95-125, ste 135-$150; 🅿 ❄ 🛜 🏊) Located inside Davis Mountains State Park (p243), this historic, 39-room inn was built by the Civilian Conservation Corps in the 1930s. It has 18in-thick adobe walls, hand-carved cedar furniture and ceilings of pine viga and *latilla* that give it the look of a Southwestern pueblo – that is, one with a swimming pool and gift shop. Reserve early.

Marfa ❸

🍴 Cochineal   American $$$

(📞432-729-3300; www.cochinealmarfa.com; 107 W San Antonio St; small plates $9-12, mains $22-42; 🕑5:30-10pm) Foodies flock to this stylish but minimalist eatery for a changing menu that showcases high-quality organic ingredients. Portions are generous, so don't be afraid to share a few small plates – maybe along the lines of brisket tacos, oyster mushroom risotto or house-made ramen with duck breast – in lieu of a full dinner.

🛏 El Cosmico   Campground $

(📞432-729-1950; www.elcosmico.com; 802 S Highland Ave; tent site per person $30, safari tents $95, tipis & yurts $165, trailers $165-210; 🅿 🛜 🏊) One of the funkiest choices in all of Texas, where you can sleep in a stylishly converted travel trailer, tipi, safari tent, or even a yurt. It's not for everyone: the grounds are dry and dusty, you might have to shower outdoors, and there's no air-con (luckily, it's cool at night). But when else can you sleep in a tipi?

Alpine ❹

🍴 Reata   Steak $$

(📞432-837-9232; www.reata.net; 203 N 5th St; lunch $10-15, dinner $13-40; 🕑11:30am-2pm & 5-10pm Mon-Sat) Reata turns on the upscale ranch-style charm – at least in the front dining

room, where the serious diners go. Step back into the lively bar area or onto the shady patio for a completely different vibe, where you can feel free to nibble your way around the menu and enjoy a margarita.

🛏 Holland Hotel   Historic Hotel $$

(📞432-837-2800; www.thehollandhoteltexas.com; 209 W Holland Ave; r incl breakfast $150-225, ste $170-250; 🚐 ❄ 🛜 🏊) Built in 1928, this beautifully renovated Spanish Colonial building has elegantly furnished rooms set with carved wood furniture, Western-style artwork and sleek modern bathrooms. The lobby, with its stuffed leather chairs and wood-beamed ceiling, is a classy place to unwind; there's a good high end restaurant attached.

Big Bend National Park ❻

🛏 Chisos Basin Campground   Campground $

(📞877-444-6777; www.nps.gov/bibe; tent & RV sites $14) The most centrally located of the main campgrounds, this 60-site place has stone shelters and picnic tables, with bathroom facilities nearby. It's located right near the **Chisos Lodge Restaurant** (www.chisosmountainlodge.com; lunch $7-12, dinner $10-22; 🕑7-10am, 11am-4pm & 5-8pm) and the **Basin Store** (📞432-477-2291; 🕑7am-9pm), as well as several popular trails. Twenty-six sites are available for advance reservations from November 15th through May at www.recreation.gov; the rest are first-come, first-served.

Terlingua ❼

🍴 Starlight Theatre   American $$

(📞432-371-3400; www.thestarlighttheatre.com; 631 Ivey Rd; mains $10-27; 🕑5pm-midnight Sun-Fri, to 1am Sat) You'd think a ghost town would be dead at night (pardon the pun), but the Starlight Theatre keeps things lively. This former movie theater fell into roofless disrepair (thus the 'starlight') before being converted into a restaurant. There's live music nearly every night in spring and fall.

Texas Gulf Coast

23

Cruise over 450 miles along the coastline with stops to spot endangered whooping cranes, party in chilled-out beach towns, or live a little Texas history.

TRIP HIGHLIGHTS

172 miles

Aransas National Wildlife Refuge
Spot whooping cranes and other wildlife

0 miles

Galveston
Beautiful beaches, rich history and architecture, plus great restaurants

START
1

West Columbia

Palacios

4

Corpus Christi

7

244 miles

Port Aransas
Beach town with mellow vibes and fun bars

12 FINISH

470 miles

South Padre Island
Bird-watching, waves to the horizon and beach-bum bars aplenty

---

4 DAYS
470 MILES/756KM

GREAT FOR...

BEST TIME TO GO
November to March, for cool weather and peak bird-watching.

 ESSENTIAL PHOTO

A whooping crane in flight at Aransas National Wildlife Refuge.

 BEST FOR BEACHES

From Port Aransas to South Padre Island are miles and miles of white sand.

Galveston Waterfront

249

23 Texas Gulf Coast

You'll never quite get the sand out of your shorts on this trip – from the Galveston Seawall through the bird-watching trails of Aransas National Wildlife Refuge and South Padre Island beach life. There's good food and good fun all the way down the curve of the Texas coast. The hardest part is finding the will to pull yourself back onto the road and leave.

TRIP HIGHLIGHT

❶ Galveston

Miles of sandy beach front Galveston's Gulf Coast seawall, starting from the empty expanses of **East Beach** (☎409-797-5111; 1923 Boddecker Dr, off Seawall Blvd; per vehicle Sat & Sun $15, Mon-Fri $12; ☉dawn-dusk) and stretching on down south. This island is part sunburned beach bum, part genteel Southern lady. Yet the massive spring-break and Mardi Gras party crowds coexist with smitten tourists wandering

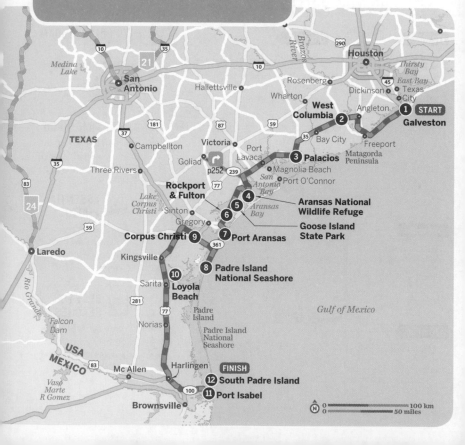

through the sizable Victorian districts (which date to the city's heyday as a port of entry for immigrants heading west) – maybe it's just that they can all get along over a table at one of the island's many great restaurants.

In the historic Strand district, old-fashioned brick-front buildings are spiffily refurbished, and there are boutiques, ice-cream parlors and general stores. Look into the history of the families that built Galveston at the **Bishop's Palace** (✆409-762-2475; www. galvestonhistory.org; 1402 Broadway Ave; adult/child $12/9; ◷10am-5pm Sun-Fri, to 6pm Sat) and **Moody Mansion** (✆409-762-7668; www.moodymansion.org; 2618 Broadway Ave; adult/child $10/8; ◷tours 11am, 1pm &

LINK YOUR TRIP

21 **Hill Country**
Head north on I-37 from Corpus Christi to San Antonio, linking with this trip through the rolling landscapes of the Texas Hill Country.

24 **Heart of Texas**
It's 180 miles west of Hwy 77 from Harlingen up the Rio Grande Valley to Laredo and the deserts of west Texas.

3pm Mon-Fri, hourly 11am-3pm Sat & Sun).

✗ 🛏 p255

The Drive » From the Seawall, head south across the San Luis pass bridge to Follets Island. At Surfside Beach, the end of the road, go 21 miles inland on TX 332/288 via Lake Jackson to TX 35. Head south for 13 miles.

---

❷ West Columbia

The lands west of modern Houston were once a hub of frontier life, among the first of Mexican lands settled by Stephen F Austin's 'Old 400' under the *empresario* migration system. Though sleepy today, the historic **Varner-Hogg Plantation** (✆979-345-4656; www.thc.texas.gov; 1702 N 13th St; adult/child $4/3; ◷8am-5pm Tue-Sun) and **Old Columbia Cemetery** (E Jackson St, at S 16th St; ◷dawn-dusk) give a glimpse into the lives of the hardy families that settled this land, while the **Aycock Crews House B&B** (✆979-345-6931; www.aycockcrews.com; 520 CR 703; r $125-175; ❈🛜) makes an interesting historical alternative inland from the chain hotels that line this stretch of the coast.

The Drive » Continue along TX 35 for 54 miles.

---

❸ Palacios

Once the domain of presidents and railroad

barons, the 1903 **Luther Hotel** (✆361-972-2312; www.lutherhotelpalacios. com; 408 S Bay Blvd; r $80-125; ❈🛜) is these days something of a diamond in the rough. The views out over Tres Palacios Bay certainly haven't lost their charm, and the occasional fisherman or 'winter Texan' still visits for a stay at a historic icon.

The Drive » Continue on TX 35 for 50 miles through Port Lavaca to just past tiny Tivoli, where you turn southeast on TX 239. Follow the signs for 12 miles through corn farms until you reach Aransas National Wildlife Refuge.

TRIP HIGHLIGHT

❹ Aransas National Wildlife Refuge

Aransas National Wildlife Refuge (✆361-286-3559; www.fws.gov/ refuge/aransas; FM 2040; per person/car $3/5; ◷sunrise-sunset, visitor center 9am-4pm, Wed-Sun only mid-Apr-mid-Oct) is a 115,000-acre wetland park that protects the wintering ground of 240 or so whooping cranes, of which in the 1940s only 15 remained in a small flock that wintered here. Standing nearly 5ft tall, with a 7ft wingspan, whooping cranes are an impressive sight. Easy hiking trails and observation platforms let you spot the birds from November to March.

To get a ground-level experience and close-up views from out on the water, take a tour with **Rockport Birding & Kayak Adventures** (☎877-892-4737; www.whoopingcranetours.com; 215 N Fulton Beach Rd, Fulton; 3hr tours per person from $55; ☺7:30am-4:30pm). It's not uncommon to spot 60 bird species on a half-day excursion by boat or kayak.

The Drive » Follow FM 774 through a series of turns 16 miles west until it rejoins TX 35. Turn south and go 13.5 miles to Lamar and turn east.

- - - - - - - - - - - - - - - - - -

5 Goose Island State Park

The main part of **Goose Island State Park**

(☎361-729-2858; www.tpwd.state.tx.us; 202 S Palmetto St; adult/child $5/free; ☺8am-10pm), where admission is charged, is right on Aransas Bay (there are beaches, but no swimming). The busiest times at the park are during the summer and whooping-crane season (November to March), but it's better for fishing than bird-watching.

The oldest tree on the coast is an oak more than 1000 years old, located near the main part of the park off 12th St, in an idyllic spot amid a sea of wildflowers. En route back to the highway, follow signs for the 1835 **Stella Maris Chapel** (☎361-790-5277; 222 Hagy Dr, Lamar).

RICHARDSEELEYPHOTOGRAPHY.COM / GETTY IMAGES ©

DETOUR: HISTORIC GOLIAD

Start: 3 Palacios

'Remember the Alamo!' is the modern icon of the Texas revolution, but contemporaries would have also recognized 'Remember Goliad!' where, on Palm Sunday, March 27, 1836, Mexican general Antonio López de Santa Anna ordered 350 Texian prisoners shot, after their surrender on the plains outside of town. The death toll was double that at the Alamo and helped inspire the Texians in their victory over Santa Anna at San Jacinto the following month.

There is a wealth of historic sites in and around the lovely town of Goliad. Start at the 1749 church and fort **Presidio La Bahia** (☎361-645-3752; www.presidiolabahia.org; Called Cinco de Mayo, off Hwy 183; adult/child $4/1; ☺9am-4:45pm). It's 36 miles each way from Tivoli.

The Drive » It's only 5 miles south on TX 35 to the twin coastal towns of Rockport and Fulton.

- - - - - - - - - - - - - - - - - -

6 Rockport & Fulton

A pedestrian-friendly waterfront, fishing boats plying their trade (plus fresh-caught seafood at restaurants nearby), and Rockport's small, revamped downtown make the adjoining towns of Rockport and Fulton an enjoyable stop.

The side streets between TX 35 and Aransas Bay are dotted

Whooping cranes

with numerous art galleries, especially in the center of Rockport; the towns claim to be home to the state's highest percentage of artists. Check in with the local creative scene at the **Rockport Center for the Arts** (📞361-729-5519; www.rockportartcenter. com; 902 Navigation Circle; 🕙10am-4pm Tue-Sat, 1-4pm Sun), just across from the harbor.

The Drive » Head 10 miles south on TX 35 to Aransas Pass, turn east on TX 361 for 6.5 miles of wetland views until you reach the free 24-hour ferries for the 10-minute transfer to Port Aransas. Be

prepared for a wait in the busy season.

- - - - - - - - - - - - - - -

TRIP HIGHLIGHT

7 Port Aransas

Port Aransas (ah-*ran*-ziss), or 'Port A,' is for many the most appealing beach town on the Texas coast. On the northern tip of Mustang Island, it's small enough that you can ride a bike or walk anywhere but large enough to have plenty of activities and nightlife. Days are relaxed, dominated by hanging out on the beach, fishing and doing nothing.

✗ ⊨ p255

The Drive » Head south 28 miles on what starts as TX 361 to Padre Island National Seashore. It's beaches all the way, and places like Mustang Island State Park make good stops.

- - - - - - - - - - - - - - -

8 Padre Island National Seashore

If you're looking for solitude, **Padre Island National Seashore** (📞361-949-8068; www.nps.gov/pais; Park Rd 22; 7-day pass per car $10; 🕙park 24hr) fits the bill. The tidal flats, shifting dunes and shallow lagoon waters provide plenty of opportunity for hiking, swimming and windsurfing. Most of the 70 miles of this island refuge are only accessible by 4WD along the undeveloped beach. Hike in a mile or two and you'll have the place all to yourself.

The Drive » Drive 15 miles back north to TX 358 and cross the John F Kennedy Causeway. Another 16 miles leads into the heart of downtown Corpus Christi.

- - - - - - - - - - - - - - - -

❾ Corpus Christi

In addition to a large marina and walkable waterfront, the 'Sparkling City by the Sea' has a small downtown strand and several good museums nearby. Anchored across the bay, in front of beach-bum restaurants and souvenir shops, is the unmissable **USS Lexington Museum** (☎316-888-4873; www. usslexington.com; 2914 N Shoreline Blvd, North Beach; adult/child $15/10; ☺9am-5pm, to 6pm Jun-Aug), a 900ft-long aircraft carrier. Explore what's under the waves next door at the **Texas State Aquarium** (☎361-881-1230; www.texasstateaquarium.org; 2710 N Shoreline Blvd, North Beach; adult/child $26/19; ☺9am-5pm, from 10am Sun; **P** 🚗), whose interactive exhibits are a hit with all ages.

🍴 p255

The Drive » Drive 18 miles west to Hwy 77. Turn south and go 35 miles past Kingsville (and the historic King Ranch) to CR 628. It's a bumpy 9 miles east to the coastal hamlet of Loyola Beach.

- - - - - - - - - - - - - - - -

❿ Loyola Beach

The little **King's Inn** (☎361-297-5265; www.marketingteammates.com/TX1338; 1116 S County Rd 2270; mains from $11-25; ☺11am-10pm Tue-Sat) is the stuff of legends, with seafood by the pound and plate after plate of avocado salad that draws visitors from up and down the Gulf Coast. Come hungry.

The Drive » Returning to Hwy 77, head 93 miles south to TX 100 and the turnoff for Los Fresnos. It's an easy side trip to the Palo Alto Battlefield, or keep on for 25 miles to Port Isabel.

- - - - - - - - - - - - - - - -

⓫ Port Isabel

The atmospheric 1852 **lighthouse** (☎956-943-7602; portisabellighthouse.com; 414 E Queen Isabella Blvd/TX 100; adult/child $4/free; ☺9am-5pm) here sets the small-town vibe in Port Isabel. It has great restaurants and is a delightful place for a waterfront stroll.

🍴 p255

The Drive » A mere 3-mile jaunt over the Queen Isabella Causeway and you're on South Padre Island.

TRIP HIGHLIGHT

⓬ South Padre Island

The town of South Padre Island (SPI) works hard to exploit its sunny climate and beaches. For most of the year mellow beach bars and waterfront restaurants let you lounge away the day. But annually in March, SPI becomes a frenetic madhouse during spring break.

Wave-runner rental and parasailing opportunities abound and there are bird-watching trails. You can learn about the slowest-moving coastal denizens at **Sea Turtle Inc** (☎956-761-4511; www.seaturtleinc.com; 6617 Padre Blvd; suggested donation adult/child $4/2; ☺10am-4pm Tue-Sun, to 5pm Jun-Aug), a rescue facility that offers tours and feeding presentations every half-hour. For a drink, try **Boomerang Billy's Beach Bar & Grill** (☎956-761-2831; www.boomerangbillysbeachbar.com; 2612 Gulf Blvd; ☺11am-late), one of the few bars right on the sand on the gulf side – 'mellow' is a bit too energetic a word for this ultimate crash pad. And as you go north up the 34-mile-long island, the beach becomes ever more quiet and remote...until the road dead-ends and only sand dunes remain.

🛏 p255

Eating & Sleeping

Galveston ❶

✕ Maceo Spice & Import Cajun $

(📞409-763-3331; www.maceospice.com;
2706 Market St; mains $7-13; ⏰11am-3pm)
This excellent importer and spice market also
happens to serve the best muffalettas and
Cajun food in town at tables crammed between
the shelves. The shop stays open till 5pm, but
lunch service ends at 3pm.

⌂ Hotel Galvez Heritage Hotel $$$

(📞409-765-7721; www.galveston.com/galvez;
2024 Seawall Blvd; r $160-315; ❄🛜🏊) Bask
in palm-fringed Spanish Colonial luxury at this
1911 historic hotel, currently managed by the
Wyndham corporation. The full-service spa
services – muscle-soaking milk bath or seaweed
contour wraps, for example – are renowned, and
the pool deck has a lovely gulf view. Ask about
special package spa deals.

Port Aransas ❼

✕ Gaff Bar $

(📞361-749-5970; gotothegaff.com; 323 Beach
St; mains $9-21; ⏰11am-11pm Sun-Thu, to
midnight Fri & Sat) Out by the beach, this
ramshackle bar (drinks from $3) is perfect
for anyone aspiring to arrested development.
Weekend fun includes belt-sander races and
chicken-poop bingo (come on bird, come on!).
There's decent pizza and subs plus live music
that includes blues and country. Most days feel
like 'talk like a pirate day' here.

⌂ Tarpon Inn Historic Hotel $$

(📞361-749-5555; www.thetarponinn.com; 200
E Cotter Ave; r $126-180, ste $180-300; ❄🛜)
Dating from 1900, when the town was still called
Tarpon, this charming if rickety place has been
rebuilt several times after hurricanes. The lobby
has more than 7000 huge silver scales from the

6ft-long namesake fish. Many rooms are small
and have no TVs or phones, but do have lots of
character and rocking chairs on the verandah.

Corpus Christi ❾

✕ Blackbeard's
On the Beach Tex-Mex $

(📞361-884-1030; blackbeards.restaurant;
3117 E Surfside Blvd, North Beach; mains $7-20;
⏰11am-9pm Sun-Thu, to 10pm Fri & Sat; 🛜)
On North Beach, this rollicking place serves
up tasty Mexican and American cuisine with a
strong seafood focus. Wash it down with cheap
margaritas while sitting back for the live music,
but watch out for the ghosts that are reputed
to haunt the place. Oh, and if it's your birthday?
Yours is on the house.

Port Isabel ⓫

✕ Joe's Oyster
Bar Restaurant Seafood $

(📞956-943-4501; 207 E Maxan St; mains $7-14;
⏰11am-7pm) Ask for recommendations on
where to eat in Port Isabel, and this combination
fishmonger and restaurant is the most common
suggestion by far. It makes a mean poor boy
sandwich, the oysters are renowned, and you
can get anything to go for picnics or packed
fresh for cooking later in the condo.

South Padre Island ⓬

⌂ Palms Resort Motel $$

(📞956-761-1316; www.palmsresortcafe.com;
3616 Gulf Blvd; r $150-230; ❄🛜🏊) This tidy
two-story motel looks right over the grass-
covered dune to the gulf. Units are large and
have fridges and microwaves. The beachfront
cafe-bar is fun.

Heart of Texas

24

From the Mexico border to the panhandle city of Amarillo you'll cross the rural length and breadth of a timeless Texas.

TRIP HIGHLIGHTS

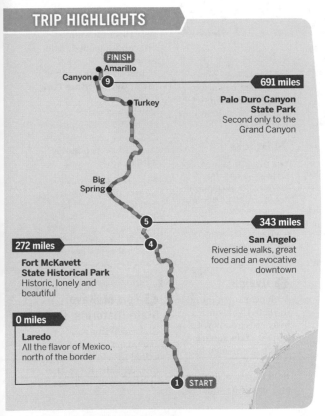

FINISH
Amarillo
Canyon
9

691 miles

Turkey

Palo Duro Canyon State Park
Second only to the Grand Canyon

Big Spring

5

343 miles

4

San Angelo
Riverside walks, great food and an evocative downtown

272 miles

Fort McKavett State Historical Park
Historic, lonely and beautiful

0 miles

Laredo
All the flavor of Mexico, north of the border

1 START

4 DAYS
709 MILES / 1141KM

GREAT FOR...

BEST TIME TO GO

March to June and September to November, to avoid scorching heat but enjoy wildflowers.

 ESSENTIAL PHOTO

Palo Duro Canyon glowing in a rainbow of colors.

 BEST FOR WIDE OPEN SPACES

The view-filling horizon of the plains.

Palo Duro Canyon State Park Lighthouse rock formation

24 Heart of Texas

The big-city sprawls of Houston, Dallas or San Antonio seem very far away as you pass through hundreds of miles of open land barely touched by humans. By the time you reach Fort McKavett, an old outpost that still seems to guard a wild and untamed frontier, you may even wonder what century you're in. At Palo Duro Canyon you'll travel back countless millennia as you wonder at timeless geologic wonders.

TRIP HIGHLIGHT

❶ Laredo

Even more than other Texas border towns, Laredo has always been tightly entwined with its sister city to the south, the fittingly named Nuevo Laredo.

While the border situation remains unsettled, Laredo's historic old downtown is evocative. Start at leafy **San Agustín Plaza** and stop into the **Republic of the Rio Grande Museum** (📞956-727-3480; webbheritage.org; 1005 Zaragoza St; $2; ⏰9am-4pm Tue-Sat) and grand **San Agustín Cathedral** (📞956-722-1382; www.dioceseoflaredo.org; 201 San Agustín Ave; ⏰hours vary). Then be sure to spend time at any of the many excellent local restaurants.

✕ 🛏 p263

The Drive » Drive 112 miles north on Hwy 83. The first 60 miles are through minimalist, arid south Texas country; the route then becomes more lush as the road begins following rivers and fertile valleys.

❷ Uvalde

A pioneer town founded in 1853, Uvalde is a busy crossroads with a great **main square**, which is crowned by the grand neoclassical 1928 courthouse. Stop and stroll the square,

pausing for something cool and refreshing along Main St.

The Drive » Continue 40 miles north on Hwy 83 through scenery that rivals the Hill Country in its oak-tree-dotted beauty.

❸ Leakey

Since prehistoric times, humans have been enjoying the beauty of the Frio River and its lovely canyon and valley. Tiny Leakey is little more than a crossroads, but what a crossroads! Hwy 83 follows the river north and south, while FM 337 runs east and west through wooded hills and secluded little valleys.

Just 10 miles south of town, **Garner State Park** (📞830-232-6132; www.tpwd.texas.gov/state-parks/garner; 234 RR 1050, off Hwy 83, Concan; adult/child under 13yr $3/free) is popular with campers.

The Drive » Go 57 miles north on Hwy 83, then jog west for 18 miles on I-10. Continue north 25 miles on Ranch Rd 1674 through hilly, uninhabited land textured with shrubs and trees.

TRIP HIGHLIGHT

❹ Fort McKavett State Historical Park

General William Tecumseh Sherman once called this fort along the San Saba River 'the prettiest post in Texas.'

Today, **Fort McKavett State Historical Park** (☏325-396-2358; www.thc.texas.gov/historic-sites/fort-mckavett-state-historic-site; 7066 FM 864; adult/child $4/3; ⏰8am-5pm) preserves the striking ruins of a once-important fort; some of the 25 buildings have been restored.

The Drive ›› Drive east on FM 864, then head west 17 miles on Hwy 190. Turn north onto the wonderfully named Toe Nail Trail/Ranch Rd 2084 (so dubbed for the toll it took on the feet of the first soldiers to march the route) and drive 27.5 miles north to Hwy 277; from there San Angelo is another 19 miles north.

TRIP HIGHLIGHT

❺ San Angelo

Situated on the fringes of the Hill Country, San Angelo is a purely Western town with an appealing overlay of gentility. The Concho River,

LINK YOUR TRIP

2 **Route 66: The Southwest**

The Mother Road passes right through Amarillo.

21 **Hill Country**
Outside of Junction, head southeast on I-10 to link to Kerrville, 54 miles away.

which scenically runs through the town, offers **walks** along its wild, lush banks on the **El Paseo de Santa Angela** (Concho River Walk; 🚶).

Fort Concho National Historic Landmark (📞325-481-2646; www.fort concho.com; 630 S Oakes St; adult/child $3/1.50; ⊙9am-5pm Mon-Sat, 1-4:30pm Sun), dating to 1867 and the years of westward expansion, may be the best-preserved Western frontier fort in the US.

At the heart of not-to-be-missed downtown, the **Concho Avenue Historic District** is a good place to stroll – be sure to pick up a historic walking tour brochure at the **visitor center** (📞325-655-4136; www.visitsanangelo.org; 418 W Ave B; ⊙9am-5pm Mon-Fri, to 4pm Sat, noon-4pm Sun). The most interesting section, known as Historic Block One, is between Chadbourne and Oakes Sts. Stop into **Miss Hattie's Bordello Museum** (📞325-653-0112; misshatties.com; 18 E Concho Ave; admission free, tours $5; ⊙2pm & 4pm Tue-Thu, hourly 1-4pm Fri-Sat) which recalls the town's wilder days.

At night you'll find great food, beer and music.

🍴 🛏 p263

The Drive ≫ Follow the green ribbon of the North Concho River 87 miles northwest on US 87, through lands on the edge of oil country.

5. GREG PANOSIAN/GETTY IMAGES ©

6 Big Spring

West of Big Spring, the land is flat and brown for 40 miles to the Permian Basin, where the cities of Midland and Odessa are at the heart of the energy boom. But here it's quiet and time moves slow. Everywhere, that is, except at the 15-story Hotel Settles (p263), a long-closed 1930s luxury hotel (the product of an oil boom) that has opened again after a lavish restoration.

Nearby, 380-acre **Big Spring State Park** (📞432-263-4931; tpwd.texas.gov/state-parks/big-spring; 1 State Park Rd; ⊙dawn-dusk) has a fine nature trail. There are few west Texas dance halls more authentic than the

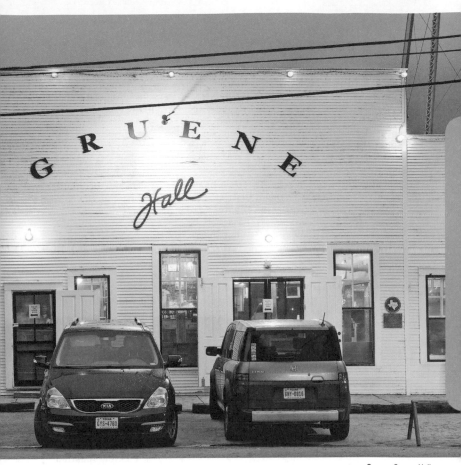

Gruene Gruene Hall

Stampede (📞432-267-2060; 1610 E Hwy 350), a bare-bones, early-1950s affair 1.5 miles northeast of Big Spring. (The schedules, however, are sporadic.)

🛏 p263

The Drive » Drive 190 miles north through some of the most lonesome terrain in Texas via TX 350, TX 208 and finally the scenic gem TX 70.

Be sure to keep your tank filled – even some county seats around here don't have gas stations anymore.

----

❼ Turkey

Tiny Turkey is one of those vanishing back-road towns that seems about to fall off the map and become a mere footnote in a history book. Bob Wills is one of Texas' most important musicians, and his life is recalled at the modest but worthwhile **Bob Wills Museum** (📞806-423-1146; www.bobwillsday.com; cnr 6th & Lyles Sts; ⏰9am-11:30am & 1-4:30pm Mon-Fri, 9am-noon Sat).

The Drive » It's 54 miles of flat, Texas two-lane driving west on TX 86. Then turn north, following the train tracks 32 miles north on Hwy 87.

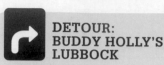

DETOUR: BUDDY HOLLY'S LUBBOCK

Start: ⑥ Big Spring

The hub for the Western music that is emblematic of the Texas plains, Lubbock is the hometown of one of the genre's greatest legends: Buddy Holly. The town celebrates his legacy at the unmissable **Buddy Holly Center** (⏺806-767-2686; www.buddyhollycenter.org; 1801 Crickets Ave; adult/child $8/5; ⏱10am-5pm Tue-Sat, from 1pm Sun). It's possible to still find the rockabilly sound that Holly made famous in the surrounding **Depot District**, at venues like the legendary **Cactus Theater** (⏺806-747-7047; www.cactustheater.com; 1812 Buddy Holly Ave). Be sure to listen to KDAV 1590AM radio, which stills plays the music of Holly's era.

See how people lived on the plains over the last 200 years at the excellent **National Ranching Heritage Center** (⏺806-742-0498; www.depts.ttu.edu/nrhc; 3121 4th St; ⏱10am-5pm Mon-Sat, 1-5pm Sun), which features dozens of restored old structures in a park-like setting.

From TX 70, Lubbuck is 58 miles west on Hwy 82.

---

⑧ Canyon

Small yet cultured, Canyon once had Georgia O'Keeffe teaching art at its West Texas A&M University. Today's campus is home to what many people figure is the best history museum in Texas: the **Panhandle-Plains Historical Museum** (⏺806-651-2244; www.panhandleplains.org; 2401 4th Ave; adult/child $10/5; ⏱9am-6pm Mon-Sat Jun-Aug, to 5pm Sep-May), where the many highlights include the myriad ways to skin a buffalo.

The Drive ›› The geologic wonders of Palo Duro Canyon are a straight 15 miles east on TX 217.

TRIP HIGHLIGHT

⑨ Palo Duro Canyon State Park

At 120 miles long and about 5 miles wide, Palo Duro Canyon is second in size in the USA only to the Grand Canyon. The cliffs striated in yellows, reds and oranges, the rock towers and other geological oddities are a refreshing surprise among the seemingly endless flatness of the plains, and are worth at least a gander.

Prehistoric American Indians lived in the canyon 12,000 years ago. The more than 26,000 acres that make up the **park** (⏺806-488-2227; www.tpwd.state.tx.us; 11450 Park Rd 5; adult/child $5/free; ⏱main gate 7am-10pm, unless camping overnight) attract hikers, horseback riders and mountain bikers.

The Drive ›› Retrace your drive 7 miles west on TX 217 and turn due north for 15 miles on FM1541 N/S Washington St.

---

⑩ Amarillo

Although Amarillo may seem as featureless as the surrounding landscape, there's plenty here to sate even the most attention-challenged. Beef, the big local industry, is at the heart of Amarillo and features in many of its attractions, including the bustling **Amarillo Livestock Auction** (⏺806-373-7464; www.amarillolivestockauction.com; 100 S Manhattan St; ⏱11am Mon).

Don't miss the **San Jacinto District** for Amarillo's best shopping, dining and entertainment.

✗ p263

Eating & Sleeping

Laredo ❶

✖ Taco N' Madre   Mexican $

(☎956-791-8226; www.tacon-madre.com; 119 E Saunders St; mains $6-12; ⊙9am-11pm) These are, without hyperbole, some of the best tacos we've ever eaten. The meat is juicy and perfectly seasoned, the tortillas fresh, the salsa piquant without being overbearing. Two or three is a reasonable meal, but good luck tearing yourself away before consuming double that. Cash only.

🛏 La Posada Hotel & Suites   Historic Hotel $$

(☎956 722 1701; www.laposada.com; 1000 Zaragoza St, San Agustín Plaza; r $110-200; ❄ @ 🛜 🏊 🐾) Far and away the nicest choice in Laredo, this hacienda-style hotel occupies a complex of buildings dating from 1916. The stylish rooms surround two large pools and gardens; the deeply shaded courtyard verandahs are a world away from the city outside.

🛏 Rialto Hotel   Historic Hotel $

(☎956-725-1800; www.therialtohotel.com; 1219 Matamoros St; r $50-70) Starting life in 1925 as a car dealership and later office space, this historic downtown building is now run as a boutique hotel. The atmosphere feels a little clinical at times, but rooms are clean and the 1st-floor restaurant serves a killer Mexican breakfast.

San Angelo ❺

✖ Peasant Village Restaurant   Deli, Bistro $$

(☎325-655-4811; 23 S Park St; lunch mains from $9, dinner mains $25-35; ⊙11am-1:30pm Mon-Fri, 6-9:30pm Tue-Sat; 🍴) Casual for lunch, luxe for dinner. Located in a beautiful 1920s house near downtown, this refined restaurant is just the place if you'd like some fine wine to go with a meal from a menu that changes with the seasons. The desserts are fab.

🛏 Inn at the Art Center   B&B $$

(☎325-659-3836; www.innattheartcenter. com; 2503 Martin Luther King Blvd, Old Chicken Farm Art Center; r $100-165; ⊕ ❄ 🛜) Funky is an understatement for this four-room B&B at the back of the bohemian Chicken Farm Art Center (☎325-653-4936; www. chickenfarmartcenter.com; ⊙10am-5pm Tue-Sat). Rooms are as artful as you'd expect at a 1970s chicken farm turned artists co-op. The Ponderosa Room has some beautiful floors made from pecan wood. The adjoining restaurant Silo House (☎325-658-3333; www.silohouse.net; lunch mains $9-15, dinner mains $28-33; ⊙11am-2pm Mon-Sat, 6-10pm Thu-Sat) is excellent for lunch and dinner.

🛏 Flamingo Flatts   Inn $$

(☎325-653-0437; www.flamingoflatts.com; 204 S Oakes St; r $100-200; ❄ 🛜) This inn is housed in a much-restored historic Antebellum hotel from 1908. The three beach-themed suites have vintage seashore decor. It's very comfortable and well-located.

Big Spring ❻

🛏 Hotel Settles   Historic Hotel $$

(☎432-267-7500; www.hotelsettles.com; 200 E 3rd St; r $130-300; ❄ 🛜 🏊) This 15-story hotel is a classic Texas story: born during a 1930s boom, it eventually closed, leaving a humungous corpse looming over an otherwise tiny town. Enter Brint Ryan, a local boy who made zillions helping corporations avoid taxes. He bought the Settles' remains and millions of dollars later it reopened in 2013 as a luxury hotel.

Amarillo ❿

✖ Big Texan Steak Ranch   Steak $$

(www.bigtexan.com; 7701 I-40 E, exit 75; mains $10-40; ⊙7am-10:30pm; 🍴) A classic, hokey Route 66 roadside attraction, the Big Texan made the move when I-40 opened in 1971 and has never looked back. Stretch-Cadillac limos with steer-horn hood ornaments offer free shuttles to and from area motels, marquee lights blink above, a shooting arcade pings inside the saloon, and a big, tall Tex road sign welcomes you.

STRETCH YOUR LEGS AUSTIN

Start/Finish Texas State Capitol

Distance 4.1 miles/6.6km

Duration Four to five hours

Get to the heart of this immensely popular city on this downtown walking tour. You'll get a peek at many of the things that have indelibly shaped Austin's character – everything from Texas politics to campus life to Mexican free-tailed bats.

Take this walk on Trip

Texas State Capitol

Built in 1888 from sunset-red granite, the **Texas State Capitol** (☎512-463-5495, tours 512-463-0063; cnr 11th St & Congress Ave; ⏰7am-10pm Mon-Fri, 9am-8pm Sat & Sun; ♿) is the largest in the US. Pick up a brochure outlining a self-guided tour of the capitol building and its grounds inside the tour-guide office on the ground floor. If nothing else, take a peek at the lovely **rotunda** and try out the **whispering gallery** created by its curved ceiling.

The Walk ≫ Head up Congress Ave towards the University; it's just a few blocks.

Bob Bullock Texas State History Museum

Big and glitzy, the **Bullock** (☎512-936-8746; www.thestoryoftexas.com; 1800 Congress Ave; adult/child $13/9; ⏰9am-5pm Mon-Sat, noon-5pm Sun) shows off the Lone Star State's history, from when it used to be part of Mexico up to the present, with high-tech interactive exhibits and fun theatrics. The museum's most famous resident is the grotesquely proportioned **Goddess of Liberty** that stood atop the capitol for nearly 100 years. Allow at least an hour or two if you stop in.

The Walk ≫ Go west one block up MLK Blvd, then turn right on University Ave and walk the two blocks to 21st St, where you'll find a postcard-perfect view of the University of Texas at Austin.

University of Texas

You could wander UT all day and still not see all of it, but this is probably the prettiest spot on campus and definitely the most iconic. **Little-field Fountain** features a dramatic, European-style sculpture, and behind it stretches the gently sloping **South Mall**, a grassy lawn flanked by 80-year-old oak trees. Topping it off is the **Main Building**, whose tower is one of the most recognizable symbols of UT and Austin.

The Walk » Stroll up the South Mall to the Main Building, then turn left and cross the West Mall to get to Guadalupe St.

The Drag

Running along the west side of campus, Guadalupe St – aka 'The Drag' – is a bustling corridor lined with restaurants and shops. Join the pedestrians streaming along the street and grab a snack at one of the cheap eateries on the west side of this stretch. Stock up on Longhorn souvenirs at the **University Co-op** (📞512-476-7211; www.universitycoop. com; 2246 Guadalupe St; ⊙9am-8pm Mon-Fri, to 7pm Sat, 10am-6pm Sun), or other school swag in burnt orange and white. The eye-catching **Hi, How Are You** (21st St & Guadalupe) mural is at the corner of W 21st and Guadalupe Sts.

The Walk » Walk down Guadalupe St to MLK, then jog over one block to Lavaca. At the corner of 11th and Lavaca Sts is the Texas Governor's Mansion. Continue south and turn right on 7th St.

Bremond Block

Part of the National Register of Historic Places, the Bremond Block preserves a concentration of elegant Victorian mansions with sprawling lawns and mature live oak trees. On the corner of Guadalupe, the 1886 **John Bremond House** is the most impressive example. Take the right fork of 7th St and circle the block clockwise to see them all.

The Walk » Walk east to Congress Ave and head south to the Colorado River.

Congress Ave Bridge

If you can time your last stop right – dusk, between late March and early November – you'll see the world's largest urban **bat colony** making their nightly exodus from under the bridge.

The Walk » Stroll back up Congress Ave (which is well lit, well populated and completely safe at night) to return to the starting point. Sixth St east of Congress is lined with bars, making it party central come nightfall.

STRETCH YOUR LEGS
SAN ANTONIO

Start The Alamo

Finish Market Square

Distance 1.5 miles/2.4km

Duration Two hours

Sprawling San Antonio has lots to offer, but it packs its best attractions into a relatively small area – perfect for exploring on foot. Head downtown to hit the highlights, including the Alamo and the River Walk.

Take this walk on Trip

The Alamo

Snap a picture of Texas' most cherished monument (📞210-225-1391; www.thealamo.org; 300 Alamo Plaza; ⊙9am-5:30pm Sep-Feb, to 9pm Mar-Aug). If you have time, go inside and learn how the former mission became a famous military fort. You might see visitors (practically pilgrims) getting downright dewy-eyed at the description of how a few hundred revolutionaries died defending the fort against thousands of Mexican troops.

The Walk » Head west two blocks on Houston St.

Buckhorn Saloon & Museum

Enjoy a beverage amidst an impressive number of mounted animals, including a giraffe, a bear and all manner of horn-wielding mammals. If that doesn't quench your thirst for taxidermy, pony up for a kitsch adventure at the adjacent **Buckhorn Museum** (📞210-247-4000; www.buckhornmuseum.com; 318 E Houston St; adult/child 3-11yr $20/15; ⊙10am-5pm, to 9pm summer) that includes wildlife from around the globe, as well as oddities like a two-headed cow and eight-legged lamb.

The Walk » Head south on Presa St. Right before the bridge, you'll find a set of stairs leading down to the River Walk, which you then follow south.

River Walk

Another of San Antonio's star attractions, the River Walk is a charming canal flowing below street level. It gets mighty crowded, but takes you past colorful cafes, landscaped hotel gardens and stone footbridges that stretch over the water. For the best overview, hop on a 40-minute **Rio San Antonio** cruise (📞210-244-5700; www.riosanantonio.com; 706 River Walk; tour $10, river taxi one-way $10, 24hr pass from $12; ⊙9am-9pm).

The Walk » From the River Walk turn right into E Commerce St. Follow it, then turn left onto N Presa St and continue to the museum.

Briscoe Western Art Museum

Western art isn't limited to paintings of cowboys and dramatic landscapes in this **museum** (📞210-299-4499; www.briscoemuseum.org; 210 W Market St; adult/

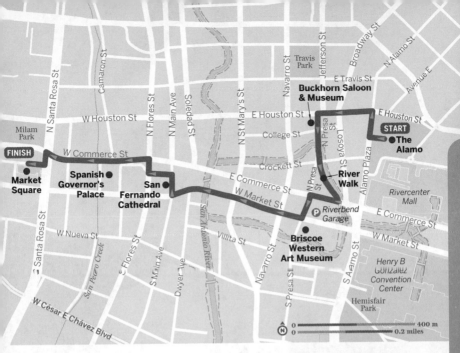

child under 13yr $10/free; 🕙10am-5pm Tue-Sun) beside the River Walk – although you will find both! Also look for a fine collection of spurs, Pancho Villa's saddle, an oral history of ranching life, photographs, sculptures, country-and-western song recordings and a fascinating diorama of the final moments of the Alamo.

The Walk >> Follow Market St west to N Main Ave.

San Fernando Cathedral

When Mexican general Santa Ana won the Battle of the Alamo, the **San Fernando Cathedral** (📞210-227-1297; www.sfcathedral.org; 115 W Main Plaza; 🕙gift shop 9am-5pm Mon-Fri, to 6:30pm Sat, 8:30am-3:30pm Sun) became an important landmark. A hundred years later, some remains were discovered – allegedly those of Davy Crockett, William Travis and James Bowie. Pay your respects to whomever they are at the marble casket near the entrance. Don't miss the dazzling gilt retablo behind the main altar.

The Walk >> Take the path to the right of the cathedral. Cross Military Plaza, then walk around the stately City Hall, built in 1892.

Spanish Governor's Palace

A National Historic Landmark, this low-profile adobe building from the 1700s was neither a palace nor the home of the Spanish governor, but the residence of the presidio captain and seat of Texas' colonial government. During the 20th century, it held businesses including a saloon and a pawn shop, but the city finally realized its significance, bought it back, and restored it (to the extent possible) to its former state.

The Walk >> Take Commerce St two blocks west. A sidewalk from Santa Rosa St leads into the square.

Market Square

Market Sq is a fair approximation of a trip south of the border. Wander the booths of the *mercado* and stock up on paper flowers, colorful pottery and the Virgin Mary in every conceivable medium. Grab some Mexican food and margaritas at the sprawling **Mi Tierra** (📞210-225-1262; www.mitierracafe.com; 218 Produce Row; mains $9-29; 🕙24hr) and enjoy the roaming mariachi band.

Utah, Colorado & Nevada

FROM ROCKY MOUNTAIN HIGHS TO ZION CANYON LOWS, it's all about extremes in Utah, Colorado and Nevada. Roads travel from ghost towns and rural America to the hyperactivity of Sin City itself. From sculpted red rock to alpine meadows strewn with wildflowers, there's powerful magic here. The grandeur beckons beyond the windshield, so take all the time you need to drink it in.

Stunning and strange, much of this rugged country has been protected as public lands. Southern Utah alone has nine national parks and monuments. The history and culture represented here stretches from the age of dinosaurs, through Ancestral Puebloan peoples and Old West mining towns, to today's Navajo Nation. Populated or barren; ancient or modern; high elevations and low: it's all in this one outdoorsy region.

Grand Staircase–Escalante National Monument (Trip 26)

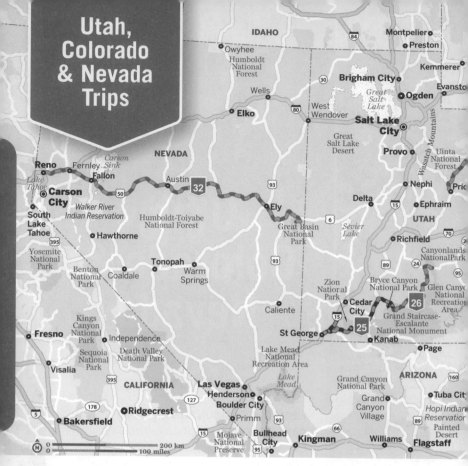

Utah, Colorado & Nevada Trips

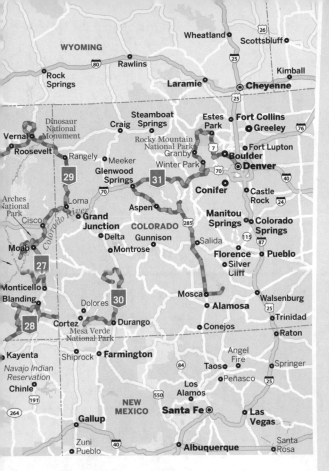

Canyoneering

Rock-climb up then rappel down through narrow slot canyons on Trips 25 27

Ancient Art Appreciation

Ancestral Puebloan cultures left traces as rock art and ruins across the region. See for yourself on Trips 26 27 28

Independence Pass

Quaking aspens surround you as you navigate hairpin turns and experience craggy-rocked mountain-pass bliss on Trip 31

Digging Dinosaurs

Visit three different working quarries and touch actual dinosaur bones in situ at several places along Trip 29

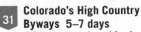

31 **Colorado's High Country Byways 5–7 days**
A heart-stopping ride through gorgeous mountain scenery. (p325)

32 **Highway 50: The Loneliest Road 3 days**
Cruise past petroglyphs, Pony Express station and, a sand dune.

Classic Trip

Zion & Bryce National Parks

25

From canyon floor to cliff-top perches, the red rock country in southwestern Utah will delight your eyes and challenge your muscles.

TRIP HIGHLIGHTS

0 miles
Kolob Canyon
A scenic drive at the top of Zion National Park

160 miles
Bryce Canyon National Park
Overlooking sorbet-colored spindles and spires

8
Tropic
FINISH

START **1**

Virgin **5**

St George

Mt Carmel

Zion Canyon
Day-hiker's heaven: stunning scenery, challenging trails

82 miles

6 DAYS
178 MILES/286KM

GREAT FOR...

BEST TIME TO GO
In April and September you'll likely have warm weather both at low and high elevations.

ESSENTIAL PHOTO

The amphitheater's color at sunrise on Fairyland Point.

BEST FOR HIKING

Zion Canyon has easy river walks to strenuous, canyon-climbing hikes.

25 | Zion & Bryce National Parks

Meet red rock country in all its heart-soaring, sculpted splendor. From the sheer wall of Zion to the pastel sentinels of hoodoos that form Bryce Canyon, these are the landscapes that no one traveling in the Southwest should miss. This trip takes in the parks' classic highlights as well as tiny Western towns and off-the-beaten-path nature sanctuaries where the screech of a hawk breaks the silence of the trail.

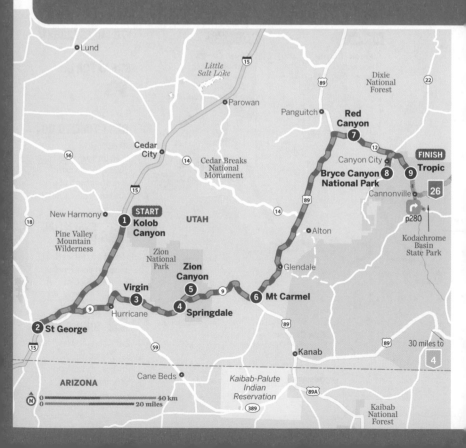

TRIP HIGHLIGHT

1 Kolob Canyons

Start your visit at the **Kolob Canyons Visitor Center** (☎435-586-0895; www.nps.gov/zion; Kolob Canyons Rd; ⌚8am-7.30pm late May-Sep, to 5pm rest of year), gateway to the less-visited, higher elevation section of Zion National Park off I-15. Even in peak season you'll see relatively few cars on the scenic 5-mile **Kolob Canyons Rd**, a high-plateau route where striking canyon and rangeland views alternate. The road terminates at **Kolob Canyons Viewpoint** (6200ft); from there the **Timber Creek Overlook Trail** (1-mile round-trip) follows a 100ft ascent to a small peak with great views of the Pine Valley Mountains beyond. In early summer the trail area is covered with wildflowers. Note that the upper section of the road may be closed due to snow from November through May.

The best longer hike in this section of the park is the **Taylor Creek Trail** (5-mile round-trip), which passes pioneer ruins and crisscrosses a creek, with little elevation change.

The Drive » Distant rock formations zoom by as you cruise along at 70-plus mph on I-15. St George is 41 miles south.

2 St George

A spacious Mormon town with an eye-catching temple and a few pioneer buildings, St George sits about equidistant between the two halves of Zion. The **Chamber of Commerce** (☎435-628-1658; www.stgeorgechamber.com; 97 E St George Blvd; ⌚9am-5pm Mon-Fri) can provide information on the historic downtown. Otherwise, use this time to stock up on food and fuel in this trip's only real city (population 77,000). Eleven miles north of town, **Snow Canyon State Park** (☎435-628-2255; stateparks.utah.gov; 1002 Snow Canyon Dr, Ivins; per vehicle $6; ⌚day use 6am-10pm; 👪) is a 7400-acre sampler of southwest Utah's famous land features. Easy trails that are perfect for kids lead to tiny slot canyons, cinder cones, lava tubes and fields of undulating slickrock.

🍴 🛏 p281

The Drive » Off the interstate, Hwy 9 leads you into canyon country. You'll pass the town of Hurricane before sweeping curves give way to tighter turns (and slower traffic). Virgin is 27 miles east of St George.

3 Virgin

The tiny-tot town of Virgin, named after the river (what else?), has an odd claim to fame – in 2000 the city council passed a largely symbolic law requiring every resident (about 600 of them) to own a gun. You can't miss **Fort Zion** (☎435-635-3455; 1000 W Hwy 9; village $2; ⌚9am-7pm), which sells homemade fudge, ice cream and every Western knickknack known to the free world. Stop and have your picture taken in the 'Virgin Jail' or 'Wild Ass Saloon' in the replica Old West village here. It's pure, kitschy fun.

The Drive » Springdale is 14 miles further along Hwy 9 (55 minutes from St George).

LINK YOUR TRIP

4 Grand Canyon North Rim & Lake Powell

Leaving Zion National Park, detour southeast down Hwy 89 for 115 miles to Page to start exploring northern Arizona.

26 Scenic Byway 12

From outside Bryce Canyon National Park, Scenic Byway 12 heads east through rugged and remote public lands and parks.

Classic Trip

❹ Springdale

Stunning orangish-red mountains, including the **Watchman** (6555ft), form the backdrop for a perfect little park town. Here eclectic cafes and eateries are big on locally sourced ingredients. Galleries and artisan shops line the long main drag, interspersed with indie motels, lodges and a few B&Bs. Make this your base for three nights exploring Zion Canyon and surrounds.

💬 LOCAL KNOWLEDGE: EAST MESA TRAIL

It feels deliciously like cheating to wander through open stands of tall ponderosa pines and then descend to Observation Point instead of hiking more than 2100ft uphill from the Zion Canyon floor. On East Mesa Trail (6.4 miles round-trip, moderate difficulty) you can do just that, because your vehicle does all the climbing. North Fork Rd is about 2.5 miles beyond the park's east entrance; follow it 5 miles north up Hwy 9 from there. Getting to the trailhead in some seasons requires 4WD; inquire about conditions and maps at the Zion Canyon Visitor Center. Nearby **Zion Ponderosa Ranch Resort** (📞800-293-5444; www.zionponderosa.com; Twin Knolls Rd; luxury tent $119, RV site $55, cabin $139-199; 📶🏊), which also has accommodations and activities, can provide hiker shuttles. Note that at 6500ft, these roads and the trail may be closed due to snow November through May.

Outfitters **Zion Guru** (📞435-632-0432; www.utahcanyonoutdoors.com; 792 Zion Park Blvd; half-day canyoneering from $150; ⏰9am-7pm) and **Zion Adventure Company** (📞435-772-1001; www.zionadventures.com; 36 Lion Blvd; canyoneering day from $177; ⏰8am-8pm Mar-Oct, 9am-noon & 4-7pm Nov-Feb) lead canyoneering, climbing and 4WD trips outside the park; the latter has inner-tube rentals for summer float trips. They both outfit for backcountry hikes through Zion National Park's popular **Narrows**.

At **Zion Canyon Giant Screen Theatre** (📞435-772-2400; www.zioncanyontheatre.com; 145 Zion Park Blvd; admission varies) the 40-minute *Zion Canyon: Treasure of the Gods* screens three times daily. The film is short on substance but long on beauty.

🍴 🛏 p281

The Drive » The entrance to the Zion Canyon section of Zion National Park is only 2 miles east of Springdale. Note that here you're at about 3900ft, the lowest (and hottest) part of your trip.

TRIP HIGHLIGHT

❺ Zion Canyon

More than 100 miles of trails cut through the surprisingly well-watered, deciduous-tree-covered Virgin River canyon section of Zion National Park. Map out your routes at the **Zion Canyon Visitor Center** (📞435-772-3256; www.nps.gov/zion; Hwy 9, Zion National Park; ⏰8am-7:30pm late May-early Sep, 8am-5pm rest of year). Your first activity should be the 6-mile **Scenic Drive**, which pierces the heart of the park. From April through October, using the free shuttle is mandatory, but you can hop off and on at any of the scenic stops and trailheads along the way.

The paved, 2.2 mile return **Riverside Walk** (👣), at the end of the road, is an easy stroll. When the trail ends, you can continue hiking along in the

Virgin River for 5 miles. Alternatively, a half-mile one-way trail leads up to the lower of the **Emerald Pools** where water tumbles from above a steep overhang stained by desert varnish.

The strenuous, 5-mile round-trip **Angels Landing Trail** (four to five hours, 1488ft elevation gain) is a vertigo-inducer with narrow ridges and 2000ft sheer drop-offs. Succeed and the exhilaration is unsurpassed. Canyon views are even more phenomenal from the top of the even higher **Observation Point** (8 miles round-trip; 2148ft elevation change).

For the longer trips down through the **Narrows** – spectacular slot canyons of the Virgin River – you need to plan ahead. An outfitter shuttle and gear plus a backcountry permit from the park are required; make advance reservations via the park website.

📖 p281

The Drive >> Driving east, Hwy 9 undulates over bridges and up 3.5 miles of tight switchbacks before reaching the impressive gallery-dotted Zion–Mt Carmel Tunnel. From there until the east park entrance, the canyon walls are made of etched, light-colored slickrock, including Checkerboard Mesa. Mt Carmel lies 26 miles (45 minutes) northwest of Zion Canyon.

❻ Mt Carmel

Several little towns line Hwy 89 north of the Hwy 9 junction. As you drive, look for little rock shops, art galleries and home-style cafes. Stop into the **Maynard Dixon Living History Museum** (www.thunderbirdfoundation. com; 2200 S State St; self-guided/docent tour $10/20; ⏰10am-5pm Mar-Nov) in Mt Carmel to explore the rustic retreat of this seminal Western artist. The Great Depression–era painter created breathtaking, light-infused landscapes and scenes of social struggle. Guides lead visitors through the log home and studio where solitude fueled the artist's imaginative drive.

The Drive >> Hwy 89 is a fairly straight shot through pastoral lands; turn off from there onto Scenic Byway 12 where the red rock meets the road. Red Canyon is 45 miles northeast of Mt Carmel.

❼ Red Canyon

Impossibly red monoliths rise up roadside as you reach **Red Canyon** (📞435-676-2676; www. fs.usda.gov/recarea/dixie; Scenic Byway 12, Dixie National Forest; ⏰park 24hr, visitor center 9am-6pm Jun-Aug, 10am-4pm May & Sep). These parklands provide super-easy access to eerie, intensely colored formations. Check out the

excellent geologic displays and pick up maps at the visitor center, where several moderate hiking trails begin. The 0.7-mile one-way **Arches Trail** passes 15 arches as it winds through a canyon. Legend has it that outlaw Butch Cassidy once rode in the area; a tough 8.9-mile hiking route, **Cassidy Trail**, bears his name.

The Drive >> Stop to take the requisite photo before you drive through two blasted-rock arches to continue on. Bryce Canyon National Park is only 9 miles down the road.

TRIP HIGHLIGHT

❽ Bryce Canyon National Park

The pastel-colored, sandcastle-like spires and hoodoos of **Bryce Canyon National Park** (📞435-834-5322; www. nps.gov/brca; Hwy 63; 7-day pass per vehicle $30; ⏰24hr, visitor center 8am-8pm May-Sep, to 4:30pm Oct-Apr) look like something straight out of Dr Seuss' imagination. The 'canyon' is actually an amphitheater of formations eroded from the cliffs. **Rim Road Scenic Drive** (18 miles one-way) roughly follows the canyon rim past the visitor center (8000ft), the lodge, incredible overlooks and trailheads, ending at **Rainbow Point** (9115ft). From early May through early October,

WHY THIS IS A CLASSIC TRIP
CAROLYN
MCCARTHY, WRITER

There's a reason these national parks have seen an enormous uptick in visitors in recent years. Zion and Bryce offer some of the most thrilling scenery out there. Wander among the odd pastel hoodoos of Bryce Canyon or wade the river through Zion's Narrows under sheer cliff walls. Welcome to the cathedrals of the American West.

Above: Zion National Park
Left: Bighorn sheep, Zion National Park
Right: Bryce Canyon National Park

Classic Trip

an optional free shuttle bus (8am until at least 5:30pm) departs from a staging area just north of the park.

The easiest walk would be to follow the **Rim Trail** that outlines Bryce Amphitheater from Fairyland Point to Bryce Point (up to 5.5 miles one-way). Several sections are paved and wheelchair accessible, the most level being the half-mile between Sunrise and Sunset Points.

A number of moderate trails descend below the rim to the maze of fragrant juniper and undulating high-mountain desert. The **Navajo Loop** drops 521ft from Sunset Point. To avoid a super-steep ascent, follow the **Queen's Garden Trail** (🥾) on the desert floor and hike up 320ft to Sunrise Point. From there take the shuttle, or follow the Rim Trail back to your car (2.9-mile round-trip).

Note that the high altitude means cooler temperatures here – 80°F (27°C) average in July – than at scorching Zion National Park.

📖 p281

The Drive » Only 11 miles east of Bryce Canyon, the town of Tropic is 2000ft lower in elevation – so expect it to be 10 degrees warmer.

----

⑨ Tropic

A farming community at heart, Tropic does offer a few services for park goers. There's a grocery store, a couple of restaurants and several motels. Basing yourself here for two nights is definitely less expensive than staying in the park. Note that the town is entirely seasonal: many businesses shut their doors tight from October through March.

🍴📖 p281

DETOUR: KODACHROME BASIN STATE PARK

Start: ⑨ Tropic

Dozens of red, pink and white sandstone chimneys punctuate **Kodachrome Basin State Park** (📞435-679-8562; www.stateparks.utah.gov; off Cottonwood Canyon Rd; day use per vehicle $8; ⊙day use 6am-10pm), named for its photogenic landscape by the National Geographic Society in 1948. The moderately easy, 3-mile round-trip **Panorama Trail** provides an overview of the otherworldly formations. Be sure to take the side trails to **Indian Cave**, where you can check out the handprints on the wall (cowboys' or Indians'?), and **Secret Passage**, a short spur through a narrow slot canyon. **Red Canyon Trail Rides** (📞800-892-7923, 435-834-5441; www.redcanyontrailrides.com; Hwy 12, Bryce Canyon Pines; 2hr ride $60; ⊙Mar-Nov) offers horseback riding in Kodachrome.

The park lies 26 miles southeast of Bryce Canyon National Park, off Cottonwood Canyon Rd, south of Cannonville.

Eating & Sleeping

St George ❷

✖ Painted Pony   Modern American $$$

(📞435-634-1700; www.painted-pony.com; 2 W St George Blvd, Ancestor Sq; lunch $10-12, dinner mains $25-36; ⏱11:30am-10pm Mon-Sat, 4-10pm Sun) Expect gourmet comfort food such as meatloaf with a port wine reduction and rosemary mashed potatoes.

🛏 Red Mountain Resort & Spa   Resort $$$

(📞435-673-4905, 877-246-4453; www.redmountainresort.com; 1275 E Red Mountain Circle; retreats per person from $220; ❄ @ 🤙 🏊 🐕) A Zen-chic sensibility pervades this low-profile yogacentric adobe resort, right down to the silk pillows that echo the copper color of surrounding cliffs. It's located 7 miles northwest of town off Snow Canyon Pkwy.

Springdale ❹

✖ King's Landing   American $$$

(📞435-772-7422; www.klbzion.com; 1515 Zion Park Blvd, Driftwood Lodge; mains $16-38; ⏱5-9pm) Bison fettuccine with truffle oil, charred octopus and verdant greens entice. Locals love its intimacy. There are also good burgers, vegetarian fare that does not bore and beautiful desserts. Reserve ahead.

🛏 Red Rock Inn   B&B $$

(📞435-772-3139; www.redrockinn.com; 998 Zion Park Blvd; cottages $199-259; ❄🤙) Five romantic country-contemporary cottages spill down the desert hillside, backed by incredible red rock. Enjoy the full hot breakfast (egg dish and pastries) that appears at the door.

Zion Canyon ❺

🛏 Zion Lodge   Lodge $$

(📞888-297-2757, 435-772-7700; www.zionlodge.com; Zion Canyon Scenic Dr; cabin/r $227/217; ❄ @ 🤙) We love the location in the middle of Zion Canyon (along with the red permit that allows you to drive to the lodge in shuttle season). But be warned: today's reconstructed lodge is not as grand as other national-park lodges (the 1920s original burned down in 1966). Nevertheless, you'll need to reserve months ahead.

Bryce Canyon National Park ❽

🛏 Bryce Canyon Lodge   Lodge $$

(📞435-834-8700, 877-386-4383; www.brycecanyonforever.com; Hwy 63; r & cabin $208-270; ⏱Apr-Oct; @ 🤙) Built in the 1920s, the main park lodge exudes rustic mountain charm, with a large stone fireplace and exposed roof timbers. The retro-cool Western cabins have gas fireplaces and creaky porches. No TVs.

Tropic ❾

✖ Stone Hearth Grille   American $$$

(📞435-679-8923; www.stonehearthgrille.com; 1380 W Stone Canyon Lane; mains $22-38; ⏱5-10pm) In a lovely rural setting staring out at the bluffs, this upscale lodge restaurant serves rib-eye steaks, quinoa-stuffed peppers and satisfying green salads alongside a decent wine list. It's the best dinner option in the area. The deck seating offers a heavy dose of romance.

🛏 Buffalo Sage B&B   B&B $$

(📞435-679-8443; www.buffalosage.com; 980 N Hwy 12; d $120; ⏱May-Sep; ❄🤙) Up on a bluff west of town, three exterior-access rooms lead out to an expansive, upper-level deck or ground-level patio with great views. The owner's background in art is evident in the decor. Do note that the communal living area is shared by cats and a dog. The full breakfast accommodates vegetarians.

Scenic Byway 12

26

Arguably Utah's most stunning drive, Scenic Byway 12 traverses moonscapes of sculpted slickrock, crosses razor-thin ridgebacks and climbs over an 11,000ft-tall mountain.

TRIP HIGHLIGHTS

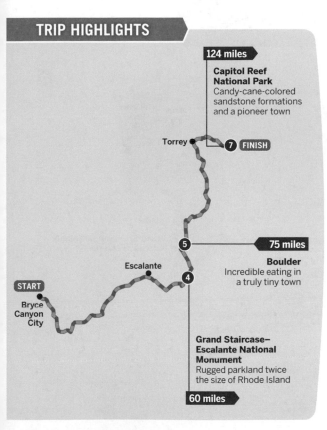

124 miles

Capitol Reef National Park
Candy-cane-colored sandstone formations and a pioneer town

Torrey — **7** FINISH

75 miles

Boulder
Incredible eating in a truly tiny town

Escalante

5

4

START

Bryce Canyon City

Grand Staircase–Escalante National Monument
Rugged parkland twice the size of Rhode Island

60 miles

**5 DAYS
124 MILES/200KM**

GREAT FOR…

BEST TIME TO GO
Summer, when the snow is gone and all attractions are open.

 ESSENTIAL PHOTO
Sandstone valley formations and distant mountains at Head of the Rocks.

 BEST FOR DRIVING
Switchbacks and narrow Hogback Ridge rule the challenging road between Escalante and Boulder.

Grand Staircase–Escalante National Monument Slot canyon

283

26 Scenic Byway 12

Bubbling slickrock formations, cool farming oases, wild side roads and rough-edged wilderness are the attraction of this once remote route. Until 1940, only wagon trails connected Escalante with Boulder and the mail was delivered by mule. Today's Scenic Byway 12 wasn't fully paved until 1985. Few people live here even today: Escalante (population 800), Boulder (population 222), Torrey (population 362). Expect rural tranquility and scenery that stuns at every turn.

❶ Bryce Canyon City

What would a road trip be without kitschy roadside stops? **Bryce Museum** (www.brycewildlifeadventure.com; 1945 W Hwy 12; $8; ⊘9am-7pm Apr–mid-Nov), a barnlike natural history exhibit, contains more than 400 taxidermied animals, in addition to American Indian artifacts, from one man's private collection. Out back, paid admission

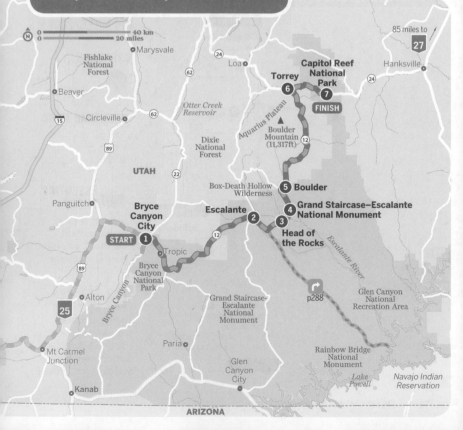

also allows you to visit the herd of exotic deer he raises. **Dixie National Forest** (www.fs.usda.gov/dixie) surrounds Scenic Byway 12 here, just northeast of Bryce Canyon National Park. The museum and several other roadside stands rent ATVs and bicycles – perfect to take advantage of the nearby **Red Canyon Bicycle Trail** ( ).

✕ ⊨ p289

The Drive ›› Past the town of Tropic, Byway 12 enters national monument parklands. A few grandfathered farming communities sit roadside as you wind your way the 41 miles (one hour) from Bryce City to Escalante.

LINK YOUR TRIP

25 Zion & Bryce National Parks

Scenic Byway 12 begins in Bryce, so you can just continue your exploration of Utah's national parks west from there.

27 Moab & Southeastern National Parks

From Capitol Reef, Moab is 145 miles to the northeast.

---

❷ Escalante

Though hardly big enough to be called a town, Escalante does cater to visitors heading out into the rugged Grand Staircase–Escalante National Monument (p286). The handful of restaurants and motels make this a good nighttime base for a day of hiking or driving in the monument. **Escalante Interagency Visitor Center** (435-826-5499; www.ut.blm.gov/monument; 775 W Main St; 8am-4:30pm daily Apr-Sep, Mon-Fri Oct-Mar) has exhibits on area geography in addition to a gift shop and information.

Escalante Outfitters (435-826-4266; www.escalanteoutfitters.com; 310 W Main St; natural history tours $45; 7am-9pm) is a traveler's oasis. The large bookstore sells maps, guides, camping supplies and liquor; the cafe has breakfasts, pizza and much-coveted wi-fi. Longtime area outfitter **Excursions of Escalante** (800-839-7567; www.excursionsofescalante.com; 125 E Main St; all-day canyoneering $175; 8am-6pm) leads canyoneering, climbing and hiking trips into the monument.

✕ ⊨ p289

The Drive ›› Monument country gets even more rough and rugged as you head further east. You'll find yourself driving up through canyons and down switchbacks to the overlook 8 miles away.

---

❸ Head of the Rocks

Don't miss the chance to pull off for one of the most arresting roadside viewpoints in Utah. Here atop the Aquarius Plateau you lord over giant mesas, towering domes, deep canyons and undulating slickrock unfurling in an explosion of color. In the far distance you can see Boulder Mountain to the northwest, the Henry Mountains to the east and Navajo Mountain to the southwest.

Continue 6 miles further east for coffee, a snack and more canyon views at **Kiva Koffeehouse** (435-826-4550; www.kivakoffeehouse.com; Hwy 12, Mile 73; dishes $4-12; 8:30am-4:30pm Wed-Mon Apr-Oct), built to resemble a traditional American Indian cliff dwelling,

The Drive ›› From Kiva Koffeehouse, Lower Calf Creek is a 2-mile, downhill drive away.

UTAH, COLORADO & NEVADA **26** SCENIC BYWAY 12

④ Grand Staircase–Escalante National Monument

At nearly 1.9 million acres, **Grand Staircase–Escalante National Monument** (GSENM; ☎435-826-5499; www.blm.gov; ☺24hr) is the largest park in the Southwest. Yet, it's one of the least visited. The harsh desert terrain *is* intimidating, but there are a few easy access points along Byway 12. The graded-dirt **Hole-in-the-Rock Road** (off Hwy 12) begins 5 miles east of Escalante; 12 miles down it is **Devils Garden** (Hole-in-the-Rock Rd, Mile 12; 👣), a giant natural playground where rock fists, orbs, spires and fingers rise to 40ft above the desert floor.

Lower Calf Creek (Hwy 12, Mile 75; day use $5; ☺day use dawn-dusk) is the most popular recreation area in the park. From the picnic area and campground, a sandy, 3-mile one-way trail follows the creekside canyon to a 126ft **waterfall** – a joy on a hot day.

The Drive » The next 16 miles are slow and winding ones as the road climbs from roughly 5300ft to 6700ft elevation in Boulder. That ridge your car is clinging to is called the 'Hogback.' Be sure to stop at the interpretive signs and the overlook of the valley just before Boulder.

⑤ Boulder

Once primarily a ranching community, this frontier outpost has attracted a diverse population of down-to-earth folks that range from artists and ecologists to farmers and cowboys. One of the reasons is Hell's Backbone Grill (p289), at Boulder Mountain Lodge. Zen Buddhists Jen Castle and Blake Spalding have been feeding the community since they opened in 2000, training staff in mindfulness and inviting the whole town to celebrations like a July 4 ice-cream social and talent show.

Be sure to stop at **Anasazi State Park Museum** (www.stateparks.utah.gov; Main St/Hwy 12; $5; ☺8am-6pm Mar-Oct, 9am-5pm Nov-Feb), which protects an ancient site inhabited from 1130 to 1175 CE and excavated in the 1950s. The petite museum is well worth seeing for the re-created six-room pueblo and excellent exhibits on the Ancestral Puebloan (or Anasazi) peoples.

🍴🛏 p289

BENEMALE / SHUTTERSTOCK ©

The Drive » Though Boulder is only 32 miles (50 minutes) south of Torrey, you have to cross over 11,317ft-high Boulder Mountain to get there. Tight switchbacks climb quickly up into the pine-forested treeline. The road is maintained, but do note that you can expect snow at these

Escalante Scenic Byway 12

elevations from November through May.

6 Torrey

Old pioneer homestead buildings line the main street of this quiet town as, in the distance, red rock cliffs catch the sunset light beautifully. The primary industry here long ago shifted from logging and ranching to outdoor tourism. Most visitors to Capital Reef National Park (11 miles away) sleep and eat here – you should do the same.

Hondoo Rivers & Trails (☎435-425-3519; www.hondoo.com; 90 E Main St; ⊗8am-8pm), one of southern Utah's longest-operating backcountry guides, offers half-, full- and multiday hiking, 4WD, rafting, horseback riding or combo trips.

✗ ⊨ p289

DETOUR: HOLE-IN-THE-ROCK ROAD

Start: ❷ Escalante

Almost as soon as the saints arrived in Salt Lake Valley, the second Mormon church president Brigham Young encouraged pioneers to settle every inch of the Utah Territory. Looking for a shortcut to more hospitable lands, in 1879 more than 200 pioneering Mormons followed this southeasterly route. When the precipitous walls of Glen Canyon on the Colorado River blocked their path, they blasted and hammered through the cliff, creating a hole wide enough to lower their 80 wagons through by rope – a feat that is honored by the road's name. An open-air memorial just west of Escalante town tells the story in greater detail. Today the 57-mile (one-way) road is still dusty and desolate. The last 7 miles require 4WD, and even then it can take almost as long to traverse those as the first 50.

The Drive » Torrey sits 1300ft above Capitol Reef, and is usually about 10°F (6°C) cooler. The 11-mile cruise through canyonlands to the valley park is all downhill from there.

TRIP HIGHLIGHT

❼ Capitol Reef National Park

Sixty-five million years ago when the earth's surface buckled and fell, the 100-mile Waterpocket Fold was created. Today **Capitol Reef National Park** (☎435-425-3791, ext 4111; www.nps.gov/care; visitor center cnr Hwy 24 & Scenic Dr; 7-day Scenic Drive pass per vehicle $10, per bicycle/pedestrian $7; tent & RV sites $20; ☉24hr, visitor center 8am-6pm Apr-Oct, to 4:30pm Nov-Mar) **protects a cross-section of geologic** history that is downright painterly: chocolate-red cliffs, yellow sandstone arches, giant cream-colored domes and stark gray monoliths.

Make sure to take the 8.2-mile, one-way **Scenic Drive** along the fold. You first pass through Mormon pioneer fruit and nut orchards, which you can freely pick from in season. The historic **Gifford Homestead** (☉8am-4.30pm mid-Mar-Oct) is a small home-stead museum, where, if you're lucky, you can buy orchard-fruit-filled minipies. At the end of the road, **Capitol Gorge Trail** (2.5 miles round-trip) leads past ancient petroglyphs. Follow the spur trail to the **Pioneer Register**, where names carved in the rock date back to 1871.

Eating & Sleeping

Bryce Canyon City ❶

✕ Bryce Canyon Lodge Restaurant
American $$$

(☎435-834-5361; Bryce Canyon Rd; breakfast & lunch $10-20, dinner $10-35; ⏱7am-10pm Apr-Oct) All food is made on-site and the certified green menu offers only sustainable seafood. The wine list is decent and, best of all, the low-lit room is forgiving if you come covered in trail dust.

🛏 Bryce Canyon Pines Campground & RV Park
Campground $

(☎435-834-5441, 800-892-7923; www.brycecanyonmotel.com; Hwy 12; tent/RV sites $38/50; ⏱Apr-Oct) Across the street from the affiliated motel, 4 miles west of the Hwy 12/63 junction, this campground sits behind a gas station and general store. The roadside location is convenient, but not exactly ambient.

Escalante ❷

✕ Circle D Eatery
American $$

(☎435-826-4125; www.escalantecircledeatery.com; 475 W Main St; mains $11-25; ⏱7am-9:30pm, limited hours Nov-Feb) Has attentive service and satisfying burgers using local beef on fresh jalapeño buns, served with shoestring fries. Smoked meats are a specialty, but there are also pastas, salads and hearty breakfasts.

🛏 Escalante Grand Staircase B&B
B&B $$

(☎435-826-4890; www.escalantebnb.com; 280 W Main St; d $142; ❄ 🛜) A wonderful find, with eight spacious rooms sporting individual entrances, skylights and porches. Tom, the host, provides vast quantities of coffee and extensive trail information, with helpful binders containing photos and directions.

Boulder ❺

✕ Burr Trail Grill & Outpost
Modern American $

(☎435-335-7511; cnr Hwy 12 & Burr Trail Rd; dishes $8-18; ⏱grill 11:30am-9:30pm, outpost 8:30am-6pm Mar-Oct; 🛜) We like the homey vibe. It's worth browsing the Outpost art gallery, gift shop and coffeehouse.

✕ Hell's Backbone Grill
Modern American $$

(☎435-335-7464; www.hellsbackbonegrill.com; 20 N Hwy 12, Boulder Mountain Lodge; breakfast $10-12, lunch $9-17, dinner $17-36; ⏱7:30-11:30am & 5-9:30pm Mar-Nov; 🥗) Earthy preparations of Southwestern dishes include gorgeous salads made from organic garden produce and braised beef in rich preparations. Dinner reservations are a must.

🛏 Boulder Mountain Lodge
Lodge $$

(☎435-335-7400, www.boulder-utah.com, 20 N Hwy 12; r $140-175, ste $325, apt $230; ❄ @ 🛜 ❄) The lodge that Hell's calls home is an ideal place for day-hikers who want to return to high-thread-count sheets, plush terry robes, spa treatments and an outdoor hot tub. Watch the birds flit by on the adjacent 15-acre wildlife sanctuary and stroll through the organic garden.

Torrey ❻

🛏 Torrey Schoolhouse B&B
B&B $$

(☎435-633-4643; www.torreyschoolhouse.com; 150 N Center St; r $120-160; ⏱Apr-Oct; ❄ 🛜) Ty Markham has done an exquisite job of bringing this rambling 1914 schoolhouse back to life as a B&B. After a full gourmet breakfast you might need to laze in the garden a while before hiking.

🛏 Muley Twist Inn B&B
B&B $$

(☎800-530-1038, 435-425-3640; www.muleytwistinn.com; 249 W 125 S, Teasdale; r $99-150; ⏱Apr-Oct; ❄ 🛜) Set against a towering red-sandstone dome in a Teasdale neighborhood, this big wooden farmhouse with a wraparound verandah looks small. It isn't. Casual rooms at the down-to-earth inn are spacious and bright.

Moab & Southeastern National Parks

27

Hiking, biking, rafting, riding (four-wheelers or horses): Moab and the surrounding parks and extensive public lands are activity central. Adrenaline, anyone?

TRIP HIGHLIGHTS

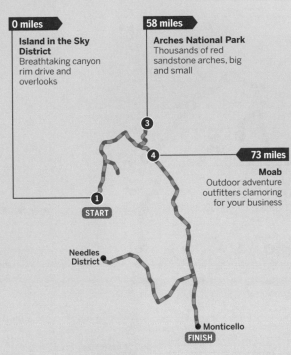

0 miles

Island in the Sky District
Breathtaking canyon rim drive and overlooks

58 miles

Arches National Park
Thousands of red sandstone arches, big and small

73 miles

Moab
Outdoor adventure outfitters clamoring for your business

START

Needles District

Monticello
FINISH

4 DAYS
196 MILES / 315KM

GREAT FOR...

BEST TIME TO GO
April and October have the most temperate weather and many events.

ESSENTIAL PHOTO
The quintessential Utah picture: Delicate Arch in Arches National Park.

BEST FOR FAMILIES
Both Arches and Canyonlands (Island in the Sky) have short trails and kids' explorer packs.

27

Moab & Southeastern National Parks

From the graceful forms of Arches National Park to the magnificent depths of Canyonlands, these views provoke stirring emotion. Stare at the swirling pattern long enough and you'll swear you can see the red rock move. Hiking through Utah's southeastern parks, you get to test your limits and bear witness to the earth's power at its most elemental. Here the story of wind and water is written in stone.

TRIP HIGHLIGHT

❶ Island in the Sky District

Roads and rivers make inroads into the 527-sq-mile desert of **Canyonlands National Park** (www.nps.gov/cany; 7-day pass per vehicle $25, per bicycle/pedestrian $10; tent & RV sites without hookups $15-20; ⏰24hr), but much of it is still untamed wilderness. Vast canyons divide the park into disparate sections. Think of Island in the Sky as the overview: an RVer's special,

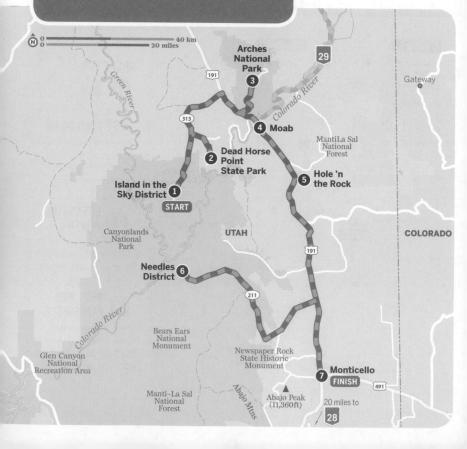

with paved drives and easy-access lookouts. Here narrow, serpentine valleys tipped with white cliffs loom high over the Colorado and Green Rivers.

A good short hike is the half-mile loop to oft-photographed **Mesa Arch**, a slender, cliff-hugging span framing a picturesque view of **Washer Woman Arch** and **Buck Canyon**. The **Grand View Overlook Trail** (2 miles round-trip) follows the canyon's edge and ends at a praise-your-maker precipice atop the mesa.

The Drive » Dead Horse Point State Park is a short detour off slow and scenic Hwy 313, 11 miles northeast of Island in the Sky. Note that

LINK YOUR TRIP

28 Monument Valley & Trail of the Ancients

From Monticello, drive 20 miles south to Blanding to start a trip around the ancient-site-filled far southeastern Utah.

29 Dinosaur Diamond Prehistoric Byway

Start a tour of Jurassic-era formations and fossils in Moab.

though your trip begins at Island, you'll be spending all the nights of this trip 42 miles away in Moab.

➋ Dead Horse Point State Park

The views pack a wallop at **Dead Horse Point State Park** (www.stateparks.utah.gov; Hwy 313; park day use per vehicle $15, tent & RV sites $35; ⊙ park 6am-10pm, visitor center 8am-6pm Mar-Oct, 9am-4pm Nov-Feb). At the end of a 4-mile drive you can peer down 2000ft to the Colorado River and 100 miles across a mesmerizing stepped red rock landscape. (You might remember this epic vista from the final scene in *Thelma & Louise*.) Legend has it that cowboys blockaded the narrow entrance to the mesa to corral wild horses, and that they forgot to release them upon leaving. The stranded equines died within view of the unreachable Colorado River below, hence the park name. Ranger-led geology talks are presented daily March through October at the point. To escape the small (but sometimes chatty) crowds, take a walk around the mesa rim.

The Drive » Retrace your tracks back to Hwy 313 and then follow Hwy 191 to Arches; it's 26 miles total.

TRIP HIGHLIGHT

➌ Arches National Park

More than 2000 red sandstone arches cover the relatively compact **Arches National Park** (☎435-719-2299; www.nps.gov/arch; Hwy 191; 7-day pass per vehicle $25; ⊙24hr, visitor center 7:30am-6:30pm Mar-Oct, 9am-4pm Nov-Feb). Add to that mazelike fins and rock-topped spires and you have one wondrous park.

There's one main road (10 miles one way) with scenic stops, and two short spurs. In the **Windows section** several arches can be seen from the pavement. Quick walks lead to other named formations, such as **Sand Dune Arch** (0.4-mile round-trip). To get to the park's most famous feature, **Delicate Arch**, take the 3-mile round-trip trail near Wolfe Ranch or you can overlook it from the viewing area. At the end of the main road, **Devils Garden** marks the beginning of a 2- to 7.7-mile round-trip hike that passes at least eight arches.

Advance reservations (at least a day or two) are necessary for the free, twice-daily ranger-led hikes into the maze of rock that is the **Fiery Furnace** (www.nps.gov/arch/planyourvisit/fiery-furnace.

htm; permits adult/child $6/3; ⊘Mar-Oct). Be prepared for fun scrambling up and over boulders, chimneying down between rocks and navigating narrow ledges.

The Drive » Red rock cliffs surround you on all sides as you drive into the town of Moab.

TRIP HIGHLIGHT

④ Moab

Southeastern Utah's largest community (population 5100) bills itself as the state's recreation capital – and man, does it deliver. The numerous outfitters here can help you find just about any type of outdoors adventure imaginable. Try **Sheri Griffith Expeditions** (☏800-332-2439; www.griffithexp.com; 2231 S Hwy 191; ⊘8am-6pm) for river rafting – family floats to class IV Cataract Canyon rapids. **Poison Spider Bicycles** (☏435-259-7882, 800-635-1792; www.poisonspiderbicycles.com; 497 N Main St; ⊘8am-7pm) will outfit you for mountain biking on the area's **Slickrock Trail** (Sand Flats Recreation Area; www.discovermoab.com/sandflats.htm; car/cyclist $5/2). **Dan Mick's Jeep Tours** (☏435-259-4567; www.danmick.com; 3-person tours from $300) specializes in impressive 4WD trips. **Moab Desert Adventures** (☏804-814-3872; www.moabdesertadventures.com; 415 N Main St; ⊘7am-7pm) offers climbing,

canyoneering and multisport packages. **Canyonlands Field Institute** (☏435-259-7750; www.cfimoab.org; 1320 S Hwy 191; ⊘May-Oct) leads all-ages interpretive hikes and canoe tours. And **Red Cliffs Lodge** (☏435-259-2002, 866-812-2002; www.redcliffslodge.com; Hwy 128, Mile 14) has daily horseback trail rides.

The town itself has an outsized offering of restaurants and motels. Look for Southwestern souvenirs around the intersection of Main and Center Sts. On a rainy day, you might peek into the **Museum of Moab** (www.moabmuseum.org; 118 E Center St; adult/child $5/free; ⊘10am-6pm Mon-Sat Apr-Oct, noon-5pm Mon-Sat Nov-Mar) to learn more about pioneer and American Indian history.

✕ ⊨ p297

The Drive » Businesses get fewer and further between until Moab ends abruptly in desert nothingness at its southern extent. Hole 'n the Rock is only 15 miles along.

----

⑤ Hole 'n the Rock

What didn't Albert and Gladys Christensen do? He was a barber, a painter, an amateur engineer and a taxidermist; she was a cook (their house once contained a restaurant) and lapidary jeweler. But what's really amazing is that they did all this

VICTOR MASCHEK / SHUTTERSTOCK ©

Dead Horse Point State Park

NEWSPAPER ROCK STATE HISTORIC SITE

This tiny, free recreation area showcases a large sandstone rock panel packed with more than 300 petroglyphs attributed to Ute and Ancestral Puebloan groups during a 2000-year period. The many humanoid and animal figures are etched out of the black, mineralized surface called desert varnish, making for great photos – late afternoon light is best. Follow the raised boardwalk along the cliffside to see them all. The site lies 12 miles west of Hwy 191 en route to Canyonlands – Needles District.

while making their home in a 5000-sq-ft cave. An unabashed tourist trap, **Hole 'n the Rock** (www.theholeintherock.com; 11037 S Hwy 191; tours adult/child $6/3.50; ☺9am-5pm; 🐾) is decorated in knockout 1950s kitsch. The couple lived in the blasted-out home until 1974. Today in addition to the cave, there's a yard full of small wooden buildings with shops, a hodgepodge of metal art and a small exotic animal zoo.

The Drive » Following Hwy 191 south 30 miles the views are in the distance and the road moves fast. The next 42 miles on Hwy 211 cross rugged parkland. Scan the sheer cliffs on the right side as you go along; they're a favorite with rock climbers.

❻ Needles District

This district is named for the thin sandstone chimneys jutting skyward in the desert. Here on the canyon floor, the jagged terrain is so different from Islands in the Sky,

it's hard to believe they're both part of Canyonlands National Park (p292). Keep your receipt, because entry to one is good for the other.

Needles District (www.nps.gov/cany; vehicle/cyclist $25/10) receives half as many visitors as other area parks, so it's a great place to get away from it all – especially if you have a 4WD or a mountain bike. Fifty miles of off-road trails (permit required) crisscross the vast landscape.

The 0.6-mile easy to moderate loop of the **Cave Spring Trail** (🐾) is especially popular with kids. The path leads up ladders and over slickrock to an abandoned cowboy camp. The handprint pictographs on the last cave's walls are haunting. To get among the namesake needle formations **Chesler Park/Joint Trail** is an 11-mile loop hike through desert grasslands, past towering red-and-white-striped

pinnacles and between deep, narrow slot canyons.

The Drive » Backtracking along cliffside Hwy 211 to Hwy 191, turn south. The valley opens up then narrows as you gain elevation getting closer to the mountains outside Monticello, 15 miles further along.

❼ Monticello

In the foothills of the Abajo (Blue) Mountains, Monticello sits at 7022ft, a good 3000ft higher (and 10°F/6°C cooler) than Moab. If you're hungry after hiking in the Needles, your closest eating options are here. In this tiny town the **Canyon Country Discovery Center** (📞435-587-2156; www.fourcornersschool.org; 1117 N Main St; adult/child $9/6; ☺10am-6pm Mon-Fri, to 9pm Sat) has interesting exhibits and educational field trips into the backcountry.

Spring wildflowers and fall tree foliage are a novelty among the arid canyonlands of this region. But here they are just west of the town boundaries in the 1.4-million-acre **Manti–La Sal National Forest** (www.fs.fed.us/r4/mantilasal; off N Creek Rd; ☺24hr), which rises to 11,360ft at Abajo Peak. **Abajo-Harts Draw**, off N Creek Rd, is the closest recreation area with trails and campgrounds.

✖ 🛏 p297

Eating & Sleeping

Moab ❹

✖ Desert Bistro   Southern US $$$

(☎435-259-0756; www.desertbistro.com; 36 S
100 W; mains $20-60; ⊘5:30-11pm Wed-Sun)
Stylized preparations of game and fresh, flown-
in seafood are the specialty at this welcoming
white-tablecloth restaurant inside an old
house. Think smoked elk in a huckleberry glaze,
pepper-seared scallops and jicama salad with
crisp pears. Everything is made on site, from
freshly baked bread to delicious pastries. Great
wine list, too.

✖ Milt's   Burgers $

(☎435-259-7424; 356 Mill Creek Dr; mains $4-9;
⊘11am-8pm Mon-Sat) Meet greasy goodness.
A triathlete couple bought this classic 1954
burger stand and smartly changed nothing.
Heaven is one of their honest burgers made
from grass-fed wagyu beef, jammed with
pickles, fresh lettuce, a side of fresh-cut fries
and creamy butterscotch milkshake. Be patient:
the line can get long. It's near the Slickrock Trail
(p294).

✖ Moab Brewery   American $$

(☎435-259-6333; www.themoabbrewery.com;
686 S Main St; mains $10-22; ⊘11:30am-11pm;
🛜) Choose from a list of nine microbrews made
in the vats just behind the bar area. The vast and
varied menu is more impressive than the food
itself. Be aware that service isn't a strong suit.

🛏 Cali Cochitta   B&B $$

(☎435-259-4961, 888-429-8112; www.
moabdreaminn.com; 110 S 200 E; cottages

$155-190; ❄🛜) Charming and central, these
adjoining brick cottages offer snug rooms fitted
with smart decor. A long wooden table on the
patio makes a welcome setting for communal
breakfasts. You can also take advantage of the
porch chairs, hammock or backyard hot tub in
the Zen garden.

🛏 Sunflower Hill Inn   Inn $$$

(☎435-259-2974; www.sunflowerhill.com; 185
N 300 E; r $208-293; ❄🛜🛁) Wow! This is
one of the best bets in town. A top-shelf B&B,
Sunflower Hill offers 12 rooms in a quaint
country setting. Grab a room in the cozier cedar-
sided early 20th-century home over the annex
rooms. All rooms come with quilt-piled beds and
antiques – some even have jetted tubs.

Monticello ❼

🛏 Abajo Haven Guest Ranch   Lodge $

(☎435-979-3126; www.abajohaven.com;
5440 N Cedar Edge Lane; cabins $89) Outdoor
adventure in the Abajo Mountains. Stay in a
nicely rustic cabin (king and two twin beds
each), have an old-fashioned cook-out and go
on a guided hike to ancient sites 1½ hours from
your cabin.

🛏 Canyonlands Lodge
at Blue Mountain   Cabin $$$

(☎435-220-1050; www.canyonlandslodge.com;
Hwy 191; cabins from $395; ❄🛜) A giant log
lodge adjacent to the national forest (p296),
10 miles south of Monticello.

Monument Valley & Trail of the Ancients

28

Extreme desert isolation has preserved rocky natural wonders and numerous Ancestral Puebloan sites in far southeastern Utah and into Arizona.

TRIP HIGHLIGHTS

210 miles

Moki Dugway
Hairpin turns, 1100ft descent – one helluva road

● Blanding

Hovenweep National Monument

8

2

FINISH
Goosenecks ●
State Park

46 miles

Bluff
A comfortable outpost in a remote and rugged landscape

START
1

Monument Valley
Monolithic buttes and mesas defining the desert Southwest

0 miles

---

5 DAYS
262 MILES/422KM

GREAT FOR...

BEST TIME TO GO
October through April to avoid scorching desert heat.

ESSENTIAL PHOTO
Monument Valley's monolithic buttes at sunrise or sunset.

BEST FOR ANCIENT SITES
Hire a guide in Bluff or Monument Valley to help you see amazing rock art and ruins.

Valley of the Gods Hot air balloons float over the desert

28

Monument Valley & Trail of the Ancients

The red rock beauty found here is no exception to southern Utah, but those who come this way want something more. Ancestral Puebloan history courses through the veins of these dusty-hued canyons, pocked with ruins of cliff dwellings and granaries and marked with rock art. Photo highlights include the Valley of the Gods and Goosenecks. Much of this area is now protected in the new Bears Ears National Monument.

TRIP HIGHLIGHT

❶ Monument Valley

Don't worry if you feel like you've seen this place before. Monument Valley's monolithic chocolate-red buttes and colossal, colorful mesas have stared in countless films, TV shows and commercials. The most famous formations are conveniently visible from the 17-mile, rough-dirt **scenic drive** looping through **Monument Valley Navajo Tribal Park** (☎435-727-5870; www.

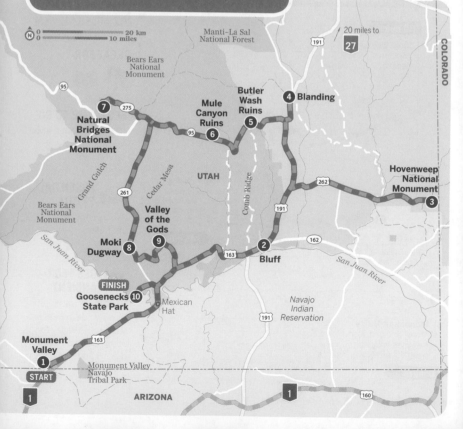

navajonationparks.org; per 4-person vehicle $20; ⊘drive 6am-7pm Apr-Sep, 8am-4:30pm Oct-Mar, visitor center 6am-8pm Apr-Sep, 8am-5pm Oct-Mar; Ⓟ), down a 4-mile spur road south of **Goulding's Lodge** (☏435-727-3231; www.gouldings.com; Hwy 163; r from $130, tent/RV sites $25/36; ▣ ▤), which has a small museum and also offers tours. Note that the park and scenery straddle the Utah–Arizona line.

The only way to get into the backcountry to see rock art, natural arches and coves is by taking a Navajo-led tour on foot, on horseback or by vehicle. Easygoing guides have booths set up in the parking lot at the visitor center. Tours are peppered with details about Diné culture, life on the reservation, movie trivia and whatever else comes to mind.

✗ ▥ p45, p305

The Drive » The monument's mesas diminish then disappear in your rearview mirror as you head north, crossing the San Juan River and continuing along its valley the 45 total miles to Bluff, UT.

- - - - - - - - - - - - - - - - - -

TRIP HIGHLIGHT

❷ Bluff

Tiny tot Bluff (population 320) isn't much, but a few good motels and a handful of restaurants – surrounded by stunning red rock – make it a cool little base for exploring. We've set up the trip for two nights in Monument Valley, two here in Bluff and one in Mexican Hat or back in the Valley. But distances are short enough that you could spend every night in Bluff and take daily forays to area sights.

Descendants of the town's pioneers re-created a tourable log cabin settlement called **Bluff Fort** (www.hirf.org/bluff.asp; 5 E Hwy 191; ⊘9am-6pm Mon-Sat). Three miles west of town on public lands, the accessible **Sand Island Petroglyphs** (www.blm. gov; Sand Island Rd, off Hwy 163; ⊘24hr) were created between 800 and 2500 years ago.

A few outfitters in town lead backcountry excursions that access rock art and ruins.

Far Out Expeditions (☏435-672-2294; www. faroutexpeditions.com; day tours $295) offers single and multiday hikes.

Wild Rivers Expeditions (☏800-422-7654; www. riversandruins.com; half-day trip adult/child $89/69), a history- and geology-minded outfit, rafts along the San Juan. And **Buckhorn Llama** (☏435-672-2466; www.llamapack. com; guided trip per day $250) leads five- and six-day, llama-supported treks – really, llamas.

✗ ▥ p305

The Drive » The best route to Hovenweep is the paved Hwy 262 (past Hatch Trading Post, turn off onto Hwy 191 and follow the signs). From Bluff to the main entrance is a slow, 42-mile drive total (1¼ hours).

- - - - - - - - - - - - - - - - - -

❸ Hovenweep National Monument

Meaning 'deserted valley' in the Ute language, the archaeological sites of **Hovenweep National Monument** (www.nps.gov/hove; Hwy 262; tent & RV sites $10; ⊘ park dusk-dawn, visitor center 8am-6pm Jun-Sep, 9am-5pm Oct-May) exist in splendid isolation. Most of the eight towers and unit houses you'll see in the **Square Towers Group**, accessed near the visitor center, were built from 1230 to 1275 CE.

LINK YOUR TRIP

1 Four Corners Cruise

In Monument Valley pick up this trip to continue exploring the geological wonders and American Indian ancestry of the region.

27 Moab & Southeastern National Parks

One hundred miles north of Bluff, Moab is your base for outdoor activity near Arches and Canyonlands National Parks.

Imagine stacking each clay-formed block to create such tall structures on tiny ledges. You could easily spend a half day or more hiking around the gorge's ruins. Other sites, which lie across the border in Colorado, require long hikes.

The Drive » Bluff is the only base in the area, so you'll have to drive both to Hovenweep and back in one day. Moving on to Blanding, 28 miles north of Bluff, Hwy 191 is a rural road unimpeded by too many twists or turns.

---

❹ Blanding

A special museum elevates small, agriculturally oriented Blanding a little above its totally drab name. The **Edge of the Cedars State Park Museum** (☏435-678-2238; www.stateparks.utah.gov; 660 W 400 N; adult/child $5/3; ⏲9am-5pm Mon-Sat, 10am-4pm Sun) is where you can learn more about the area's ancients, with its trove of archaeological treasures that have been gathered from across southeastern Utah. Outside, climb down the rickety ladder into a dark, earthy-smelling ceremonial kiva (an Ancestral Puebloan ceremonial structure) from c 1100 CE. Can you feel a power to the place? (Just ignore the encroaching subdivision noise.)

Blue Mountain Artisans (www.bluemountain artisans.com; 215 E Center St;

JULIEN HAUTOGEUR / SHUTTERSTOCK ©

⏲11am-6pm Wed-Sat) sells professional photographs of area archaeological and geological sites, plus local jewelry.

🛏 p305

The Drive » Heading west on Hwy 95, the scenery gets up close and personal. Butler Wash is only 14 miles along on free public lands; look for the signs.

---

❺ Butler Wash Ruins

No need to hike for days into the backcountry here: it's only a half-mile tramp to views of the freely accessible Butler Wash Ruins, a 20-room cliff dwelling on public lands. Scramble over the slickrock boulders (follow the cairns) to see

Monument Valley

the sacred kivas, habitation and storage rooms associated with the Ancestral Puebloan (or Anasazi) Kayenta group of northern Arizona c 1300 CE.

The Drive ⟫ Continue west on Hwy 95. After the road veers north, look for a sign announcing more ruins – about 25 miles along.

⑥ Mule Canyon Ruins

Though not particularly well preserved or evocative, the base of the tower, kiva and 12-room Mule Canyon Ruins sit almost roadside. Pottery found here links the population (c 1000 to 1150 CE) to the Mesa Verde group in southern Colorado.

The Drive ⟫ Continue along through the cliffs and canyons of Hwy 95 until you branch off onto the even smaller Hwy 275. The monument is 26 miles west of Mule Canyon.

⑦ Natural Bridges National Monument

The views at **Natural Bridges** (www.nps.gov/ nabr; Hwy 275; 7-day pass per vehicle $10, tent & RV

TAKE ONLY PICTURES

Sadly enough, many invaluable archaeological sites in the area have been vandalized by thieves. Even casual visitors do irreparable damage by climbing on old dwelling walls or picking up 'just one' little pot shard. The old maxim 'take only pictures' bears repeating. Do not touch, move or remove any artifacts; it's against the law. The best way to explore ancient backcountry sites is with a well-informed, responsible guide.

sites $10; 🕑24hr, visitor center 8am-6pm May-Sep, 9am-5pm Oct-Apr) are of a white sandstone canyon (it's not red!). All three impressive and easily accessible bridges are visible from a 9-mile winding **Scenic Drive** loop with overlooks. The oldest is also the closest: take a half-mile hike to the beautifully delicate **Owachomo Bridge**, spanning 180ft at only 9ft thick. Note that trails to Kachina and Siapu bridges are not long, but they require navigating super-steep sections or ladders. Near the end of the drive, don't skip the 0.3-mile trail to the **Horsecollar Ruin** cliff dwelling overlook.

The Drive >> Ocher-yellow to reddish-orange sandstone canyons surround you as you wend your way south on Rte 261. To your right is Cedar Mesa–Grand Gulch primitive area, a seriously challenging wilderness environment now part of the new Bears Ears National Monument. To drive the 36 miles to Moki Dugway will take at least an hour.

TRIP HIGHLIGHT

8 Moki Dugway

Along a roughly paved, hairpin-turn-filled section of road, Moki Dugway descends 1100ft in just 3 miles. Miners 'dug out' the extreme switchbacks in the 1950s to transport uranium ore. Note that the road is far from wide by today's standards, but there are places to pull out. You can't always see what's around the next bend, but you can see down the sheer drop-offs. Those afraid of heights (or in trailers over 24ft long), steer clear.

The Drive >> At the bottom of the dugway, prepare yourself for another wild ride. The turnoff for Valley of the Gods is less than 5 miles ahead on your left.

9 Valley of the Gods

Think of the gravel road through the freely accessible **Valley of the Gods** (www.blm.gov) as a do-it-yourself roller coaster,

with sharp, steep hills and quick turns around some amazing scenery. Locals call it 'mini–Monument Valley.' Download the public lands office pamphlet from www.blm.gov to identify the strangely shaped sandstone monoliths and pinnacles (Seven Sailors, Lady on a Tub, Rooster Butte...). Allow an hour-plus for the 17 miles between Hwys 261 and 163. Do not attempt it without a 4WD if it's rained recently.

The Drive >> Once you emerge from the valley, follow Hwy 163 back west and take the little jog up Hwy 261 to the Goosenecks State Park spur, a total of 8 miles away.

10 Goosenecks State Park Overlook

Following the 4-mile spur to **Goosenecks State Park** (stateparks.utah. gov; vehicle $5, campsite $10) brings you to a mesmerizing view. From 1000ft above you can see how the San Juan River's path carved tight turns through sediment, leaving gooseneck-shaped spits of land untouched. The dusty park itself doesn't have much to speak of besides pit toilets and picnic tables.

Eating & Sleeping

Monument Valley ❶

✗ Stagecoach
Dining Room   American $$

(☎435-727-3231; www.gouldings.com;
Goulding's Trading Post Rd; mains $12-20;
🕓6:30am-9:30pm, shorter hours in winter)
Goulding Lodge's restaurant, Stagecoach
Dining Room, is a replica of a film set built for
John Ford's 1949 Western *She Wore a Yellow
Ribbon*. Get a vitamin kick from the salad bar
before tucking into the steaks or Navajo tacos
piled high with chile and cheese. At lunchtime
it often swarms with coach tourists.

Blutt ❷

✗ Comb Ridge Bistro   Cafe $

(☎435-485-5555; www.combridgebistro.
com; 680 S Hwy 191; breakfast mains $5-7,
dinner mains $10-17; 🕓8am-3pm & 5-9pm
Tue-Sun; 🛜🅿) An adobe gallery and cafe
with standout single-pour coffee, blue-corn
pancakes and breakfast sandwiches loaded
with peppers and eggs. Dinner includes
pasture-raised beef in the form of homemade
meatloaf or whiskey burgers, organic salads
and good vegetarian options.

🛏 Valley of the Gods B&B   B&B $$

(☎970-749-1164; www.valleyofthegodsbandb.
com; off Hwy 261; s/d $145/175, cabin $195)
Spend a secluded night at one of the original
ranches in the area, 6.5 miles north of Hwy
163. Exposed wood-and-stone rooms have
simple rustic beds, and the on-site cabin is just
magical. Water is trucked in and solar power
is harnessed out of necessity here (leave your
hair dryer at home).

Blanding ❹

🛏 Stone Lizard Lodge   Motel $$

(☎435-678-3323; www.stonelizardlodging.
com; 88 W Center St; r $104-109, ste $155-249;
🛜) More than a motel, with spacious rooms
sporting Southwestern themes, homemade
cinnamon rolls for breakfast and a huge back
garden with strawberries for the picking. The
suites feel like a welcoming home. Wander
into the office to borrow a book from the great
regional library.

Mexican Hat ❺

🛏 San Juan Inn   Motel $

(☎435-683-2220; www.sanjuaninn.net; Hwy
163; r from $84, apt $265, yurt from $90;
❄🛜) The cliffside San Juan Inn perches high
above the river. These basic motel rooms are
the nicest in town, with quilted comforters and
flat-screen TVs. There's also a **trading post**
(🕓7am-9pm) and restaurant on-site. Yurt
accommodations are in round tents decked out
with air-conditioning, wi-fi and views.

Vernal
UTAH'S DINOSAUR LAND

Dinosaur Diamond Prehistoric Byway

29

Take a trip back in time to when allosaurus walked the earth. Cruise through this incredibly fossil-rich landscape, then dig into the many museums and quarries to learn more.

TRIP HIGHLIGHTS

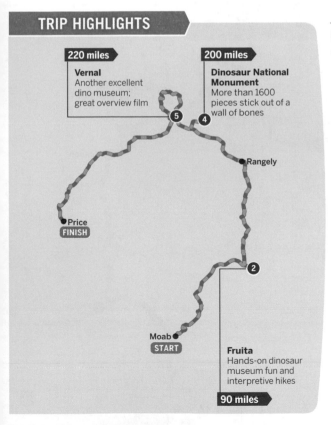

220 miles

Vernal
Another excellent dino museum; great overview film

200 miles

Dinosaur National Monument
More than 1600 pieces stick out of a wall of bones

Rangely

Price
FINISH

Moab
START

Fruita
Hands-on dinosaur museum fun and interpretive hikes

90 miles

6 DAYS
408 MILES / 656KM

GREAT FOR...

BEST TIME TO GO
May and September have temperate weather, but activities for kiddos happen June to August.

ESSENTIAL PHOTO
A lower leg bone big as your body at Dinosaur National Monument.

BEST FOR FAMILIES
Digging to find 'dinosaur bones' at the Dinosaur Journey museum.

29 Dinosaur Diamond Prehistoric Byway

Imagine the most remote and rugged place you've seen. Driving the diamond you'll conquer high plateaus, traverse scenic canyons and cross tall mountains. Though arid now, in the late Jurassic period (154 to 147 million years ago) this mostly Morrison Formation terrain was a lush, subtropical forest. Eighty different vertebrates have been found within this one region. Utah and Colorado combined represent the most complete fossil record in the US.

❶ Moab

Situated between two national parks and surrounded by even more public land, Moab makes a good base for outdoor adventure. If you want to track area dinosaurs, pick up the topical pamphlets from the **Moab Information Center** (www.discovermoab.com; 25 E Center St; ⏲8am-7pm; 📶). The half-mile **Mill Canyon Dinosaur Trail**, 15 miles north of town, follows a Jurassic-era stream bed where fossils and petrified wood are

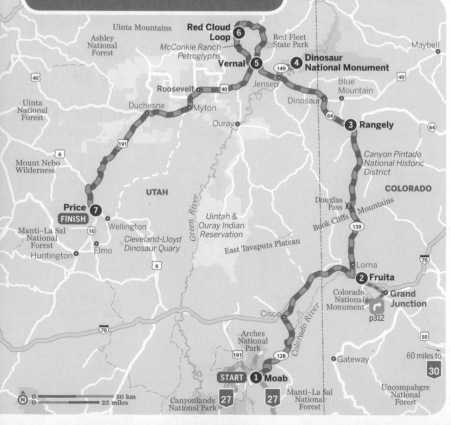

to be seen. Plus there's a detour to a track site. **Comb Ridge Sauropod Trackway**, 23 miles north, contains four different sets of fossilized footprints.

Numerous outdoor operators lead excursions into the region. **Adrift Adventures** (☎435-259-8594, 800-874-4483; www.adrift.net; 378 N Main St) offers 4WD trips that focus on prehistoric sites – both dinosaur bones and ancient rock art. With **Canyonlands by Night & Day** (☎435-259-5261, 800-394-9978; www.canyonlandsbynight.com; 1861 N Hwy 191; adult/child $69/59; ☺Apr-Oct; 🚌), an evening dinner cruise

LINK YOUR TRIP

27 Moab & Southeastern National Parks

Before your dinosaur odyssey, spend a few activity-filled days exploring the national parks around Moab.

30 San Juan Skyway & Million Dollar Highway

For incredible vistas and old mining towns, detour 105 miles southwest on Hwy 50 to start this trip in Ouray, CO.

down the Colorado comes complete with a sound-and-light show.

🛏 p313

The Drive » Two miles north of Moab, follow the long and winding River Rd (Hwy 128) through the Colorado River gorge for 44 miles (1¼ hours) before exiting at Cisco, which is a further 42 speedy, interstate miles from Fruita.

TRIP HIGHLIGHT

❷ Fruita

Two miles inside the Colorado state line, stop at the **Trail Through Time** (www.blm.gov; I-70, exit 2, McInnis Canyons National Conservation Area; ☺dawn-dusk), the best of four interpretive dinosaur trails around town. On the 1.5-mile loop you can learn loads about the prehistoric landscape from interpretive panels, touch in-situ bones and, in summer, check out the active **Mygatt-Moore Quarry**.

Maybe it's the desolation of the dry, rumbling country; maybe it's the lack of anything human-made in your view. Whatever the reason, it seems entirely possible to imagine dinosaurs roaming **Fruita Paleontological Area** (www.blm.gov; Horsethief Rd, off Kings View Rd; ☺dawn-dusk). A half-mile loop trail leads past helpful signs illustrating the environment and the six dinosaurs found here during 100

years of off-and-on excavation.

Dinosaur Journey (☎970-858-7282; www.museumofwesternco.com; 550 Jurassic Ct; adult/child $9/5; ☺9am-5pm Mon-Sun May-Sep, 10am-4pm Mon-Sat & from noon Sun Oct-Apr; 🚼) is a fantastic little family-friendly museum where kiddos can make their own dinosaur tracks, dig for bones and be surprised by a spitting and spurting, animatronic dilophosaurus. Unlike many big-city museums, the fossils here are actually from the region.

✕ 🛏 p313

The Drive » Backtracking 4 miles west on I-70, take exit 15 north to CO 139. You start out in Loma, but soon enough the gray cliffs emerge and the road rises to wind its way up and over Douglas Pass (8268ft). Driving the 71 miles to Rangely will take 1½ hours.

---

❸ Rangely

South of Rangely, **Canyon Pintado National Historic District** (www.blm.gov; CO 139; ☺24hr) protects the ancient archaeology of the area's Freemont and Ute cultures. Seven rock-art sites are easily accessible off CO 139. Stop at the South Orientation Center sign (Mile 52.8) for information or pick up an interpretive brochure at the **Rangely Chamber of Commerce**

(📞970-675-5290; www.
rangely.com; 209 E Main St;
🕑1-5pm Mon-Fri). The lat-
ter also has a list of other
rock-art sites scattered
along area back roads.

An oil-service town,
Rangely itself isn't much
to look at, but its handful
of motels and restaurants
make it a good stop
en route to Dinosaur
National Monument.

The Drive » Follow CO 64
out of Rangely, through a stark
landscape; after 18 miles be
sure to turn east (right) on
Hwy 40 to get to the Colorado
section of the monument.

- - - - - - - - - - - - - - - - -

TRIP HIGHLIGHT

❹ Dinosaur National Monument

Straddling the Utah–
Colorado state line,
**Dinosaur National
Monument** (www.nps.
gov/dino; off Hwy 40, Vernal;
7-day passes per vehicle $20;
🕑24hr) protects one of
North America's largest
dinosaur fossil beds,
discovered here in 1909.
Though each state's sec-
tion is beautiful, Utah
has the bones.

Start at the **Canyon
Area Visitor Center** in
Colorado where you can
pick up an interpre-
tive brochure for the
**Harpers Corner Scenic
Drive** (31 miles one-way),
which cruises from
5921ft to 7625ft with
several overlooks along
the way.

Visitors need to
backtrack to Hwy 40 to
access the Utah section,

30 miles west. Abso-
lutely do not miss the
Quarry Exhibit, which
is an enclosed, partially
excavated rock wall with
more than 1600 actual
bones sticking out –
an amazing, almost
unbelievable sight to
see. (The area was once
a stream bed where
remains collected.) Fol-
low the **Fossil Discovery
Trail** (2.2 miles round-
trip) to touch a few more
rock-bound giant femurs
and such.

The Drive » From the Utah
side of the national monument,
Vernal is 15 miles away via
UT 149 and Hwy 40.

- - - - - - - - - - - - - - - - -

TRIP HIGHLIGHT

❺ Vernal

The only town of any
size around, Vernal, UT,
serves as the gateway for
the national monument.
Not that you'd notice
with a giant pink sauro-
pod statue welcoming
you or anything.

The informative film
at the **Utah Field House
of Natural History State
Park Museum** (📞435-789-
3799; stateparks.utah.gov;
496 E Main St; 🕑9am-7pm
Apr-Aug, to 5pm low season;
🚻) provides a great
all-round overview of
the region's paleonto-
logical history. Interac-
tive exhibits, expert
interview videos, and, of
course, giant mounted
fossils, further tell the
story.

Before you go, stop at
the **Dinosaurland Tourist

Board (Vernal Chamber
of Commerce; 📞800-477-
5558; www.dinoland.com;
134 W Main St; 🕑9am-5pm
Mon-Fri) for pamphlets on
the Red Cloud Loop and
other regional driving
tours.

🍴 🛏 p313

The Drive » Following the
detailed directions you picked
up in Vernal, drive the Red
Cloud Loop, keeping your eyes
peeled for deer and elk. Note
that a substantial portion of
this drive is on unpaved roads
and you should check on road
conditions before you depart.

- - - - - - - - - - - - - - - - -

❻ Red Cloud Loop

Take a slowly scenic,
74-mile drive on the Red
Cloud Loop backway
to explore the ancient
environs. Check out
hundreds of fossilized
dinosaur tracks at **Red
Fleet State Park** (📞435-
789-4432; stateparks.utah.
gov; day use $7, tent/RV
sites $15/25; 🕑6am-10pm
Apr-Oct, 8am-5pm Nov & Dec).
The 200ft of **McConkie
Ranch Petroglyphs**
(Dry Fork Canyon Rd; by
donation; 🕑dawn-dusk)
are also fascinating.
Generous ranch owners
built a little self-serve
info shack with posted
messages and a map,
but be advised that the
800-year-old Fremont
Indian art here requires
some rock-scrambling
to see. Being on private
land has really helped;
these alien-looking
anthropomorphs are in

McConkie Ranch Petroglyphs

DETOUR:
COLORADO NATIONAL
MONUMENT

Start: ❷ Fruita

The **Colorado National Monument** (☎970-858-3617, ext 360; www.nps.gov/colm; Hwy 340; 7-day per vehicle $15; ⏱24hr, visitor center 9am-6pm) is the crown jewel of the Western Slope, a place where the setting sun seems to set fire to otherworldly red rock formations and hikers test themselves against a starkly beautiful environment. Rising 2000ft above the river valley, these colorful canyons expose the geologic history of the area. Learn more about the different sedimentary layers at the visitor center, then step out to overlook the stratification in real life.

The monument contains a variety of hiking trails starting on the 23-mile **Rim Rock Drive**, most of them relatively short, such as the half-mile hike starting from the **Coke Ovens Trailhead** or a quarter-mile stroll starting at the **Devils Kitchen Trailhead**. The park's highest, **Black Ridge Trail** (5.5 miles one-way) traipses up and down through the Morrison Formation of Jurassic dinosaur fame. The west entrance to this 32-sq-mile scenic wonder is 2 miles south of Fruita, off I-70.

much better shape than the many that have been desecrated by vandals on public lands.

The Drive » Red Cloud Loop ends where you started, in Vernal. From there follow Hwy 191 south. The next 110 miles (around two hours) snake through canyons and over ridges to reach Price. For Cleveland-Lloyd quarry, take CO 10 south to the Elmo-Cleveland turnoff and follow signs 15 miles southeast on dirt roads.

❼ Price

Though limited in scope, the **College of Eastern Utah Prehistoric Museum** (☎435-613-5060; www.usueastern.edu/museum; 155 East Main St; adult/child $6/3; ⏱9am-5pm Mon-Sat) has worked to make its fossil displays a bit more dynamic. Get directions there for the remote **Cleveland-Lloyd Dinosaur Quarry** (☎435-636-3600; www.blm.gov; off Hwy 10; adult/child $5/2; ⏱10am-5pm Thu-Sat, noon-5pm Sun late Mar–Oct), 32 miles south of Price. More than 12,000 bones have been taken from the ground there, the largest concentration of which belonged to meat-eating allosaurs. Excellent exhibits examine why so many of one species was found in one place. Salt Lake City is 110 miles northeast.

🛏 p313

Eating & Sleeping

Moab 1

3 Dogs and a Moose — B&B $$

(☎435-260-1692; www.3dogsandamoosecottages.com; 171 W Center St; cottages $135-305; ❄ 📶 🐾) Lovely and low-key, these four downtown cottages make an ideal base camp for groups and families who want a little socializing in situ. The style is French country meets playful modern. Even better, you can pick your own tomatoes in the landscaped yard, where there are also hammocks, a bike wash, a grill and a hot tub.

Fruita 2

Aspen Street Coffee — Cafe $

(☎970-858-8888; 136 E Aspen Ave; dishes $2-8; ⏰6:30am-5pm Mon-Sat, 7am-1pm Sun; 📶) With simple wraps, strong coffee and homemade granola, this is a great spot to stock up before the ride.

Hot Tomato Cafe — Pizza $

(☎970-858-1117; www.hottomatocafe.com; 124 N Mulberry St; small pizzas $12-16; ⏰11am-9pm Tue-Sat) This pizza joint and cyclist hangout is run by Jen and Anne, a pair of bike enthusiasts who espouse a sustainable business ethos. Pizza comes in thick slices, and there's a good salad selection and a row of Colorado beer on tap. When it gets late, there's a fun scene on the small outdoor patio.

Balanced Rock Motel — Motel $

(☎970-858-7333, ext 4; www.balancedrockmotel.com; 126 S Coulson St; d $65; ❄ 📶) Tidy and well maintained, the independent Balanced Rock is an excellent value for the price. The two-story, exterior-access motel is popular with mountain bikers.

Vernal 5

Vernal Brewing Company — Pub Food $$

(☎435-781-2337; www.vernalbrewingco.com; 55 S 500 E; mains $11-20; ⏰11:30am-9pm Mon-Sat) This craft brewery has come to dinosaur town and it's a home run. There are five house brews on tap, including a peach-infused wheat ale. Dine on gooey mac and cheese, green salad topped with grilled salmon or a red-blooded American burger.

Holiday Inn Express & Suites — Hotel $$

(☎800-315-2621, 435-789-4654; www.holidayinn.com/vernal; 1515 W Hwy 40; r $119-176; ❄ 📶 🏊) One of the nicest chain hotels in town, the HI Express has loads of amenities (fitness center, business center, laundry, morning newspapers and turn-down service). Kids' laughter often fills the indoor pool and jacuzzi..

Price 7

San Rafael Swell Bed & Breakfast — B&B $$

(☎435-381-5689; www.sanrafaelbedandbreakfast.com; 15 E 100 N, Castle Dale; r incl breakfast $85-140; ❄ 📶) San Rafael Swell Bed & Breakfast offers a personal touch with imaginative themed rooms that transport you to Asia, Hawaii and an English garden. Less expensive rooms share a bathroom.

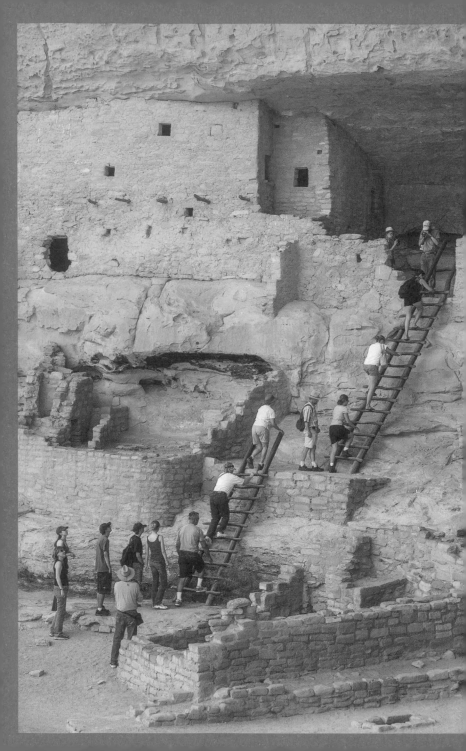

Classic Trip

San Juan Skyway & Million Dollar Highway

30

Encompassing the vertiginous Million Dollar Hwy, the San Juan Skyway loops southern Colorado, traveling magnificent passes to alluring Old West towns.

TRIP HIGHLIGHTS

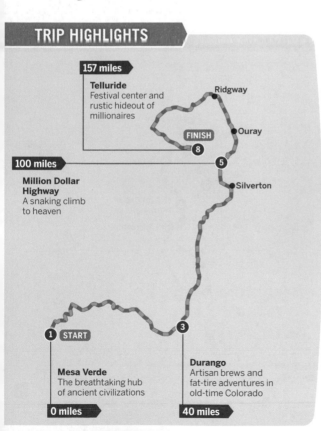

157 miles

Telluride
Festival center and rustic hideout of millionaires

Ridgway

FINISH
8

Ouray

100 miles

Million Dollar Highway
A snaking climb to heaven

5

Silverton

1 **START**

3

Mesa Verde
The breathtaking hub of ancient civilizations

Durango
Artisan brews and fat-tire adventures in old-time Colorado

0 miles

40 miles

6–8 DAYS
157 MILES/253KM

GREAT FOR...

BEST TIME TO GO
Visit from June to October for clear roads and summer fun.

 ESSENTIAL PHOTO
Snap Mesa Verde's dramatic cliff dwellings.

 BEST FOR FOODIES
The farm-to-table options in Mancos and Durango.

Mesa Verde National Park Ancestral Puebloan cliff dwellings

Classic Trip

30 San Juan Skyway & Million Dollar Highway

This is the West at its most rugged: a landscape of twisting mountain passes and ancient ruins, with burly peaks and gusty high desert plateaus, a land of unbroken spirit. Beyond the thrills of outdoor adventure and the rough charm of old plank saloons, there remains the lingering mystery of the region's earliest inhabitants whose awe-inspiring cliff dwellings make up Mesa Verde National Park.

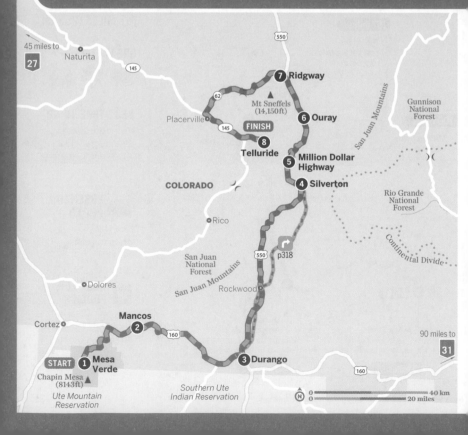

❶ Mesa Verde

More than 700 years after Ancestral Puebloans left, the mystery behind their last known home remains. Amateur anthropologists love it; the incredible cultural heritage makes it unique among American national parks. Ancestral Puebloan sites are scattered throughout the canyons and mesas, perched on a high plateau south of Mancos, though many remain off-limits to visitors.

If you only have a few hours, stop at **Mesa Verde Visitor & Research Center**

LINK YOUR TRIP

27 Moab & Southeastern National Parks

It's a three-hour drive from Telluride. Take CO 145 north to CO 90 west, which becomes UT 26 west. It ends at UT 141; head north.

31 Colorado's High Country Byways

From Durango it's a four-hour drive on the CO 160 to Alamosa; from here take CO 285 north to Great Sand Dunes National Park.

(📞970-529-5034; www.nps. gov/meve; ⏰8am-7pm Jun– early Sep, to 5pm early Sep– mid-Oct, closed mid-Oct–May; 📶♿) and drive around **Chapin Mesa** where you can take a ranger-led tour to **Balcony House** (www.recreation.gov; Cliff Palace Loop; 1hr guided tour $5; P ♿), climbing to a well-preserved, hidden cliff dwelling via an exposed ladder. Purchase your ticket a day in advance at the visitor center.

If you have a day or more, buy tickets in advance for popular ranger-led tours of Cliff Palace and Balcony House. These active visits involve climbing rung ladders and scooting through ancient passages. The heat in summer is brutal – go early if you want to hike or cool off at the informative **Chapin Mesa Museum** (📞970-529-4475; www.nps. gov/meve; Chapin Mesa Rd; admission included with park entry; ⏰8am-6:30pm Apr– mid-Oct, 8am-5pm mid-Oct– Apr; P ♿) near Spruce Tree House.

The Drive ❯❯ Entering Mesa Verde, go immediately left for the visitor center. Return to the main access road. It takes 45 minutes to reach the main attractions on Wetherill Mesa and the road is steep and narrow in places. Leaving the park, head east on Hwy 160 for Mancos, exit right for Main St and follow to the intersection with Grand Ave.

❸ Durango

A regional darling, Durango's style straddles its ragtime past and a cool, cutting-edge future where townie bikes, caffeine and farmers

❷ Mancos

Blink and you'll miss this hamlet embracing the offbeat, earthy and slightly strange (witness the puppets dangling through the roof of the local coffee shop). With a vibrant arts community and love for locavore food, Mancos is the perfect rest stop. You will find most points of interest in a three-block radius. These include a custom hat shop, galleries and good cooking. During the last Friday of each month, the Arts Walk fires up what locals deem 'downtown.'

The area's oddest accommodations is **Jersey Jim Lookout Tower** (📞970-533-7060; r $40; ⏰mid-May–mid-Oct), a watch tower standing 55ft high with panoramic views. This sought-after lodging is 14 miles north of Mancos at 9800ft. It comes with an Osborne Fire Finder and topographic map.

The Drive ❯❯ Drive east on Hwy 160. Reaching Durango turn left onto Camino del Rio and right onto W 11th St in half a mile. Main Ave is your second right.

Classic Trip

markets rule. Outdoor enthusiasts get ready to be smitten. The **Animas River** floats right through town; float it or fly-fish it, while hundreds of mountain-bike rides range from scenic dirt roads to steep singletrack. When you've gotten your kicks, you can join the summer crowds strolling **Main Ave**, stopping at book stores, boutiques and breweries.

Leave town heading north on the **San Juan Skyway** (Hwy 550), which passes farms and stables as it starts the scenic climb toward Silverton. Bring your hunger to the family-run **James Ranch** (Animas

River Valley; mains $6-13; ⏰11am-7pm Mon-Sat) just 10 miles out of Durango. The outstanding farmstand grill features the farm's own organic grass-fed beef, cheese and fresh produce market. Steak sandwiches and focaccia cheese melts with caramelized onions simply rock. Kids dig the goats. Thursday features Burgers & Bands from July to October (adult/child $20/10). A two-hour farm tour ($18) is held on Mondays and Fridays at 9:30am and Tuesdays at 4pm.

The Drive » Take Main Ave heading north. Leaving Durango it becomes Hwy 550, also part of the San Juan Skyway. James Ranch is 10 miles in on the right side. A band of 14,000ft peaks becomes visible to the right and frequent pullouts offer scenic views. Before Silverton the

road climbs both Coal Banks Pass (10,640ft) and Molas Pass (10,910ft).

----

4 Silverton

Ringed by snowy peaks and proudly steeped in tawdry mining-town lore, Silverton would seem more at home in Alaska than the lower 48. At 9318ft the air is thin, but that discourages no one from hitting the bar stool.

Explore it all and don't shy away from the mere 500 locals – they're happy to see a fresh face. It's a two-street town, but only respectable **Greene St**, now home to restaurants and trinket shops, is paved. One block over, notorious **Blair St** was a silver-rush hub of brothels and boozing establishments, banished to the back street where real ladies didn't stroll.

Stop at the **Silverton Museum** (☎970-387-5838; www.silvertonhistoricsociety. org; 1557 Greene St; adult/child $8/3; ⏰10am-4pm Jun-Oct; P ♿), housed in the old San Juan County Jail, to see the original cells. It tells the Silverton story from terrible mining accidents to prostitution, drinking, gambling and robbery, showing the many ways to meet a grisly end in the West.

Most visitors use Silverton as a hub for Jeep tours – sketchy mining

---

DETOUR:
NARROW GAUGE
RAILROAD

Start: 3 Durango

Climb aboard the steam-driven **Durango & Silverton Narrow Gauge Railroad** (☎970-247-2733; www.durangotrain.com; 479 Main Ave; return adult/child 4-11yr from $89/55; ⏰May-Oct; ♿) for the train ride of the summer. The train, running between Durango and Silverton, has been in continuous operation for 123 years, and the scenic 45-mile journey north to Silverton, a National Historic Landmark, takes 3½ hours one-way. Most locals recommend taking it one way and returning from Silverton via bus; it's faster. It's most glorious in late September and early October when the Aspens go golden.

roads climbing in all directions offer unreal views. In winter, **Silverton Mountain** (☎970-387-5706; www.silvertonmountain.com; State Hwy 110; daily lift ticket $59, all-day guide & lift ticket $159) offers experts the best in untamed, ungroomed terrain.

 p323

The Drive » Leaving Silverton head north on Hwy 550, the Million Dollar Hwy. It starts with a gentle climb but becomes steeper. Hairpin turns slow traffic at Molas Pass to 25mph. The most hair-raising sections follow, with 15mph speed limits in places. The road lacks guardrails and drops are huge, so stay attentive. Pullouts provide relief between mile markers 91 and 93.

- - - - - - - - - - - - - - - - - -

TRIP HIGHLIGHT

❺ Million Dollar Highway

The origin of the name of this 24-mile stretch between Silverton and Ouray is disputed – some say it took a million dollars a mile to build it in the 1920s; others purport the roadbed contains valuable ore.

Among America's most memorable drives, this breathtaking stretch passes old mine head frames and larger-than-life alpine scenery. Though paved, its blind corners, tunnels and narrow turns would put the Roadrunner on edge. It's often closed in winter, when it's said to have more avalanches than

the entire state of Colorado. Snowfall usually starts in October.

Leaving Silverton, the road ascends Mineral Creek Valley, passing the Longfellow mine ruins 1 mile before **Red Mountain Pass** (11,018ft), with sheer drops and hairpin turns slowing traffic to 25mph.

Descending toward Ouray, visit **Bear Creek Falls**, a large turnout with a daring viewing platform over the crashing several-hundred-foot falls. A difficult 8-mile trail here switchbacks to even greater views – not for vertigo sufferers.

Stop at the **lookout** over Ouray at mile marker 92. Turn right for the lovely **Amphitheater Campground**

LOCAL KNOWLEDGE: COLORADO'S HAUTE ROUTE

An exceptional way to enjoy hundreds of miles of singletrack in summer or virgin powder slopes in winter, **San Juan Hut System** (☎970-626-3033; www.sanjuanhuts.com; per person $30) continues the European tradition of hut-to-hut adventures with five backcountry mountain huts. Bring just your food, flashlight and sleeping bag – amenities include padded bunks, propane stoves, wood stoves for heating and firewood.

Mountain-biking routes go from Durango or Telluride to Moab, winding through high alpine and desert regions. Or pick one hut as your base. There's terrain for all levels, though skiers should have knowledge of snow and avalanche conditions or go with a guide. The website has helpful tips and information on rental skis, bikes and (optional) guides based in Ridgway or Ouray.

(☎877-444-6777; www.recreation.gov; Hwy 550; tent sites $20; ◷Jun-Aug).

The Drive » The Million Dollar Hwy makes a steep descent into Ouray and becomes Main St.

- - - - - - - - - - - - - - - - - -

❻ Ouray

A well-preserved mining village snug beneath imposing peaks, Ouray breeds enchantment. It's named after the legendary Ute chief who kept the peace between the white settlers and the crush of miners invading the San Juan Mountains in the early 1870s, by relinquishing the Ute tribal lands. The area is rife with hot springs. One cool cave spring, now located underneath the **Wiesbaden Hotel** (☎970-325-4347; www.

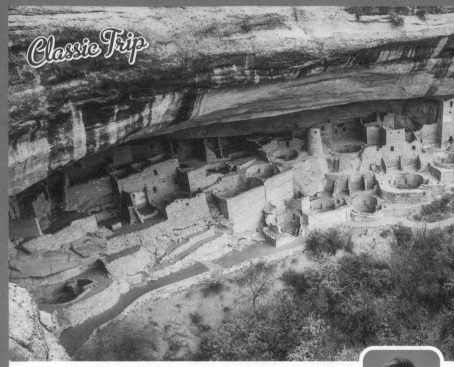

Classic Trip

ERIC LIMON / SHUTTERSTOCK ©

WHY THIS IS A CLASSIC TRIP
CAROLYN MCCARTHY, WRITER

This trip is Colorado at its most breathtaking, with winding country roads and spunky mining towns backed by the chiseled San Juan Mountains. Want to feel the Wild West? Try making small talk with the barkeeps and hotel hosts in Ouray, Silverton and Telluride. In these parts, every 19th-century saloon or historic hotel has a ghost story to share. Check out the bullet holes in Telluride's New Sheridan Bar.

Above: Cliff Palace, Mesa Verde
Left: Gondola, Telluride
Right: Hiking near Telluride

wiesbadenhotsprings.com; 625 5th St; r $132-347; ☺🛜🏊), was favored by Chief Ouray. Now you can soak there by the hour.

The annual **Ouray Ice Festival** (📞970-325-4288; www.ourayicefestival.com; donation for evening events; ⊙Jan; 👨) draws elite climbers for a four-day competition. But the town also lends thrills to hikers and 4WD fans. If you're skittish about driving yourself, **San Juan Scenic Jeep Tours** (📞970-325-0089; www.sanjuanjeeptours.com; 206 7th Ave; adult/child half-day $59/30; 👨) takes open-air Jeeps into the high country, offering special wildflower or ghost-town trips. It's worth hiking up to **Box Canyon Falls** (off Box Canyon Rd; adult/child $4/2; ⊙8am-8pm Jun-Aug; P 👨) from the west end of 3rd Avenue. A suspension bridge leads you into the belly of this 285ft waterfall. The surrounding area is rich in birdlife – look for the protected black swift, which nests in the rock face.

🍴 🛏️ p323

The Drive » Leave Ouray heading north via Main St, which becomes Hwy 550 N. It's a flat 10-mile drive to Ridgway's only traffic light. Turn left onto Sherman St. The center of town is spread over the next half-mile.

❼ Ridgway

Wide open meadows backed by snowcovered San Juans and the stellar Mt Sneffels, Ridgway is an inviting blip of a burg. The backdrop of John Wayne's 1969 cowboy classic *True Grit*, today it sports a sort of neo-Western charm.

Sunny rock pools at **Orvis Hot Springs** (☎970-626-5324; www. orvishotsprings.com; 1585 County Rd 3; per hour/day $18/22) make this clothing-optional hot spring hard to resist. Though it gets its fair share of exhibitionists, a variety of soaking areas (100°F to 114°F/37°C to 45°c) mean you can probably scout out the perfect quiet

spot. Less appealing are the private indoor pools lacking fresh air. It's 9 miles north of Ouray, outside Ridgway.

The Drive 》 Leaving town heading west, Sherman St becomes CO 62. Take this easy drive 23 miles. At the crossroads go left onto CO 145 S for Telluride. Approaching town there's a traffic circle; take the second exit onto W Colorado Ave. The center of Telluride is in half a mile.

TRIP HIGHLIGHT

❽ Telluride

Surrounded on three sides by mastodon peaks, exclusive Telluride was once a rough mining town. Today it's dirtbag-meets-diva – where glitterati mix with ski bums, and renowned music and film festivals create a frolicking summer atmosphere.

The very renovated center still has palpable old-time charm. Stop into

the plush **New Sheridan Bar** (☎970-728-3911; www. newsheridan.com; 231 W Colorado Ave, New Sheridan Hotel; ☺5pm-2am) to find out the story of those old bullet holes in the wall and the plucky survival of the bar itself, even as the adjoining hotel sold off chandeliers to pay the heating bills during waning mining fortunes.

Touring downtown, check out the **free box** where you can swap unwanted items; the tradition is a point of civic pride. Then take a free 15-minute **gondola** (S Oak St; ☺7am-midnight; 🎿) ride up to the Telluride Mountain Village, where you can rent a mountain bike, dine or just bask in the panoramas.

If you are planning on attending a festival, book your tickets and lodging months in advance.

✕ 🏠 p323

TELLURIDE FESTIVALS

Telluride is mountain magic in the summer when bluebird skies converge with stellar festival opportunities. For more information, see www. visittelluride.com/festivals-events.

Mountainfilm (late May) A four-day screening of high-caliber outdoor adventure and environmental films.

Telluride Bluegrass Festival (late Jun) Thousands enjoy a weekend of top-notch rollicking alfresco bluegrass going well into the night.

Telluride Film Festival (early Sep) National and international films are premiered throughout town, and the event attracts big-name stars.

Eating & Sleeping

Silverton ❹

🛏 Inn of the Rockies at the Historic Alma House   B&B $$

(📞970-387-5336, toll-free 800-267-5336; www.innoftherockies.com; 220 E 10th St; r $129-173; 🅿️ ☻ ❊) Opened by a local named Alma in 1898, this inn has nine unique rooms furnished with Victorian antiques. The hospitality is first-rate and its New Orleans–inspired breakfasts, served in a chandelier-lit dining room, merit special mention. Cheaper rates are available without breakfast. There's also a garden hot tub for soaking after a long day.

Ouray ❻

🍴 Don Ton Restaurant   French, Italian $$$

(📞970-325-4419; www.bontonrestaurant.com; 426 Main St; mains $16-40; ⏱5:30-11pm Thu-Mon, brunch 9:30am-12:30pm Sat & Sun; 🍴) Bon Ton has been serving supper for a century in a beautiful room under the historic St Elmo Hotel. The French-Italian menu includes specialties like roast duck in cherry peppercorn sauce and tortellini with bacon and shallots. The champagne brunch comes recommended.

🛏 Box Canyon Lodge & Hot Springs   Lodge $$

(📞800-327-5080, 970-325-4981; www.boxcanyonouray.com; 45 3rd Ave; r $189; 🛜) It's not every hotel that offers geothermal heating, not to mention pineboard rooms that are spacious and fresh, and spring-fed barrel hot tubs – perfect for a romantic stargazing soak. With good hospitality that includes free apples and bottled water, it's popular, so book ahead.

Telluride ❽

🍴 Chop House   Modern American $$$

(📞970-728-4531; www.newsheridan.com; 231 W Colorado Ave, New Sheridan Hotel; mains $26-62; ⏱5pm-2am) With superb service and a chic decor of embroidered velvet benches, this is an easy pick for an intimate dinner. Start with a cheese plate, but from there the menu gets Western with exquisite elk shortloin and ravioli with tomato relish and local sheep-milk ricotta.

🛏 Telluride Town Park Campground   Campground $

(📞970-728-2173; 500 E Colorado Ave; campsite with/without vehicle space $28/17; ⏱ mid-May–mid-Oct; 🏕🏊) Right in the center of town, this convenient creekside campground has 43 campsites, along with showers, swimming and tennis. Sites are all on a first-come, first-served basis, unless it's festival time (consult ahead with festival organizers). Fancy some nightlife with your camping? Why not.

Colorado's High Country Byways

31

This breathtaking trip takes you from the front range to the high-country byways that connect the Rocky Mountains with the continental divide and scudding mountains of the south.

TRIP HIGHLIGHTS

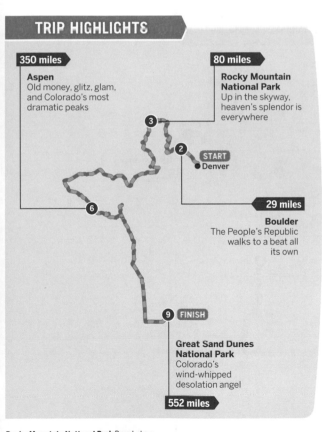

350 miles

Aspen
Old money, glitz, glam, and Colorado's most dramatic peaks

80 miles

Rocky Mountain National Park
Up in the skyway, heaven's splendor is everywhere

3

2

START
● Denver

6

29 miles

Boulder
The People's Republic walks to a beat all its own

9 **FINISH**

Great Sand Dunes National Park
Colorado's wind-whipped desolation angel

552 miles

5–7 DAYS
552 MILES/888KM

GREAT FOR...

BEST TIME TO GO
June to September for clear roads, wildflowers, aspens and great views.

 ESSENTIAL PHOTO
Maroon Bells.

 BEST FOR WILDLIFE
Capture Colorado's signature peaks in all their alpenglow glory.

Colorado's High Country Byways

This high-country Rocky Mountain thriller brings wild-world explorers across the continental divide through hairpin turns, lost alpine lakes, exhilarating landscapes, broken-down mining towns and some of the state's most tanned and toned towns. You'll climb to 12,096ft and dusty-bottom your way past towering snowcapped peaks, then end up in a vast sand-dune wonderworld of arching skies, howling winds and surreal landscapes.

❶ Denver

Spirited and urbane, Denver is the West's cosmopolitan capital, and well worth a day of exploration (p342). This city is blessed with great museums, tons of sunshine and spectacular parks and bike trails.

✕ 🛏 p331

The Drive ⟫ Take I-25 N on this 30-mile drive, veering west onto Hwy 36 W, which will take you past the worthwhile Butterfly Pavilion on your way to crunched-out Boulder.

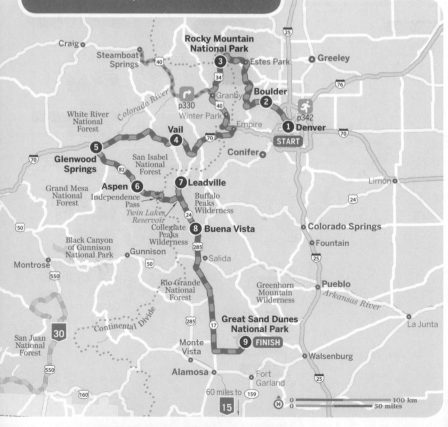

❷ Boulder

Tucked up against its soaring signature Flatirons, this idyllic college town has a sweet location and a palpable eco-sophistication.

If you only have a couple of hours, head straight to **Chautauqua Park** (📞303-442-3282; www.chautauqua.com; 900 Baseline Rd) for some of the best hikes and views on the Front Range. Then it's down past the University of Colorado at Boulder campus to the **Boulder Creek Bike Path** (🚲) and its riverfront parks. The pedestrian-only **Pearl**

LINK YOUR TRIP

15 **Enchanted Circle & Eastern Sangres**
Head 100 miles directly south on bumpy backroads to Taos, joining the New Mexico crimson-hued Enchanted Circle.

30 **San Juan Skyway & Million Dollar Highway**
From the Great Sand Dunes National Park, head up to Hwy 50 and past the mysterious Black Canyon of the Gunnison to Ouray.

Street Mall (Pearl St, btwn 9th & 15th Sts; 🚻 🚼) is lively and perfect for strolling.

✂ p331

The Drive » From downtown, head west on Canyon Blvd (Hwy 119) winding your way up Boulder Canyon, past towering rock formations and the Barker Reservoir to the hippie mountain enclave of Nederland. From there, it's north on the stunning Peak-to-Peak Hwy 72, past Long's Peak to Estes Park, the eastern entrance to Rocky Mountain National Park. It'll take over an hour (45 miles).

❸ Rocky Mountain National Park

With one foot on either side of the continental divide and behemoths of granite in every direction, **Rocky Mountain National Park** (📞970-586-1242; www.nps.gov/romo; 1000 W Hwy 36, Estes Park) takes you to the wild-tufted top of the United States.

Estes Park, with its bumper-to-bumper main drag and plethora of kitsch shopping, is a necessary gateway into the park. From there, head into the park to the **Moraine Park Museum** (📞970-586-1206; Bear Lake Rd; ⏰9am-4:30pm Jun-Oct; 🚻), before deciding on your route and a day hike.

🛏 p331

The Drive » On this day-long drive (165 miles) from downtown Estes, head up Trail Ridge Rd (generally open late May to October, depending on snow). From there, it's down past the resort towns of Grand Lake and Winter Park, over Berthoud Pass, up I-70, over Vail Pass, and down into Vail.

❹ Vail

If you have a day, hop on the **Vail to Brecken-ridge Bike Path** (www.summitbiking.org) and ride it for as far as your lungs will take you. You can also grab one of the gondolas to a cool mountain-top summit and **Epic Discovery** (📞970-496-4910; www.epicdiscovery.com; day pass Ultimate/Little Explorer $94/54; ⏰10am-6pm Jun-Aug, Fri-Sun only Sep; 🚻) for family fun, take a ride at the **Stables** (📞970-445-8204; www.vailstables.com; 915 Spraddle Creek Rd; rides $70-355; ⏰May-Sep), or a soar with **Vail Valley Paragliding** (📞970-845-7321; www.vailvalleyparagliding.com; per person $205-275) or **Zip Adventures** (📞970-926-9470; www.zipadventures.com; 4098 Hwy 131, Wolcott; per person $170; ⏰May-Nov).

🛏 p331

The Drive » From Vail, it's a straight 60-mile shot west along I-70 to Glenwood Springs. Along the way, you pass through the amazing Glenwood Canyon – marvel at the hanging bridge construction and fractured canyon walls.

❺ Glenwood Springs

DAVID A LITMAN/SHUTTERSTOCK ©

Perched at the confluence of the Colorado and Roaring Fork Rivers at the end of Glenwood Canyon, **Glenwood Hot Springs** (☏970-947-2955; www.hotspringspool.com; 401 N River St; adult/child $23.25/14.25, lower rates off-peak; ⊙7:30am-10pm, from 9am off-peak; ♿) have been a travel destination for centuries. The Ute Indians meditated in steamy **thermal caves** (☏970-945-0667; www. yampahspa.com; 709 E 6th St; incl towel rental $15; ⊙9am-9pm) here, then called Yampah (Great Medicine). Before or after your hot springs or thermal caves treatment, you can rent a bike with **Canyon Bikes** (☏800-439-3043; www.canyonbikes. com; 319 6th St; bike rental per day adult/child $32/24; ⊙8am-8pm Jun-Aug; ♿) or charge class III and IV rapids with **Colorado Whitewater Rafting** (☏800-993-7238; www. coloradowhitewaterrafting. com; 2000 Devereux Rd; half-day adult/child from $57/47; ⊙May-Aug) through Glenwood Canyon.

🛏 p331

The Drive » From Glenwood, cruise south through the Roaring Fork Valley on CO 82 for about 40 miles to Aspen. The further up the valley you go, the bigger the homes. Stop in old mining towns such as Carbondale and Basalt, to ground yourself before hitting glitzed-out Aspen.

TRIP HIGHLIGHT

❻ Aspen

Aspen is a singular town unique to the world. Rich, famous, beautiful and brainy, yet somehow down-to-earth and welcoming to all. Flash your best smile and you'll fit right in.

In summer, winter, spring or fall, the four mountains of **Aspen Snowmass Ski Resort** (☏800-525-6200; www. aspensnowmass.com; 4-mountain lift ticket adult/ child $164/105; ⊙9am-4pm Dec–mid-Apr; ♿) offer world-class skiing and mountain adventures. Hikers won't want to miss a day trip to the **Maroon Bells** – quite

Aspen Aspen Snowmass Ski Resort

simply one of the most beautiful summits in the world. Downtown Aspen has some of the Southwest's best restaurants, plenty of galleries and the noteworthy **Aspen Center for Environmental Studies** (ACES; 📞970-925-5756, www.aspennature. org; 100 Puppy Smith St, Hallam Lake; 🕤9am-5pm Mon-Fri; 👪).

🗙 🛏 p331

The Drive » During the summer, it'll only take a few hours to go over Independence Pass (CO 82) to Leadville. Wintertime, you'll need to backtrack clear to Vail to get here on the slow road (130 miles). No matter which route you take, this is spectacular country.

- - - - - - - - - - - - - - - - - -

7 Leadville

Leadville was once the second-biggest city in Colorado. But unlike other historic towns with mining roots, Leadville never made the switch to resort status.

Dive into town history at the **National Mining Hall of Fame** (www. mininghalloffame.org; 120 W 9th St; adult/student $12/10;

DETOUR: STEAMBOAT SPRINGS

Start: ❸ Rocky Mountain National Park

You can easily extend your trip by heading west from Granby for 80 miles on Hwy 40, to the ski resort and peaced-out mountain village of Steamboat Springs. When you're in town, don't miss hikes and bikes in the nearby wilderness, followed by a soak in **Strawberry Park Hot Springs** (☎970-879-0342; www.strawberryhotsprings. com; 44200 County Rd; per day adult/child $15/8; ⊙10am-10:30pm Sun-Thu, to midnight Fri & Sat; 🚻).

⊙9am-5pm, closed Mon Nov-Apr; 🚻) or bike the **Mineral Belt Trail** (www. mineralbelttrail.com) before a wilderness outing to nearby **Mt Massive** (www.14ers.com; ⊙Jun-Oct), Twin Lakes, **Ski Cooper** (☎800-707-6114; www. skicooper.com; Hwy 24; lift ticket adult/child $52/32; ⊙9am-4pm Dec–mid-Apr; 🚻) or the **Matchless Mine** (☎719-486-1229; www.mininghalloffame. org; E 7th Rd; adult/student with tour $12/10, without tour $6/5; ⊙noon-4:45pm mid-May–Sep).

The Drive » It's only 35 miles south from Leadville to Buena Vista, although you could spend a few days exploring here. First, you pass the headwaters of the Arkansas as you descend into the Arkansas River Valley. The Collegiate Peaks tower to your right, while Buffalo Peaks Wilderness is well worth a stop on your left.

---

❽ Buena Vista

With the 14,197ft **Mt Princeton** (www.14ers. com; Mt Princeton Rd) and the rest of the **Collegiate Peaks** providing a dramatic backdrop to the west, and the icy Arkansas River rushing by the boulder-filled hills east of town, Buena Vista certainly lives up to its name. Whether you're after hiking, biking, paddling through Browns Canyon National Monument, achy-bones-soaking at **Mt Princeton Hot Springs Resort** (☎719-395-2447; www. mtprinceton.com; 15870 County Rd 162; day pass adult/child $22/16; ⊙9am-10pm Mon-Thu, to 11pm Fri-Sun; 🚻 🍽) or simply stupendous landscapes, this is a town that has adventure playground written all over it.

The Drive » It gets pretty flat for a while, but don't worry, as you head down more than 100 miles south to the Great Sand Dunes, things start to get more interesting at every mile marker. Salida is a fun town worth a stop along the way.

TRIP HIGHLIGHT

❾ Great Sand Dunes National Park

For all of Colorado's striking natural sights, this sea of sand is a place where nature's magic is on full display.

At the center of the **park** (☎719-378-6399; www. nps.gov/grsa; 11999 Hwy 150; adult/child $3/free; ⊙visitor center 8:30am-5pm Jun-Aug, 9am-4:30pm Sep-May) is a 55-sq-mile dune of sand surrounded by rigid mountain peaks on one side and glassy wetlands on the other. After long drives on the straight highways of high plains or twisting byways through the Rocky Mountains, it's a bit unnerving to find yourself so suddenly standing amid the landscape of the Sahara. While you're here, take a while to head out for a hike or mountain bike, or continue north to the spectacular Crestone Needle.

Eating & Sleeping

Denver ❶

✕ Root Down   Modern American $$$

(☎303-993-4200; www.rootdowndenver.com; 1600 W 33rd Ave; mains $14-35; ⏱5-10pm daily, 11am-2pm Fri, 10am-2:30pm Sat & Sun; ✈; 🚌19, 52) In a converted gas station, chef Justin Cucci has undertaken one of the city's most ambitious culinary concepts, marrying sustainable 'field-to-fork' practices, high-concept culinary fusions and a low-impact, energy-efficient ethos.

🛏 Crawford Hotel   Hotel $$$

(☎855-362-5098; www.thecrawfordhotel.com; 1701 Wynkoop St; r $349-469, ste $589-709; ❄🛜🏊; 🚌55L, 72L,120L, FF2, 🚆A, B, C, E, W) Set in the historic Union Station (p342), the Crawford Hotel is an example of Denver's amazing transformation. Rooms are luxurious and artful, with high ceilings and throwbacks like the art-deco headboards and clawfoot tubs.

Boulder ❷

✕ Oak at
Fourteenth   Modern American $$

(☎303-444-3622; www.oakatfourteenth.com; 1400 Pearl St; mains $13-30; ⏱11:30am-10pm Mon-Sat, 5:30-10pm Sun; 🚌205, 206) Zesty and innovative, Oak has top-notch cocktails and tasty small plates. The only downside: it tends to be noisy, so save your intimate confessions.

Rocky Mountain National Park ❸

🛏 Aspenglen
Campground   Campground $

(☎877-444-6777; www.recreation.gov; State Hwy 34; summer tent & RV sites $26) With only 54 sites, this is the smallest of the park's reservable camping grounds. There are many tent-only sites, including some walk-ins, and a limited number of trailers are allowed.

Vail ❹

🛏 Sebastian Hotel   Hotel $$$

(☎800-354-6908; www.thesebastianvail.com; 16 Vail Rd; r winter/summer from $800/300; 🅿❄🛜🏊🍴) Deluxe and modern, this sophisticated hotel showcases tasteful contemporary art and an impressive list of amenities. Room rates dip in the summer, the perfect time to enjoy the tapas bar and spectacular pool area.

Glenwood Springs ❺

🛏 Sunlight Lodge   Lodge $$

(☎970-945-5225; www.sunlightlodge.com; 10252 County Rd 117; d $109-159; ⏱seasonal; ❄) This adorable mountain lodge has 20 Western-style rooms with quilted beds and fireplaces. Somehow, the hustle of the outside world doesn't make it through the door – there are no TVs and no cell-phone reception, and when it's blanketed by snow, it achieves a languid coziness.

Aspen ❻

✕ Pine Creek
Cookhouse   American $$$

(☎970-925-1044; www.pinecreekcookhouse.com; 12700 Castle Creek Rd; mains $16-68; ⏱lunch & dinner Dec-Mar & mid-Jun–Sep; ✈🍴) This log-cabin restaurant boasts the best setting around. In summer you can hike here; in winter it's cross-country skis or horse-drawn sleigh in the shadow of glorious white-capped peaks. Sample alpine delicacies like house-smoked trout, buffalo tenderloin and grilled elk brats.

🛏 Little Nell   Hotel $$$

(☎970-920-4600; www.thelittlenell.com; 675 E Durant Ave; r winter/summer from $1200/700; 🅿❄🛜🏊🍴) A legendary ski-in, ski-out Aspen landmark offering understated, updated elegance and class at the foot of Aspen Mountain. .

Highway 50: The Loneliest Road

32

Wanted: Intrepid travelers unafraid of vast, empty, isolated spaces. History lovers willing to embrace the weird. Solo adventurers preferred.

TRIP HIGHLIGHTS

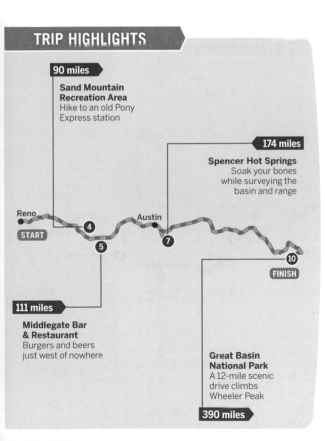

90 miles

Sand Mountain Recreation Area
Hike to an old Pony Express station

174 miles

Spencer Hot Springs
Soak your bones while surveying the basin and range

Reno
START

Austin

FINISH

111 miles

Middlegate Bar & Restaurant
Burgers and beers just west of nowhere

Great Basin National Park
A 12-mile scenic drive climbs Wheeler Peak

390 miles

3 DAYS
390 MILES/628KM

GREAT FOR...

BEST TIME TO GO
Spring for snow-capped mountains, fall for colorful leaves.

 ESSENTIAL PHOTO
Rolling along Hwy 50 toward the South Snake Range.

☑ **BEST FOR HISTORY**
Old Pony Express stations link visitors to the past.

32 Highway 50: The Loneliest Road

If you thought central Nevada was flat to the horizon, this road trip will dispel that misconception, as majestic peaks appear from nowhere to defy the desert. Look for subtle reminders of earlier wayfarers. Prehistoric tribes left rock carvings. The Pony Express abandoned its stone stations. And chunks of the Lincoln Hwy, the nation's first transcontinental road, bake in the sun.

❶ Reno

Nicknamed 'The Biggest Little City in The World,' Reno is the best place to rest up, load up and blow some cash before entering the sandy wilds of the Great Basin, a series of bowl-shaped depressions between the Sierra Nevada Mountains and the Rockies. Downtown, try your luck at the mining-themed **Silver Legacy** (☎775-329-4777; www.silverlegacyreno.com; 407 N Virginia St; ⊙24hr), one of several casinos on Virginia St, then walk

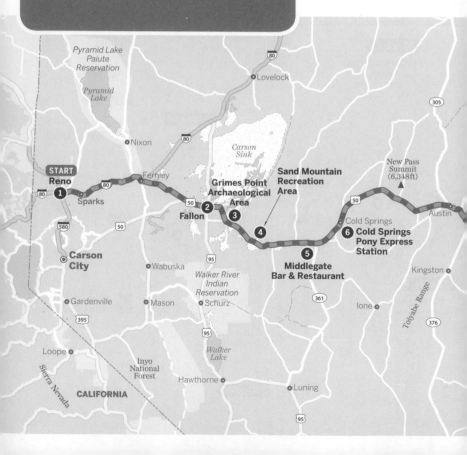

south to the Riverwalk District (www.renoriver.org) to watch kayakers run class II and III rapids at the 1.5-mile **Truckee River Whitewater Park** (www.reno.gov; Wingfield Park). Enjoy the river view while you can; rivers don't flow to the sea in the Great Basin. They meander into lakes, marshes and squishy sinks.

🍴 🛏 p339

The Drive » Hop on I-80 east. In Sparks, just east of Reno, fuel up on gas and Elvis kitsch at Sierra Sid's Casino (200 N McCarran Blvd, off I-80), which

exhibits guns and jewelry owned by Elvis. From I-80, pick up Hwy 50A east in Fernley.

----

❷ Fallon

Look up and you might spot an F-16 flying over Fallon, home of the US Navy's Top Gun

fighter-pilot school. On the ground, dragsters compete at the **Top Gun Raceway** (☎775-423-0223; www.topgunraceway.com; 15550 Schurz Hwy; adult/child 6-12yr $10/5) between March and November. The **Churchill County Museum** (☎775-423-3677;

LINK YOUR TRIP

1 Four Corners Cruise

To loop through the Four Corners region, drop south on Hwy 93 to Las Vegas.

25 Zion & Bryce National Parks

Trade mountain peaks for fiery spires by driving I-50 east to I-15 south in Utah.

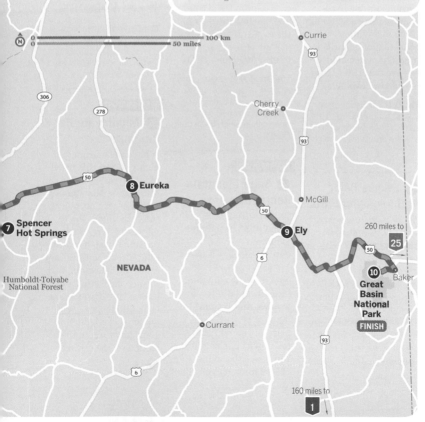

THE PONY EXPRESS

Wanted: Young, skinny, wiry fellows not over 18. Must be expert riders willing to risk death daily. Orphans preferred.

The Pony Express (1860–61) was the FedEx of its day, using a fleet of young riders and swift horses to carry mail between Missouri and California in an astounding 10 days. Each horseman rode full-bore for almost six hours – changing horses every 10 miles – before passing the mail to the next rider. The Pony Express lasted only 18 months, made obsolete by the telegraph.

www.ccmuseum.org; 1050 S Maine St; ☺10am-5pm Mon-Sat, to 4pm Dec-Feb) is a bit like Fallon's attic. Here you can see a Paiute hut and a Model T Ford, learn about the hardships of pioneers and flip through an impressive collection of historic photographs. You can also reserve tickets for tours of **Hidden Cave** here.

The Drive » Head east on Hwy 50 for 7 miles. You'll pass cattle, barbed-wire fences and a methamphetamine warning sign or two.

- - - - - - - - - - - - - - - - -

❸ Grimes Point Archaeological Area

A 0.75-mile interpretive trail at this **archaeological site** (☎775-885-6000; www.blm.gov/nv; ☺24hr; P) loops past 200 or so petrolgyphs, or rock carvings, some of them dating back 9000 years. For another archaeologically significant site, follow the entrance road back to **Hidden Cave**, a possible cache site in prehistoric times. A short but steep interpretive trail leads to the cave (closed without a guide), or you can join a free, docent-guided cave tour on the second and fourth Saturdays of the month. They begin at 9:30am at the Churchill County Museum (p335).

The Drive » Continue east about 16 miles. In the spring, the pavement ahead might shimmer in the heat while snowy mountains beckon in the distance.

- - - - - - - - - - - - - - - - -

TRIP HIGHLIGHT

❹ Sand Mountain Recreation Area

That 600ft-high yellow monolith? That's **Sand Mountain** (☎775-885-6000; www.blm.gov/nv; 7-day permit $40, entry free Tue & Wed; ☺24hr; P), a sand dune measuring 1.5 miles by 2 miles. And if you think it might be a peaceful place to ponder nature, roll down your window. Yep, that's the sound of swarming ATVers

revving their dune buggies. They're a mesmerizing sight as they zip up and down the dune.

The ruins of the **Sand Springs Pony Express Station** (admission free) are also here. British explorer Sir Richard Burton stopped at the station in 1860. He described it as '…roofless and chairless, filthy and squalid, with a smoky fire in one corner and a table in the centre of an impure floor, the walls open to every wind and the interior full of dust.' Nice!

Covered by sand for a century, the station was rediscovered by archaeologists in 1976.

The Drive » Continue 21 miles east. The Pony Express Re-Ride re-creates the full run every June (www.xphomestation.com).

- - - - - - - - - - - - - - - - -

TRIP HIGHLIGHT

❺ Middlegate Bar & Restaurant

What's the marquee menu item at this woodplank watering hole? The Middlegate Monster, a 1⅓lb burger that's hard to finish unless you're one of the Navy Seals passing through or dropping in – sometimes they arrive by helicopter. A former stage stop, and later a Pony Express station, Middlegate (p339) is a fine place to loiter. Add your dollar bill to the collection on the ceiling.

✕ p339

Sand Mountain

The Drive » Continue on Hwy 50 and drive east for 15 miles. Watch for ghostly spirits out in the sagebrush: this stretch has seen a lot of untimely death.

TRIP HIGHLIGHT

❻ Cold Springs Pony Express Station

A 2-mile trail leads to the stone ruins of this spooky Pony Express station, close to where Jose Zowgaltz was wounded in an ambush. He made it to the station... then perished. On another occasion, the station master was murdered. Cross Hwy 50 for the foundations of the second Cold Springs Station, which doubled as a stagecoach stop and telegraph station. Stop at the new **Cold Springs Station** (📞775-423-1233; 52300 Hwy 50; meals $6-16; ⏰8am-8pm; 🚻) if you're hungry

The Drive » From Cold Springs Station, Hwy 50 twists up to the 6348ft New Pass Summit then drops into another basin. Another climb leads into the Toiyabe Mountains. Fifty miles takes you to Austin, once a mid-19th-century boomtown; blow through and head 20 miles southeast to the next stop..

TRIP HIGHLIGHT

❼ Spencer Hot Springs

Twenty miles southeast of Austin (the latter half down a dirt track) lies this pool of sulfuric mineral water that will cure whatever ails you. Enterprising locals have shaped the muddy spring into a stone tub. But locals and weary travelers looking to soak the tired out of their bones aren't the only ones who love these springs; if it's been raining, mosquitoes swarm around here, too. Bring DEET-based repellent and a Nevada-size sense of humor.

The Drive » Rejuvenated from your soak, get back on Hwy 50 and roll over basin and range for 58 miles to Eureka,

LOCAL KNOWLEDGE: COLD SPRINGS PONY EXPRESS STATION

The Bureau of Land Management calls the vault toilet at the Cold Springs Pony Express Station '*The Loneliest Rest Stop on the Loneliest Road.*' But we hear it gets a lot of use.

337

'I SURVIVED HWY 50' CERTIFICATE

For travelers who like a challenge, the Nevada Tourism Commission has issued a *Hwy 50 Survival Guide* (www.travelnevada.com/travel-guides). The guide includes a basic map, details about Hwy 50 towns and a postcard. Your goal? To get the postcard stamped in five communities along the route. Return the completed card, and you'll receive a personalized 'I Survived Hwy 50' certificate along with a pin. Pre-order a survival guide at www.ponyexpressnevada.com or pick one up at chambers of commerce, hotels, motels and gas stations along the route.

a blink-and-you'll-miss-it old mining town that now relies on tourists. Like you!.

8 Eureka

In the late 19th century, $40 million worth of silver was extracted from the hills around Eureka. Pride of place goes to the **county courthouse** (775-237-5540; 10 S Main St; 8am-noon & 1-5pm Mon-Fri), with its handsome pressed-tin ceilings and walk-in vaults, and the beautifully restored **opera house** (775-237-6006; 31 S Main St; 8am-noon & 1-5pm Mon-Fri), also dating from 1880, which hosts an art gallery and concerts. The **Eureka Sentinel Museum** (775-237-5010; 10 N Monroe St; 10am-6pm Tue-Sat Nov-Apr, daily May-Oct) displays yesteryear newspaper technology and colorful examples of period reportage.

The Drive » Continue east over rolling scrubby hills and

watch for deer. It's 77 miles to Ely.

9 Ely

The biggest town for miles around, Ely was established as a mining town in the 1860s. Its old downtown has beautiful regional history murals and awesome vintage neon signs. Downtown, kitsch lovers will dig the Hotel Nevada (p339); its funky casino and eclectically Western lobby are worth a look even if you don't spend the night. The bar defines the term 'local color.' You can also buy 'I Survived the Loneliest Road' T-shirts here.

The **Ely Renaissance Village** (800-496-9350; 400 Ely St; 10am-4pm Sat Jul-Sep) is a collection of 1908 period homes built by settlers from France, Slovakia, China, Italy and Greece.

🍴 🛏️ p339

The Drive » Continue east on Hwy 50.

TRIP HIGHLIGHT

10 Great Basin National Park

Near the Nevada–Utah border, this uncrowded **national park** (775-234-7331; www.nps.gov/grba; 24hr) encompasses 13,063ft Wheeler Peak, rising abruptly from the desert and creating an awesome but compact range of life zones and landscapes. A seasonal 12-mile scenic drive twists up to the summit.

Hiking trails near the summit take in superb country made up of glacial lakes, groves of ancient bristlecone pines (some more than 5000 years old) and even a permanent ice field. June through August, stick around for the **Dark Rangers** astronomy programs (Tuesday, Thursday and Saturday nights). The guided **full-moon hikes** are also popular.

The **Lehman Caves Visitor Center** (775-234-7331, tour reservations 775-234-7517; www.nps.gov/grba; 5500 NV-488, Baker; tours adult $8-10, child $4-5; 8am-4:30pm, tours 8:30am-4pm) organizes guided tours of the caves, which are brimming with limestone formations. Reservations are recommended. Next to the visitor center, a simple cafe stays open from May through October.

Eating & Sleeping

Reno ❶

✖ Great Basin Brewing Co   Pub Food $

(📞775-284-7711; www.greatbasinbrewingco.
com; 5525 S Virginia St; mains $8-20; ⏰11am-
midnight Sun-Thu, 11am-1:30am Fri & Sat) The
pub grub here includes burgers, sausage
sandwiches, pizza and fish tacos. There's a
debate in town over who brews the best beer,
Great Basin or Sierra Nevada. We're not picking
sides, but we do give extra points to 20-year-old
Great Basin for its outdoorsy ambience, which
includes a mountain scene splashed across the
wall. It's 6 miles south of downtown.

✖ Old Granite
Street Eatery   American $$

(📞775-622-3222; www.oldgranitestreeteatery.
com; 243 S Sierra St; dinner mains $12-29;
⏰11am-10pm Mon-Thu, to 11pm Fri, 10am-11pm
Sat, to 3pm Sun; 🖊) A lovely well-lit place for
organic and local comfort food, old-school
artisanal cocktails and craft beers, this antique-
strewn hot spot enchants diners with its stately
wooden bar, water served in old liquor bottles
and lengthy seasonal menu. Forgot to make
a reservation? Check out the iconic rooster
and pig murals and wait at a communal table
fashioned from a barn door.

🛏 Sands Regency   Hotel $

(📞775-348-2200; www.sandsregency.com;
345 N Arlington Ave; Sun-Thu r from $49, Fri
& Sat from $89; 🅿 ❄ 📶 🏊 🐾) The Sands
Regency has some of the largest standard
digs in town. Its rooms are decked out in a
cheerful tropical palette of upbeat blues,
reds and greens – a visual relief from typical
motel decor. Empress Tower rooms are
best. The 17th-floor gym and Jacuzzi are
perfectly positioned to capture the drop-dead
panoramic mountain views, and an outdoor
pool opens in summer.

🛏 Whitney Peak   Design Hotel $$

(📞775-398-5400; www.whitneypeakhotel.com;
255 N Virginia St; d from $129; 🅿 ❄ 📶) What's
not to love about this independent, inventive,
funky, friendly, non-smoking, non-gambling
downtown hotel? Spacious guest rooms have
a youthful, fun vibe celebrating the great
outdoors and don't skimp on designer creature
comforts. With an executive-level concierge
lounge, free use of the external climbing wall (if
you're game), a noteworthy on-site restaurant
and friendly, professional staff, Whitney Peak is
hard to beat.

Middlegate ❺

✖ Middlegate Station   Burgers $

(📞775-423-7134; www.facebook.com/
middlegate.station; 42500 Austin Hwy, cnr Hwys
50 & 361; mains $6-17; ⏰6am-2am) A legendary
pit stop on the 'Loneliest Road in America,'
47 miles from Fallon, this quirky, ramshackle
ranch-style saloon is famous for its Middlegate
Monster Burger and general Wild West vibe. While
burgers are king here, there's plenty of other high-
calorie, high-cholesterol delights to dismantle
and devour. Dr Atkins would be so proud!

Ely ❾

✖ La Fiesta   Mexican $$

(📞775-289-4114; 700 Ave H; mains $8-24;
⏰11am-9pm; 🖊) La Fiesta serves up cheesy
enchiladas and frozen margaritas.

🛏 Hotel Nevada   Hotel $

(📞775-289-6665; www.hotelnevada.com; 501
Aultman St; r from $79; 🅿 ❄ @ 📶) Ely's most
famous building, the historic Hotel Nevada,
which opened with 100 guest rooms in 1929, is
both hotel and casino. Despite the smoky casino
on the ground floors and the compact size of the
rooms, the hotel is at least worth a look for its
iconic appeal, if not charm.

STRETCH YOUR LEGS
LAS
VEGAS

Start/Finish Bellagio

Distance 1.8 miles/2.9km

Duration Four hours

This loop takes in the most dazzling sites on the Strip: the canals of Venice, the graceful Eiffel Tower, the world's tallest Ferris wheel and a three-story chandelier. And remember, objects on the Strip are further away than they appear.

Take this walk on Trip

Bellagio

For floral inspiration, pause in the lobby at the ever-stylish **Bellagio** (☑888-987-6667; www.bellagio.com; 3600 S Las Vegas Blvd; ☺24hr; P🐾) to admire the room's showpiece: a Dale Chihuly sculpture composed of 2000 hand-blown glass flowers in vibrant colors. Just beyond the lobby, the **Bellagio Conservatory & Botanical Gardens** (☺24hr; P🚹) dazzles passersby with gorgeously ostentatious floral designs that change seasonally. If you're hankering for fine art, see what's on display at the **Bellagio Gallery of Fine Art** (☑702-693-7871; adult/child under 12yr $18/free; ☺10am-8pm, last entry 7:30pm; P🚹), which hosts blockbuster traveling exhibits.

The Walk ≫ Walk north on S Las Vegas Blvd (The Strip) and cross E Flamingo Rd. Caesar's Palace will be just ahead on your left.

Caesars Palace

It's easy to get lost inside this labyrinth-like Greco-Roman **fantasyland** (☑866-227-5938; www.caesarspalace.com; 3570 S Las Vegas Blvd; ☺24hr; P) where maps are few (and not oriented to the outside). The interior is captivating, however, with marble reproductions of classical statuary, including a 4-ton Brahma shrine near the front entrance. Towering fountains, goddess-costumed cocktail waitresses and the swanky haute couture of the Forum Shops ante up the glitz. For lunch, consider the fantastic buffet at **Bacchanal** (☑702-731-7928; www.caesars.com; buffet per adult $30-58, child 4-10yr $15-27; ☺8am-10pm; P❄🍴🚹), a gastronomic celebration of global proportions. You'll love every bite of it.

The Walk ≫ Continue north on S Las Vegas Blvd, passing the Mirage. At night, its faux-Polynesian volcano erupts. Just north, take the walkway over The Strip.

Venetian

The spectacular **Venetian** (☑702-414-1000; www.venetian.com; 3355 S Las Vegas Blvd; ☺24hr; P) is a facsimile of a doge's palace, inspired by the splendor of

Italy's most romantic city. It features roaming mimes and minstrels in period costume, hand-painted ceiling frescoes and full-scale reproductions of the Italian port's famous landmarks. Flowing canals, vibrant piazzas and stone walkways attempt to capture the spirit of La Serenissima Repubblica, reputedly the home of the world's first casino. Take a **gondola ride** or stroll through the atmospheric **Grand Canal Shoppes**.

The Walk » It's a 0.7-mile trek to Paris, but sights along the way should keep it interesting, particularly the $55 million LINQ shopping and entertainment district, home to the 550ft-tall High Roller, billed as the world's tallest Ferris wheel.

Paris Las Vegas

Evoking the gaiety of the City of Light, **Paris Las Vegas** (☏877-603-4386; www. parislasvegas.com; 3655 S Las Vegas Blvd; ⊗24hr; P) strives to capture the essence of the grande dame by recreating her landmarks. Fine likenesses of the Opera, the Arc de Triomphe, the Champs-Élysées, the soaring Eiffel Tower and even the Seine frame the property. The signature attraction is the **Eiffel Tower Experience** (☏888-727-4758; www.caesars.com; adult/ child 12yr & under/family $19/14/49, after 7:15pm $22/17/67; ⊗9:30am-12:30am Mon-Fri, to 1am Sat & Sun, weather permitting; P ♿). Ascend in a glass elevator to the observation deck for panoramic views of the Strip, notably the Bellagio's dancing fountains.

The Walk » Walk a short distance south on S Las Vegas Blvd. Cross the boulevard on Paris Dr.

The Cosmopolitan

The twinkling three-story chandelier inside this sleek addition to the Strip isn't purely decorative. Nope, it's a 'step inside, sip a swanky cocktail and survey your domain' kind of place, worthy of your wildest fairy tale. A bit much? Not really. Like the rest of Vegas, the **Cosmopolitan** (☏702-698-7000; www. cosmopolitanlasvegas.com; 3708 S Las Vegas Blvd; ⊗24hr; P ❄) is just having fun.

The Walk » From here, walk north on S Las Vegas Blvd to catch the dazzling choreographed dancing fountain show at Bellagio.

STRETCH YOUR LEGS DENVER

Start/Finish LoHi neighborhood

Distance 4 miles/6.4km

Duration Three hours

The Mile High City has winsome walking paths, world-class art museums, brewpubs aplenty, urban white-water parks, Rocky Mountain–chic boutiques and eateries, and a new urban scene that is transforming this classic Western city.

Take this walk on Trip

LoHi

One of Denver's hottest neighborhoods, Lower Highlands – LoHi to locals – sits conveniently next to I-70, offering a bird's-eye view of the city and free parking (two-hour on the main drag, unlimited on side streets). Here, check out some hipster boutiques, laid-back brewpubs and great lunchtime restaurants, like **Tamales by La Casita** (☎303-477-2899; www.tamalesbylacasita.net; 3561 Tejon St; dishes $3-10; ☺7am-7pm Mon-Fri, from 9am Sat; 🖍 👫; ☐44), before heading into the city.

The Walk ›› Trundle over to the 16th St pedestrian bridge, which passes over I-70, and past John McEnroe's pile of public art known as National Velvet. Cross another pedestrian bridge to Commons Park.

Commons Park

Affording views of the city and a bit of fresh air, spacious and hilly **Commons Park** (www.denvergov.org/parksandrecreation; cnr 15th & Little Raven Sts; 👫 🐾; ☐10, 28, 32, 44) has bike paths, benches, river access and plenty of people-watching. A lyrical curving stairway to nowhere known as **Common Ground** by artist Barbara Grygutis is an undeniable centerpiece.

The Walk ›› Meander through the park, then cross over the pedestrian-only Millennium Bridge, with its 200ft sloped 'mast' and laser-like cables. Take in the views of Coors Field and Union Station, before plunging into Lower Downtown (LoDo).

Union Station

Beautifully restored, the 19th-century **Union Station** (☎303-592-6712; www.unionstationindenver.com; 1701 Wynkoop St; ℙ; ☐55L, 72L,120L, FF2, ☒A, B, C, E, W) is LoDo's crown jewel. A transportation hub, the waiting area doubles as an urban chic lounge. Swanky restaurants and bars line the building along with classy boutiques and cool coffee shops.

The Walk ›› Poke around Union Station – sip a cappuccino or window-shop. From here, head southeast to 16th Street Mall. The town's favorite bookstore, the Tattered Cover, marks its start.

16th Street Mall

The 16th St pedestrian mall is a bustling stretch of downtown Denver with restaurants, retail shops and old-school tourist traps. There are a few gems though – **I Heart Denver** (www.iheartdenverstore.com; ⊙10am-9pm Mon-Sat, 11am-6pm Sun; 🚌10, 28, 32, MALLRIDE) for one – and the occasional street performer too.

The Walk » Cruise southeast on 16th St to the end of the pedestrian mall. From there, hop across Colfax Ave to Civic Center Park. To save time, take the free bus that runs the length of the mall.

Civic Center Park

In the shadow of the State Capitol's golden dome, **Civic Center Park** (cnr Broadway & Colfax Ave; ♿; 🚌0, 9, 10, 52) hosts food trucks, public events and some of the most iconic sculptures in the city, including the 1920 **Bronco Buster**, whose model was arrested for cattle rustling before the statue was finished (the artist bailed him out). If you have time, head to the **State Capitol** for a free tour plus a selfie with

the 13th step, which sits exactly a mile above sea level.

The Walk » Head south past the whimsical Yearling statue (how did that horse get onto that chair?) and the postmodern Denver Public Library before you hit the iconic Denver Art Museum.

Denver Art Museum

Truly a don't-miss museum, **DAM** (📞720-865-5000; www.denverartmuseum.org; 100 W 14th Ave; adult/child $13/free; 1st Sat of month free; ⊙10am-5pm Tue-Thu, Sat & Sun, to 8pm Fri; 🅿 ♿; 🚌0, 52) is home to one of the largest American Indian art collections in the country plus it hosts a variety of special multimedia exhibits. There's a large family area, and it always has several interactive exhibits, which kids love. When you're done, head back to LoHi.

The Walk » Go past the Convention Center's Big Blue Bear, continuing west down Champa St past the Denver Performing Arts Complex and its signature Dancers statue. From there, take the Cherry Creek Bike Path to Confluence Park and back to LoHi.

ROAD TRIP ESSENTIALS

Southwest USA Driving Guide

The interstate system is thriving in the Southwest, but a well-maintained network of state roads and scenic byways offers unparalleled opportunities for exploration.

DRIVING LICENSE & DOCUMENTS

➡ Foreign visitors can legally drive a car in the USA for up to 12 months using their home country's driving license.

➡ An IDP (International Driving Permit) will have more credibility with US traffic police, especially if your normal license doesn't have a photo or isn't in English. Your home country's automobile association can issue an IDP, valid for one year. Always carry your license together with the IDP.

➡ To ride a motorcycle in the US, you need either a valid US state motorcycle license or an IDP endorsed for motorcycles.

INSURANCE

➡ Liability insurance covers people and property that you might hit.

➡ For damage to a rental vehicle, a collision damage waiver (CDW) is available for about $27 to $29 per day. If you have collision coverage on your vehicle at home, it might cover damage to rental cars; inquire before departing.

➡ Some credit cards offer reimbursement coverage for collision damages when you use the card to rent a car; check before departing. There may be exceptions for rentals of more than 15 days or for exotic models, jeeps, vans and 4WD vehicles. Check your policy.

➡ Many rental agencies stipulate that damage a car suffers while being driven on unpaved roads is not covered by the insurance they offer. Check with the agent when you make your reservation.

➡ Consult your insurance policy before leaving home to confirm whether or not you are insured for theft of items in your car while traveling.

Driving Fast Facts

➡ **Right or left?** Drive on the right.

➡ **Legal driving age** 16 (New Mexico: 15½)

➡ **Top speed limit** 85mph (Hwy 130 between Austin and San Antonio, TX)

➡ **Best bumper sticker** We're all here because we're not all there (Jerome, AZ)

Southwest USA Playlist

Border Town Chris Whitley

Rocky Mountain High John Denver

Take it Easy The Eagles

Texas, Texas Red Meat

Viva Las Vegas Elvis Presley

RENTING A CAR

➡ Rental cars are readily available at all airports and many downtown city locations.

➡ With advance reservations for a small car, the daily rate with unlimited mileage is about $30 to $60.

➡ Larger companies don't require a credit-card deposit, which means you can cancel without a penalty if you find a better rate.

➡ Midsize cars are often only a tad more expensive.

➡ Deals abound and the business is competitive so it pays to shop around. Aggregator sites such as www.kayak.com can provide a good cross-section of options. You can often snag great last-minute deals via the internet; rental reservations made in conjunction with an airplane ticket often yield better rates.

➡ Most companies require that you have a major credit card, are at least 25 years old and have a valid driver's license. Some national agencies may rent to drivers between the ages of 21 and 25 but may charge a daily fee.

➡ If you decide to fly into one city and out of another, you may incur drop-off charges. Check the amount before finalizing your plans. Dropping off the car in another state may raise the rate.

MOTOR HOMES (RVS)

➡ Rentals range from ultra-efficient VW campers to plush land yachts.

➡ After the size of the vehicle, consider the impact of gas prices, gas mileage, additional mileage costs, insurance and refundable deposits; these can add up quickly. It pays to shop around and read the fine print.

➡ Base rate for a four-person vehicle can be anywhere from $420 to $1800 weekly in the summer, plus 34¢ for each additional mile not included in your package. Get out a good map and a calculator to determine if it's practical.

Road Distances (miles)

	Amarillo, TX	Austin, TX	Bryce Canyon NP, UT	Carlsbad, NM	Cortez (Mesa Verde NP), CO	Denver, CO	Grand Canyon (North Rim), AZ	Grand Canyon (South Rim), AZ	Las Vegas, NV	Phoenix, AZ	Reno, NV	Salt Lake City, UT	Santa Fe, NM
Austin, TX	495												
Bryce Canyon NP, UT	835	1250											
Carlsbad, NM	285	480	820										
Cortez (Mesa Verde NP), CO	540	960	390	530									
Denver, CO	435	930	565	580	380								
Grand Canyon (North Rim), AZ	750	1175	130	740	340	690							
Grand Canyon (South Rim), AZ	695	1110	290	685	370	675	210						
Las Vegas, NV	855	1300	250	850	570	755	270	280					
Phoenix, AZ	705	1005	430	590	400	790	340	220	290				
Reno, NV	1305	1740	565	1295	840	990	680	725	450	735			
Salt Lake City, UT	880	1300	260	870	350	520	390	520	420	710	520		
Santa Fe, NM	280	700	660	270	280	390	530	470	640	520	1080	630	
Tucson, AZ	735	890	540	480	470	890	470	350	410	120	855	820	560

The Border Patrol

Officers of the United States Border Patrol (USBP) are ubiquitous in southern Arizona and New Mexico. Border patrol officers are law enforcement personnel who have the ability to pull you over, ask for ID and search your car if they have reasonable cause. There's a good chance they'll flash you to the side of the road if you're driving down back roads in a rental or out-of-state car. These roads have been used to smuggle both people and drugs north from Mexico.

➡ Always carry ID, including a valid tourist visa if you're a foreign citizen, and car registration (if it's a rental car, your rental contract should suffice).

➡ Be polite and they should be polite to you.

➡ If they ask, it's best to allow the agents to see inside your trunk (boot) and backseat.

It's almost guaranteed that you'll drive through checkpoints down here. If you've never done so before, the 'stop side' of the checkpoints is the route going from south (Mexico) to north (USA).

You may just be waved through the checkpoint; otherwise slow down, stop, answer a few questions (regarding your citizenship and the nature of your visit) and possibly pop your trunk and roll down your windows so officers can peek inside your car. Visitors may consider this intrusive, but grin and bear it. For better or worse, this is a reality of traveling on the border.

➡ Before heading out, consult www.rvtravel.com for tips galore.

➡ Purchase a campground guide from **Woodall's** (www.woodalls.com), which also has a great all-round website. Or check **KOA** (koa.com) for a free annual campground directory listing its US and Canadian campgrounds.

Cities and towns in Arizona where you can cross the US–Mexico border include San Luis (south of Yuma), Lukeville (Hwy 85), Nogales and Douglas. From New Mexico, travel south to El Paso, TX, to reach Ciudad Juarez. US Customs and Border Protection tracks current wait times (see apps.cbp.gov/bwt) at every border crossing.

BORDER CROSSING

It is not worth the hassle of driving overland from Mexico unless you are on a long-distance trip with your own vehicle. The website www.dmv.org has information about crossing the US–Mexico border by car. Foreign visitors should review US entry requirements at the State Department (www.travel.state.gov) and the US Customs and Border Protection (www.cbp.gov) websites.

To enter the US via Mexico driving you will need the following:

➡ passport
➡ vehicle title
➡ Mexican Vehicle Import Permit
➡ receipts for associated fees
➡ Mexican tourist permit 'FMT'
➡ appropriate visa to enter the US

MAPS

Detailed state highway maps are distributed free by state governments. Call or send an email to state tourism offices (typically through their websites) to request maps or pick them up at highway tourism information offices when you enter a state on a major highway. For exploring American Indian reservations in the Four Corners region, buy the popular AAA Indian Country map. It's for sale at **Books 'n' More** (☏800-858-2808; www.grandcanyon.org; Visitor Center Plaza; ⊙8am-8pm Jun-Aug, shorter hours rest of year; 🚻Village, Kaibab/Rim), which is across the plaza from Grand Canyon Visitor Center on the South Rim, and from various outlets online.

ROAD CONDITIONS

Be extra defensive while driving in the Southwest. Everything from dust storms to snow to roaming livestock can make conditions dangerous. Near Flagstaff, AZ, watch for elk at sunset on I-17. The animals like to soak up warmth from the blacktop (or so we've heard). You don't want to hit an elk, which can weigh between 500lb and 900lb.

Distances are great in the Southwest and there are long stretches of road without gas stations. Running out of gas on a hot and desolate stretch of highway is no fun, so pay attention to signs that caution 'Next Gas 98 Miles.'

Road conditions for interstates and rural highways are typically very good. Unpaved roads to ghost towns, petroglyph sites and remote trailheads are generally well-graded but can be challenging after storms or if they lead to very remote sites. Unpaved roads across American Indian reservations are of varying quality. Consider using four-wheel-drive vehicles for extended trips on dirt roads and ask locally about conditions.

For updates on road conditions, call ☑511 (excluding Texas) while traveling within the region, or try the following:

Arizona (☑888-411-7623; www.az511.com)

Colorado (www.codot.gov)

Nevada (☑877-687-6237; www.nvroads.com)

New Mexico (☑800-432-4269; www.nmroads.com)

Texas (☑800-452-9292; www.txdot.gov)

Utah (☑801-965-4000; www.udot.utah.gov)

ROAD RULES

➡ Driving laws are slightly different in each state, but all require the use of safety belts.

➡ In every state, children under five years of age must be placed in a child safety seat secured by proper restraints.

➡ The maximum speed limit on all rural interstates is 75mph, with Texas and Utah allowing

---

Road Trip Websites

American Automobile Association (AAA; ☑ 800-222-4357; www.aaa.com) Provides maps and other information, as well as travel discounts and 24-hour emergency assistance for members.

America's Byways (www.fhwa.dot.gov/byways) Descriptions and maps for designated national scenic byways.

Gas Buddy (www.gasbuddy.com) Find the cheapest gas in town.

---

higher speeds on a handful of specified sections of road. The speed limit drops to 65mph on urban freeways in Arizona, Colorado, Nevada and Utah; New Mexico and Texas allow urban interstate drivers to barrel through at 75mph. But no matter your location, watch for speed limit signs requiring a lower speed than the maximums listed here.

➡ Bans on cell-phone use and texting while driving are becoming more common. Currently, you cannot talk on a hand-held device in Nevada and parts of New Mexico. In Utah and Colorado cell-phone use for drivers under the age of 18 is prohibited. Texting while driving is banned in Colorado, Utah, Nevada and New Mexico. These laws are becoming stricter and are subject to change.

PARKING

Public parking is readily available in most Southwest destinations, whether on the street or in parking lots. In rural areas and small towns it is often free of charge. Many towns have metered parking, which will limit the amount of time you can leave your car.

Parking can be a challenge in urban areas. Street parking is limited so you will

---

California Inspection Stations

When entering California, agricultural inspection stations at the state border may ask you to surrender fruit in an attempt to stop the spread of pests associated with produce.

Driving Problem-Buster

What should I do if my car breaks down? Call the service number provided by the rental-car company, and it will make arrangements with a local garage. If you're driving your own car, it's advisable to join AAA, which provides emergency assistance.

What if I have an accident? If serious damage occurs, you'll have to call the local police (📞911) to come to the scene of the accident and file an accident report, for insurance purposes.

What should I do if I get stopped by the police? Always pull over to the right at the first available opportunity. Stay in your car and roll down the window. Show the officer your driver's license and automobile registration. For any violations, you cannot pay the officer the ticket; payment must be made by mail or online.

What happens at a border patrol checkpoint? See p347 for information on making border crossings.

What if I can't find anywhere to stay? In summer it's advisable to make reservations in advance. Most towns have tourist information centers or chambers of commerce that will help travelers find accommodations in a pinch. Public lands managed by the Bureau of Land Management and the Forest Service often allow dispersed camping, which means you can camp where you want on undeveloped land as long as you stay 900ft from a developed water source and follow other guidelines (www.blm.gov).

probably have to pay to leave your car in private lots. See the City Guide (p24) for more information about parking in Las Vegas, Phoenix, Santa Fe and Austin.

FUEL

Gas stations are common in urban areas and along interstates. Many are open 24 hours. Small-town stations may be open only from 7am to 8pm or 9pm.

At most stations, you must pay before you pump. The more modern pumps have credit/debit card terminals built into them, so you can pay right at the pump. At more expensive 'full service' stations, an attendant will pump your gas for you; no tip is expected.

SAFETY

When leaving the car, travelers are advised to remove valuables and lock all car doors, especially in urban areas and at isolated trailheads. Be extra careful driving on rural roads at night, which may not be well-lit and may be populated by deer, elk, livestock and other creatures that can often total your car if you hit them.

Take these precautions when driving:
➡ Pull off to the side of the road in dust storms and wait it out. They don't usually last long.
➡ Watch for livestock on highways and on American Indian reservations and areas marked 'Open Rangelands.'
➡ Lock car doors and don't leave any valuables visible, especially at trailhead parking lots.

RADIO

Arizona On the Hopi Reservation KUYI (88.1FM) plays reggae, honky-tonk, Cajun and American Indian music, with Hopi news.

New Mexico KTAO (101.9FM) in Taos is a solar-powered station airing American Indian music, astrology reports, local news, outlaw country and world music.

Texas In Lubbock, KDAV (1590AM), where Buddy Holly once worked, plays nothing but classic rockabilly.

Southwest USA Travel Guide

GETTING THERE & AWAY

Most travelers to the Southwest arrive by air and car, with bus running a distant third place. The train service is little used but available. Major regional transportation hubs include Las Vegas, Phoenix, Albuquerque and Salt Lake City.

Flights, car rentals, tours and accommodations can be booked online at lonelyplanet.com/bookings.

AIR

Unless you live in or near the Southwest, flying in and renting a car is the most time-efficient option. Most domestic visitors fly into Phoenix, Las Vegas or Albuquerque. International visitors, however, usually first touch down in Los Angeles, New York, Miami, Denver or Dallas/Fort Worth before catching an onward flight to any number of destinations.

BUS

Greyhound (☑800-231-2222; www.greyhound.com) is the main carrier to and within the Southwest, operating buses several times a day along major highways between large towns.

TRAIN

Three **Amtrak** (☑800-872-7245; www.amtrak.com) trains cut a swath through the Southwest, but they are not connected to one another. Use them to reach the region but not for touring.

Southwest Chief Runs daily between Chicago and Los Angeles, via Kansas City. Significant stations include Albuquerque, NM, and Flagstaff and Williams, AZ. On-board guides provide commentary through national parks and American Indian regions.

California Zephyr Runs daily between Chicago and San Francisco (Emeryville) via Denver, with stops in Salt Lake City and Reno, NV.

Sunset Limited Runs thrice weekly from Los Angeles to New Orleans and stops in Tucson, AZ.

ARRIVING IN SOUTHWEST USA

Denver International Airport

Rental Car Courtesy shuttles to and from rental car offices stop on Level 5, Island 4 at Jeppesen Terminal. The Ground Transportation Center is also on Level 5.

Train The University of Colorado A Line train departs from the airport every 15 to 30 minutes. It passes through downtown's Union Station, making this the easiest and most cost-effective airport transit to town.

Bus Available by door 506 in West Terminal and door 511 in East Terminal. Costs $9 to $13 one way to Stapleton, downtown and suburbs.

Taxi Around $60 to downtown.

Shuttle From $33 to Denver area.

McCarran International Airport (Las Vegas)

Rental Car Blue-and-white McCarran Rent-a-Car shuttles run from Terminals 1 and 3 to the rental car center 3 miles away.

Taxi From $23 to $28 to the Strip, taking 30 minutes in heavy traffic; per NV Taxi Authority, taking the tunnel will result in a higher fare.

Shuttle Costs $11 to the Strip; take exit door 9 to Bell Trans.

DRIVING TO THE SOUTHWEST

Getting to the Southwest from other regions of the US is easy. Be aware that the distances between towns can be big so fill up on gasoline at every opportunity. In rural areas repair services may be limited, it's best to contract AAA services or similar for emergency service, towing and repairs.

DIRECTORY A–Z

ACCOMMODATIONS

Definitely book accommodations in advance during summer, the winter holidays and spring break.

➡ **Apartment & House Rentals** Often good-value and unique properties, with kitchens and good wi-fi connections.

➡ **Camping** From RV parks to the backcountry, the Southwest is a camper's dream destination. You should always reserve months ahead where possible – particularly for national parks and if you're in an RV.

➡ **Hotels** Great range of choices in urban centers, not so much in rural areas.

➡ **B&Bs** These family-run homes generally offer value and personality.

➡ **Motels** Chain motels line the roadsides everywhere, catering to a range of budgets and comfort levels.

Most places are nonsmoking, although some national chains and local budget motels may offer smoking rooms.

Sleeping Price Ranges

The following price ranges are based on standard double occupancy in high season. Unless otherwise noted, breakfast is not included, bathrooms are private and lodging is open year-round. Rates generally don't include taxes, which vary considerably between towns and states.

$	less than $100
$$	$100-250
$$$	more than $250

ELECTRICITY

Type A
120V/60Hz

Type B
120V/60Hz

FAMILIES & CHILDREN

The Southwest is a blast for families, with entertaining attractions for all ages: national parks, aquariums, zoos, science museums, theme parks, lively campgrounds, and hiking and biking in

Practicalities

Discount Cards From printable internet coupons to coupons found in tourist magazines, there are price reductions aplenty. For lodging, pick up one of the coupon books stacked outside highway visitor centers. These typically offer some of the cheapest rates out there.

Card-carrying members of automobile associations are entitled to travel discounts. The **American Automobile Association** (AAA; ☏800-874-7532; www.aaa.com) has reciprocal agreements with several international auto associations, so bring your membership card from home.

Emergency & Important Numbers If you need any kind of emergency assistance, call ☏911. Some rural phones might not have this service, in which case dial ☏0 for the operator and ask for emergency assistance.

Country code	☏1
International access code	☏011
Emergency	☏911
National sexual assault hotline	☏800-656-4673
Statewide road conditions	☏511

Smoking Arizona, Colorado, New Mexico and Utah ban smoking in enclosed work spaces, including restaurants and bars. Nevada's statewide ban permits smoking in bars, casinos and designated restaurant smoking rooms. More than 100 cities in Texas – including the largest metro areas – have passed smoke-free laws that limit the activity in some or all public venues. Inquire locally before lighting up.

outrageously scenic places. Geology, history and wildlife are accessible in concrete ways at every turn, making the Southwest as educational as it is fun.

Best Regions for Kids

ARIZONA
Outdoorsy families can bike the Greenway near Grand Canyon Village and study saguaros outside Tucson. Water parks lure kids to Phoenix, while dude ranches, ghost towns and cliff dwellings are only a scenic drive away.

NEW MEXICO
Swoop up a mountain on the Sandia Peak Tramway, drop into Carlsbad Caverns or scramble to the Gila Cliff Dwellings.

TEXAS
Historic sites with activity books, plus theme parks, make San Antonio especially family-friendly. Beaches line the southern Gulf

Coast; Houston's Hermann Park contains a zoo, a natural history museum, a manicured Japanese garden and a train ride; while the zoo, aquarium and science museum in Dallas all attract young attention.

UTAH
National parks sprawl across swaths of red rock country, offering fantastic hiking, biking and rafting. In the mountains, skis, alpine slides or snow tubes are equally fun.

SOUTHWESTERN COLORADO
Chug through the San Juan Mountains on a historic steam train, relax in Ouray's hot springs or choose your adventure – hiking, fishing, skiing – in low-key Telluride.

NEVADA
Children are not allowed in the gaming areas of casinos, but roller coasters and animal exhibits cater to the kiddies in Las Vegas. For outdoor adventure, head to Great Basin National Park or Valley of Fire State Park.

Helpful Resources for Families

For all-around information and advice, check out Lonely Planet's *Travel with Children*. For outdoor advice, read *Kids in the Wild: A Family Guide to Outdoor Recreation* by Cindy Ross and Todd Gladfelter, and Alice Cary's *Parents' Guide to Hiking & Camping*.

FOOD

Whoever advised 'moderation in all things' has clearly never enjoyed a Sonoran dog in Tucson. Same goes for a messy plate of *huevos rancheros* at a small-town Arizona diner. Or a loaded green-chile cheeseburger in New Mexico. Food in the Southwest is a tricultural celebration not suited for the gastronomically timid, or anyone on a diet. One or two dainty bites? Not likely. But admit it, isn't food part of the reason you're here?

Eating Price Ranges

The following price ranges refer to a main course excluding taxes and tip.

$	less than $15
$$	$15-25
$$$	more than $25

HEALTH

When it comes to health care, the US has some of the finest in the world. The problem? Unless you have good insurance, it can be prohibitively expensive. It's essential to purchase travel health insurance if your regular plan doesn't cover you when you're abroad. At a minimum you need coverage for medical emergencies and treatment, including hospital stays and an emergency flight home if necessary.

There is good hospital and emergency care in populated areas, but remote areas in and around some national parks may be far from services. For this reason, accident evacuation insurance is an important add-on.

Recommended Vaccinations

Check www.cdc.gov for updated recommendations. Currently, vaccines for these diseases are required for US immigration:

➡ Mumps
➡ Measles
➡ Rubella
➡ Polio
➡ Tetanus and diphtheria
➡ Pertussis
➡ Haemophilus influenzae type B (Hib)
➡ Hepatitis A
➡ Hepatitis B
➡ Rotavirus
➡ Meningococcal disease
➡ Varicella
➡ Pneumococcal disease
➡ Seasonal influenza

INSURANCE

If your health insurance does not cover you for medical expenses abroad, consider supplemental insurance. Find out in advance if your insurance plan will make payments directly to providers or reimburse you later for overseas health expenditures.

For information on car rental insurance, see the Southwest USA Driving Guide (p345).

INTERNET ACCESS

➡ Public libraries in most cities and towns offer free internet access, either at computer terminals or through a wireless connection, usually for 15 minutes to an hour (a few may charge a small fee). In some cases you may need to obtain a guest pass or register.

➡ If you can bring your laptop do so, as most places that serve coffee also offer free wi-fi as long as you order a drink.

➡ You may be charged for wi-fi use in nice hotels and resorts.

➡ Check www.wififreespot.com for a list of free wi-fi hot spots nationwide.

LEGAL MATTERS

➡ If you are arrested for a serious offense in the US, you are allowed to remain silent, are entitled to have an attorney present during any interrogation and are presumed innocent until proven guilty.

➡ You have the right to an attorney from the very first moment you are arrested. If you can't afford one, the state must provide one for free.

➡ All persons who are arrested are legally allowed to make one phone call. If you don't have a lawyer or family member to help you, call your embassy or consulate.

➡ If you are stopped by the police for everyday matters, there is no system of paying fines on the spot. The officer should explain to you how the fine can be paid; many matters can be handled by mail or online.

LGBTIQ+ TRAVELERS

The most visible LGTBIQ+ communities are in major cities. Utah and southern Arizona are typically not as freewheeling as San Francisco. LGBTIQ+ travelers should be careful in predominantly rural areas – simply holding hands could provoke aggressive responses.

The most active LGTBIQ+ community in the Southwest is in Phoenix. Santa Fe and Albuquerque have active LGTBIQ+ communities, and Las Vegas has an active LGTBIQ+ scene. Conservative Utah has little LGTBIQ+ life outside Salt Lake City. The following are useful resources:

Damron (www.damron.com) Publishes classic LGTBIQ+ travel guides.

OutTraveler (www.outtraveler.com) News, tips and in-depth stories about LGTBIQ+ travel for destinations around the world.

Gay Yellow Network (www.glyp.com) Has listings for numerous US cities including Phoenix and Las Vegas.

Purple Roofs (www.purpleroofs.com) Lists LGTBIQ+ owned and welcoming B&Bs/hotels.

National Gay & Lesbian Task Force (⌨Washington, DC 202-393-5177; www.thetaskforce.org) The website of this national activist group covers news and politics.

Lambda Legal Defense Fund (⌨in Los Angeles 213-382-7600; www.lambdalegal.org) The website lists legal protections for LGTBIQ+ people and their families by state.

MONEY

Most locals do not carry large amounts of cash for everyday transactions, and rely instead on credit cards, ATMs and debit cards. Small businesses may refuse to accept bills larger than $50.

ATMs & Cash

➡ ATMs are great for quick cash influxes and can negate the need for traveler's checks entirely. Watch out for ATM surcharges as they may be $3 to $5 per withdrawal. Some ATMs in Vegas may charge more.

➡ The Cirrus and Plus systems both have extensive ATM networks that will give cash advances on major credit cards and allow cash withdrawals with affiliated ATM cards.

➡ Look for ATMs outside banks and in large grocery stores, shopping centers, convenience stores and gas stations.

➡ To avoid possible account-draining scams at self-serve gas stations, consider paying with cash instead of using your debit card at the pump.

Bargaining

Gentle haggling is generally reserved for flea markets; otherwise, expect to pay the stated price.

Credit Cards

Major credit cards are widely accepted throughout the Southwest, including at car-rental agencies and most hotels, restaurants, gas stations, grocery stores and tour operators. It's highly recommended that you carry at least one card.

Currency Exchange

➡ Banks are usually the best places to exchange currency. Most large city banks offer currency exchange, but banks in rural areas do not.

➡ Currency-exchange counters at the airports and in tourist centers typically have the worst rates; ask about fees and surcharges first.

Exchange Rates

Australia	A$1	$0.75
Canada	C$1	$0.74
Europe	€1	$1.09
Japan	¥100	$0.90
Mexico	10 pesos	$0.59
New Zealand	NZ$1	$0.69
UK	£1	$1.28

For current exchange rates see www.xe.com.

Tipping

Airport & Hotel Porters Tip $2 per bag, minimum $5 per cart.

Bartenders Tip 10% to 15% per round, minimum per drink $1.

Housekeeping Tip $2 to $4 per night, left under card provided.

Restaurant Servers Tip 15% to 20%, unless gratuity is included in the bill.

Taxi Drivers Tip 10% to 15%, rounded up to the next dollar.

Valet Parking Tip minimum $2 when keys handed back.

NATIONAL & STATE PARKS

Before visiting any national park, check out its website using the search tool on the National Park Service (NPS) home page (www.nps.gov). On the Grand Canyon's website (www.nps.gov/grca), you can download the seasonal newspaper, *The Guide*, for the latest information on prices, hours and ranger talks. There is a separate edition for both the North and South Rims.

Some state parks in Arizona operate on a five-day schedule, closed Tuesdays and Wednesdays. Before visiting an Arizona state park, check its website to confirm opening times.

➡ At the entrance of a national or state park, be ready to hand over cash (credit cards may not always be accepted). Costs range from nothing at all to $30 per vehicle for a seven-day pass.

➡ If you're visiting several parks in the Southwest, you may save money by purchasing the **America the Beautiful** annual pass ($80). It admits all passengers in a vehicle (or four adults at per-person fee areas) to all national parks and federal recreational lands for one year. With the pass, children under 16 are admitted free.

➡ US citizens and permanent residents aged 62 and older are eligible for a lifetime Senior Pass.

➡ US citizens and permanent residents with a permanent disability may qualify for a free Access Pass.

➡ Check the park's website for notices about Fee-Free Days, when no admission is charged.

PETS

When it comes to pet-friendly travel destinations, the Southwest is one of the best. More and more hotels accept pets these days, although some charge extra per night, others make you leave a deposit and still others have weight restrictions – less than 35lb is usually the standard.

Some hotels have additional pet fees, or limited rooms that accept pets – call in advance to check their policies. One of the most unique pet-friendly options in the Southwest is in Santa Fe: head to the swank **Ten Thousand Waves** (☑505-992-5003; www.tenthousandwaves.com; 3451 Hyde Park Rd; r $249-299; 🅿 ❄ 🛜 🐾).

At national parks, check first before you let your pet off the leash – many forests and park lands have restrictions on dogs. If you're planning a long day in the car, vets recommend stopping at least every two hours to let your dog pee, stretch their legs and have a long drink of water. If your dog gets nervous or nauseated in the car, it is safe and effective to give them Benadryl (or the generic equivalent) to calm them down. The vet-recommended dosage is 1mg per pound. For information on pet care, consult www.humanesociety.org.

When stopping to eat during a downtown stroll, don't immediately tie your dog up outside the restaurant. Ask first about local laws.

PHOTOGRAPHY

Print film can be found in drugstores and at specialty camera shops. Digital-camera memory cards are available at chain retailers such as Best Buy and Target.

Some American Indian reservations prohibit photography and video recording completely; when it's allowed you may be required to purchase a permit. Always ask permission to photograph someone close-up; anyone who agrees may expect a small tip.

Lonely Planet's *Guide to Travel Photography* is full of helpful tips for photography while on the road.

POST

➡ The US Postal Service provides great service for the price. For 1st-class mail sent and delivered within the US, postage rates are 49¢ for letters up to 1oz (21¢ for each additional ounce) and 34¢ for standard-size postcards.

→ If you have the correct postage, drop your mail into any blue mailbox. To send a package weighing 13oz or more, go to a post office.

→ International airmail rates are $1.15 for a 1oz letter or postcard.

→ Call private shippers such as United Parcel Service (UPS) and Federal Express to send more important or larger items.

PUBLIC HOLIDAYS

New Year's Day January 1

Martin Luther King Jr Day 3rd Monday of January

Presidents Day 3rd Monday of February

Easter March or April

Memorial Day Last Monday of May

Independence Day July 4

Labor Day 1st Monday of September

Columbus Day 2nd Monday of October

Veterans Day November 11

Thanksgiving 4th Thursday of November

Christmas Day December 25

SAFE TRAVEL

Southwestern cities generally have less violent crime than larger US cities but it is present.

Take the following precautions in the great outdoors:

→ Avoid open areas, canyon rims or hilltops during lightning storms.

→ Avoid riverbeds and canyons when storm clouds gather; flash floods are deadly.

→ When camping in bear country, place your food inside a food box (one is often provided by the campground).

→ Step carefully on hot summer afternoons and evenings, when rattlesnakes like to bask on the trail.

→ Scorpions lurk under rocks and woodpiles; use caution.

TELEPHONE

→ Always dial ☏1 before toll-free (☏800, ☏888 etc) and domestic long-distance numbers.

→ Some toll-free numbers may only work within the region or from the US mainland. But you'll only know if it works by making the call.

→ All phone numbers in the US consist of a three-digit area code followed by a seven-digit local number.

→ All five Southwestern states require you to dial the full 10-digit number for all phone calls because each state has more than one area code. You will not be charged for long-distance fees when dialing locally.

→ When calling a cell phone anywhere in the USA you need to always dial the 10-digit number; however, you do not need to dial the country code (☏1) when calling from within the United States.

→ Pay phones aren't as readily found now that cell phones are more prevalent. But keep your eyes peeled and you'll find them. If you don't have change, you can use a calling card.

→ To make international calls direct, dial ☏011 + country code + area code + number. An exception is to Canada, where you dial ☏1 + area code + number. International rates apply for Canada.

→ For international operator assistance, dial ☏0. The operator can provide specific rate information and tell you which time periods are the cheapest for calling.

→ If you're calling the Southwest from abroad, the international country code for the US is ☏1. All calls to the Southwest are then followed by the area code and the seven-digit local number.

→ Private prepaid phonecards are available from convenience stores, supermarkets and pharmacies. AT&T sells a reliable phone card that is widely available in the US.

TOILETS

Public toilets are common in parks and town centers; otherwise, service stations, restaurants and hotels have bathrooms for guest use.

TOURIST INFORMATION

Larger cities and towns have tourist information centers run by local convention and visitor bureaus. In smaller towns, local chambers of commerce often perform the same functions.

Great online resources include:

American Southwest (www.americansouthwest.net) Covers parks and natural landscapes.

Bureau of Land Management (www.blm.gov) Oversees public lands with recreational uses for the public.

Family Travel Files (www.thefamilytravelfiles.com) Ready-made vacation ideas, destination profiles and travel tips.

Grand Canyon Association (www.grandcanyon.org) Has an extensive online bookstore for the park.

Kids.gov (www.kids.gov) Eclectic, enormous national resource where you can download songs and activities, and learn a bit about each state's history.

Woodall's (www.woodalls.com) RV website with information on campgrounds and forum for the RV community.

TRAVELERS WITH DISABILITIES

Travel within the Southwest is getting better for people with disabilities, but it's still not easy. Public buildings are required to be wheelchair accessible and to have appropriate restroom facilities. Public transportation services must be made accessible to all and telephone companies have to provide relay operators for the hearing impaired. Many banks provide ATM instructions in braille, curb ramps are common, many busy intersections have audible crossing signals, and most chain hotels have suites for guests with disabilities. Still, it's best to call ahead to check.

➡ US residents and permanent residents with disabilities may be eligible for the lifetime Access Pass, a free pass to national parks and more than 2000 recreation areas managed by the federal government. Visit store.usgs.gov/pass/access.html.

➡ Accessing Arizona (www.accessingarizona.com) has information about wheelchair-accessible activities in Arizona. It's slightly out-of-date but still useful.

➡ For reviews about the accessibility of hotels, restaurants and entertainment venues in metropolitan Phoenix, check out www.brettapproved.com.

➡ **Arizona Raft Adventures** (☑800-786-7238, 928-526-8200; www.azraft.com; 6-day Upper Canyon hybrid/paddle trips $2097/2197, 10-day Full Canyon motor trips $3160) can accommodate travelers with disabilities on rafting trips through the Grand Canyon.

➡ The Utah tourism office has a list of programs and resources for disabled travelers in Utah at travel.utah.gov/publications/onesheets/Accessible_Utah_web.pdf.

➡ **Wheelchair Getaways** (☑Arizona & Las Vegas 888-824-7413, Colorado 800-238-6920, New Mexico 800-408-2626, main office 800-642-2042; www.wheelchairgetaways.com) rents accessible vans in cities across the Southwest including Phoenix, Tucson, Albuquerque, Las Vegas and Boulder City.

➡ Download Lonely Planet's free Accessible Travel guide from lptravel.to/AccessibleTravel.

➡ **Society for Accessible Travel & Hospitality** (SATH; ☑212-447-7284; www.sath.org) is a useful global resource for information on traveling with a disability.

BEHIND THE SCENES

SEND US YOUR FEEDBACK

We love to hear from travelers – your comments help make our books better. We read every word, and we guarantee that your feedback goes straight to the authors. Visit lonelyplanet. com/contact to submit your updates and suggestions.

Note: We may edit, reproduce and incorporate your comments in Lonely Planet products such as guidebooks, websites and digital products, so let us know if you are happy to have your name acknowledged. For a copy of our privacy policy visit lonelyplanet.com/legal.

WRITERS' THANKS

HUGH MCNAUGHTAN

My sincere thanks to everyone who helped me through an epic research trip through Arizona – Tas and my girls, editor Alex, the ever-helpful support crew at LP, and the kind people of the Grand Canyon State. And Matt for the mescal.

AMY C BALFOUR

Thank you for your Austin recommendations and hospitality: Chris McCray, Doug Kilday, Ken Wiles and family, John Apperson and Amanda Bachman. For fine party throwing and fierce BBQ opinions, thanks to the Austin W&L crew and their families: Jenny Stratton, Anna Salas, Kelly Rogers, Lucy Anderson, Bitsy and David Young, Chris Casey and John Pipkin. Thank you Paul and Crystal Sadler for the San Antonio and West Texas tips. To Mary, Ron and Gina in Drip, can we do it again? In West Texas, an appreciative shout out to Jenny Moore, Michelle Cromer, Anne Mitchell and Anne and Keene Haywood. With help from Mariella Krause, Jeff Kelsey, Melissa Reid and Sarah Bunn. Finally, thanks Alex Howard for entrusting me with this awesome assignment, and cheers to my talented co-writers.

STEPHEN LIOY

Many thanks to many people, but specifically to these: Aileen for the thousand tips, Anthony for the co-pilot miles and company, Jess and Kevin for always being there, Kalli and Tonie for helping me enjoy inefficiency, Shane for tips and time and sometimes beer, Cindy/Payton/Pres for being so bad at Catan, Dav and Nan and UpChuck for the very many nights and meals and help, and Jack.

CAROLYN MCCARTHY

My many thanks go out to the Utah tourism office and friends Drew and Zinnia, Francisco Kjolseth and Meg and Dave. Thanks also to my co-writers, especially Chris Pitts. Utah worked its magic once more. It is a privilege to go back year after year.

CHRISTOPHER PITTS

Thanks to the inordinately kind people of New Mexico, in particular Michael Benanav in Dixon, John Feins and Cynthia Delgado in Santa Fe, and all the rangers at the national parks – especially the guy who led the incredible Carlsbad Cave tour – keep up the great work! At the writing desk, thanks to co-authors Carolyn McCarthy, Benedict Walker and Hugh McNaughtan for suggestions and Alex Howard for keeping the whole project on track.

THIS BOOK

This 4th edition of Lonely Planet's *Southwest USA's Best Trips* guidebook was curated by Hugh McNaughtan and researched and written by Hugh, Amy C Balfour, Stephen Lioy, Carolyn McCarthy, Christopher Pitts, Ryan Ver Berkmoes and Benedict Walker. The previous edition was written by Amy, Michael Benanav, Greg Benchwick, Lisa Dunford, Mariella Krause, Carolyn and Ryan.

This guidebook was produced by the following:

Commissioning Editor Kirsten Rawlings

Destination Editor Alexander Howard

Product Editors Andrea Dobbin, Hannah Cartmel

Book Designers Clara Monitto, Katherine Marsh

Cartographers Julie Sheridan, Corey Hutchison, Alison Lyall

Assisting Editors James Bainbridge, Michelle Bennett, Janice Bird, Nigel Chin, Carly Hall, Kate James, Ali Lemer, Gabrielle Stefanos, Simon Williamson

Cover Researcher Hannah Blackie

Thanks to Kate Chapman, Joel Cotterell, Evan Godt, Liz Heynes, Sonia Kapoor, Indra Kilfoyle, Virginia Moreno, Mazzy Prinsep, Dianne Schalmeiner

RYAN VER BERKMOES

Like the seasons of a Texas bluebonnet, life can go full circle. In 1997, *Texas* was the second book I ever did for Lonely Planet. And now here's Texas again. Happily this time around I didn't have the worst meal of my life in Nacogdoches. Fond thanks to those many people who were so helpful more than two decades ago and again this time. And fond love to Alexis Ver Berkmoes, who is proof that as some things fade away, other things just get better.

BENEDICT WALKER

A huge thank you to Alex Howard from LP for granting me this amazing opportunity and sticking by me until I got 'er done. I dedicate this update to Mr and Mrs Bruce and Cheryl Cowie, my self-adopted Canadian parents and the original high rollers of my world. Thanks to Mum for giving Nanna's prayer-chair a workout; to Kirk, Alex and friends for showing me their Vegas; to Justin and the burners in Reno; my birthday buddy Nicole in Carson City; and my favorite American, Brad, for speaking my language and keeping me sane. You all rock.

ACKNOWLEDGMENTS

Climate map data adapted from Peel MC, Finlayson BL & McMahon TA (2007) 'Updated World Map of the Köppen-Geiger Climate Classification', *Hydrology and Earth System Sciences*, 11, 1633–44.

Front cover photographs (clockwise from top): Monument Valley, Arizona, Zhukova Valentyna/ Shutterstock ©; Blue Swallow Motel, New Mexico, Nick Fox/Shutterstock ©; Valley of Fires, New Mexico, franckreporter/Getty ©

Back cover photograph: The Wave, Paria Canyon-Vermilion Cliffs Wilderness, Arizona, pick-uppath/ Getty ©

INDEX

N

O

P

Q

R